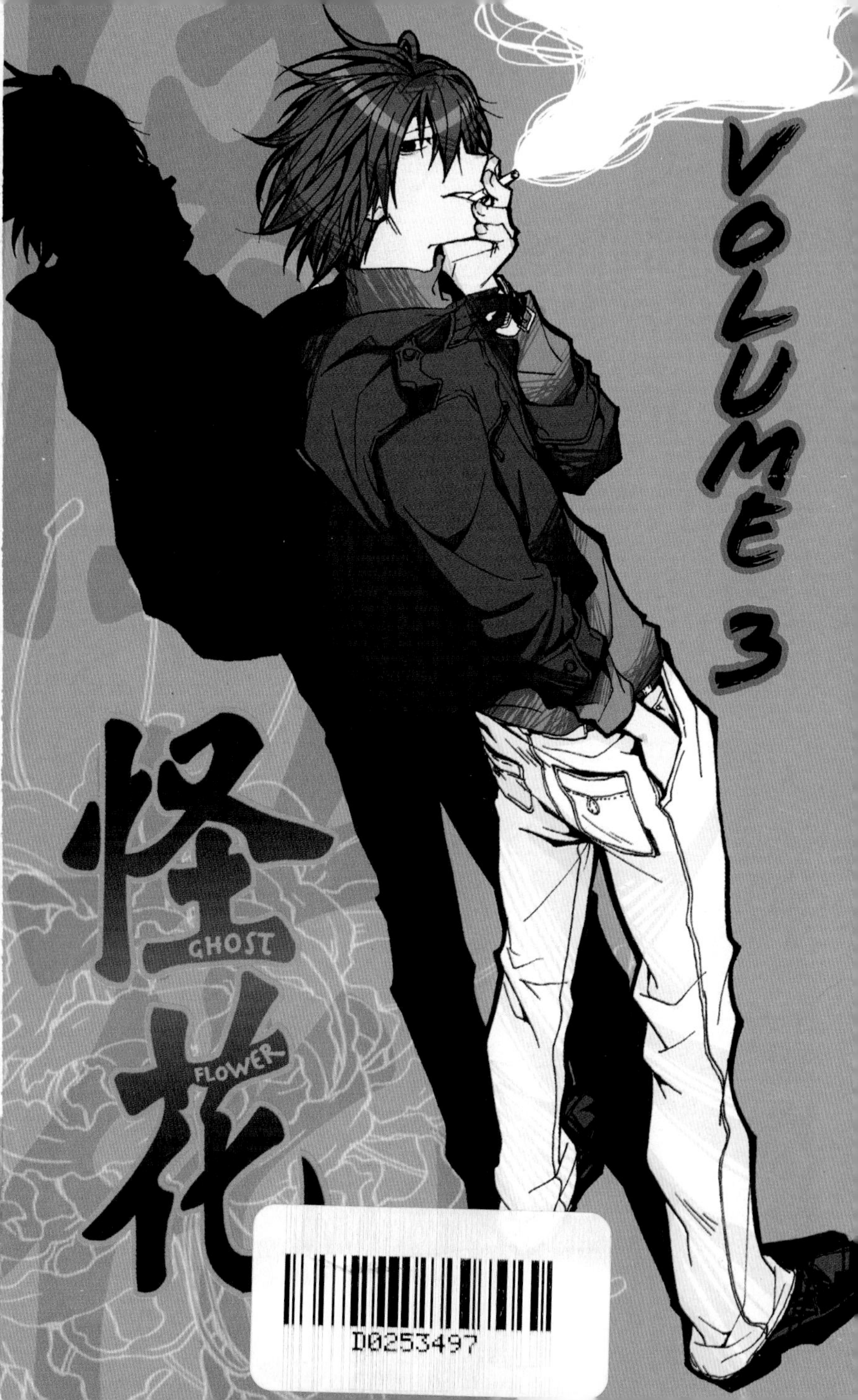
VOLUME 3
怪 GHOST
花 FLOWER

PROLOGUE

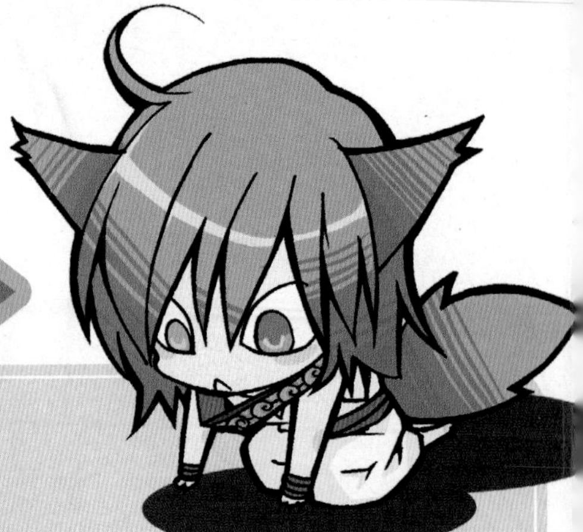

Laon is a fox that used to live in the heavens under the care of Queen Mago. She became a gumiho after collecting nine tails, each tail requiring one hundred years of energy and effort. Laon only needed one more tail to become a deity before she incurred Queen Mago's wrath and was expelled to Earth with all her tails and her ears taken away.

This is the story of Laon finding her first tail after being banished to Earth.

When a woman survives the attack of a serial rapist-murderer, the media, in search of ratings, splashes the news all over without any regard to the victim's well-being. Laon's tail punishes the press by killing off the responsible media personnel one by one, but in return, it also takes the woman's life. The tail also uses the woman's daughter, wishing to harvest the girl's womb, which bears the secret to the creation of the universe. But the tail leaves traces of itself at the crime scene, which Laon discovers...

VICTIM LIST

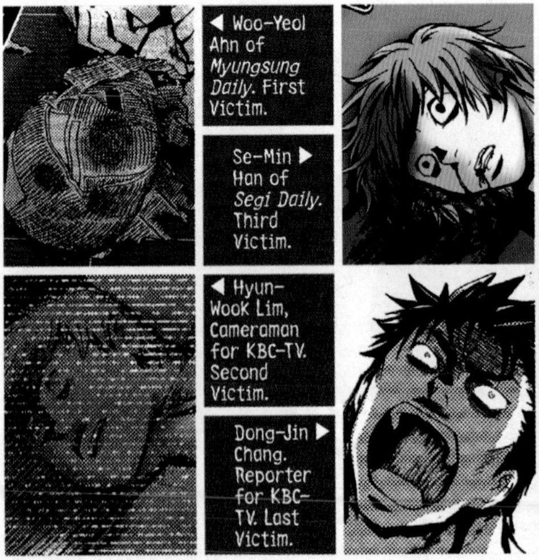
◀ Woo-Yeol Ahn of *Myungsung Daily*. First Victim.
Se-Min Han of *Segi Daily*. Third Victim. ▶
◀ Hyun-Wook Lim, Cameraman for KBC-TV. Second Victim.
Dong-Jin Chang. Reporter for KBC-TV. Last Victim. ▶

SUSPECTS

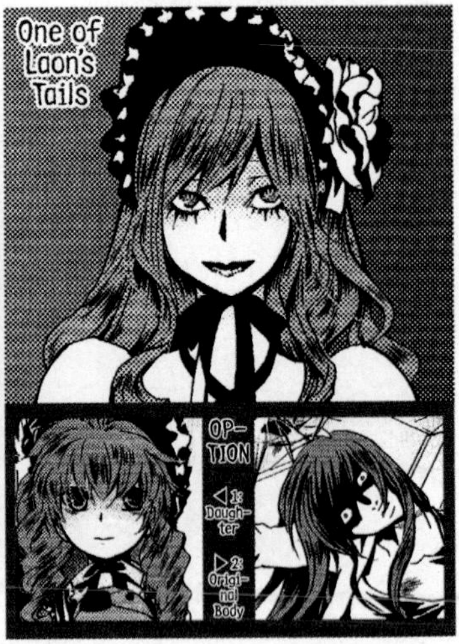
One of Laon's Tails
OPTION
◁ 1: Daughter
▷ 2: Original Body

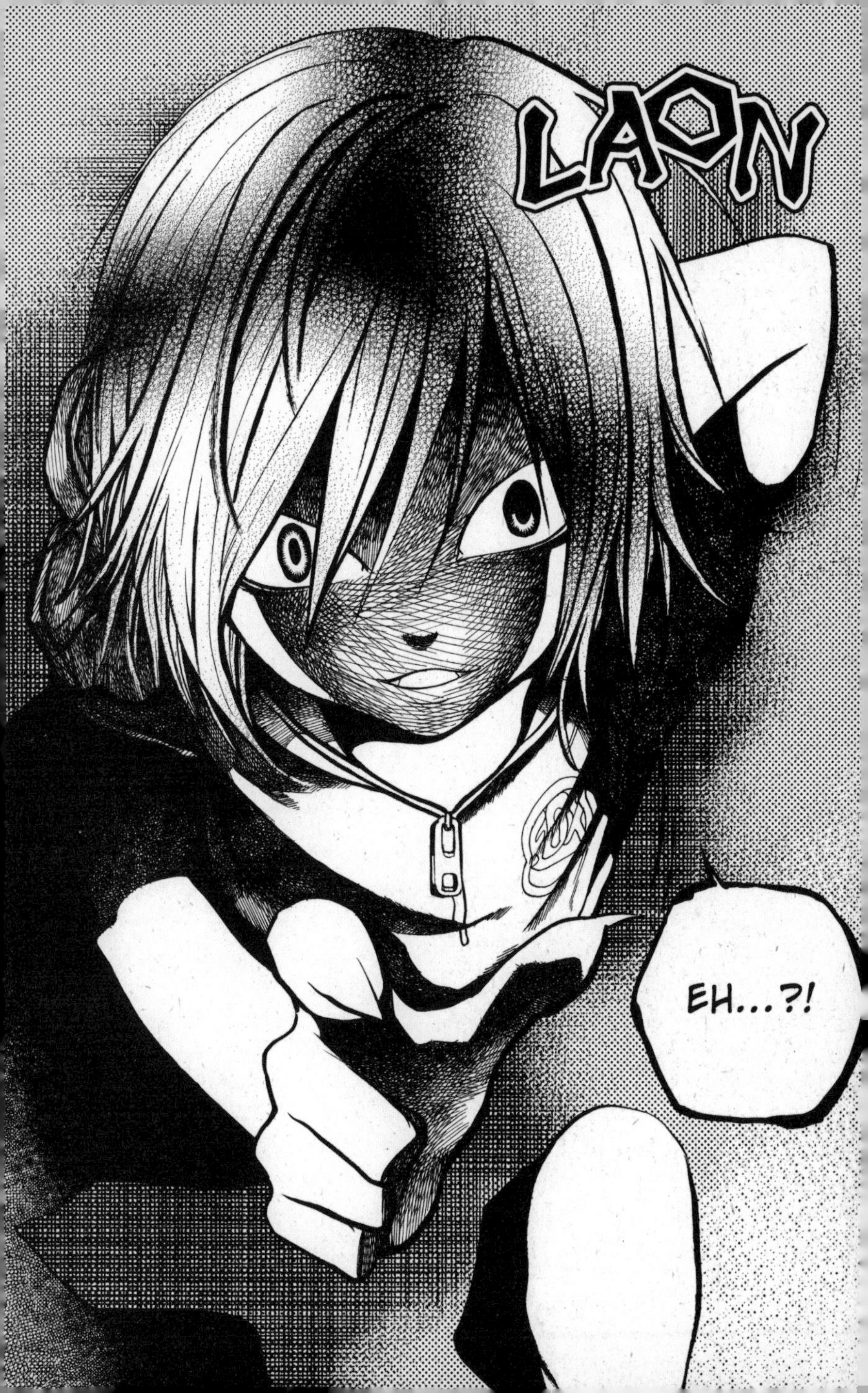
LAON
EH...?!

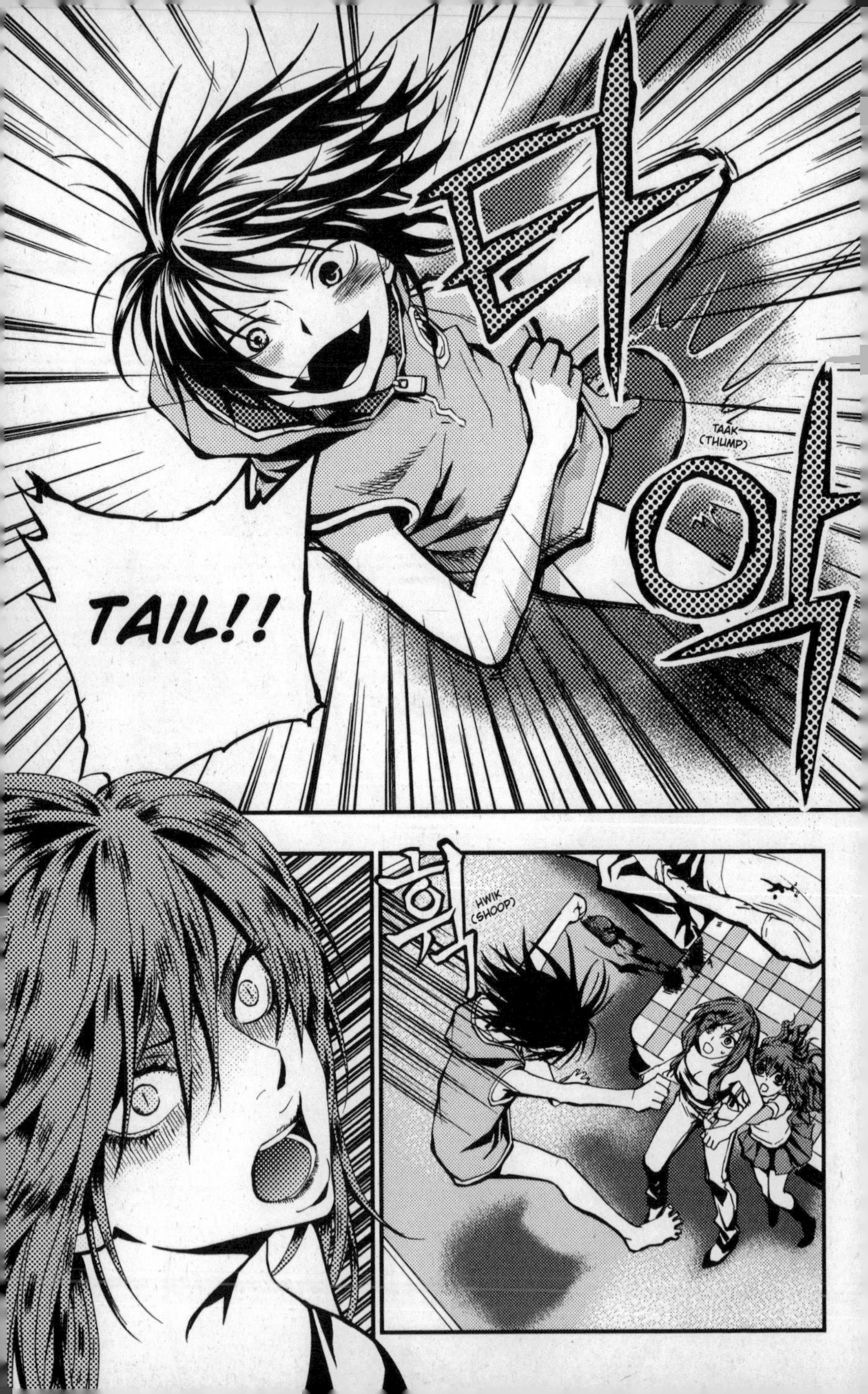
TAIL!!
TAAK (THUMP)
HWIK (SHOOP)

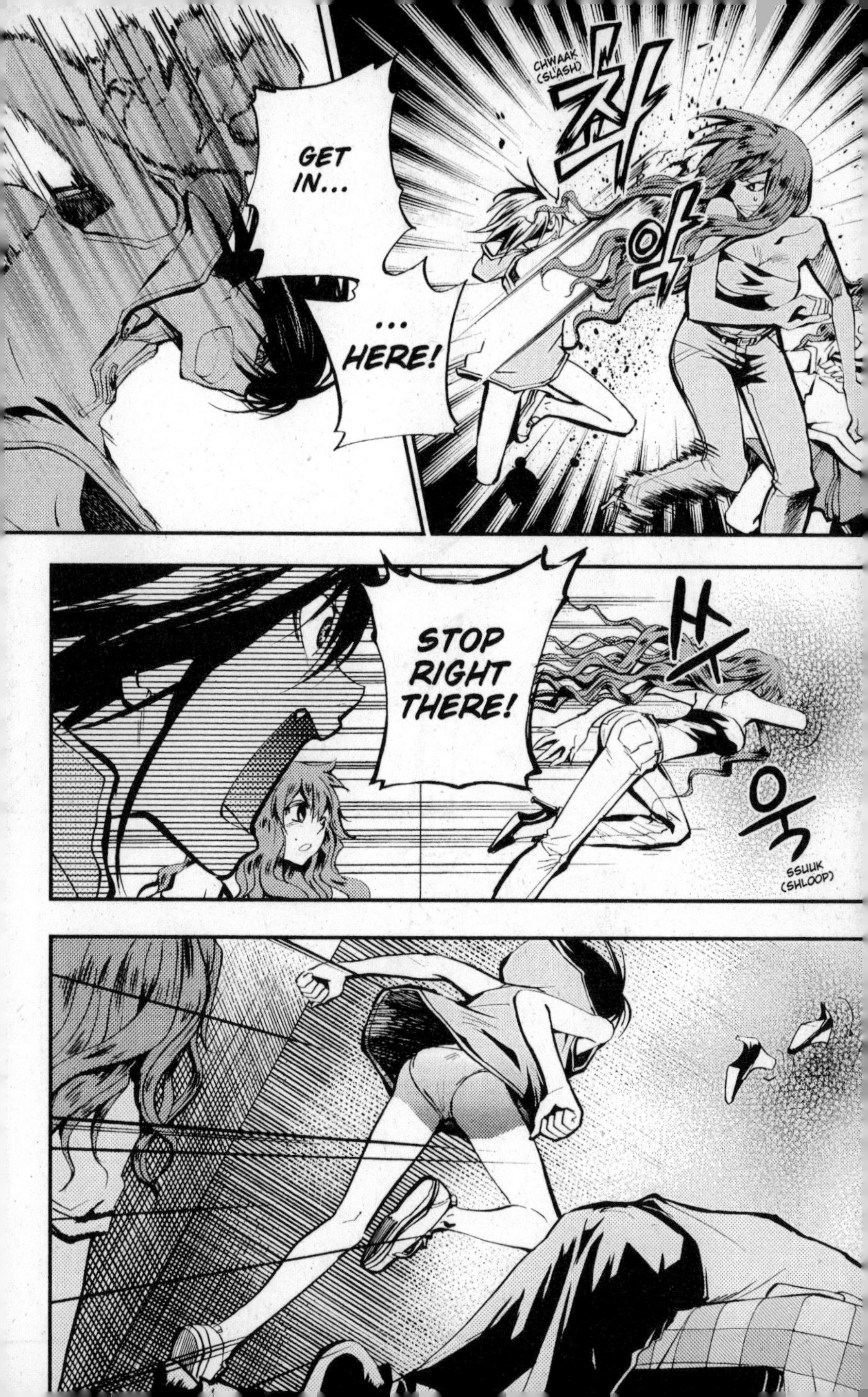
CHWAAK (SLASH)
GET IN...
...HERE!
STOP RIGHT THERE!
SSUUK (SHLOOP)

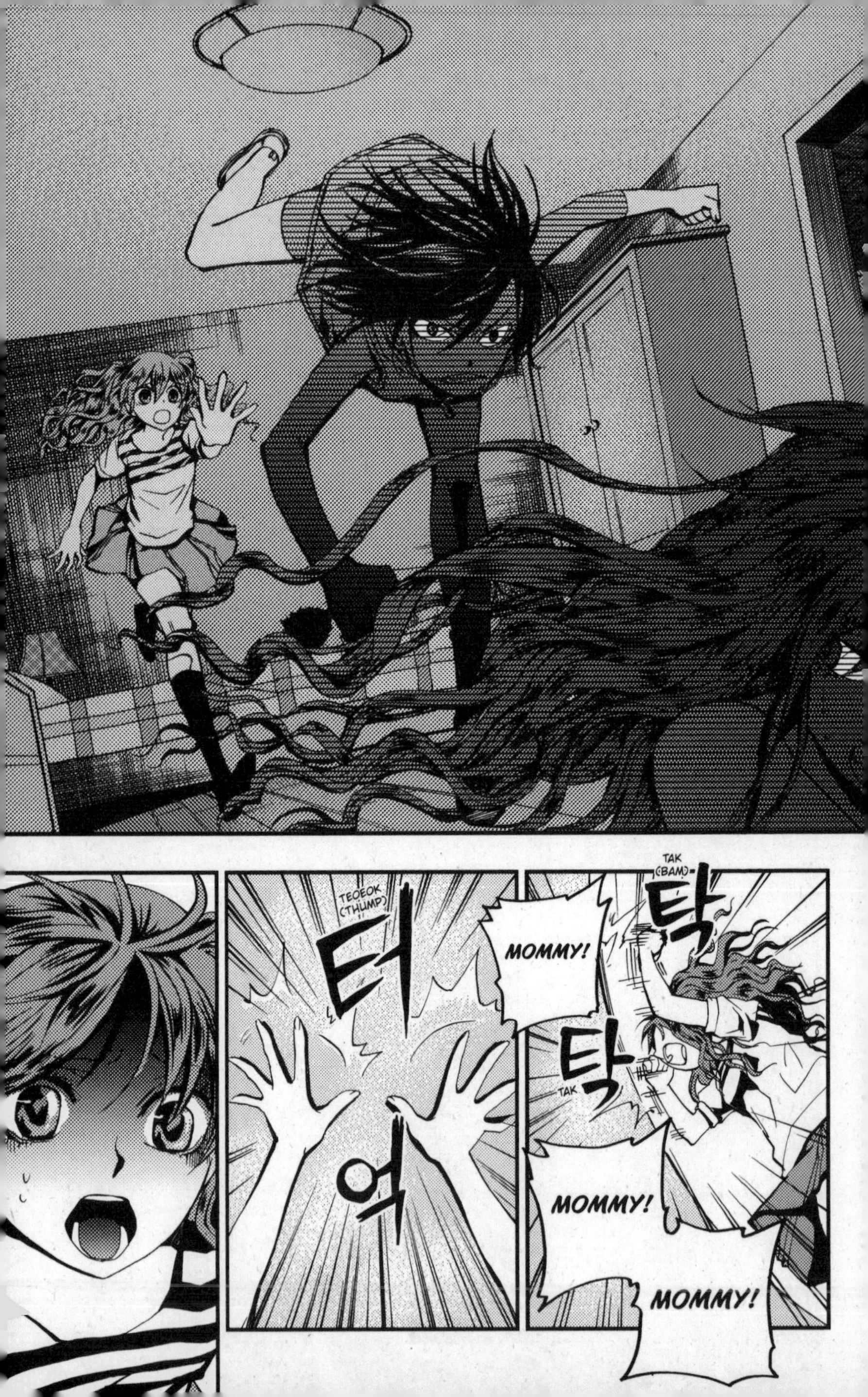
TEOEOK (THUMP)
터
어
TAK (BAM)
탁
MOMMY!
탁
TAK
MOMMY!
MOMMY!

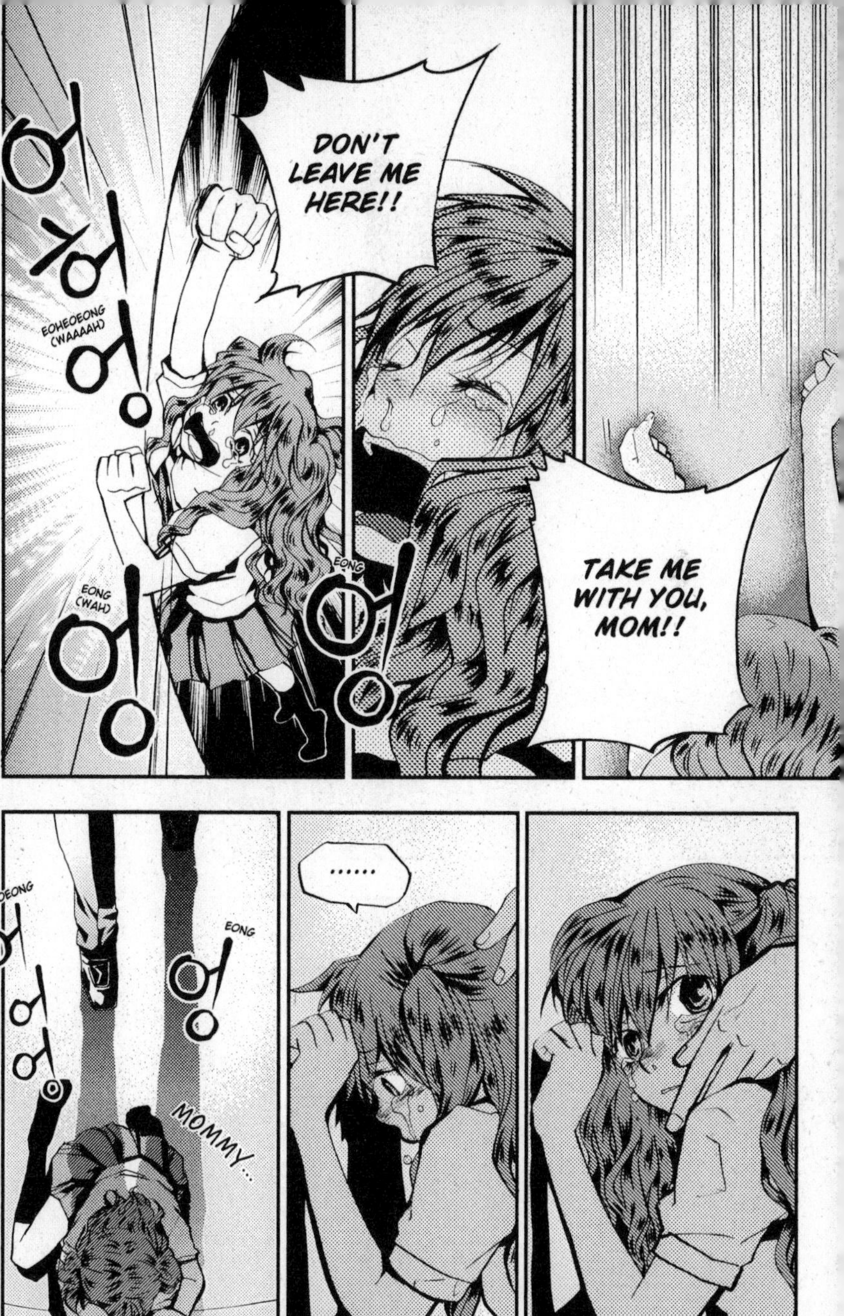
어허엉!
EOHEOEONG (WAAAAH)
DON'T LEAVE ME HERE!!
엉!
EONG (WAH)
엉!
EONG
TAKE ME WITH YOU, MOM!!
어엉...
EOEONG
엉!
EONG
MOMMY...
......

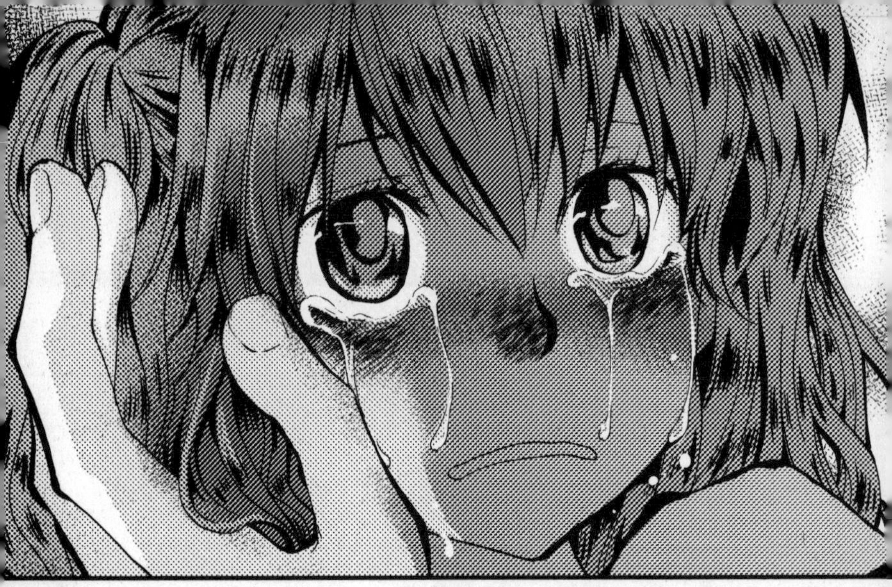

SIGNS: RECHARGE BUS CARD HERE / CIGARETTES

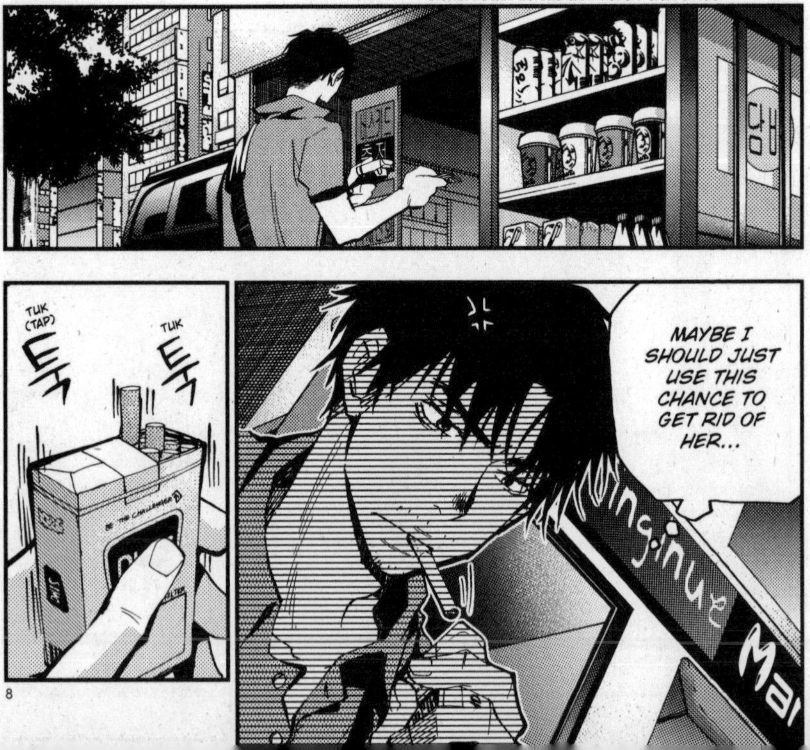
TUK (TAP)
툭
TUK
툭
BE THE CHALLENGER
MAYBE I SHOULD JUST USE THIS CHANCE TO GET RID OF HER...

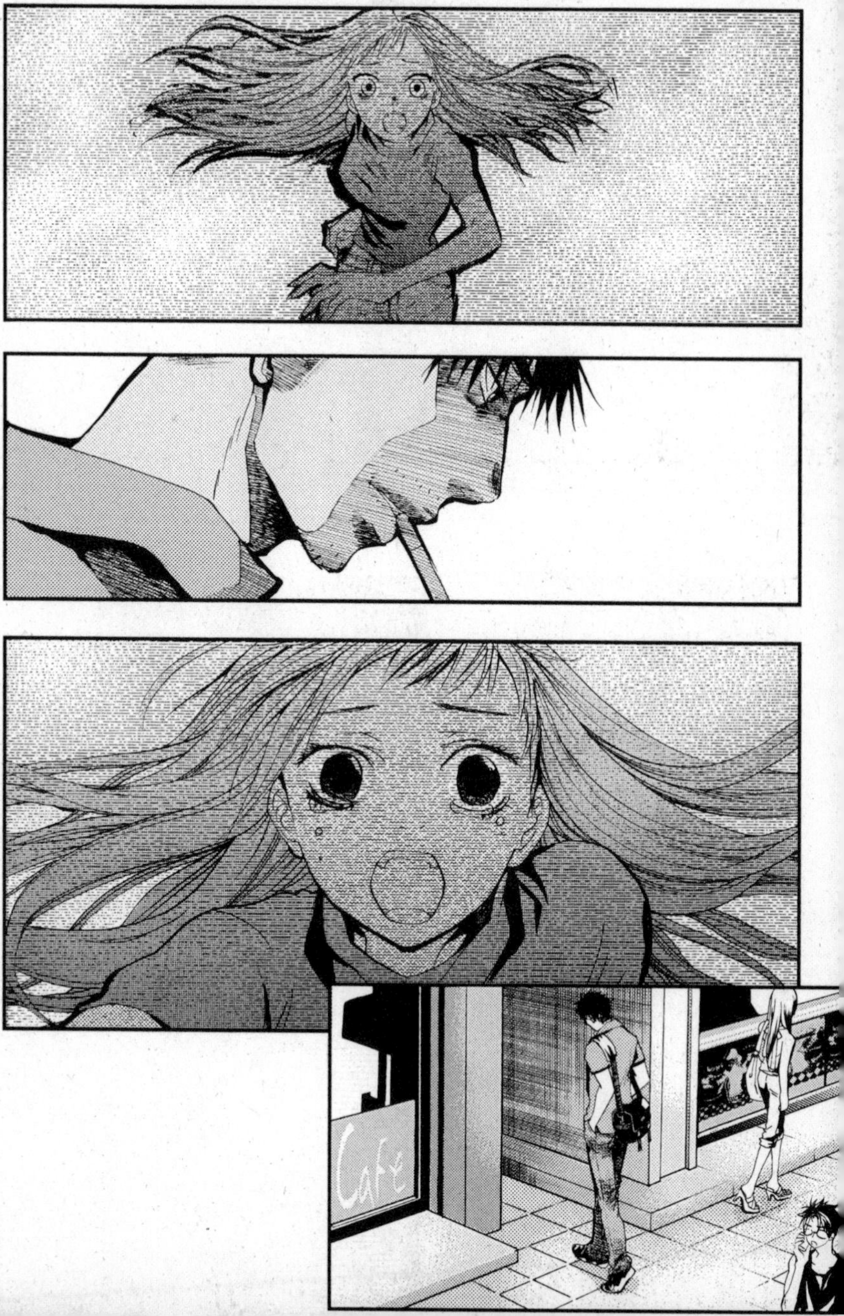
Cafe

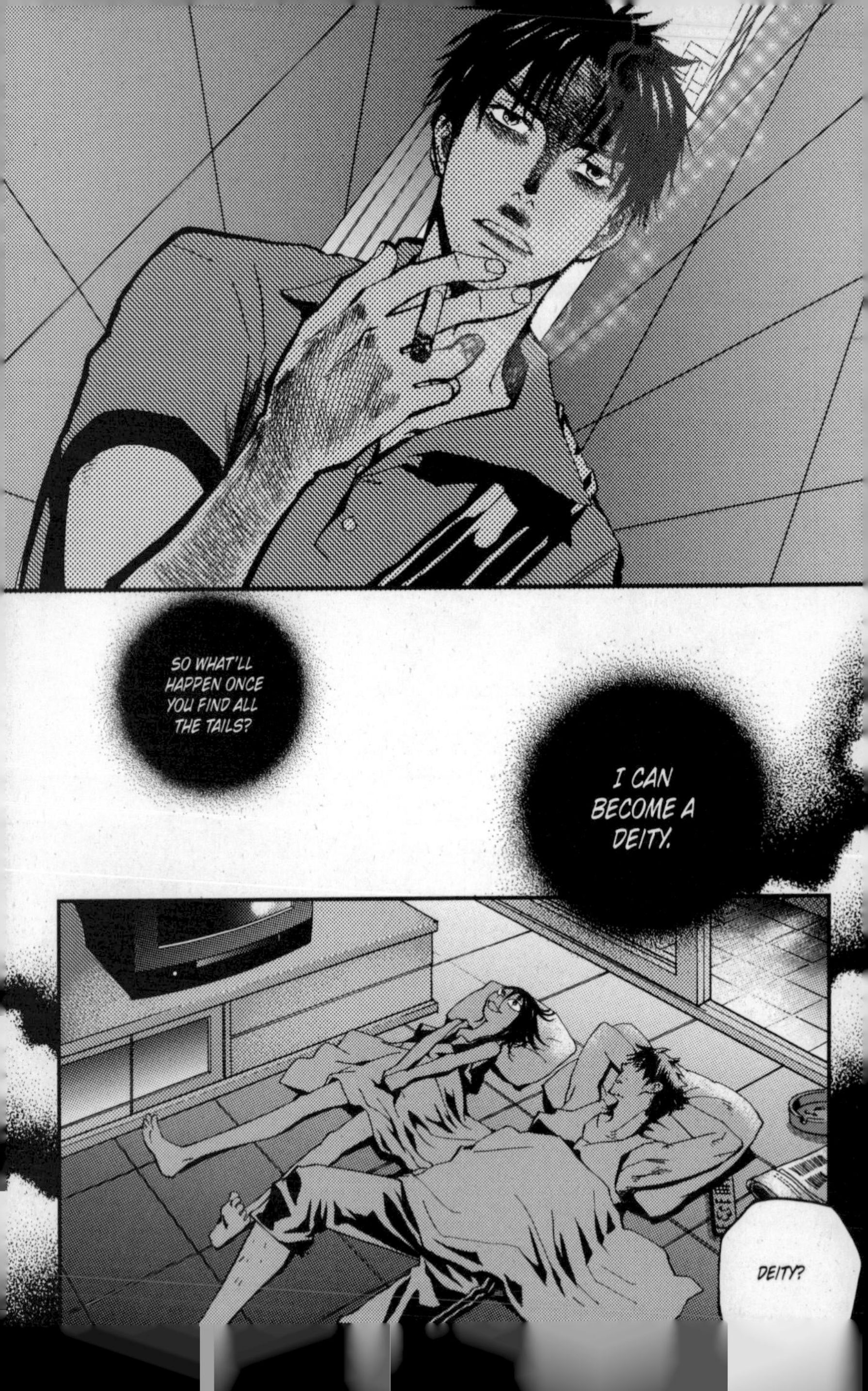
SO WHAT'LL HAPPEN ONCE YOU FIND ALL THE TAILS?
I CAN BECOME A DEITY.
DEITY?

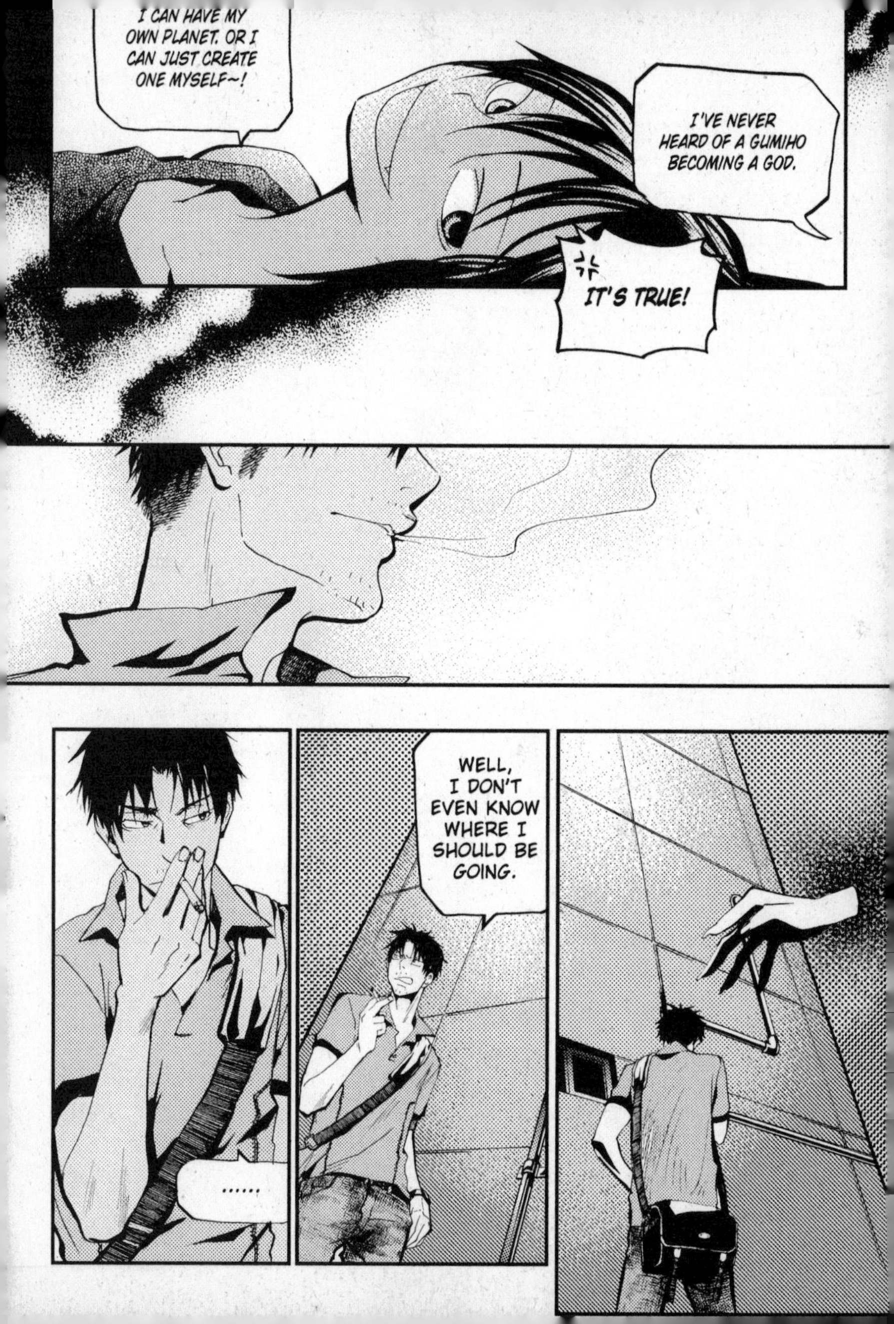
I CAN HAVE MY OWN PLANET. OR I CAN JUST CREATE ONE MYSELF~!
I'VE NEVER HEARD OF A GUMIHO BECOMING A GOD.
IT'S TRUE!
......
WELL, I DON'T EVEN KNOW WHERE I SHOULD BE GOING.

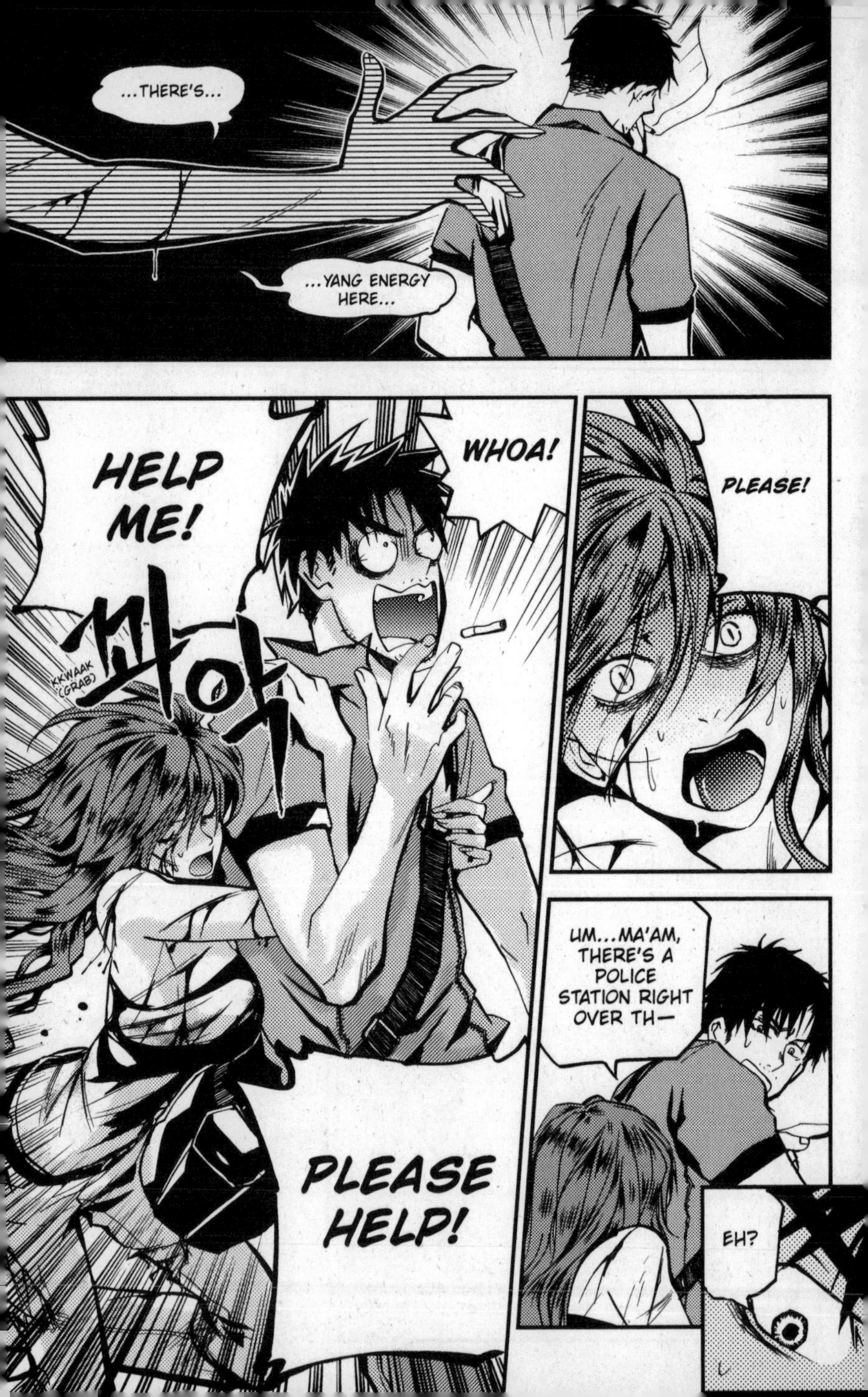
...THERE'S...
...YANG ENERGY HERE...
HELP ME!
WHOA!
KKWAAK (GRAB)
PLEASE HELP!
PLEASE!
UM...MA'AM, THERE'S A POLICE STATION RIGHT OVER TH—
EH?

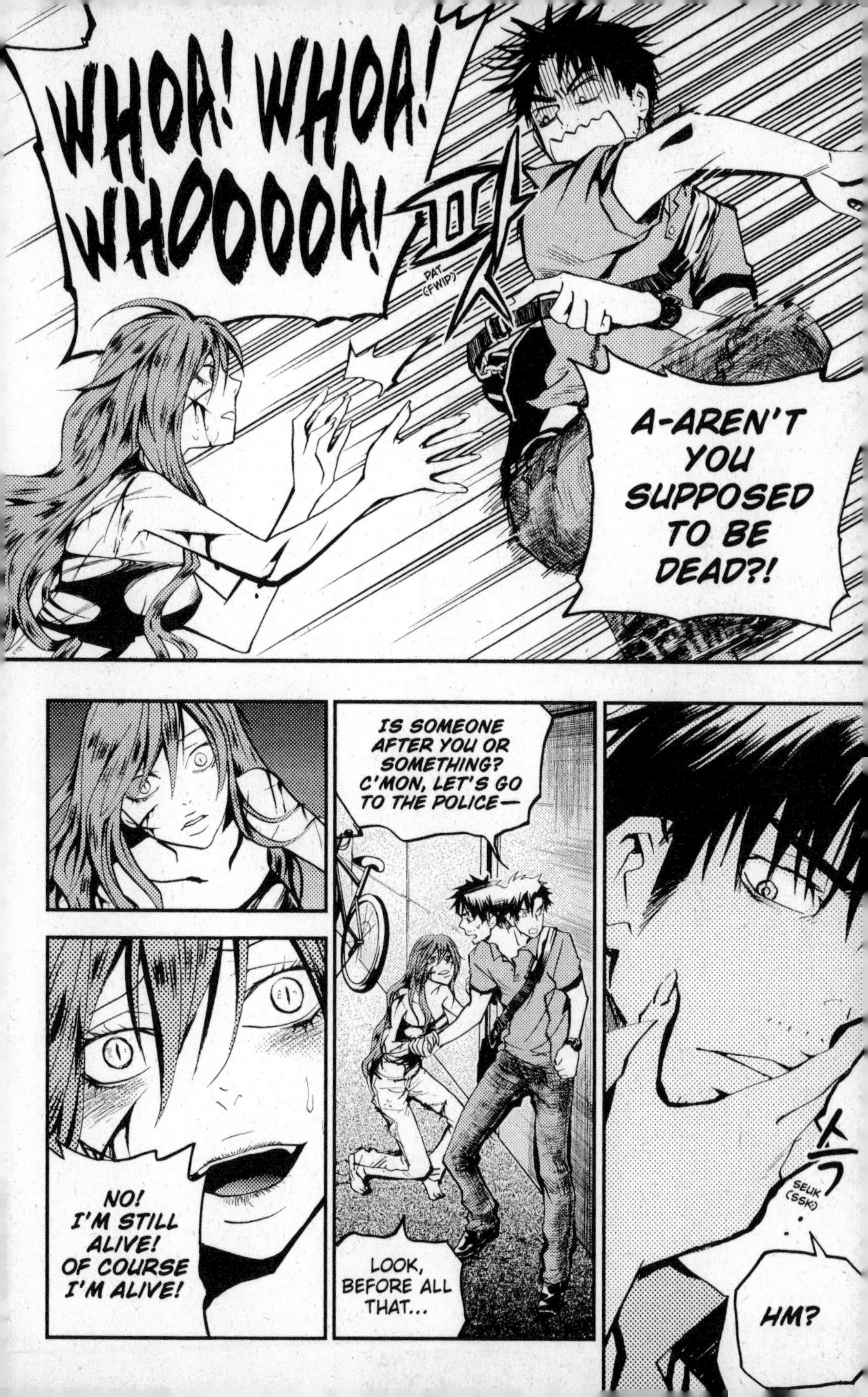
WHOA! WHOA! WHOOOOA!
PAT (FWIP)
A-AREN'T YOU SUPPOSED TO BE DEAD?!
NO! I'M STILL ALIVE! OF COURSE I'M ALIVE!
IS SOMEONE AFTER YOU OR SOMETHING? C'MON, LET'S GO TO THE POLICE—
LOOK, BEFORE ALL THAT...
SEUK (SSK)
HM?

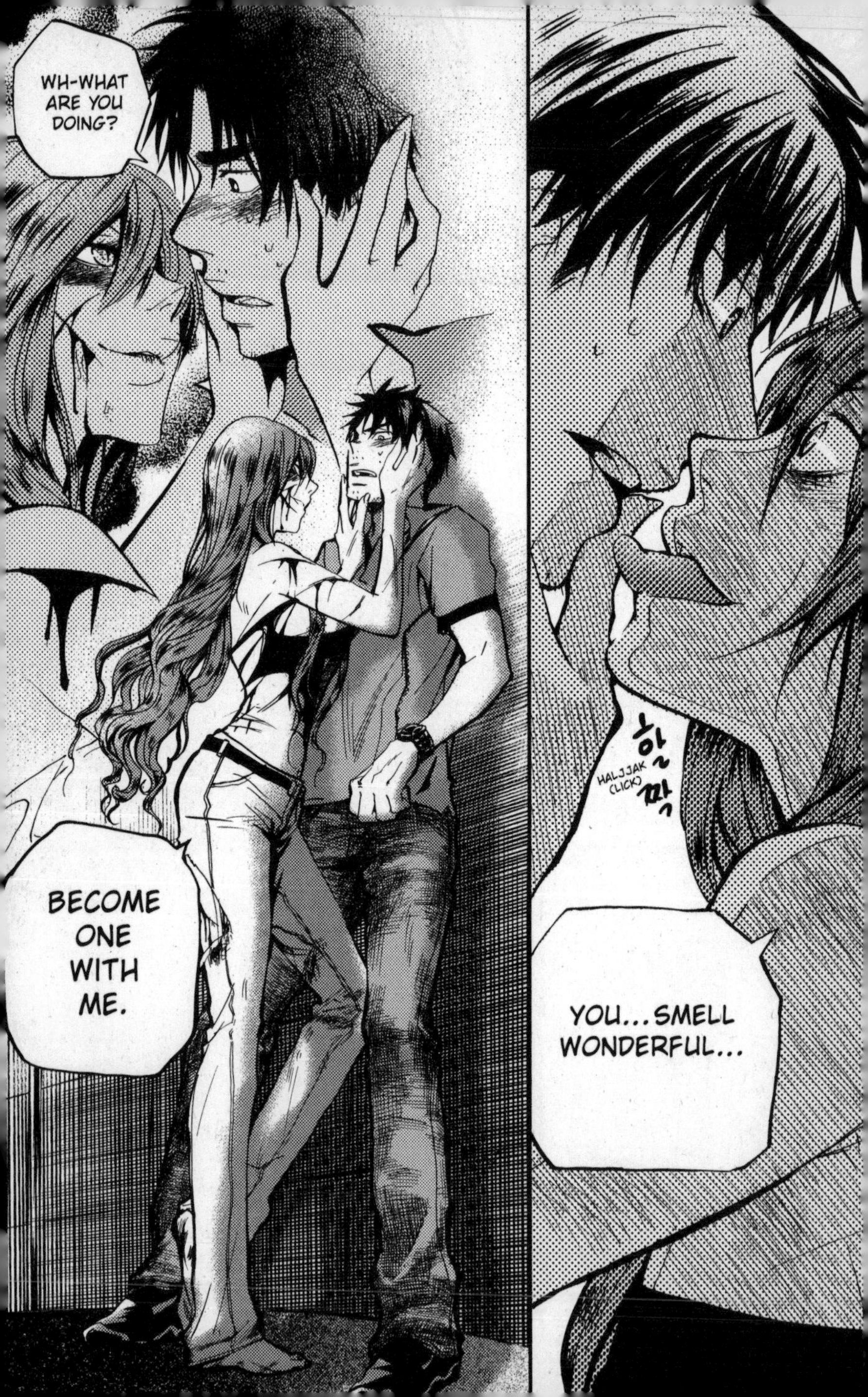
WH-WHAT ARE YOU DOING?
BECOME ONE WITH ME.
할짝
HALJJAK (LICK)
YOU...SMELL WONDERFUL...

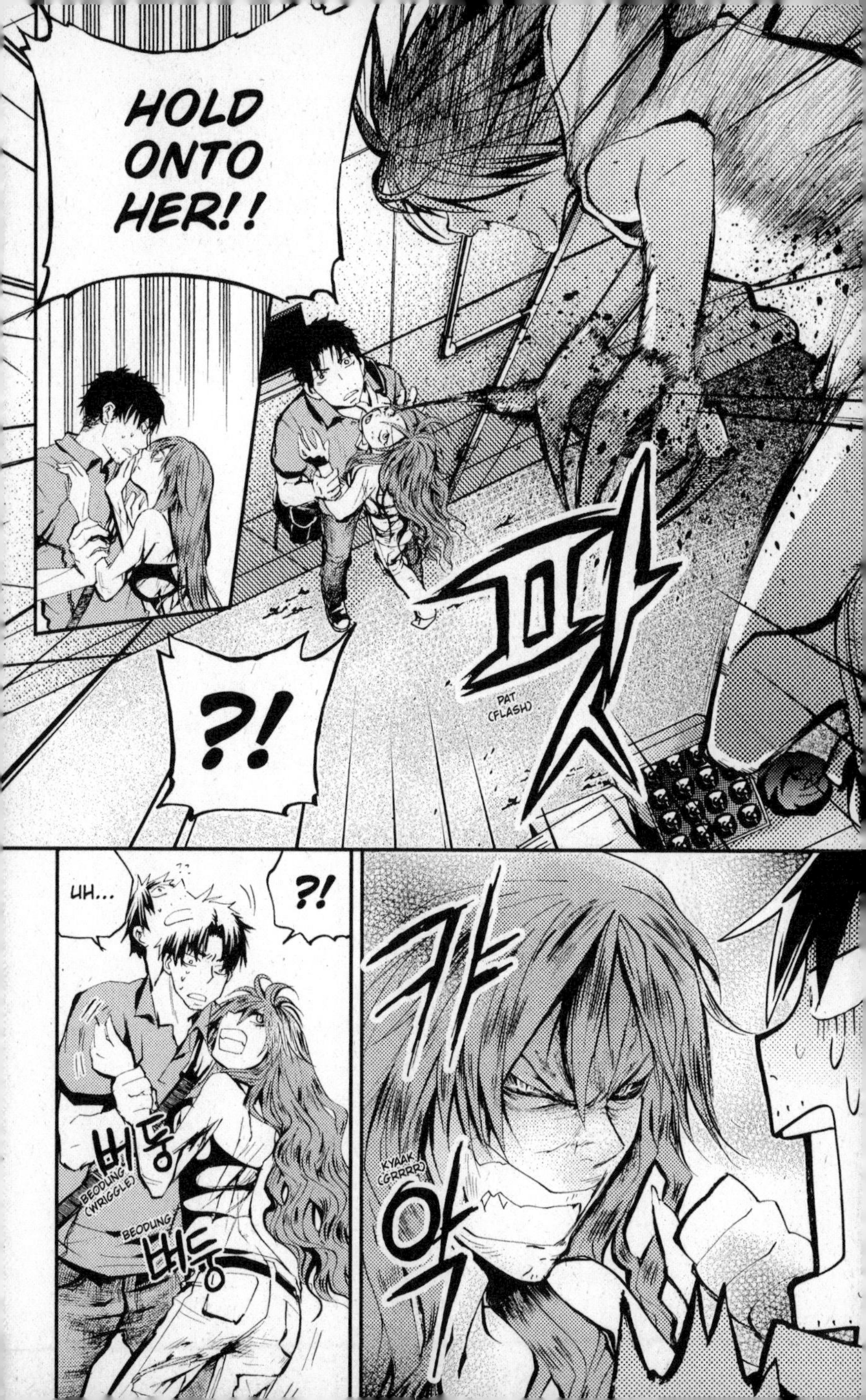
HOLD ONTO HER!!
?!
PAT
(FLASH)
UH...
?!
버둥
BEODUNG
(WRIGGLE)
BEODUNG
버둥
카
악
KYAAK
(GRRRR)

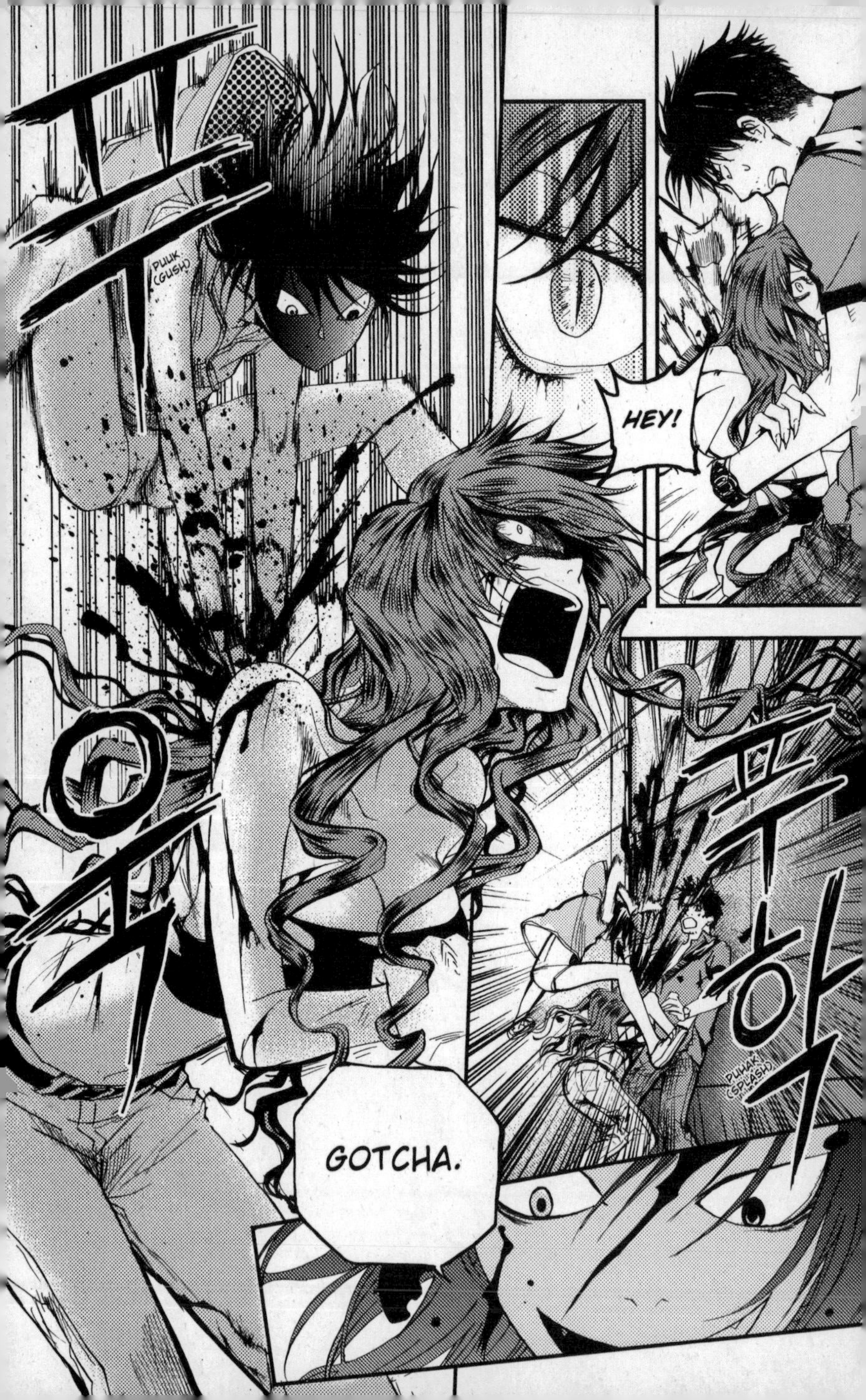

푸욱
PUUK (GUSH)
HEY!
푸학
PUHAK (SPLASH)
GOTCHA.

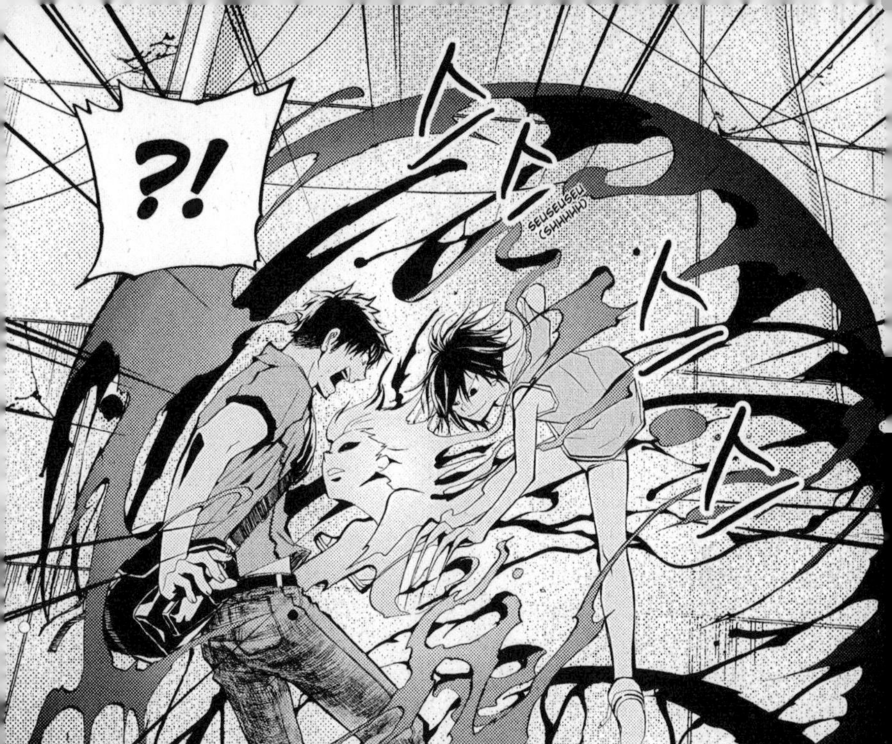
?!
SEUSEUSEU (SHHHHH)
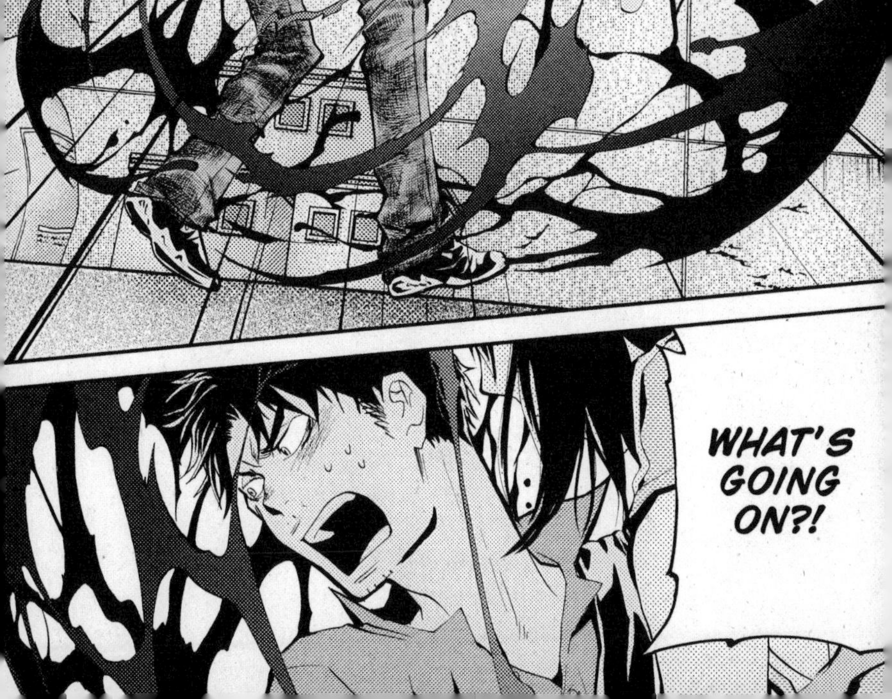
WHAT'S GOING ON?!

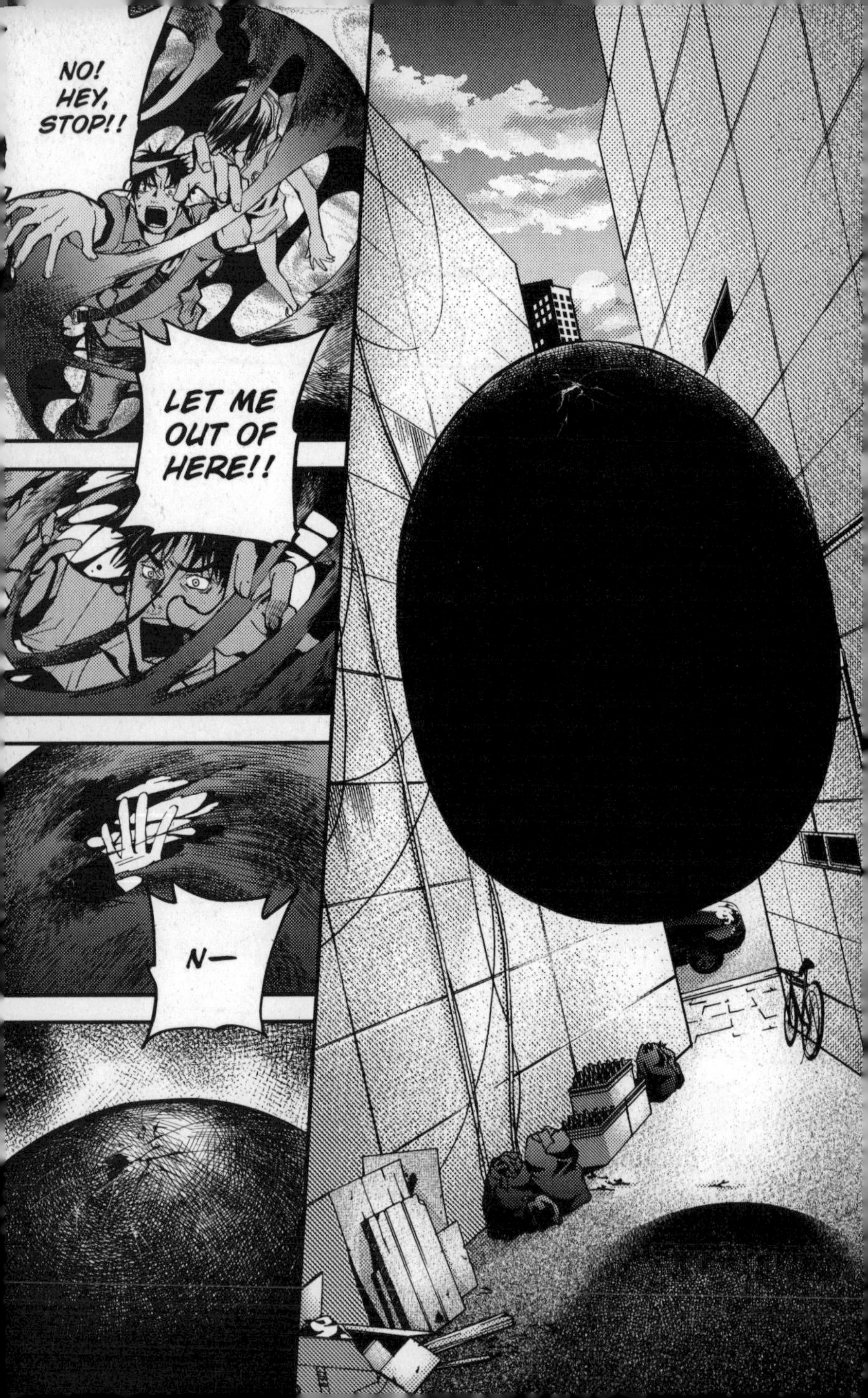
NO! HEY, STOP!!
LET ME OUT OF HERE!!
N—

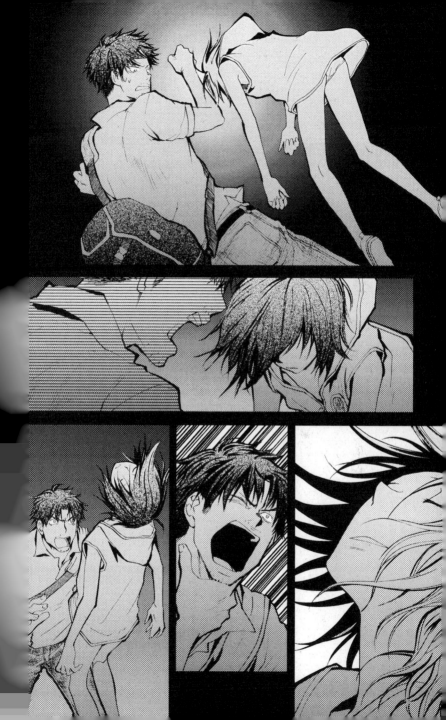

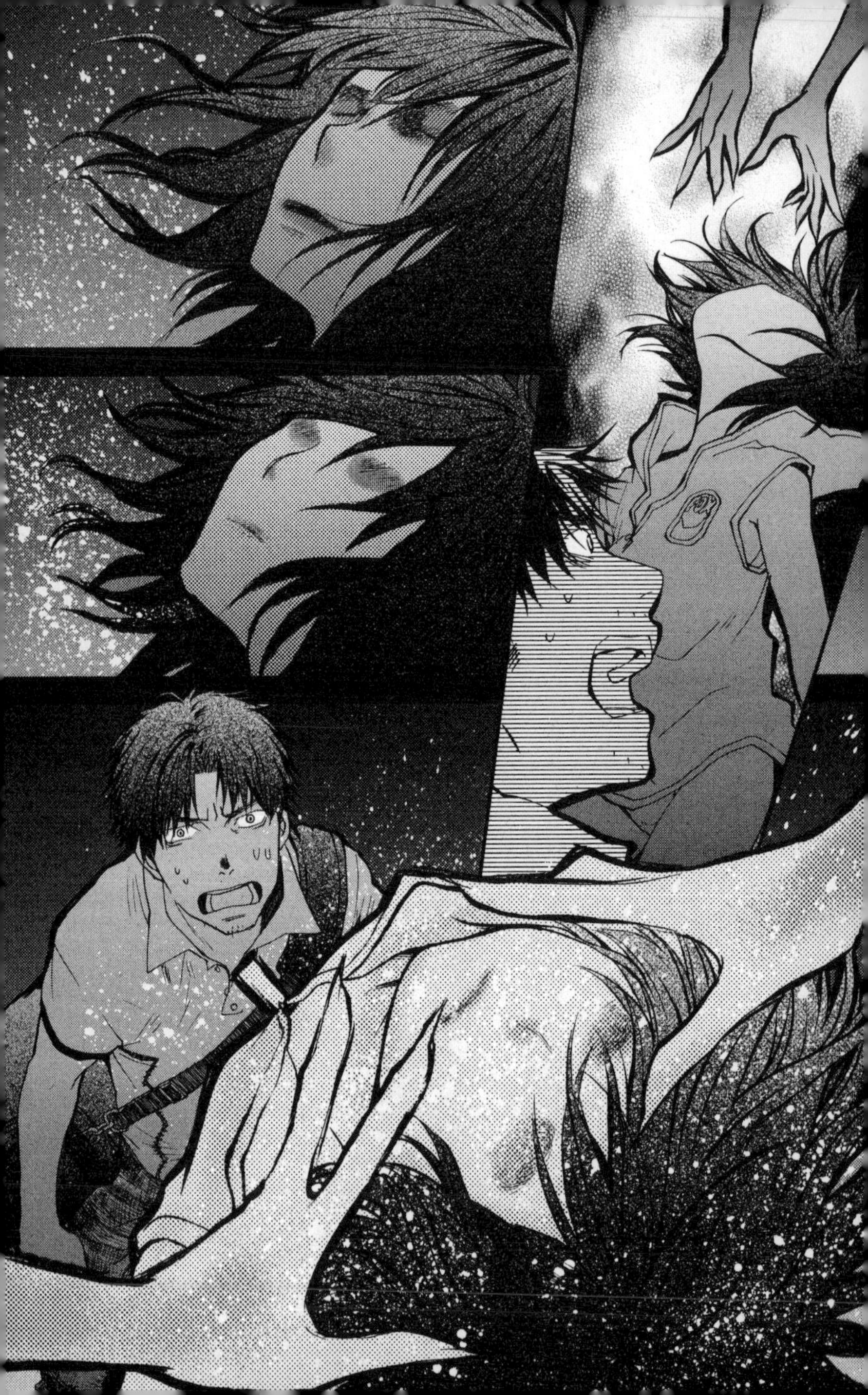

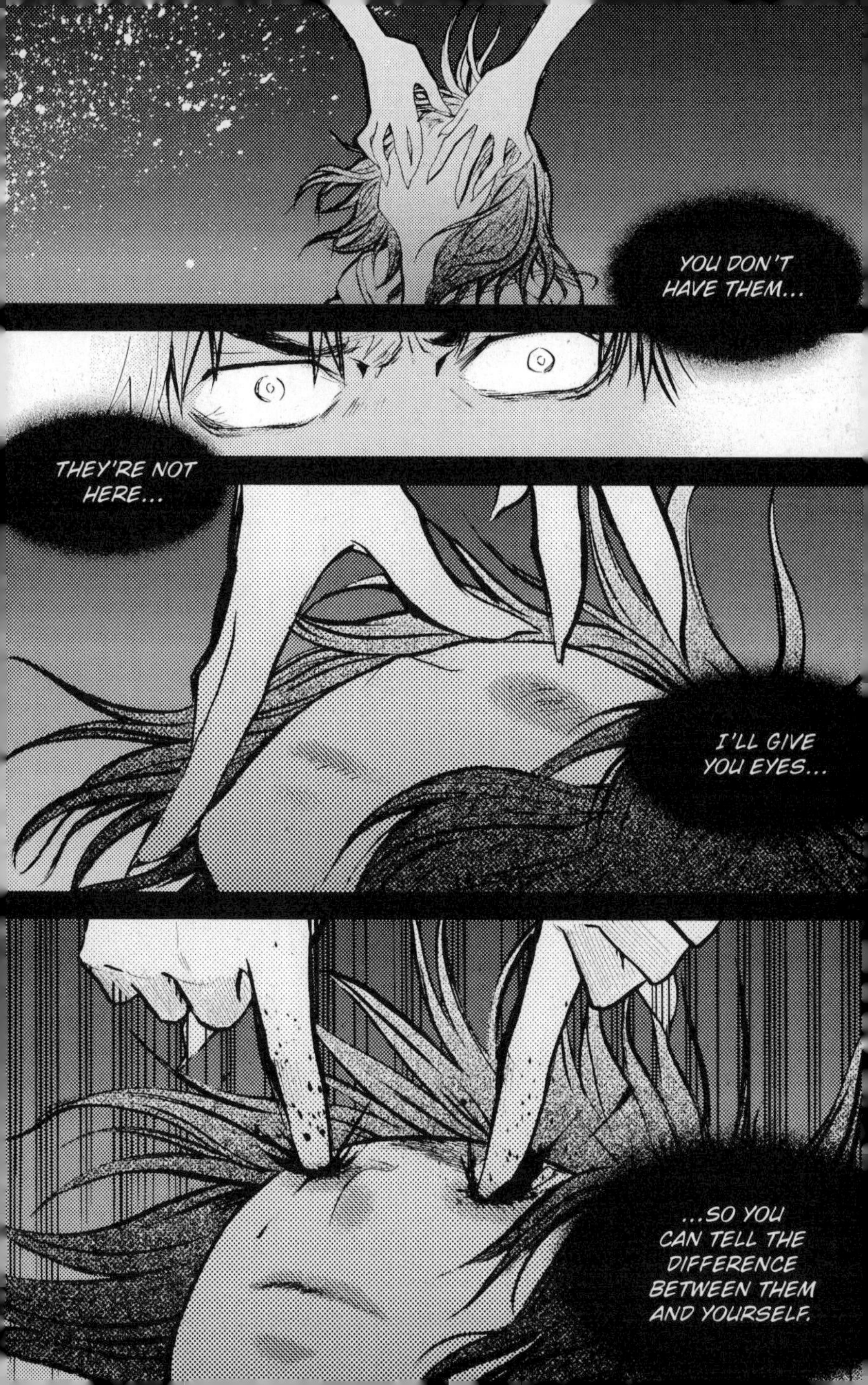
YOU DON'T HAVE THEM...
THEY'RE NOT HERE...
I'LL GIVE YOU EYES...
...SO YOU CAN TELL THE DIFFERENCE BETWEEN THEM AND YOURSELF.

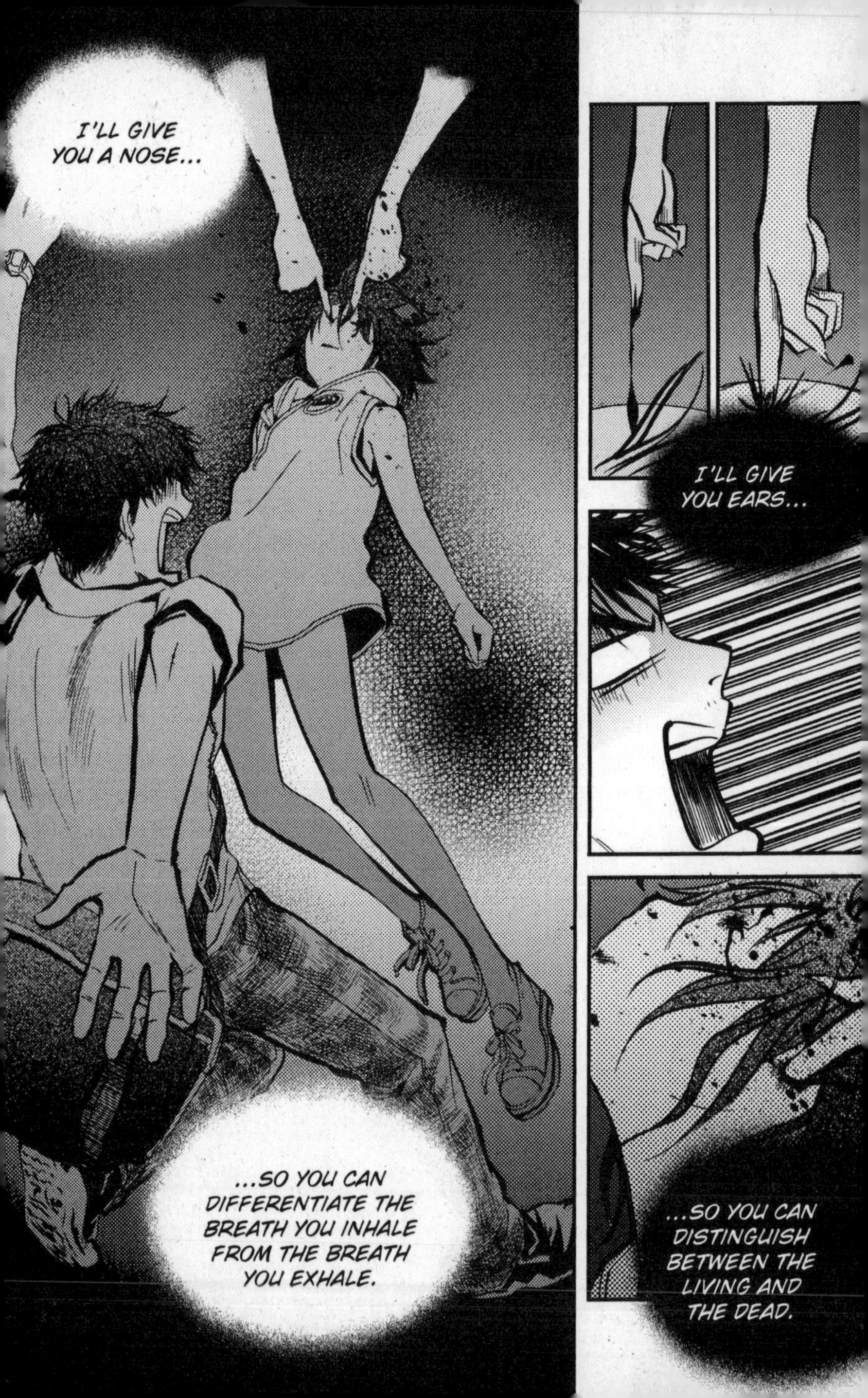
I'LL GIVE YOU A NOSE...
...SO YOU CAN DIFFERENTIATE THE BREATH YOU INHALE FROM THE BREATH YOU EXHALE.
I'LL GIVE YOU EARS...
...SO YOU CAN DISTINGUISH BETWEEN THE LIVING AND THE DEAD.

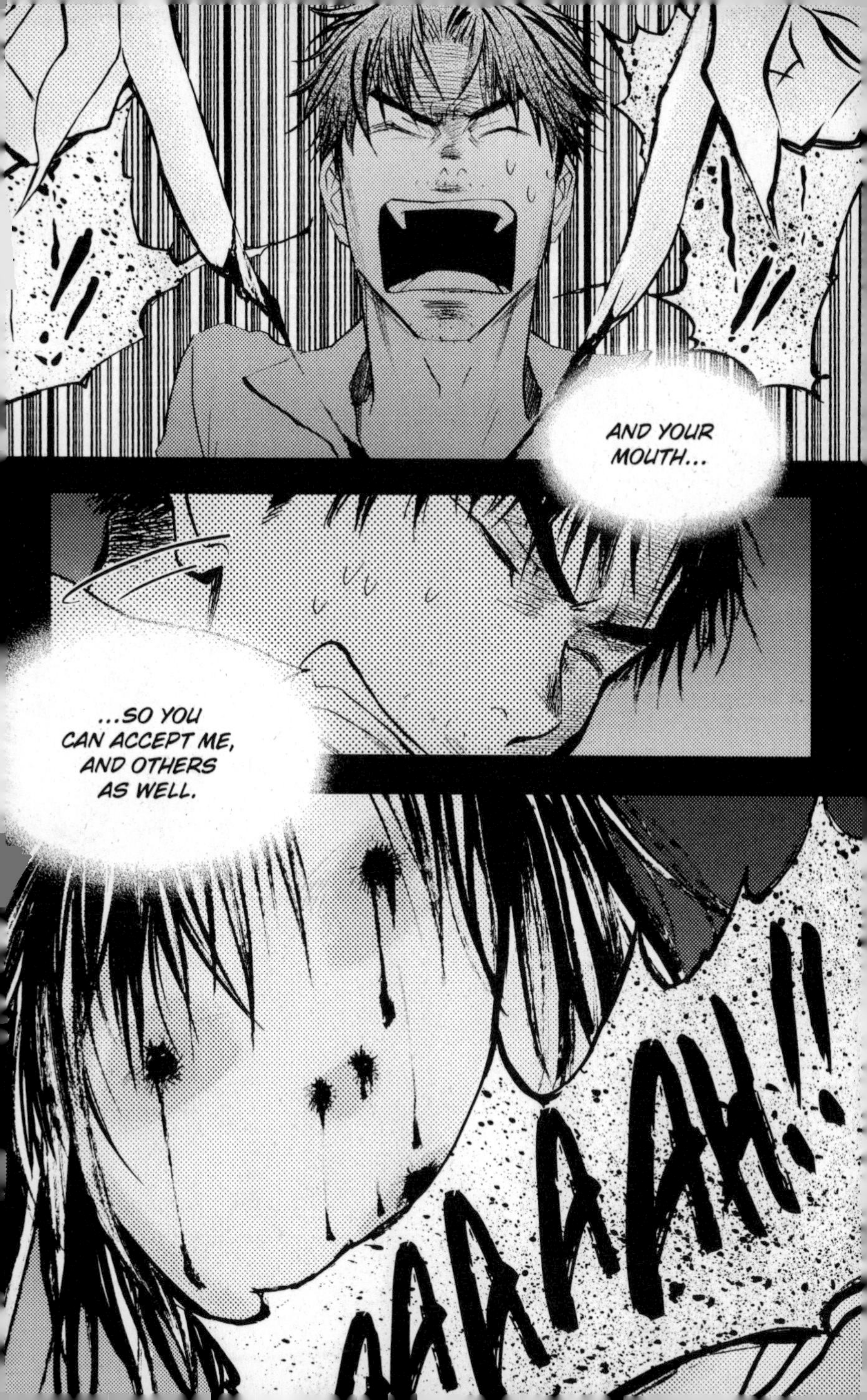
AND YOUR MOUTH...
...SO YOU CAN ACCEPT ME, AND OTHERS AS WELL.
AAAAAH!!

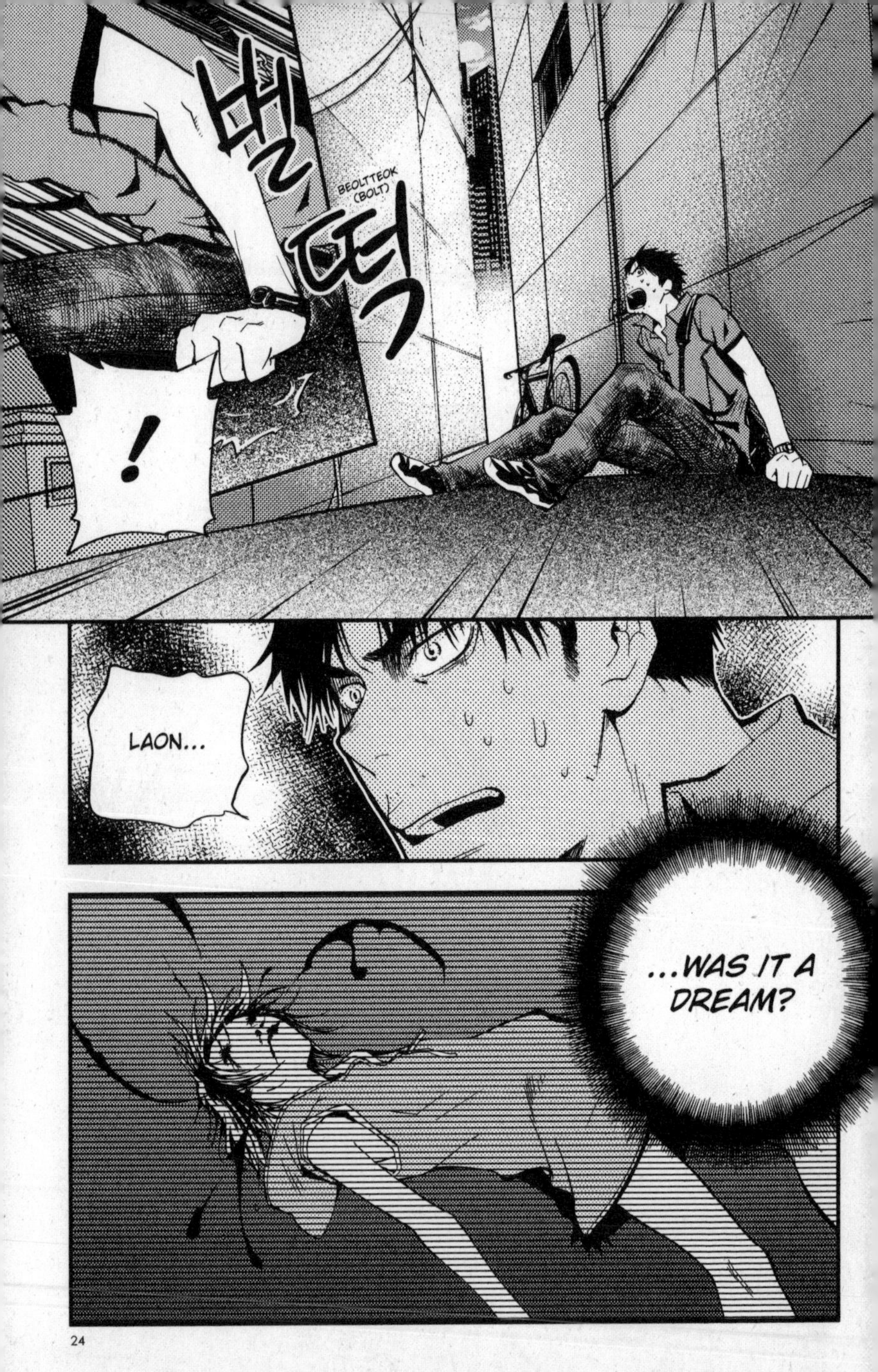
벌떡
BEOLTTEOK (BOLT)
!
LAON...
...WAS IT A DREAM?

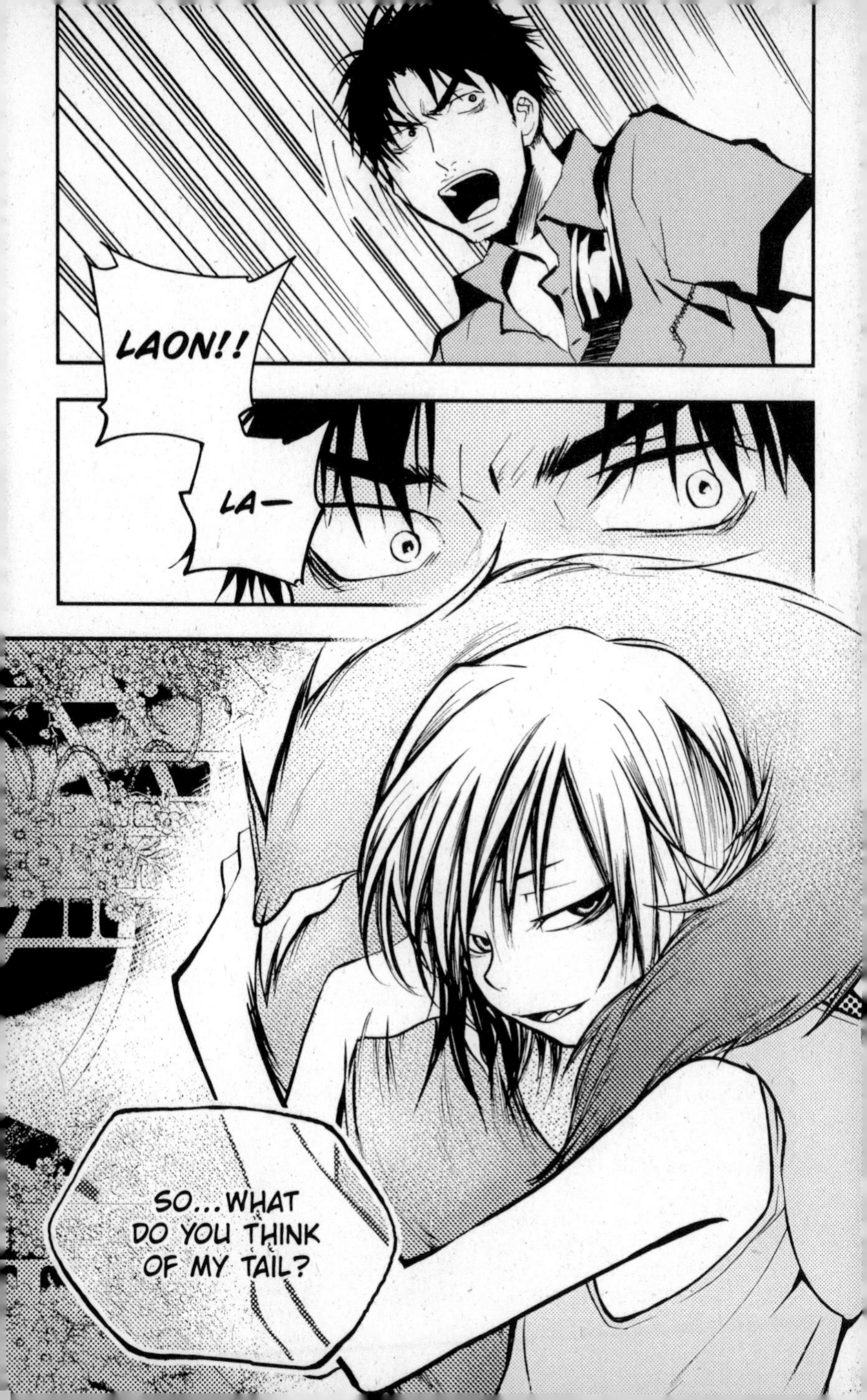
LAON!!
LA—
SO...WHAT DO YOU THINK OF MY TAIL?

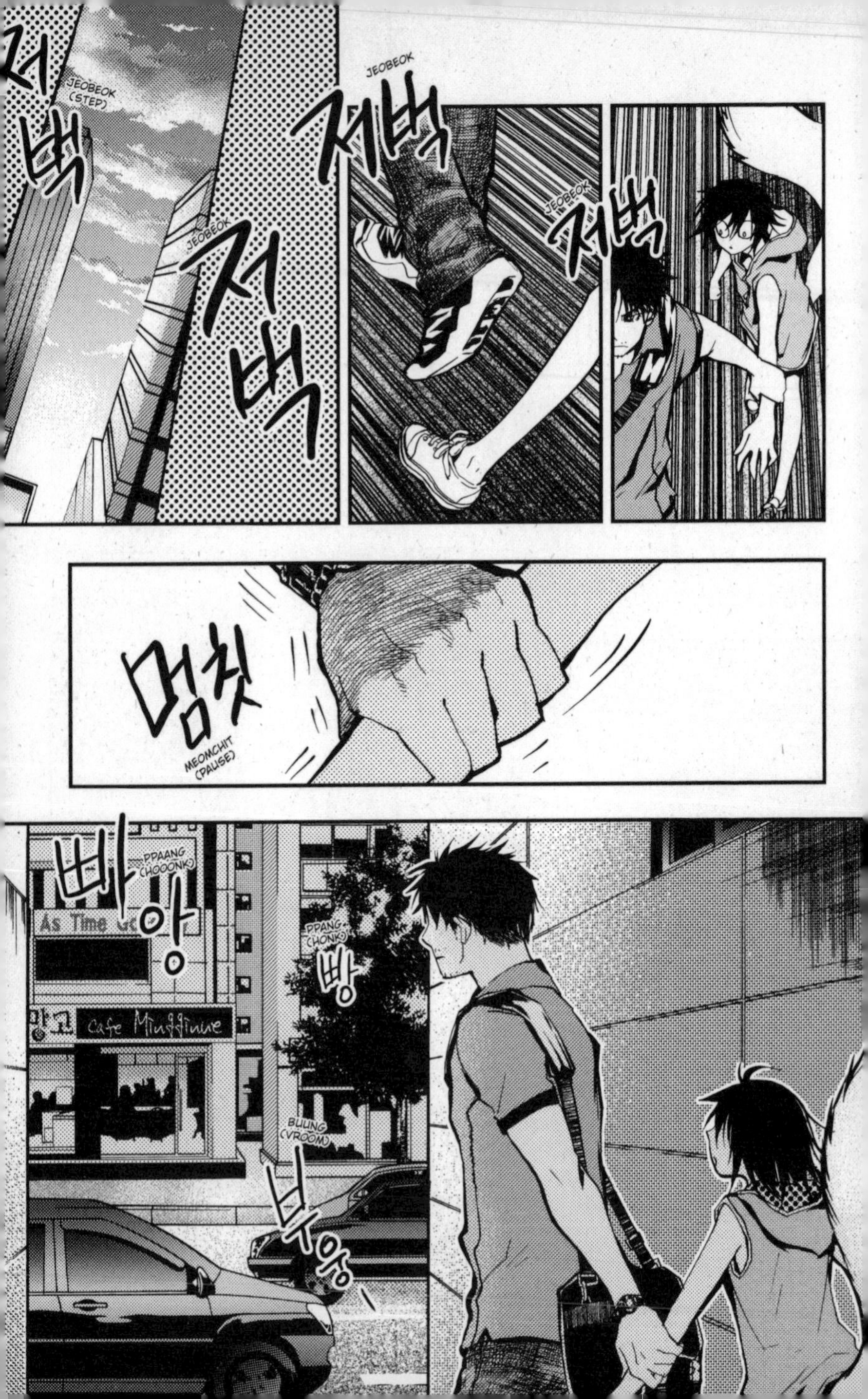

저벅
JEOBEOK (STEP)
저벅
JEOBEOK
저벅
JEOBEOK
저벅
JEOBEOK
멈칫
MEOMCHIT (PAUSE)
빠앙!
PPAANG (HOOONK)
빵
PPANG (HONK)
부웅
BUUNG (VROOM)

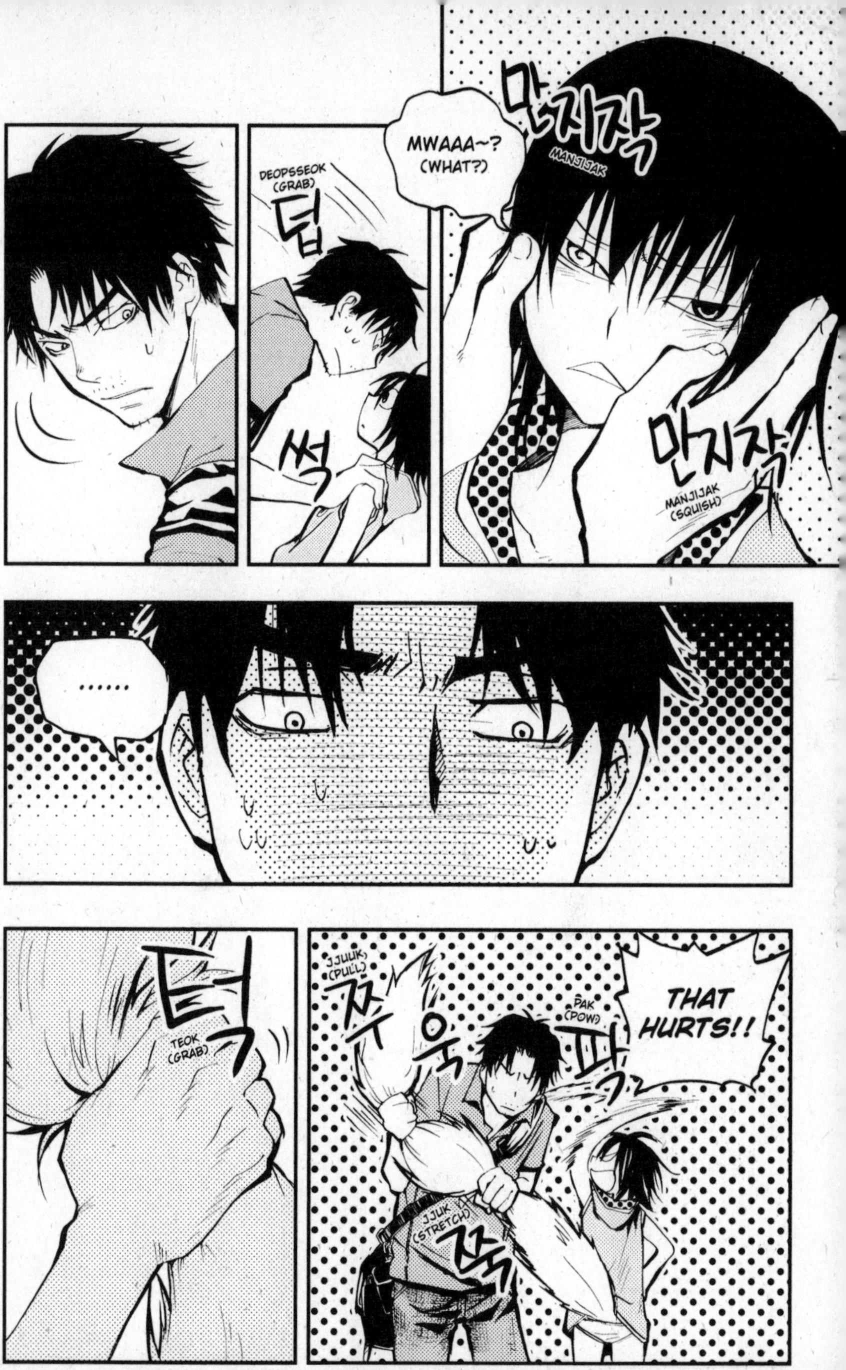
DEOPSSEOK (GRAB)
덥
석
MWAAA~? (WHAT?)
만지작
MANJIJAK
만지작
MANJIJAK (SQUISH)
......
턱
TEOK (GRAB)
JJUUK (PULL)
쭈욱
PAK (POW)
팍
THAT HURTS!!
JJUK (STRETCH)
쭉

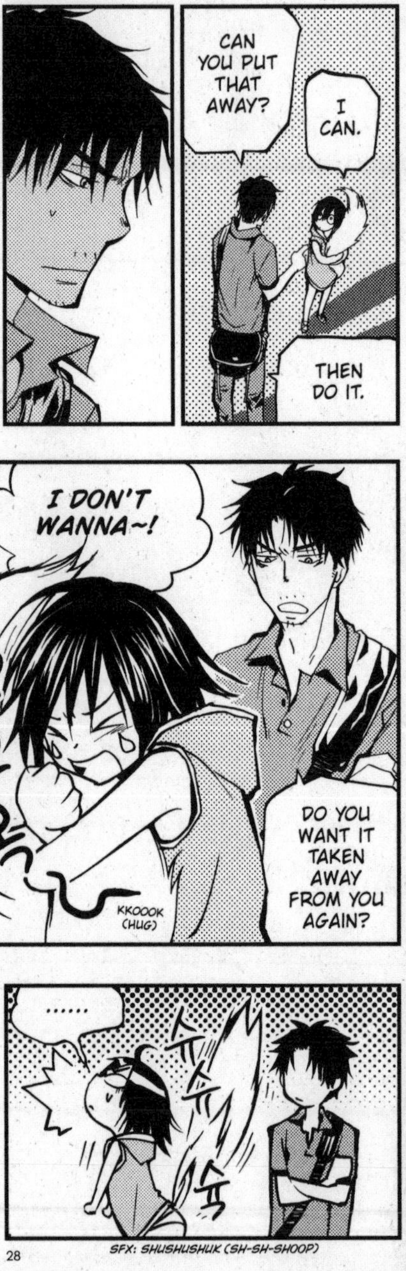
CAN YOU PUT THAT AWAY?
I CAN.
THEN DO IT.
I DON'T WANNA~!
꼬오옥
KKOOOK (HUG)
DO YOU WANT IT TAKEN AWAY FROM YOU AGAIN?
......
슈슈슉

SFX: SHUSHUSHUK (SH-SH-SHOOP)

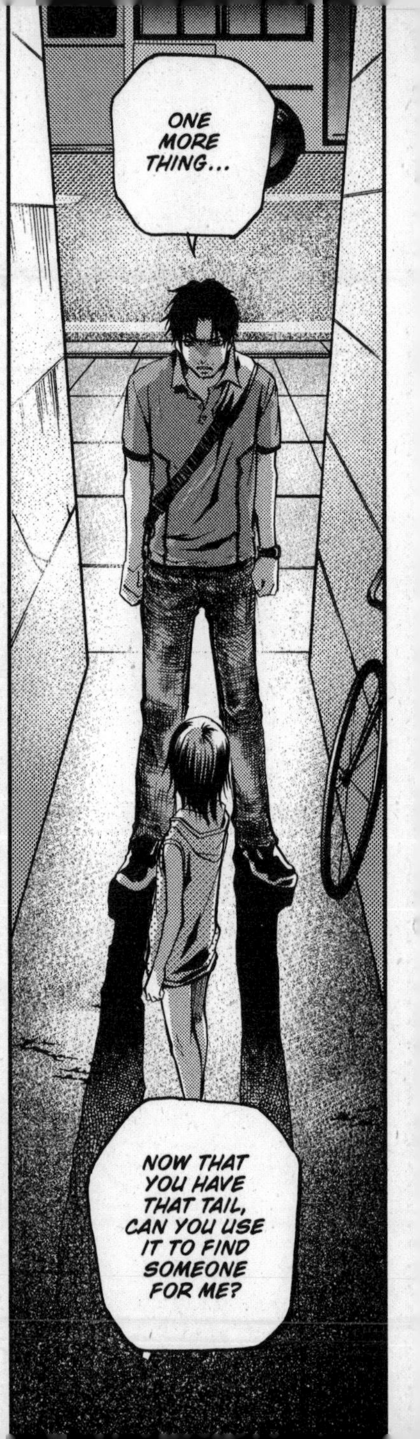
ONE MORE THING...
NOW THAT YOU HAVE THAT TAIL, CAN YOU USE IT TO FIND SOMEONE FOR ME?

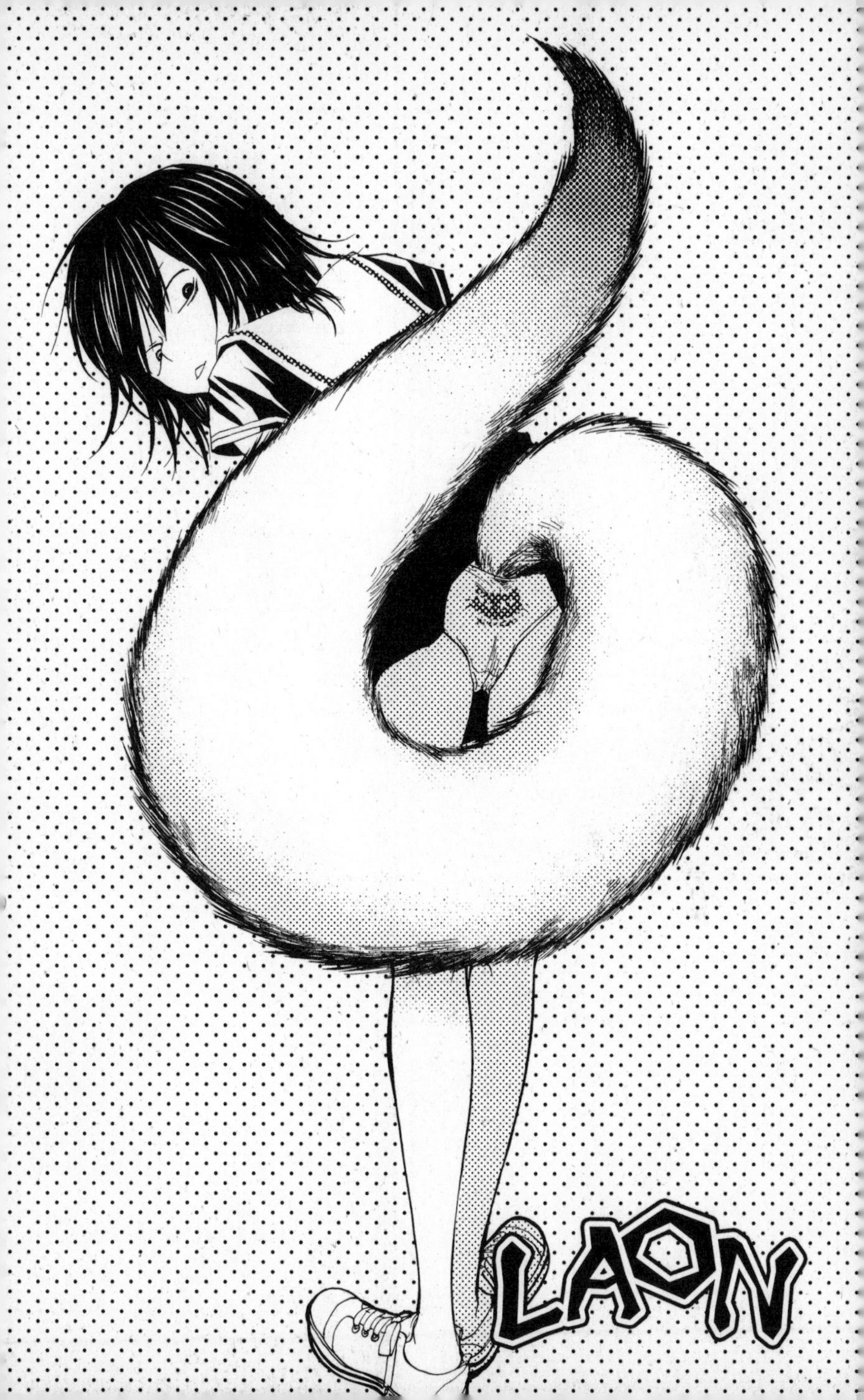
LAON

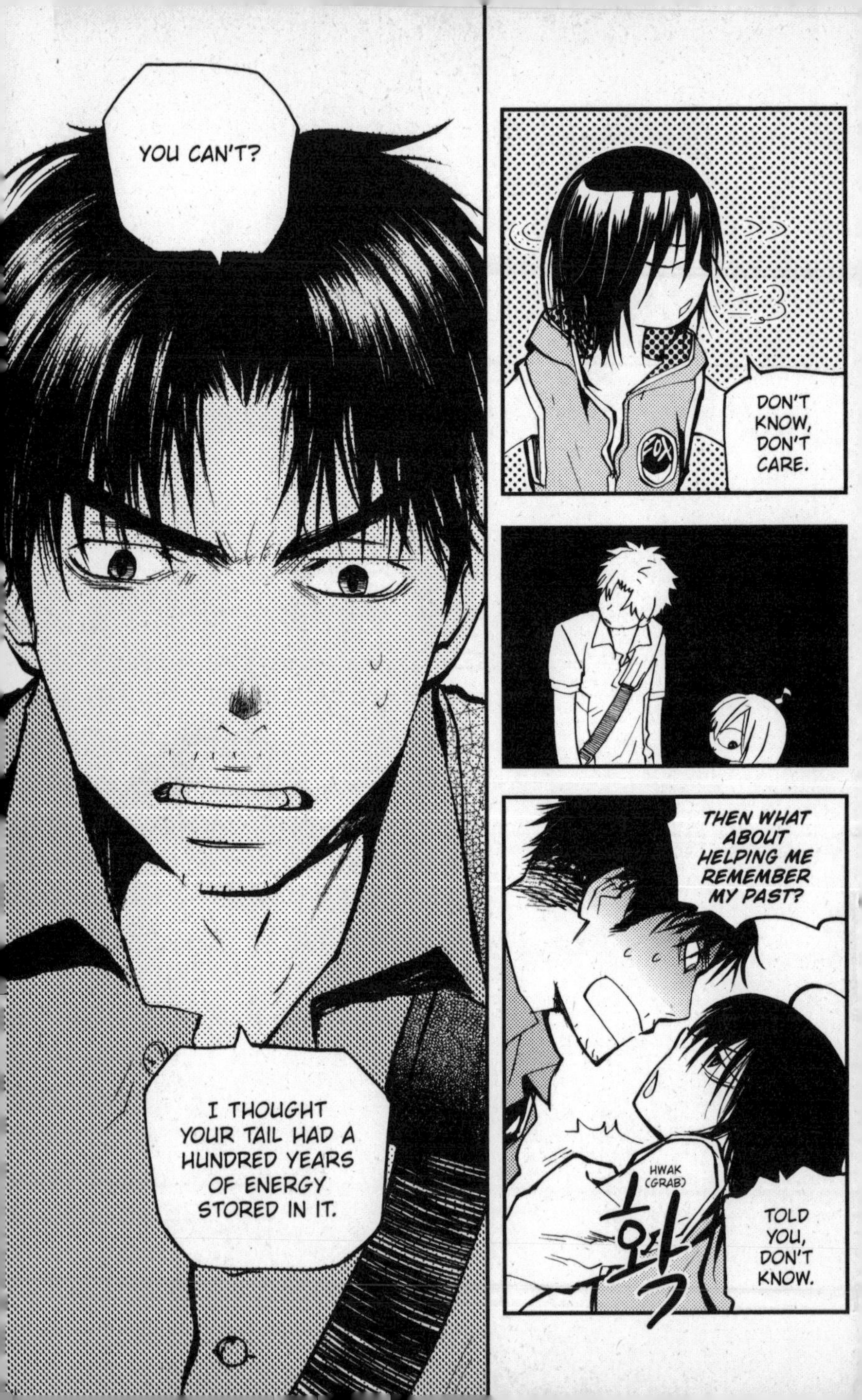
YOU CAN'T?
I THOUGHT YOUR TAIL HAD A HUNDRED YEARS OF ENERGY STORED IN IT.
DON'T KNOW, DON'T CARE.
THEN WHAT ABOUT HELPING ME REMEMBER MY PAST?
HWAK (GRAB)
TOLD YOU, DON'T KNOW.

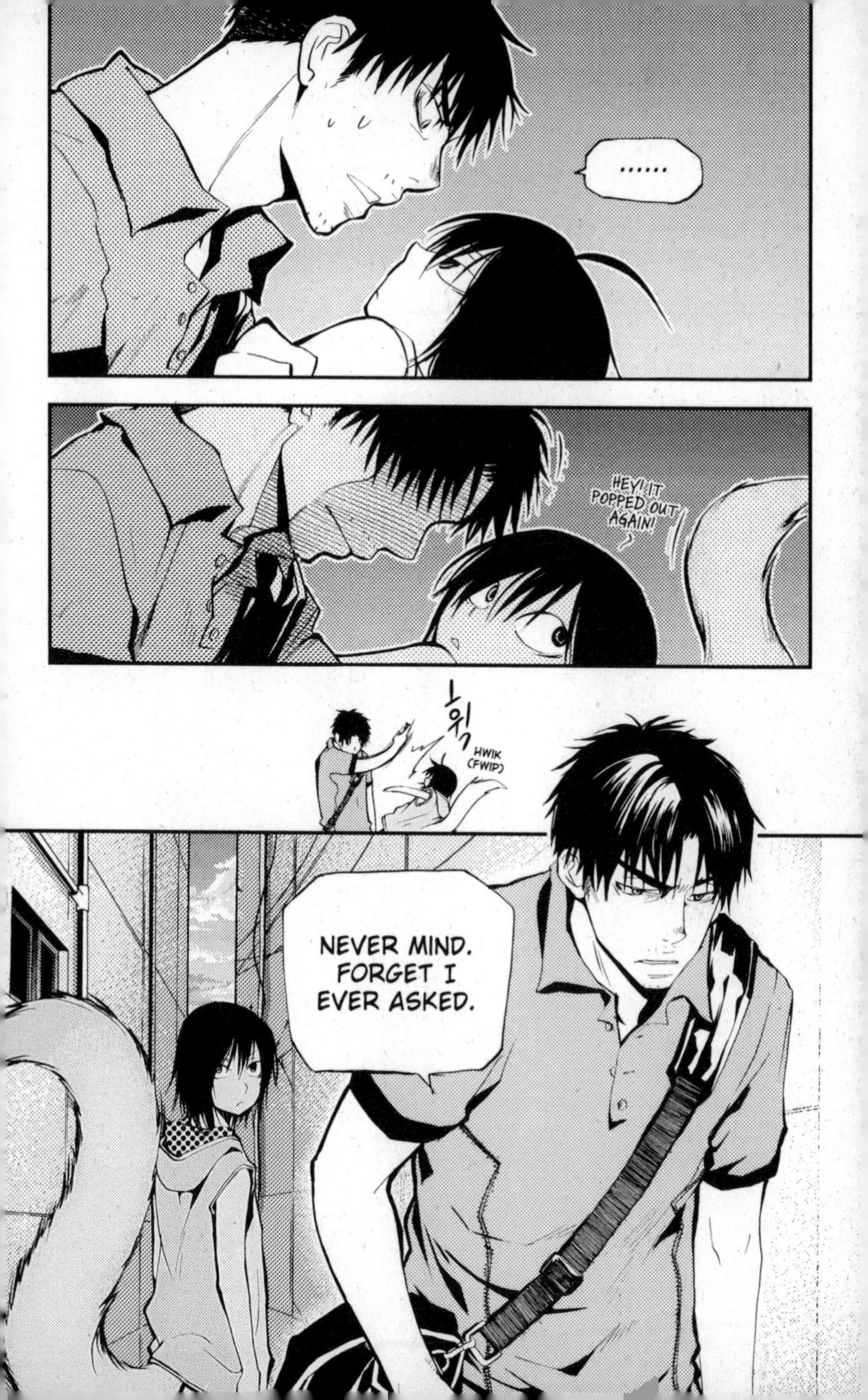
......
HEY! IT POPPED OUT AGAIN!
휘익
HWIK (FWIP)
NEVER MIND. FORGET I EVER ASKED.

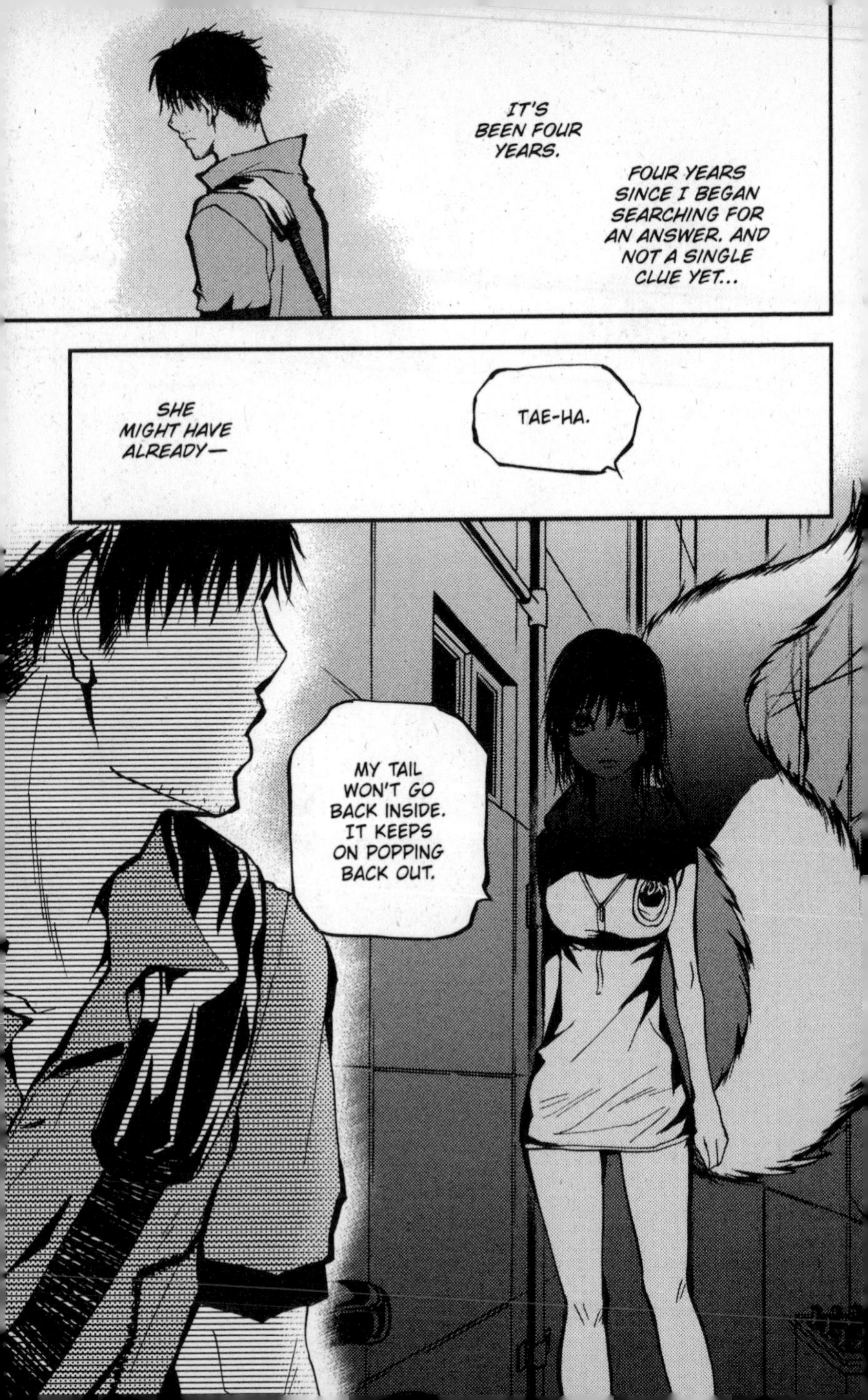
IT'S BEEN FOUR YEARS.
FOUR YEARS SINCE I BEGAN SEARCHING FOR AN ANSWER. AND NOT A SINGLE CLUE YET...
SHE MIGHT HAVE ALREADY—
TAE-HA.
MY TAIL WON'T GO BACK INSIDE. IT KEEPS ON POPPING BACK OUT.

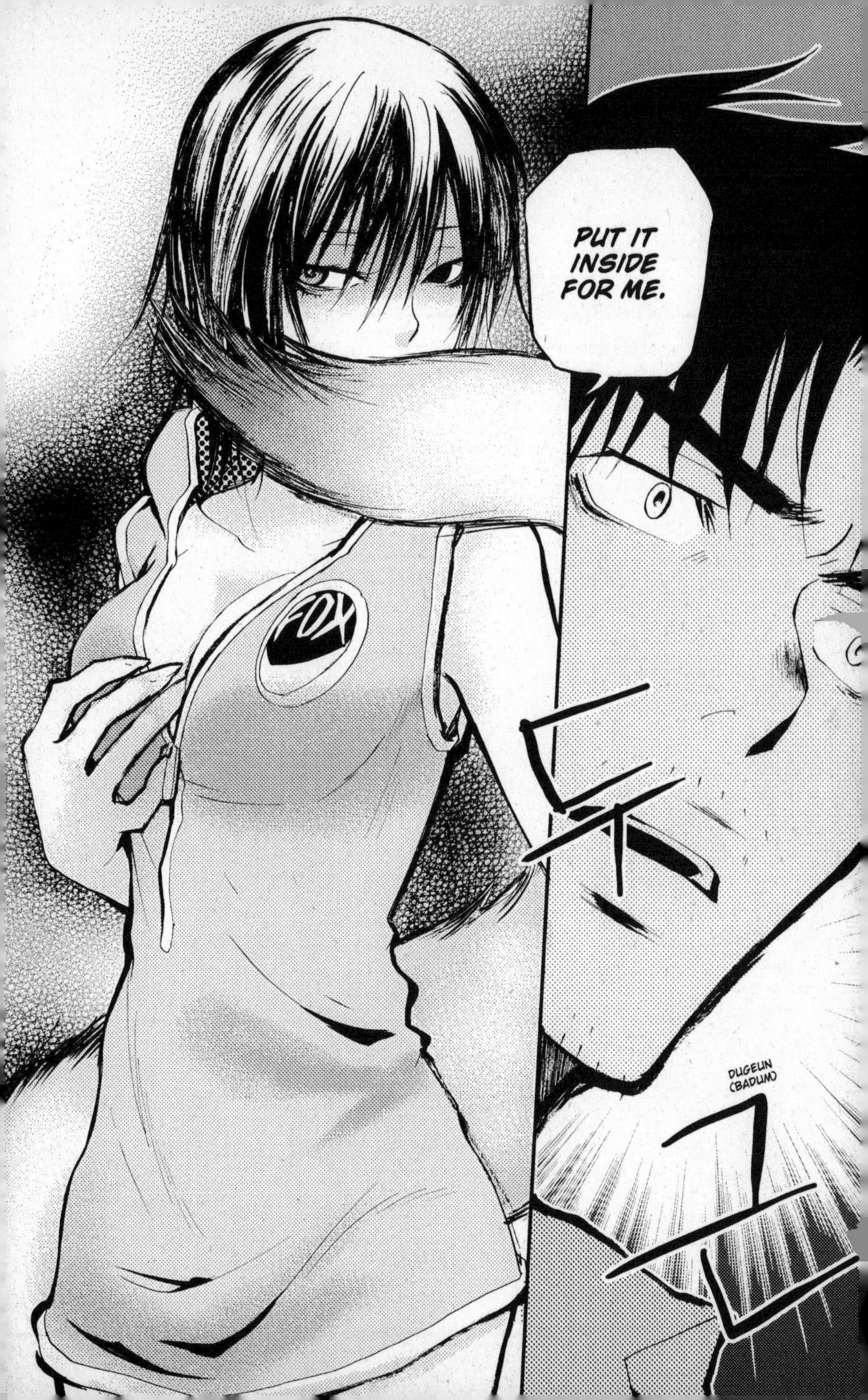
PUT IT INSIDE FOR ME.
DUGEUN (BADUM)

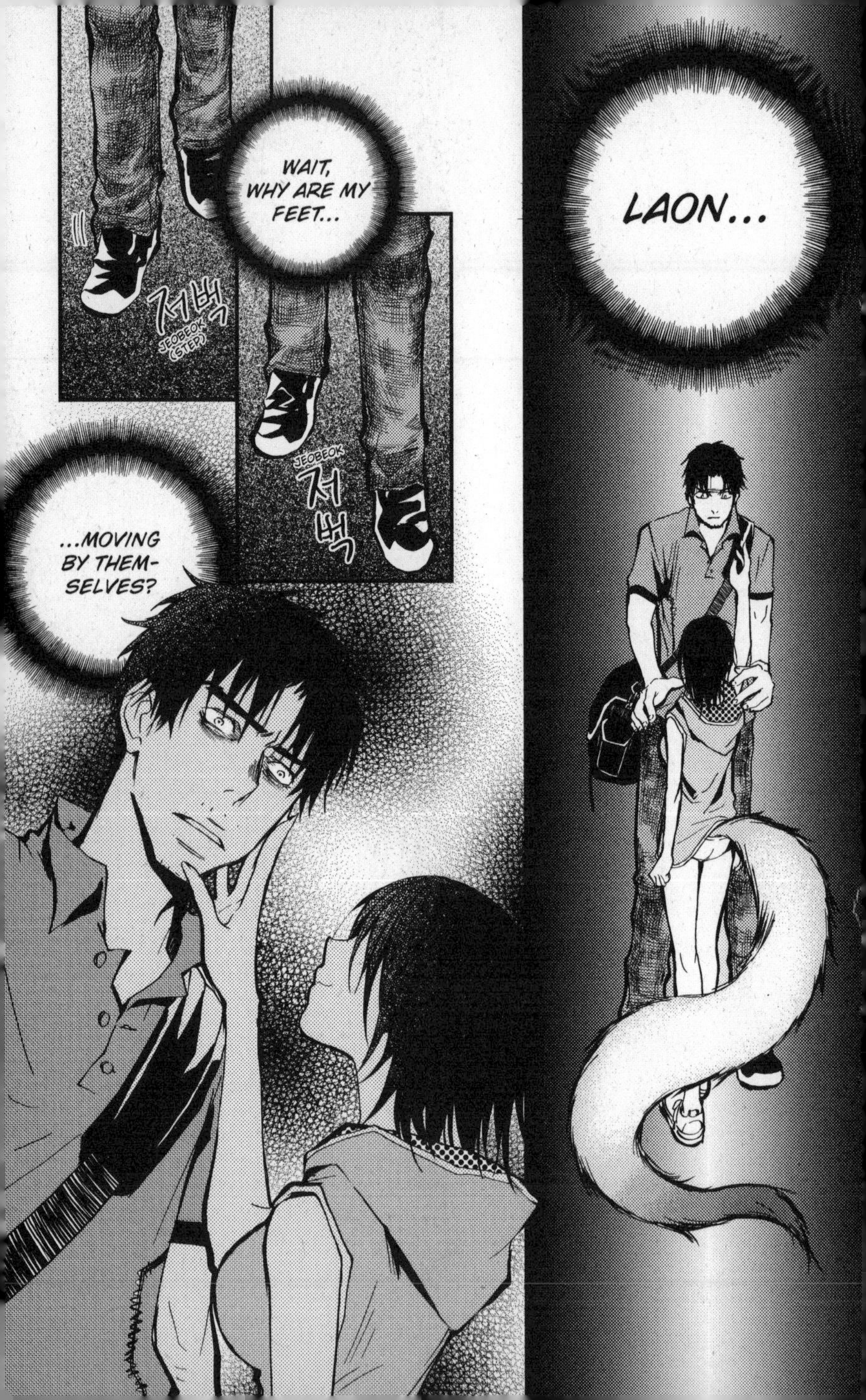

저벅
JEOBEOK (STEP)
WAIT, WHY ARE MY FEET...
JEOBEOK
저벅
...MOVING BY THEM-SELVES?
LAON...

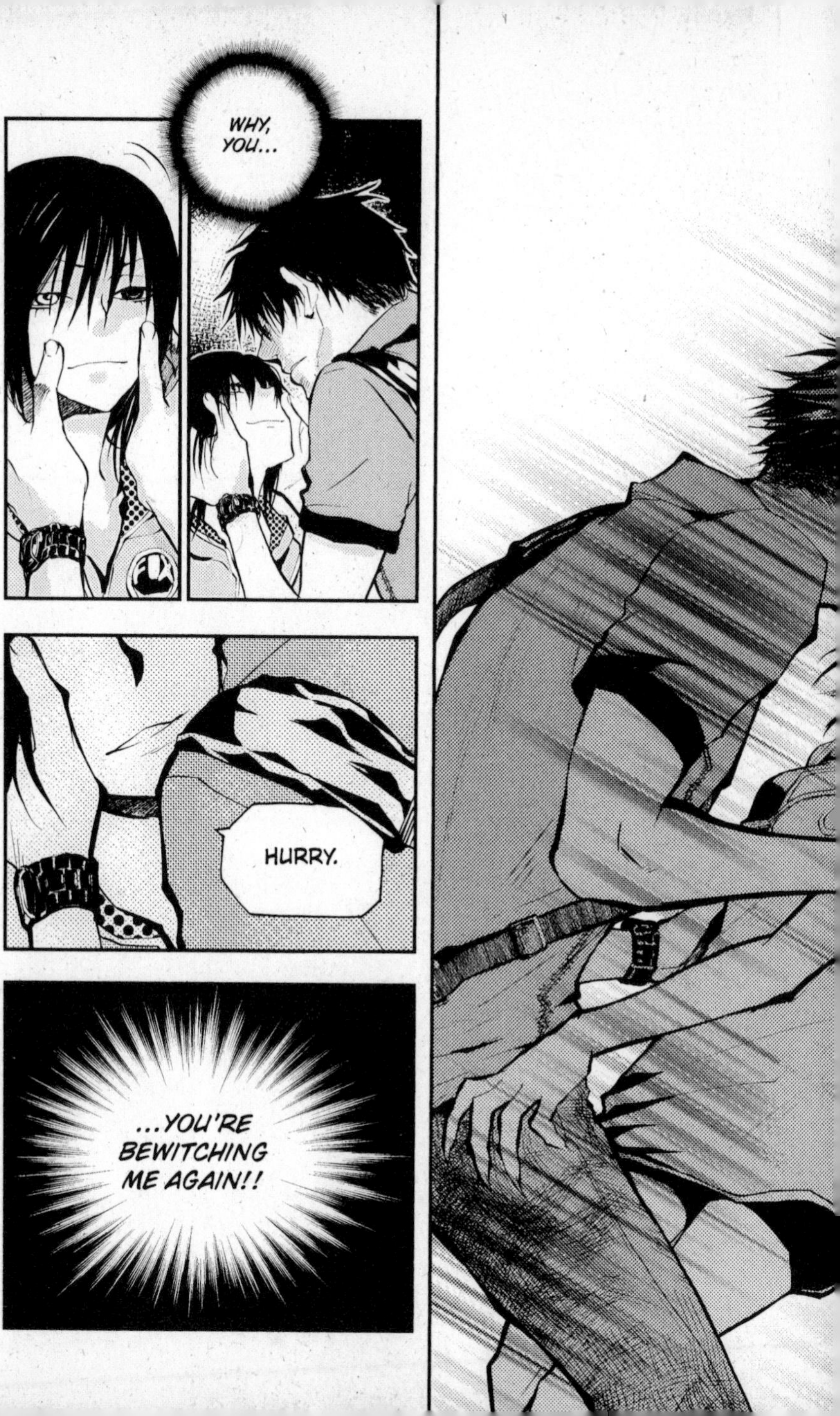
WHY, YOU...
HURRY.
...YOU'RE BEWITCHING ME AGAIN!!

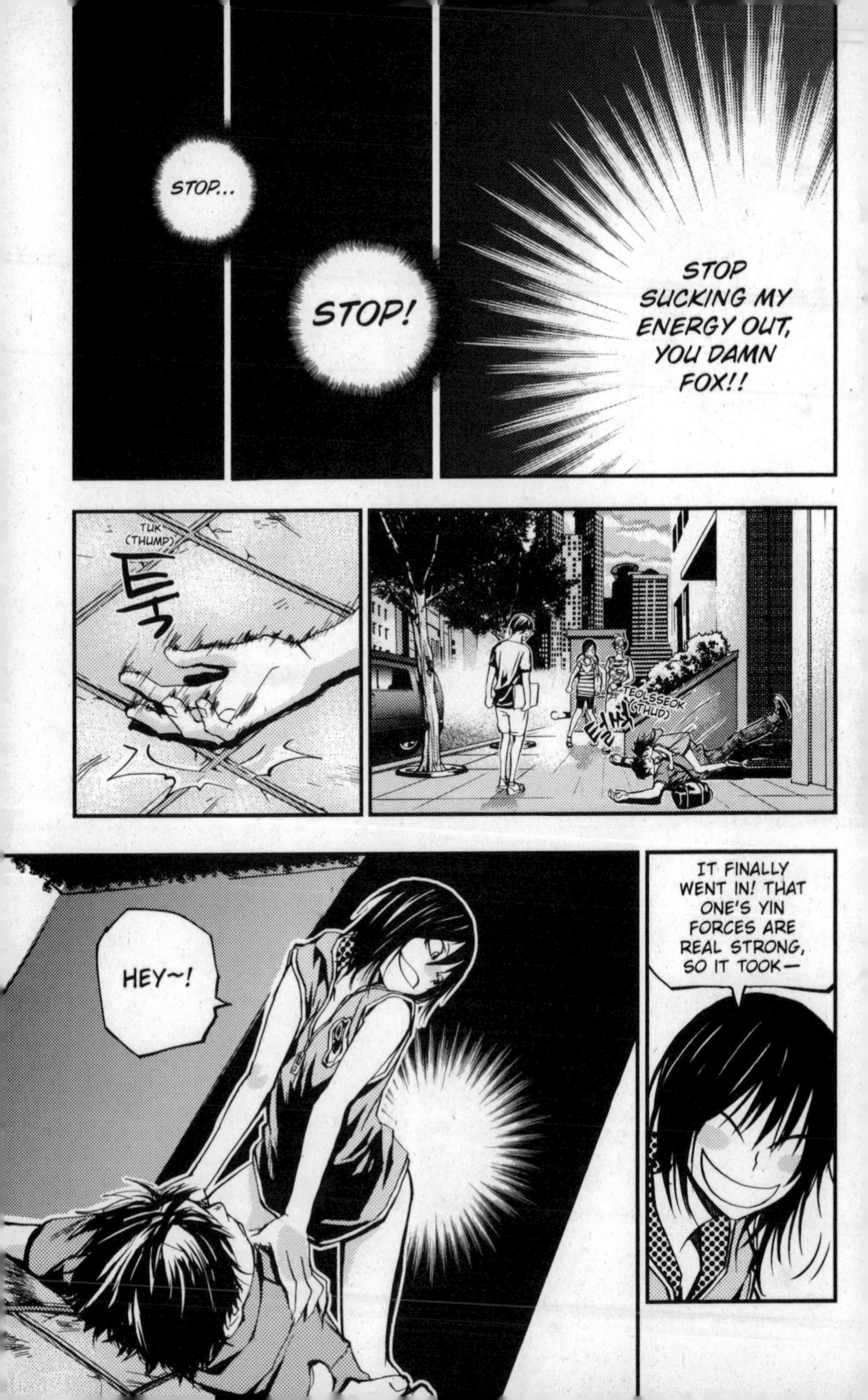
STOP...
STOP!
STOP SUCKING MY ENERGY OUT, YOU DAMN FOX!!
TUK (THUMP)
TEOLSSEOK (THUD)
HEY~!
IT FINALLY WENT IN! THAT ONE'S YIN FORCES ARE REAL STRONG, SO IT TOOK—

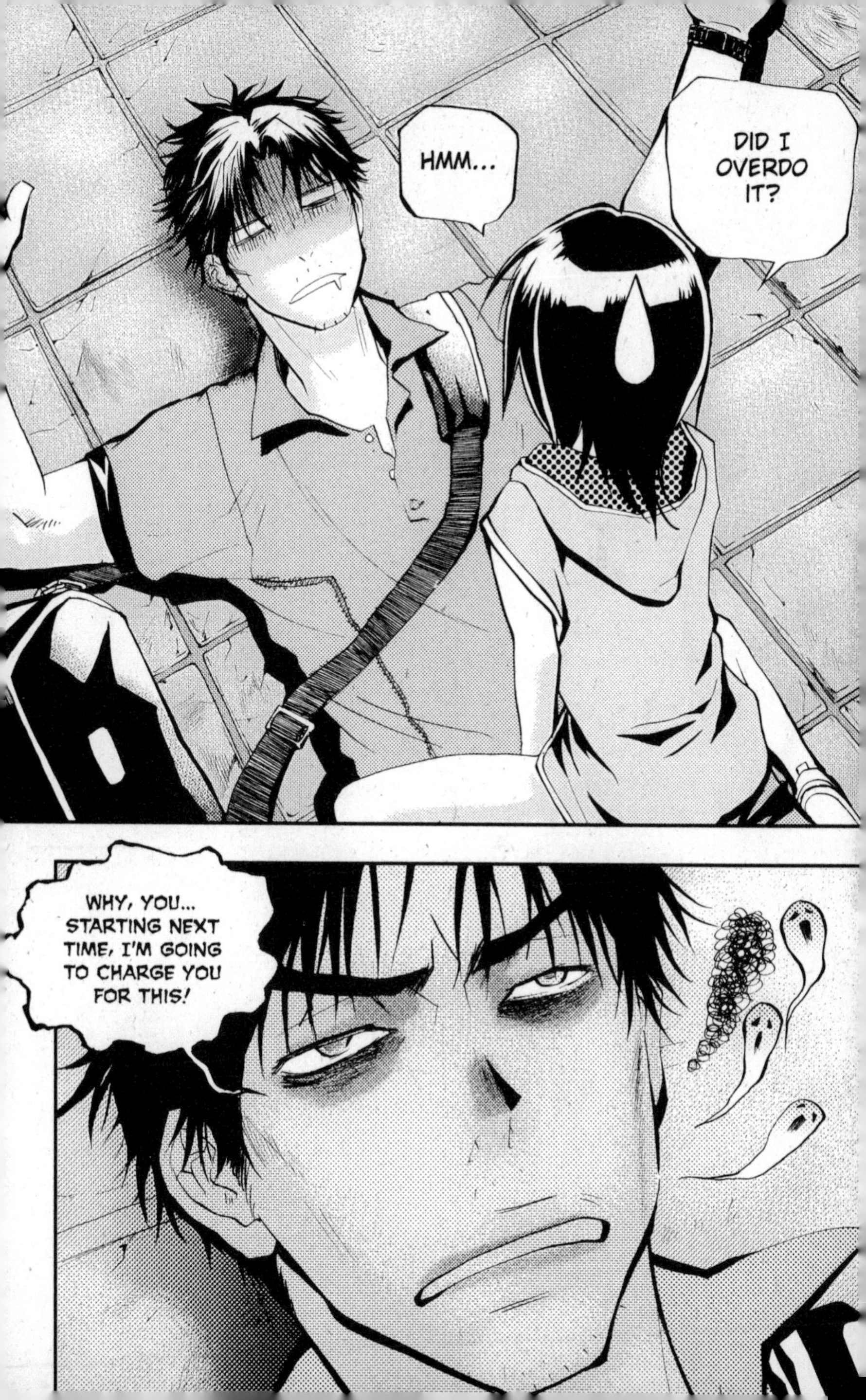
HMM...
DID I OVERDO IT?
WHY, YOU... STARTING NEXT TIME, I'M GOING TO CHARGE YOU FOR THIS!

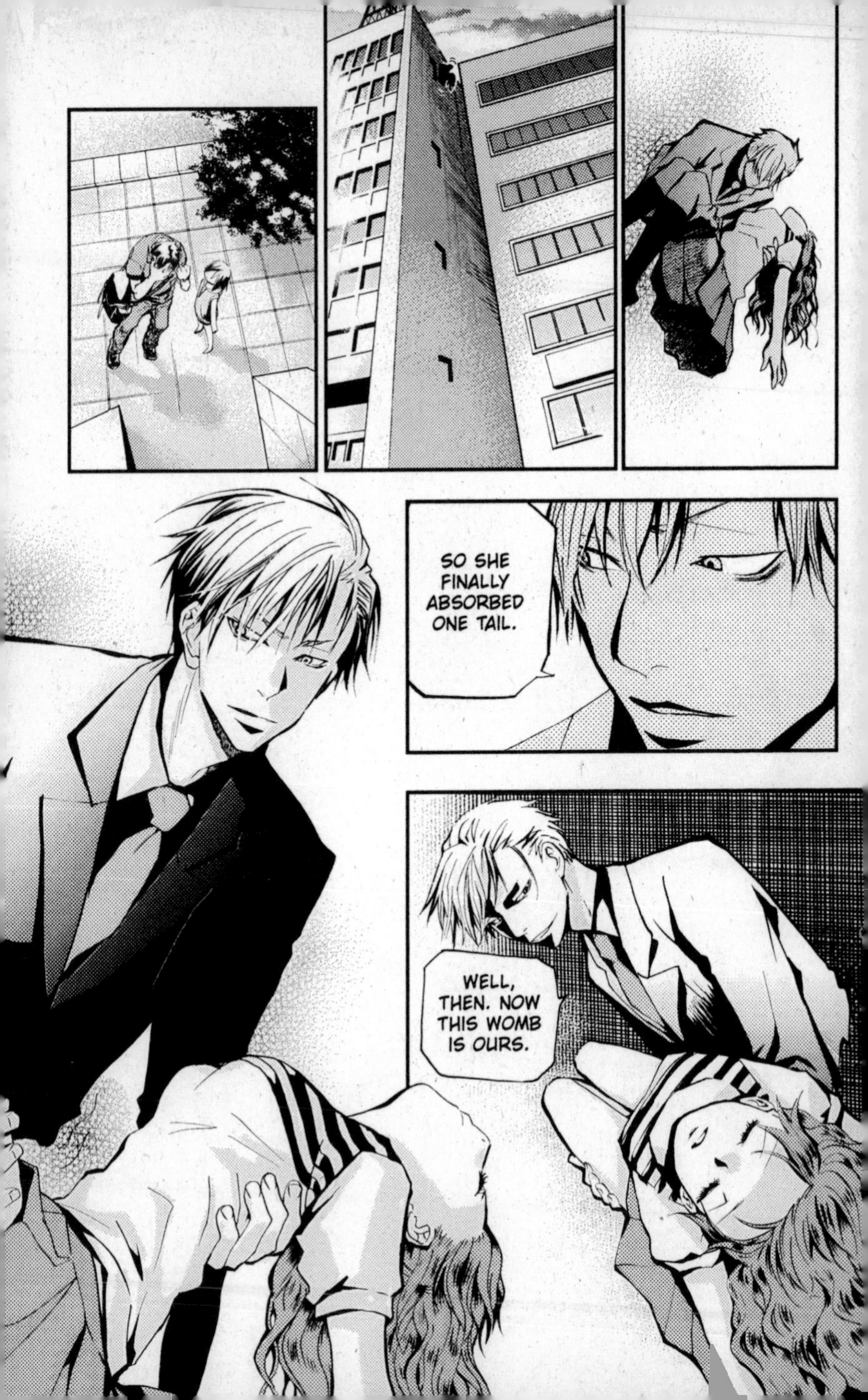
SO SHE FINALLY ABSORBED ONE TAIL.
WELL, THEN. NOW THIS WOMB IS OURS.

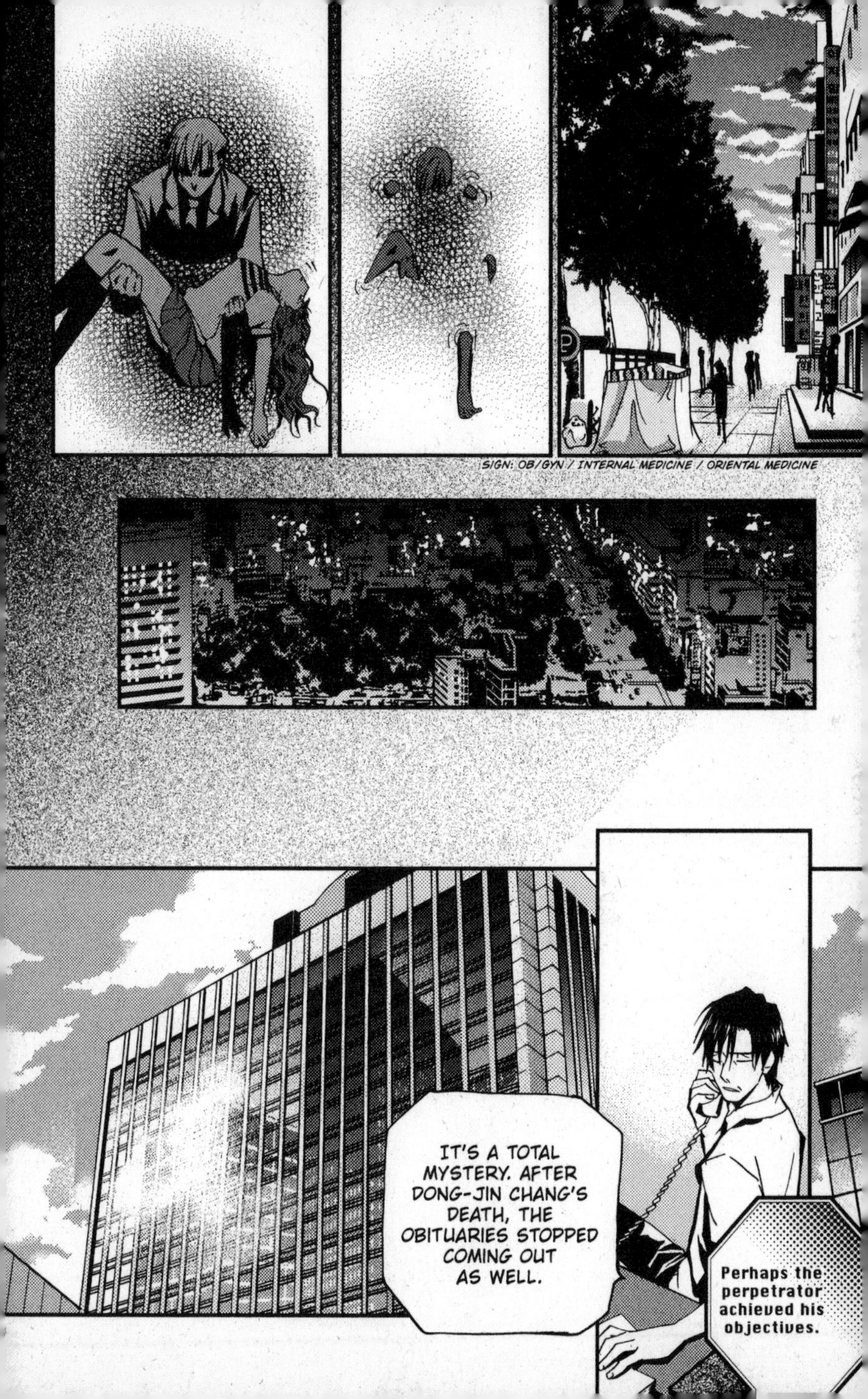
SIGN: OB/GYN / INTERNAL MEDICINE / ORIENTAL MEDICINE
IT'S A TOTAL MYSTERY. AFTER DONG-JIN CHANG'S DEATH, THE OBITUARIES STOPPED COMING OUT AS WELL.
Perhaps the perpetrator achieved his objectives.

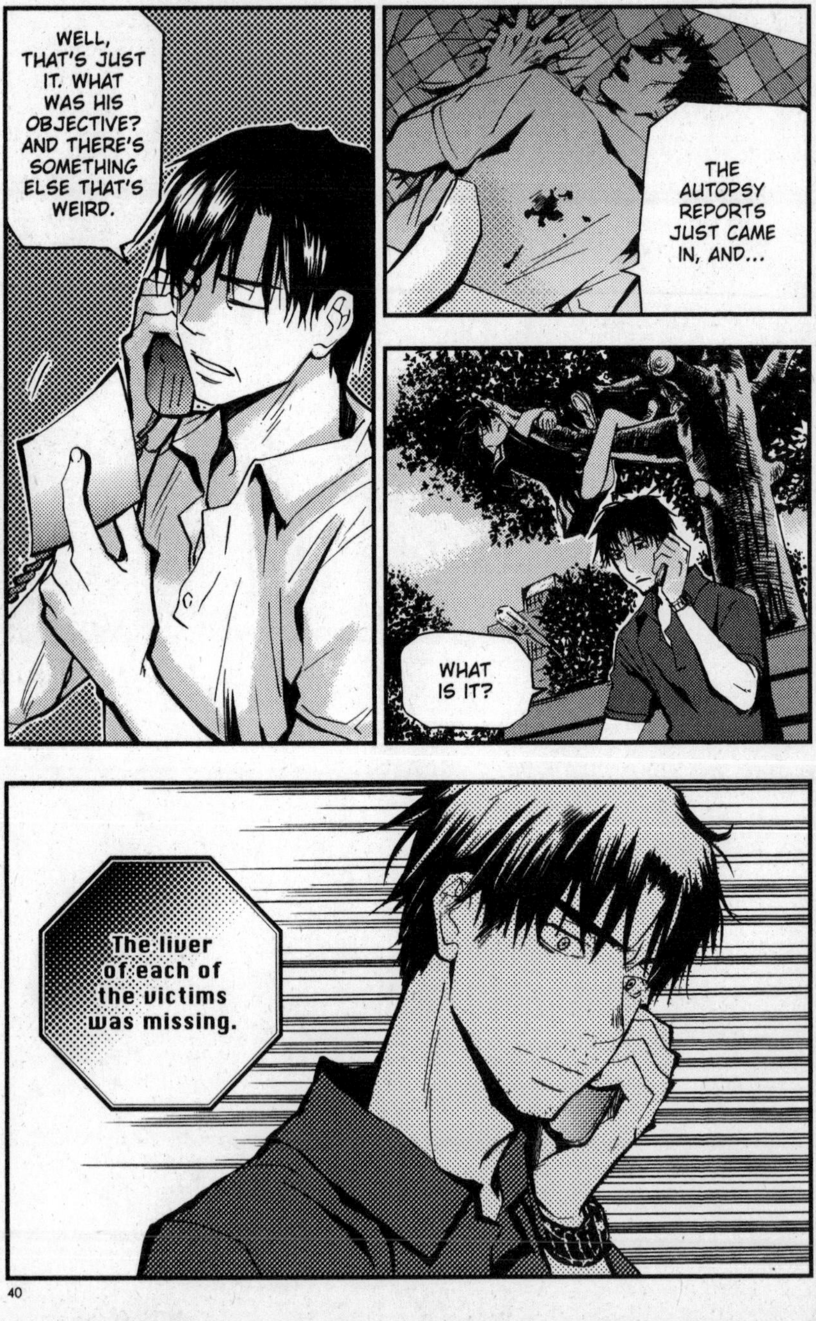
WELL, THAT'S JUST IT. WHAT WAS HIS OBJECTIVE? AND THERE'S SOMETHING ELSE THAT'S WEIRD.
THE AUTOPSY REPORTS JUST CAME IN, AND...
WHAT IS IT?
The liver of each of the victims was missing.

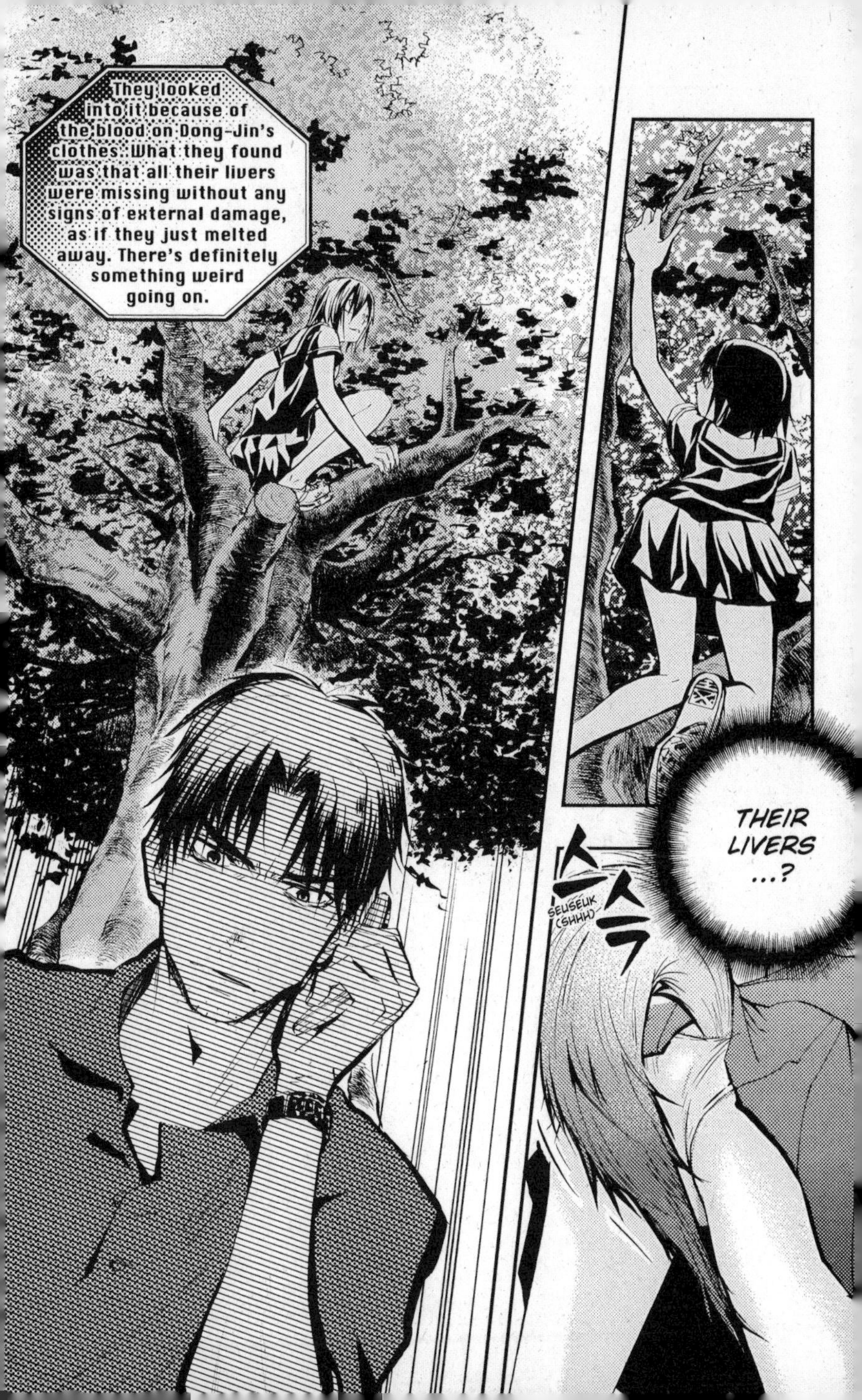
They looked into it because of the blood on Dong-Jin's clothes. What they found was that all their livers were missing without any signs of external damage, as if they just melted away. There's definitely something weird going on.
THEIR LIVERS ...?
SEUSEUK (SHHH)

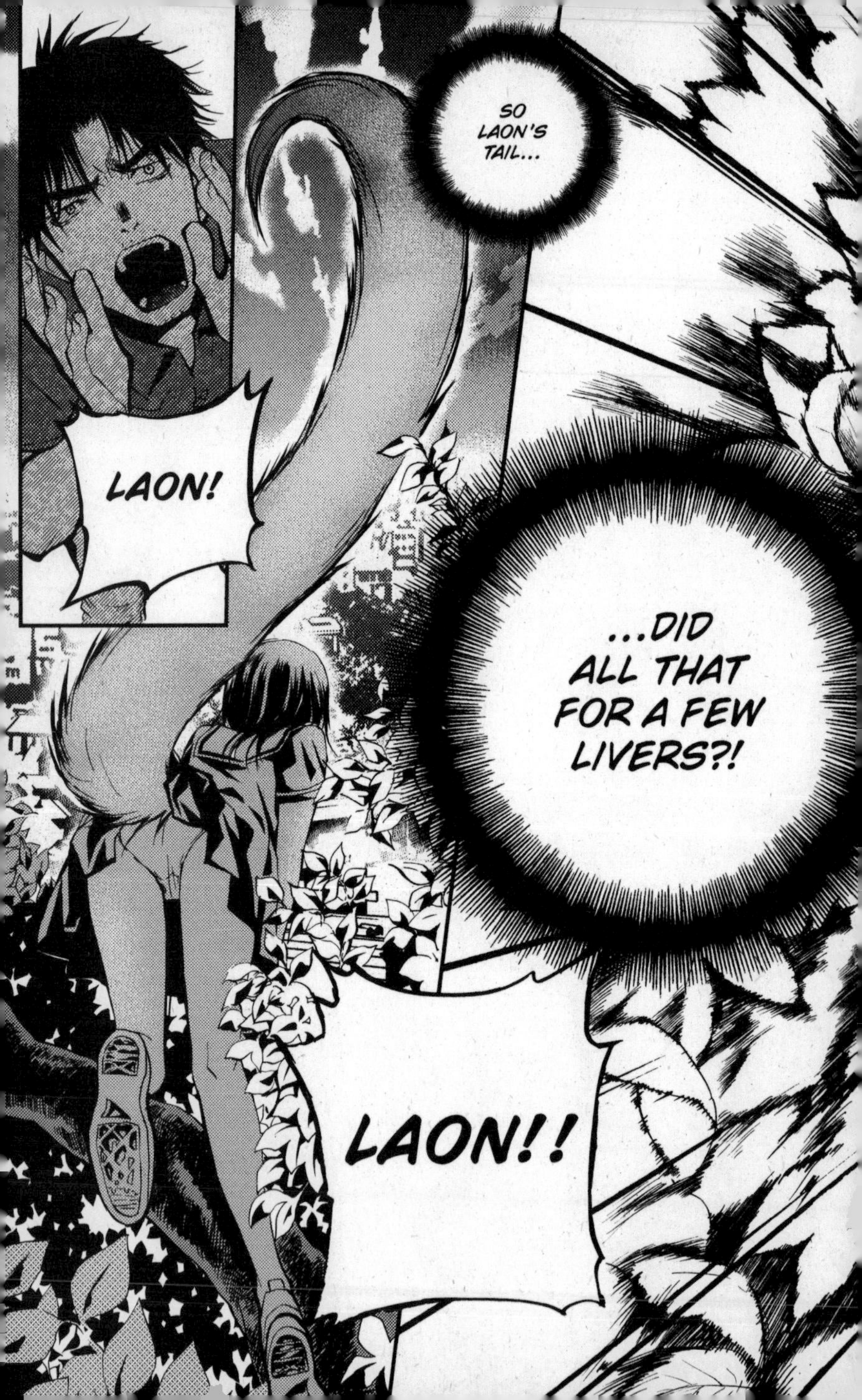
LAON!
SO LAON'S TAIL...
...DID ALL THAT FOR A FEW LIVERS?!
LAON!!

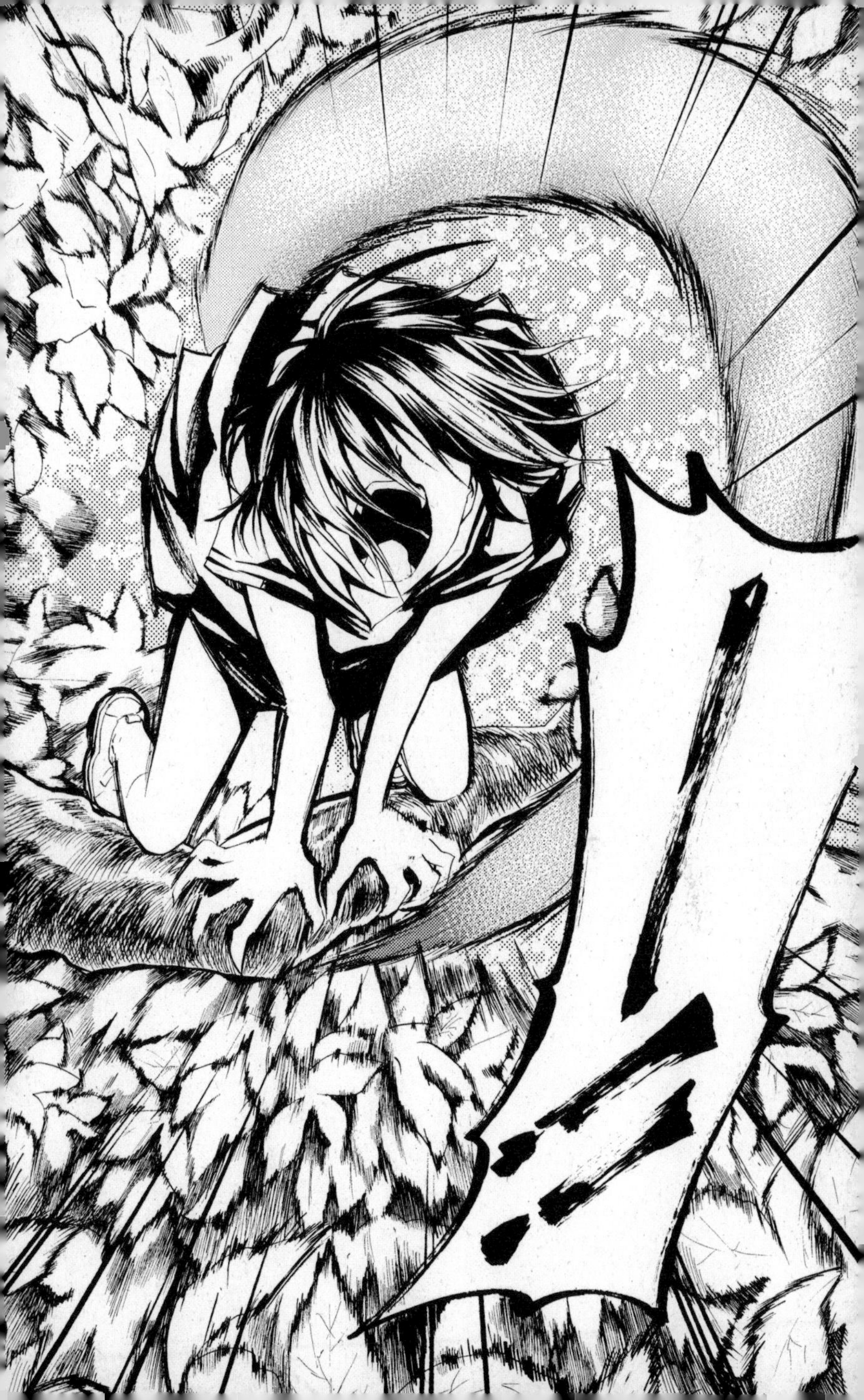

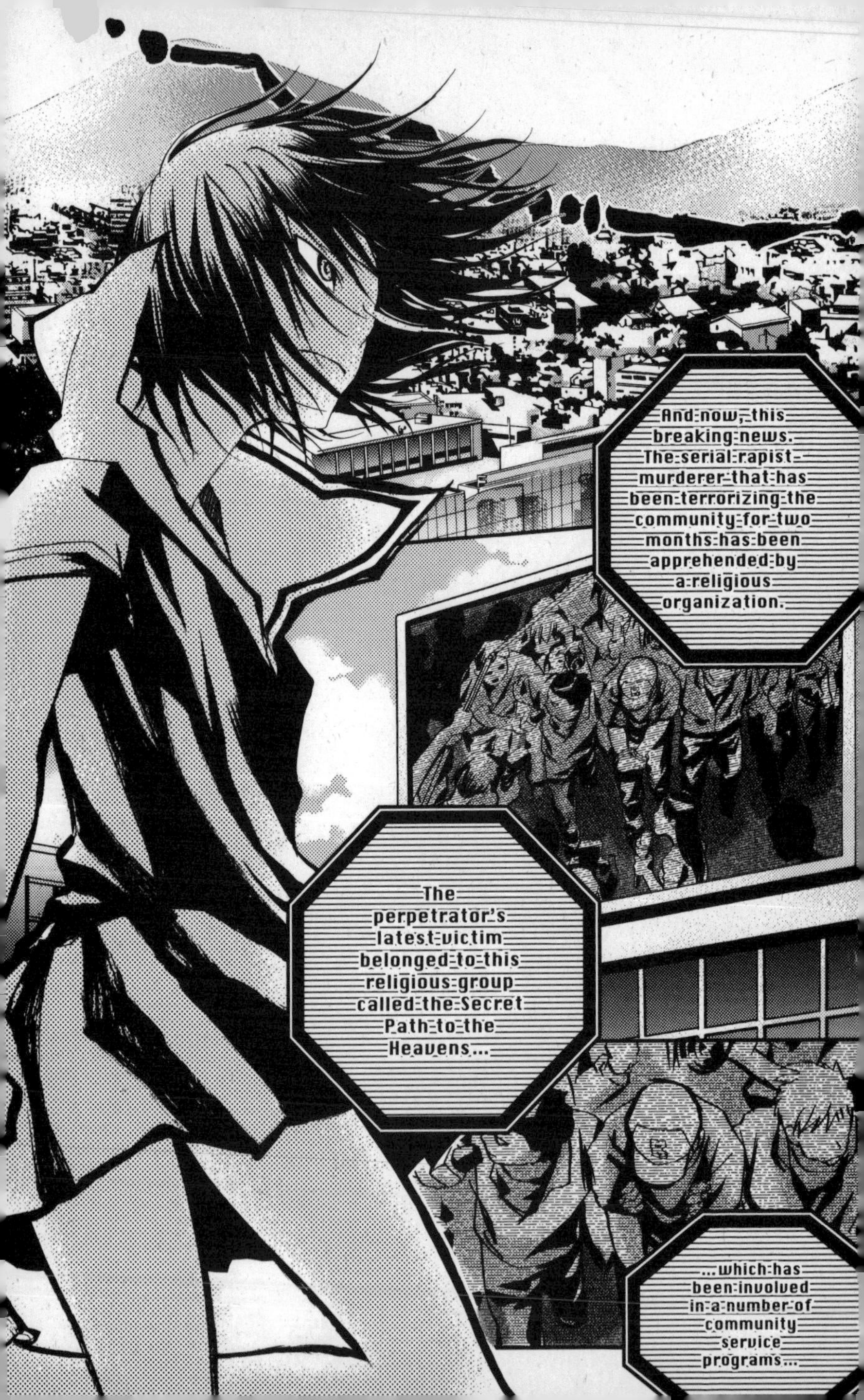
And now, this breaking news. The serial rapist-murderer that has been terrorizing the community for two months has been apprehended by a religious organization.
The perpetrator's latest victim belonged to this religious group called the Secret Path to the Heavens...
...which has been involved in a number of community service programs...

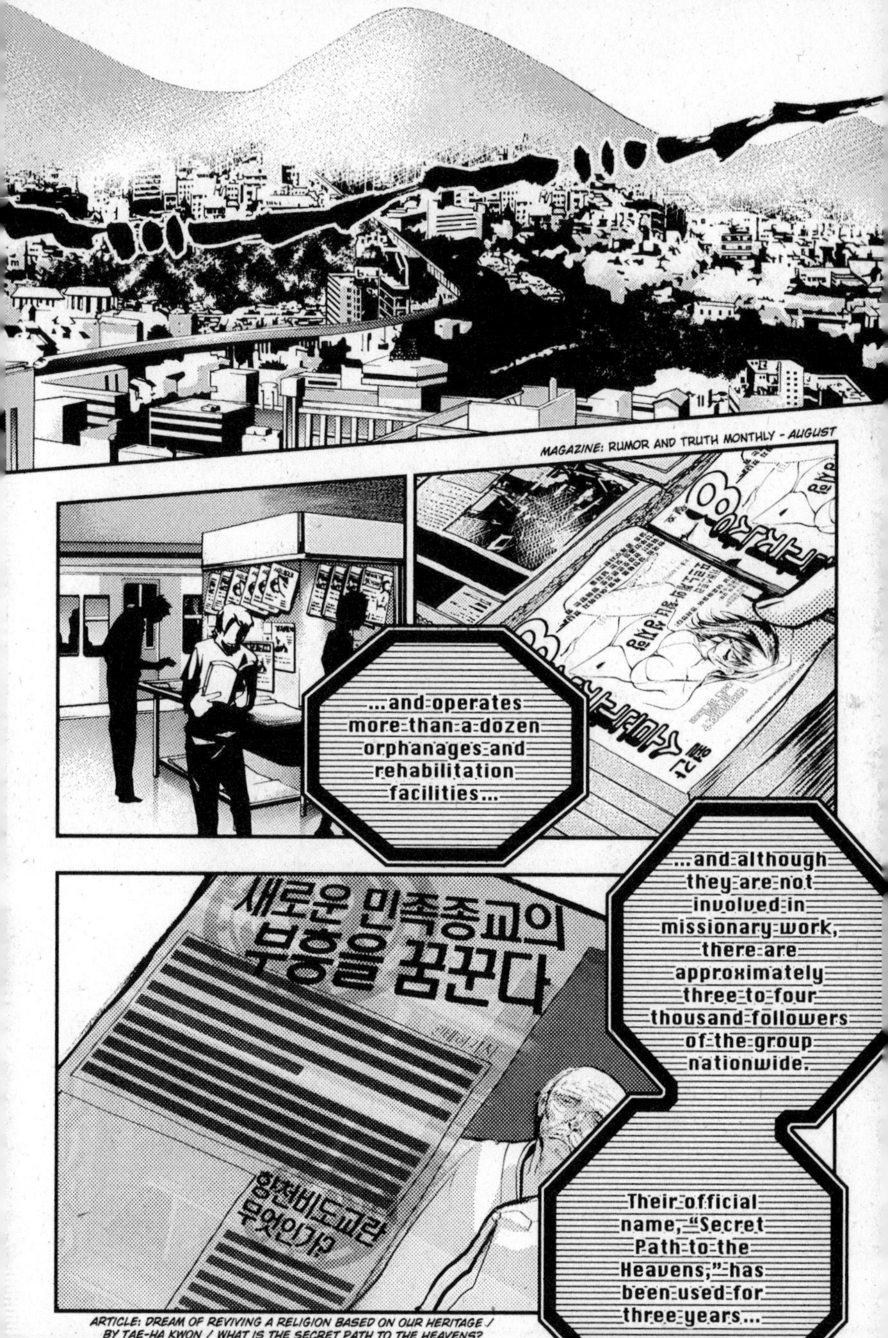
MAGAZINE: RUMOR AND TRUTH MONTHLY - AUGUST
...and operates more than a dozen orphanages and rehabilitation facilities...
새로운 민족종교의 부흥을 꿈꾼다
향천비도교란 무엇인가?
...and although they are not involved in missionary work, there are approximately three to four thousand followers of the group nationwide.
Their official name, "Secret Path to the Heavens," has been used for three years...
ARTICLE: DREAM OF REVIVING A RELIGION BASED ON OUR HERITAGE / BY TAE-HA KWON / WHAT IS THE SECRET PATH TO THE HEAVENS?

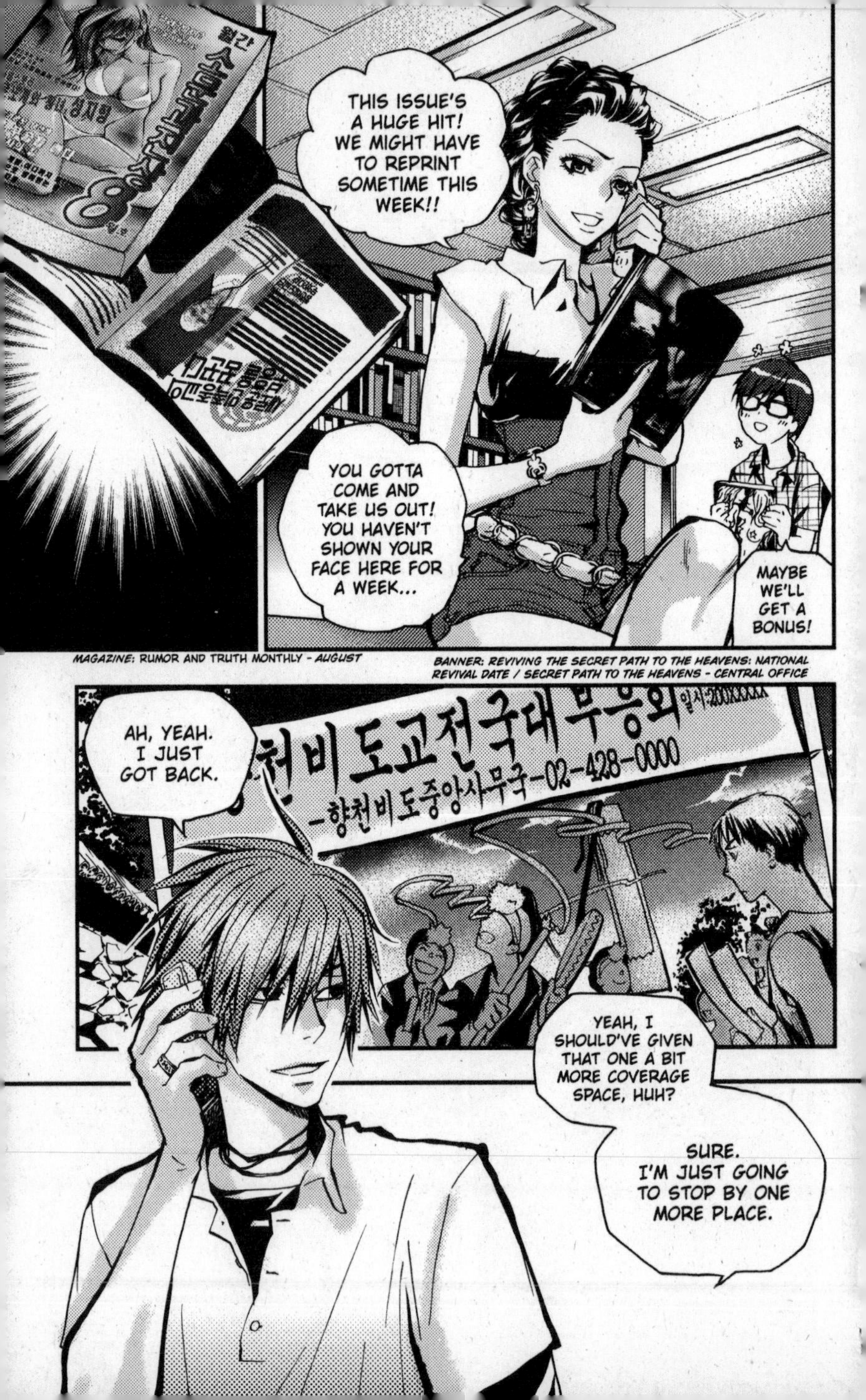
THIS ISSUE'S A HUGE HIT! WE MIGHT HAVE TO REPRINT SOMETIME THIS WEEK!!
YOU GOTTA COME AND TAKE US OUT! YOU HAVEN'T SHOWN YOUR FACE HERE FOR A WEEK...
MAYBE WE'LL GET A BONUS!
MAGAZINE: RUMOR AND TRUTH MONTHLY - AUGUST
BANNER: REVIVING THE SECRET PATH TO THE HEAVENS: NATIONAL REVIVAL DATE / SECRET PATH TO THE HEAVENS - CENTRAL OFFICE
AH, YEAH. I JUST GOT BACK.
YEAH, I SHOULD'VE GIVEN THAT ONE A BIT MORE COVERAGE SPACE, HUH?
SURE. I'M JUST GOING TO STOP BY ONE MORE PLACE.

PLEASE TAKE ONE! MAY YOU FIND HAPPINESS.

PAMPHLET: SECRET PATH TO THE HEAVENS: NATIONAL REVIVAL EVENT / WE WILL CHANGE EVERYTHING / WE WILL TEACH YOU THE ROOTS OF OUR PEOPLE.

HMPH.

향선기도교 제 1회 전국 대부흥회
모든 것을 변화시킬 것입니다

□□□□□□□□□□□□□
□□□□□□□□□□□
□□□□□□□□□□□□
왕림한 만족의 기원을 알려드립니다

□□에서 모입시다

THEY HAVE GOOD BUSINESS SENSE.

"NOW IS THE TIME TO STRIKE," HUH?

HEY, IT'S BEEN A WHILE, YOUNG-SHIN.

HOW'VE YOU BEEN?

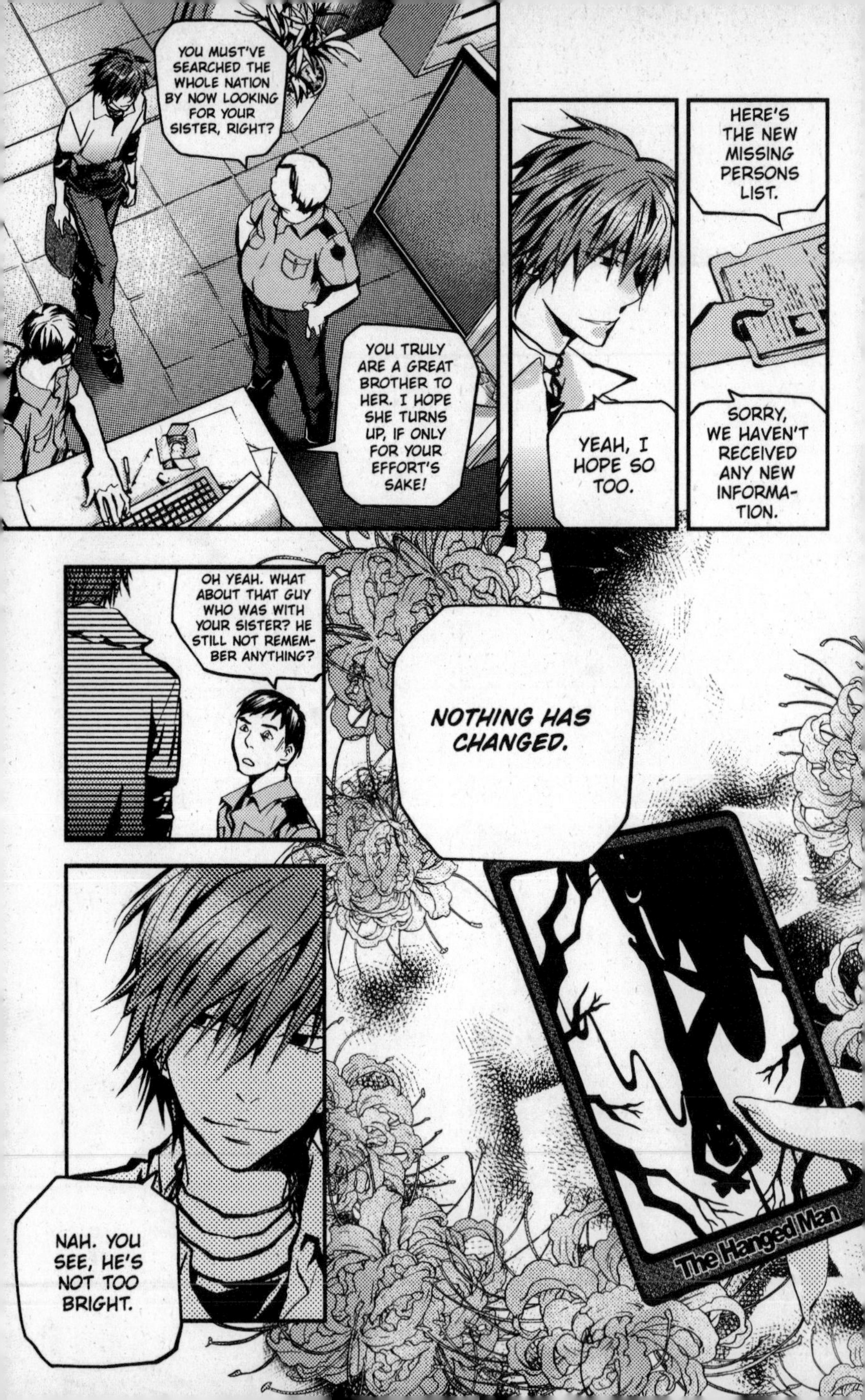
YOU MUST'VE SEARCHED THE WHOLE NATION BY NOW LOOKING FOR YOUR SISTER, RIGHT?
YOU TRULY ARE A GREAT BROTHER TO HER. I HOPE SHE TURNS UP, IF ONLY FOR YOUR EFFORT'S SAKE!
YEAH, I HOPE SO TOO.
HERE'S THE NEW MISSING PERSONS LIST.
SORRY, WE HAVEN'T RECEIVED ANY NEW INFORMATION.
OH YEAH. WHAT ABOUT THAT GUY WHO WAS WITH YOUR SISTER? HE STILL NOT REMEMBER ANYTHING?
NAH. YOU SEE, HE'S NOT TOO BRIGHT.
NOTHING HAS CHANGED.
The Hanged Man

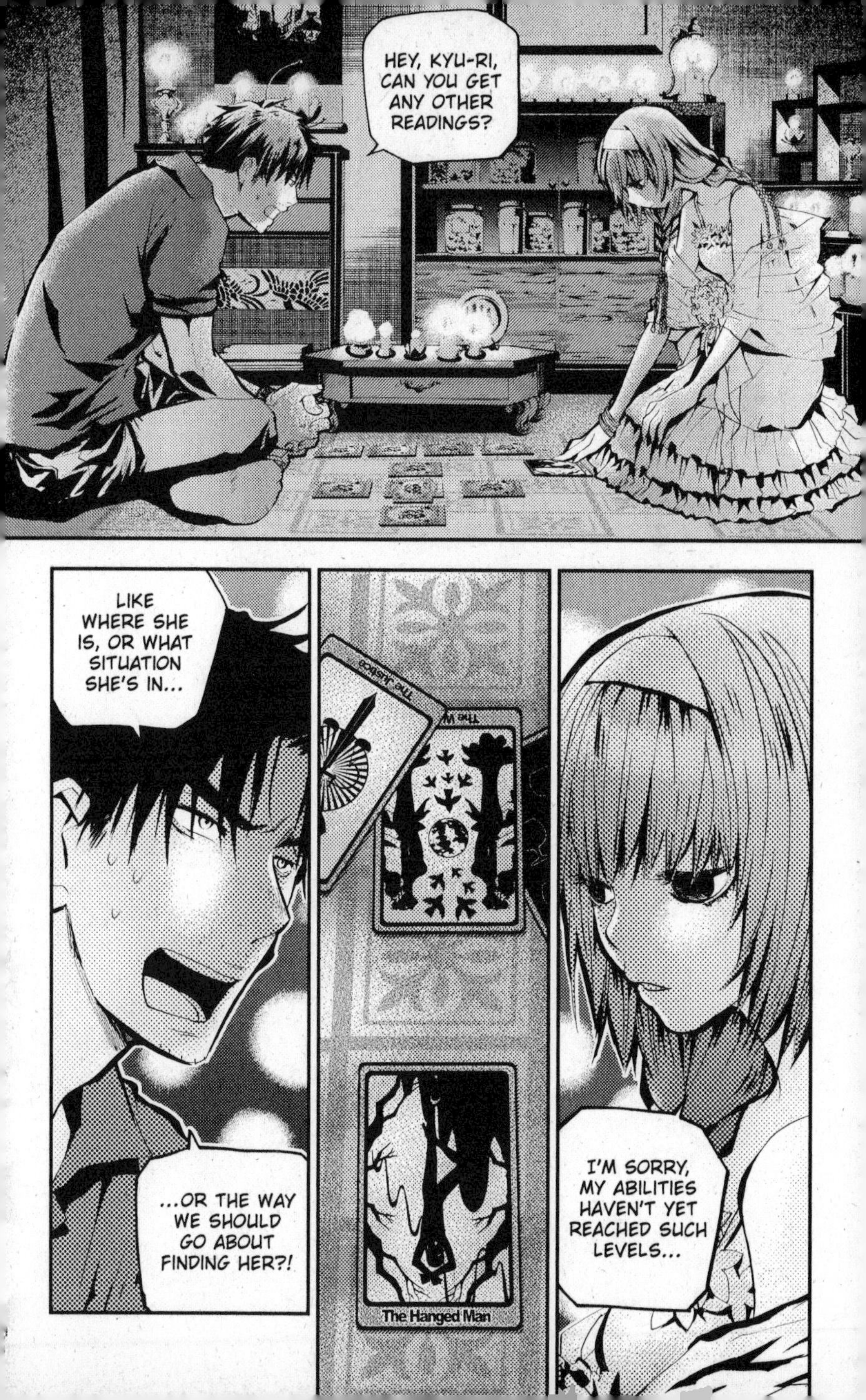
HEY, KYU-RI, CAN YOU GET ANY OTHER READINGS?
LIKE WHERE SHE IS, OR WHAT SITUATION SHE'S IN...
...OR THE WAY WE SHOULD GO ABOUT FINDING HER?!
The Justice
The Hanged Man
I'M SORRY, MY ABILITIES HAVEN'T YET REACHED SUCH LEVELS...

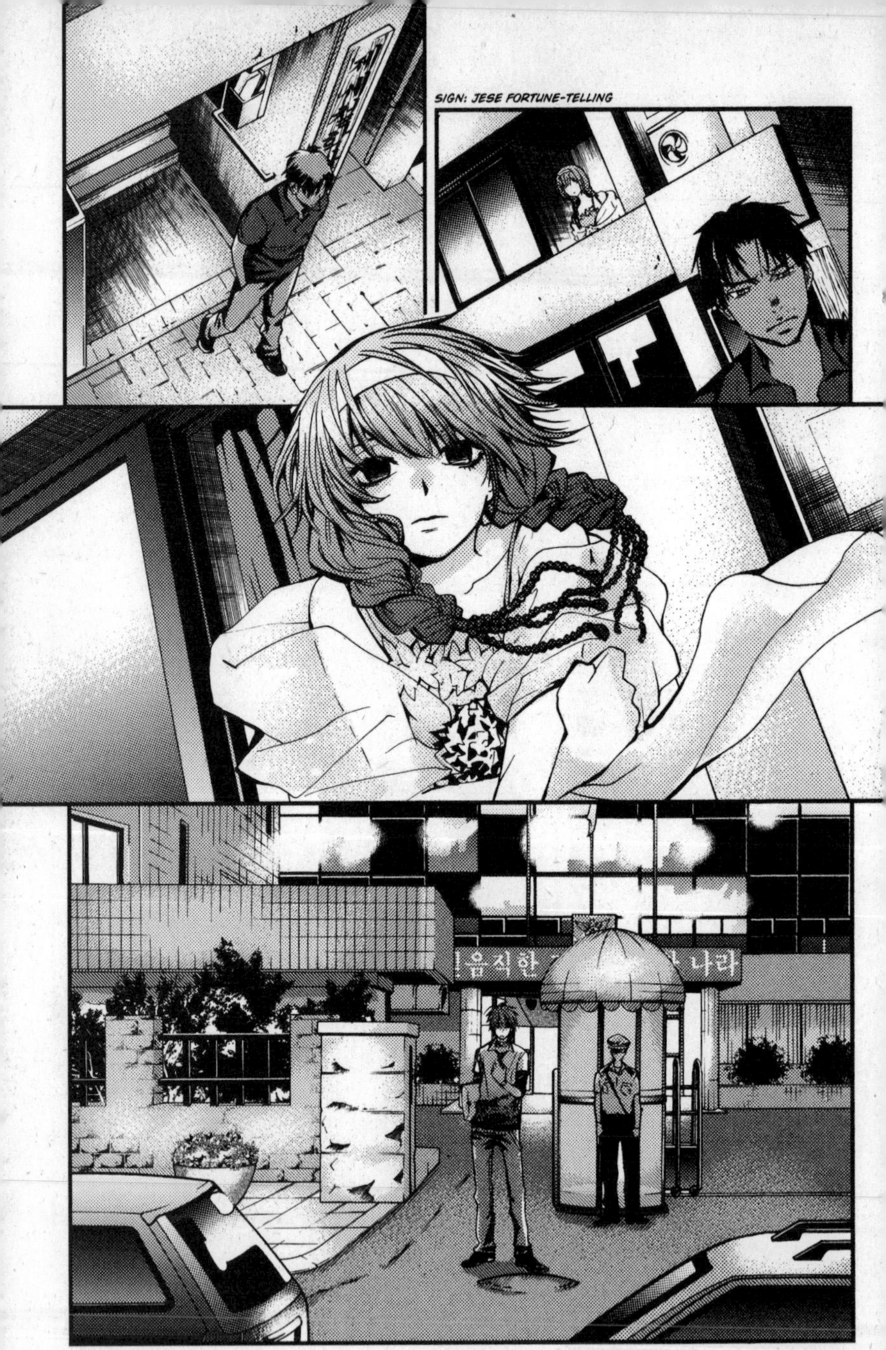
SIGN: JESE FORTUNE-TELLING

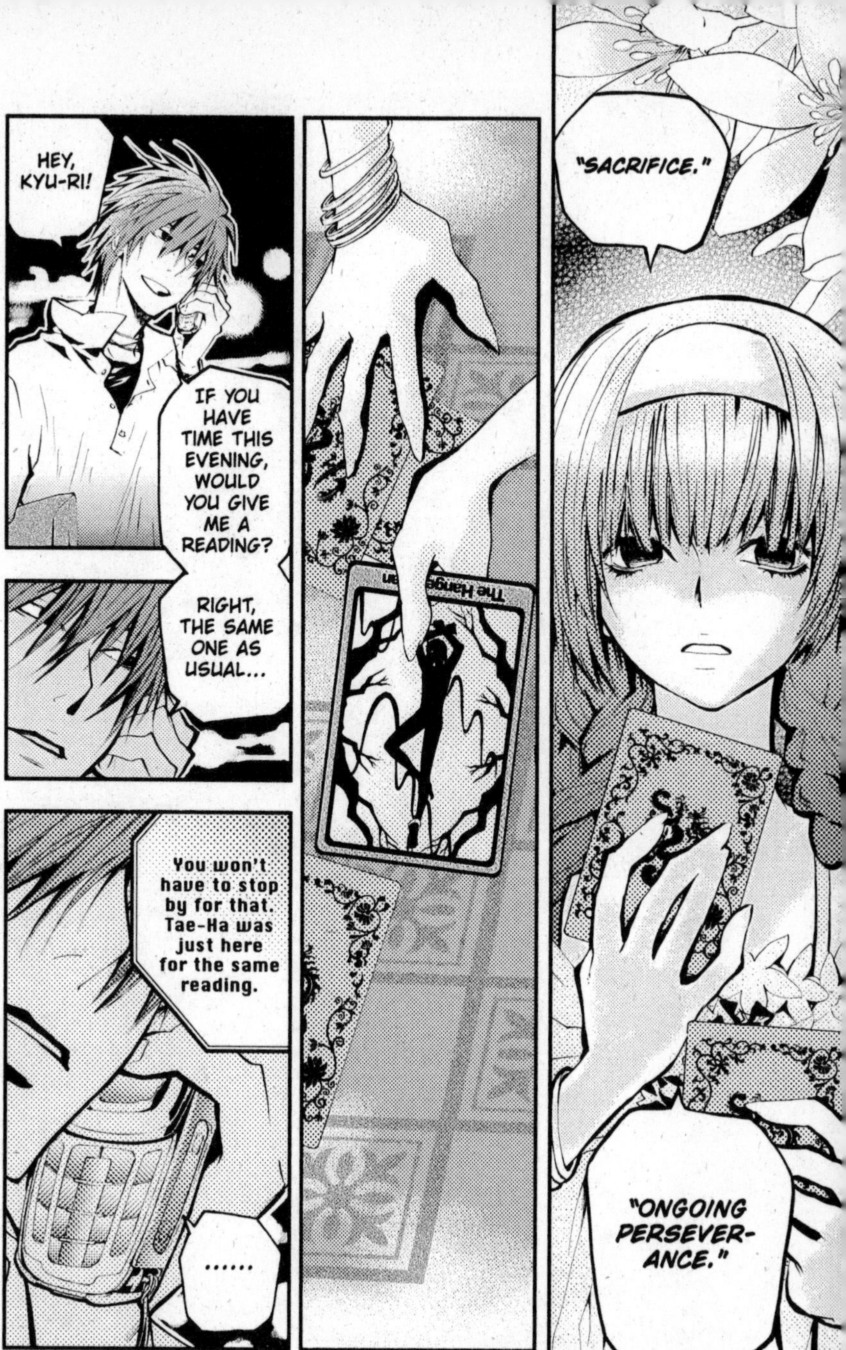
HEY, KYU-RI!
IF YOU HAVE TIME THIS EVENING, WOULD YOU GIVE ME A READING?
RIGHT, THE SAME ONE AS USUAL...
You won't have to stop by for that. Tae-Ha was just here for the same reading.
......
"SACRIFICE."
"ONGOING PERSEVER-ANCE."

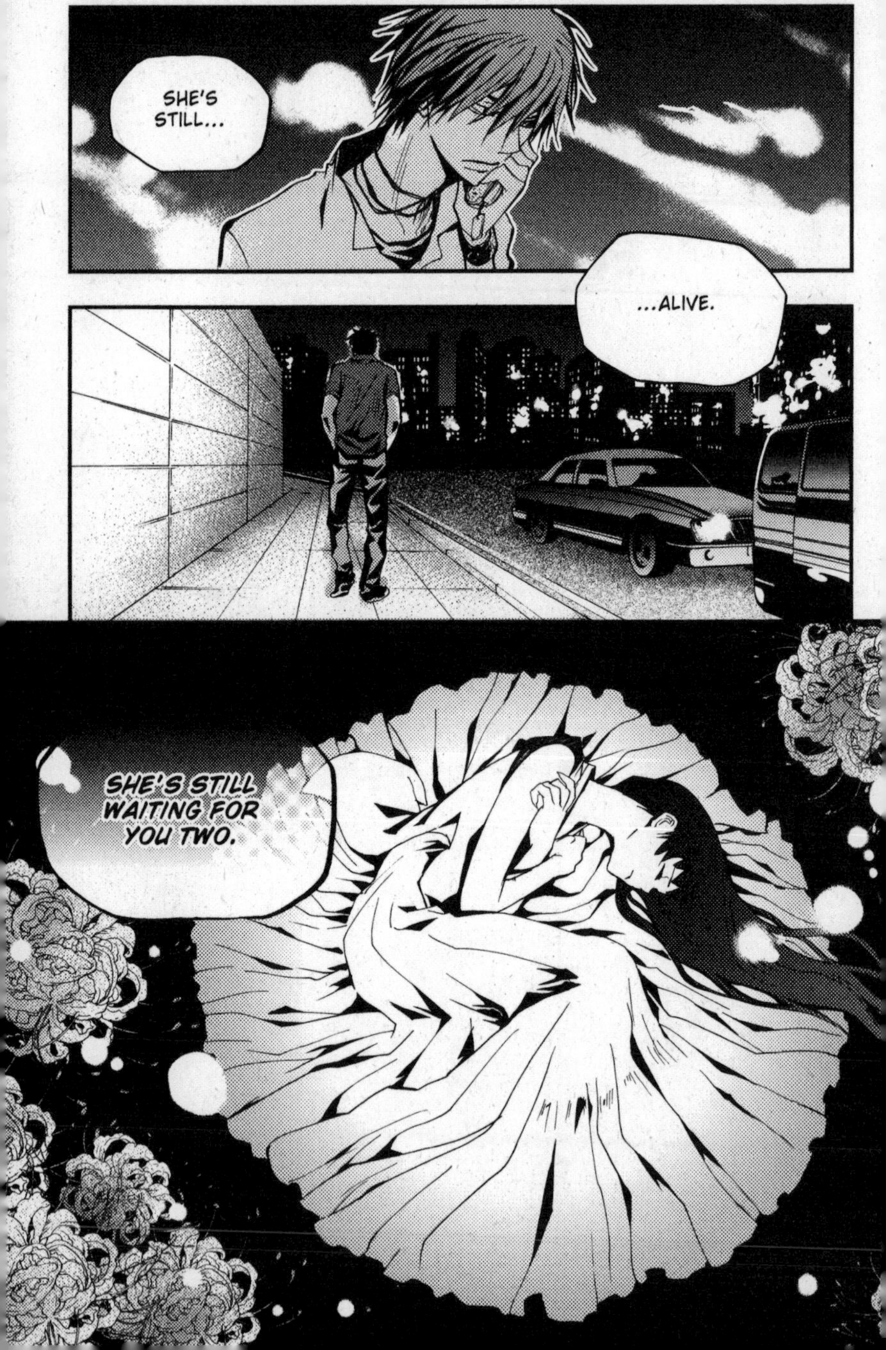
SHE'S STILL...
...ALIVE.
SHE'S STILL WAITING FOR YOU TWO.

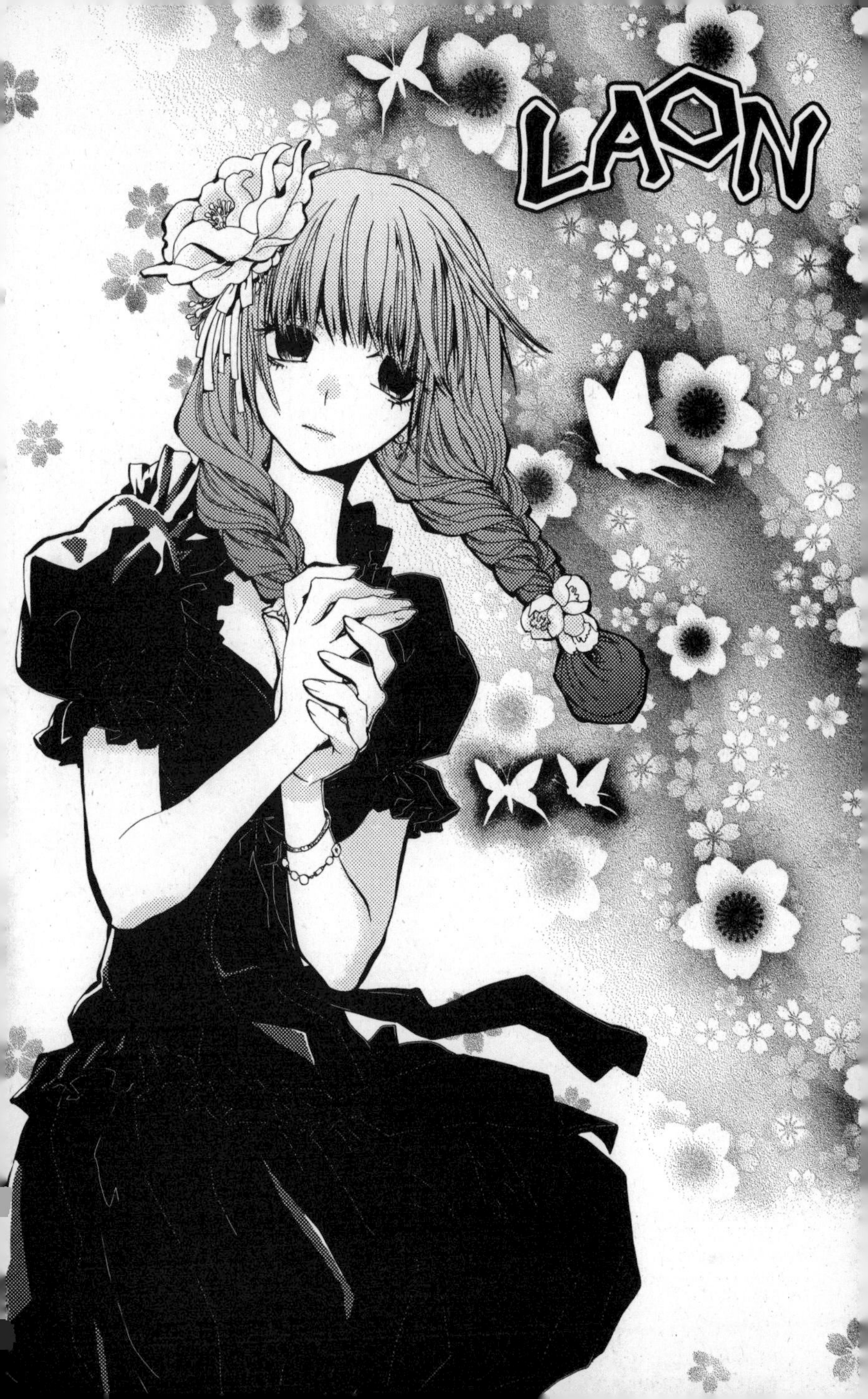
LAON

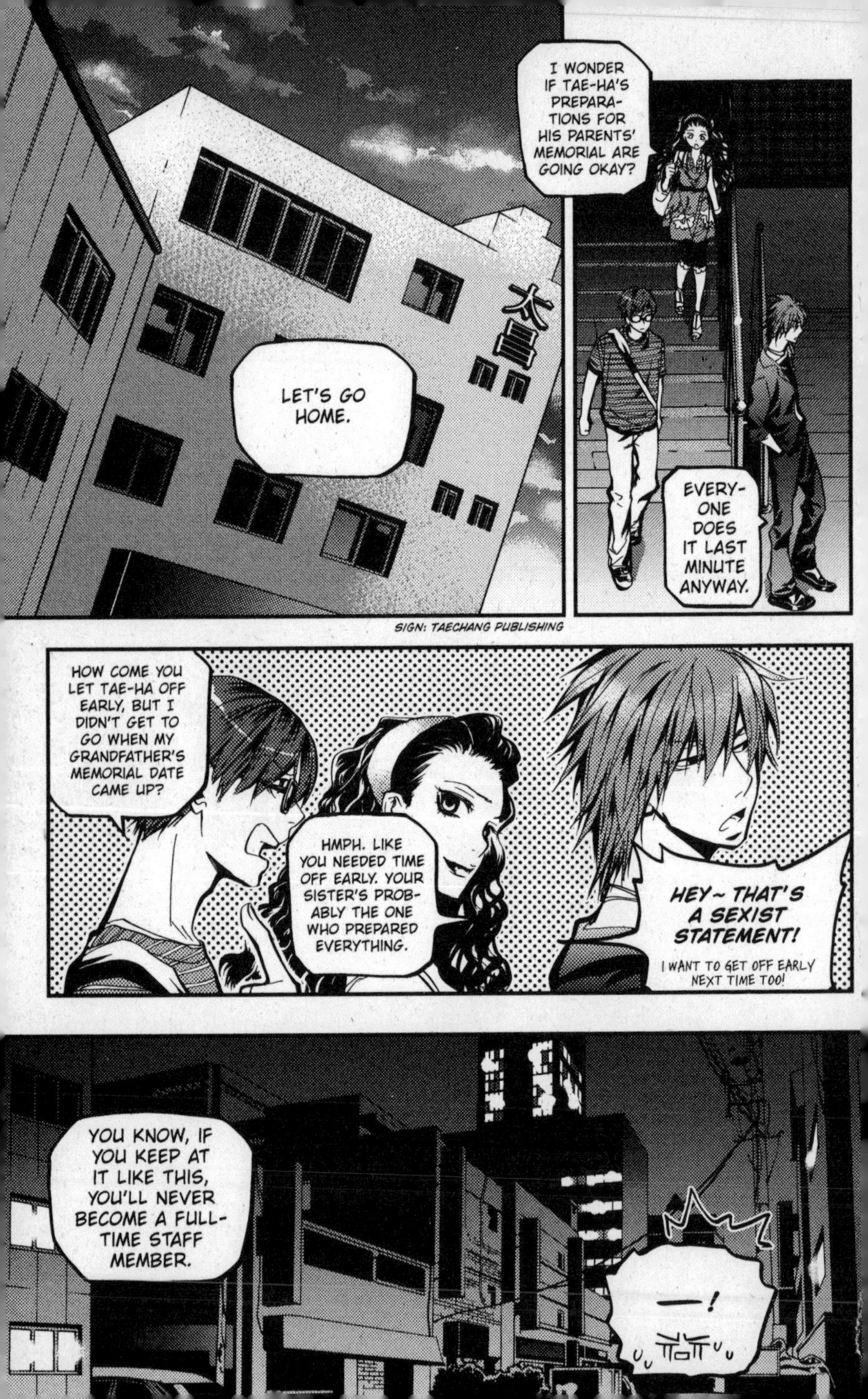
LET'S GO HOME.
I WONDER IF TAE-HA'S PREPARATIONS FOR HIS PARENTS' MEMORIAL ARE GOING OKAY?
EVERYONE DOES IT LAST MINUTE ANYWAY.
SIGN: TAECHANG PUBLISHING
HOW COME YOU LET TAE-HA OFF EARLY, BUT I DIDN'T GET TO GO WHEN MY GRANDFATHER'S MEMORIAL DATE CAME UP?
HMPH. LIKE YOU NEEDED TIME OFF EARLY. YOUR SISTER'S PROBABLY THE ONE WHO PREPARED EVERYTHING.
HEY~ THAT'S A SEXIST STATEMENT!
I WANT TO GET OFF EARLY NEXT TIME TOO!
YOU KNOW, IF YOU KEEP AT IT LIKE THIS, YOU'LL NEVER BECOME A FULL-TIME STAFF MEMBER.
—!

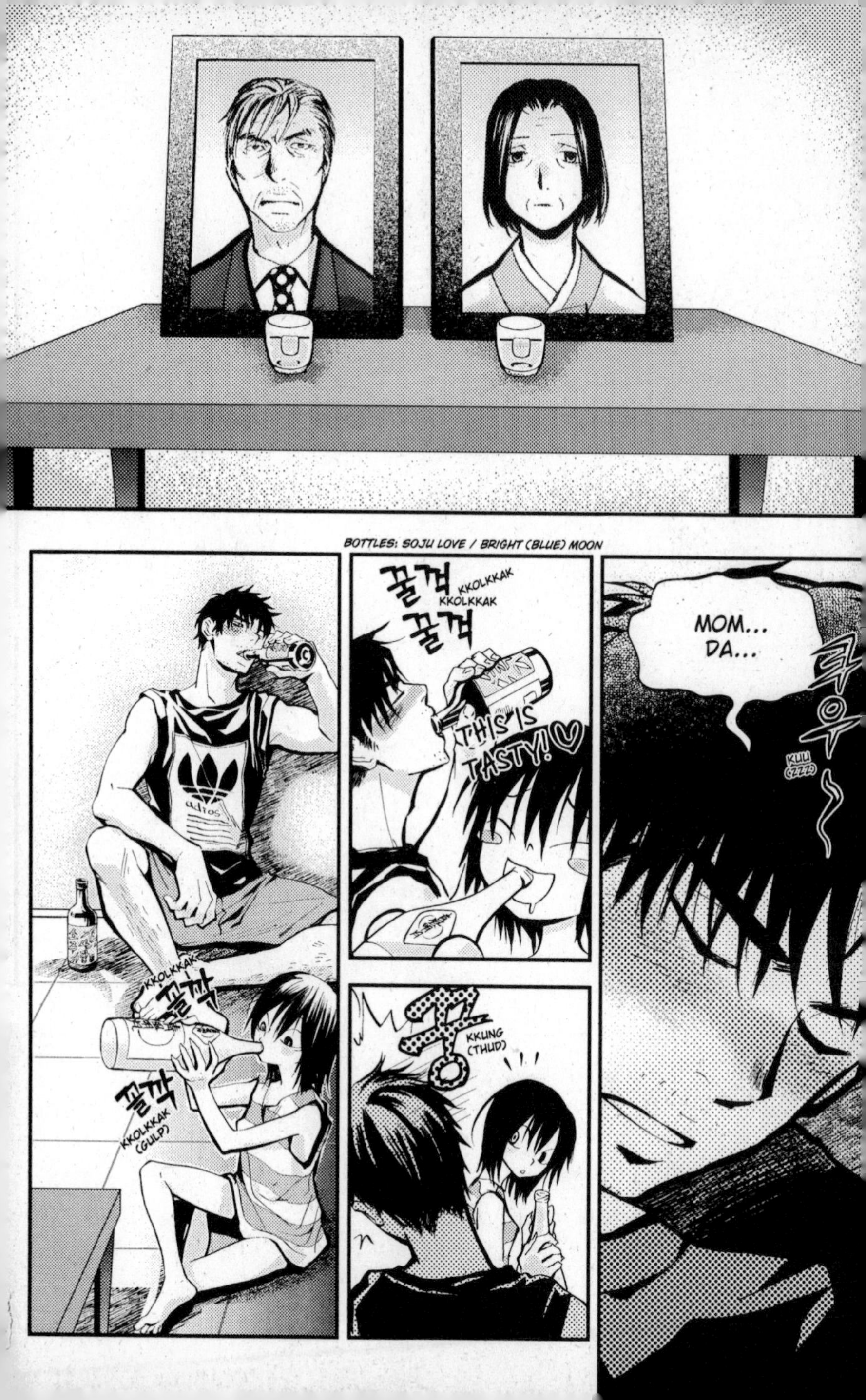
BOTTLES: SOJU LOVE / BRIGHT (BLUE) MOON
꼴깍 KKOLKKAK
꼴깍 KKOLKKAK (GULP)
꿀꺽 KKOLKKAK
꿀꺽 KKOLKKAK
THIS IS TASTY! ♡
쿵 KKUNG (THUD)
MOM... DA...
쿠우~ KUU (ZZZ)

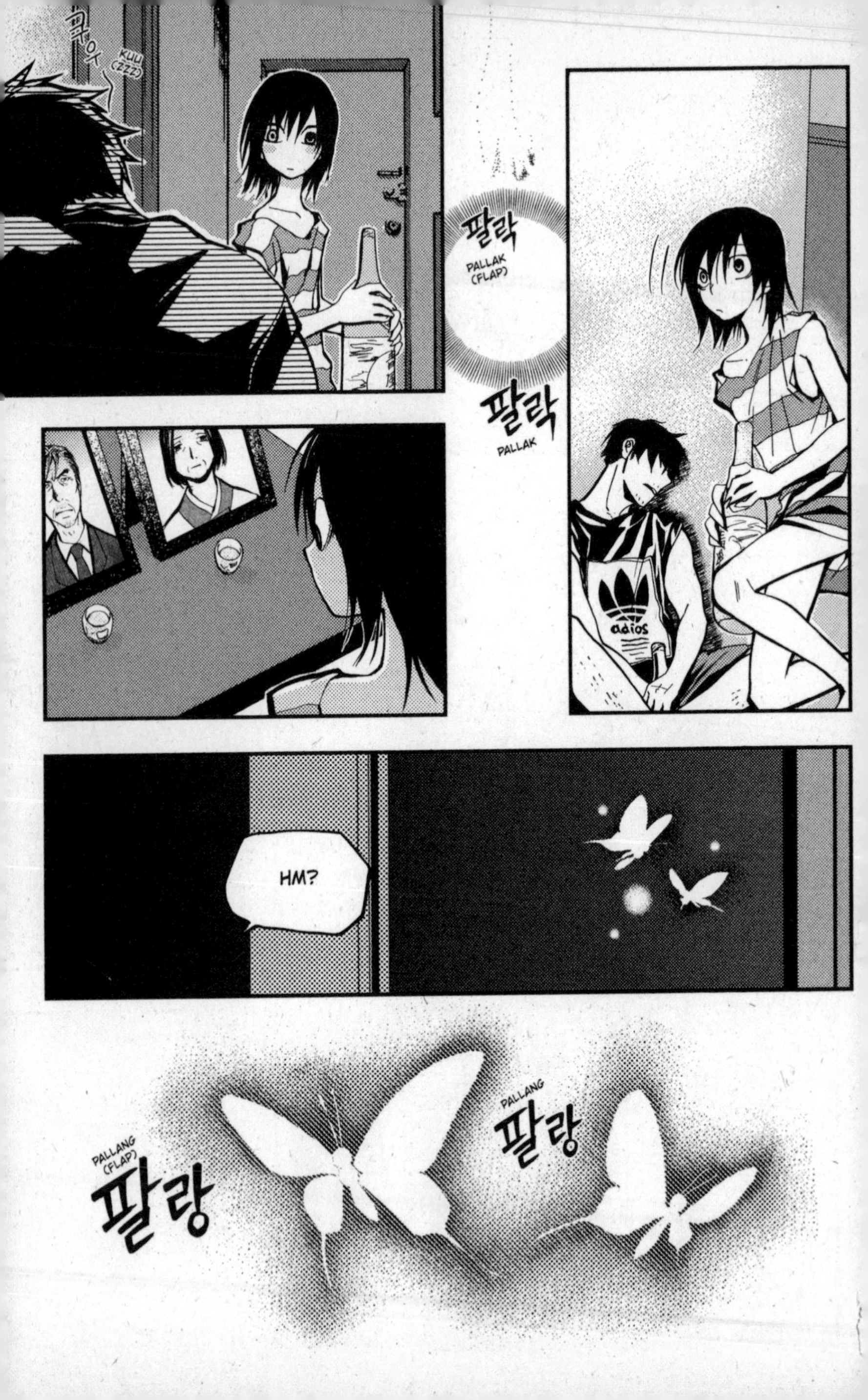
쿠우
KUU (ZZZ)
팔락
PALLAK (FLAP)
팔락
PALLAK
adios
HM?
PALLANG (FLAP)
팔랑
PALLANG
팔랑

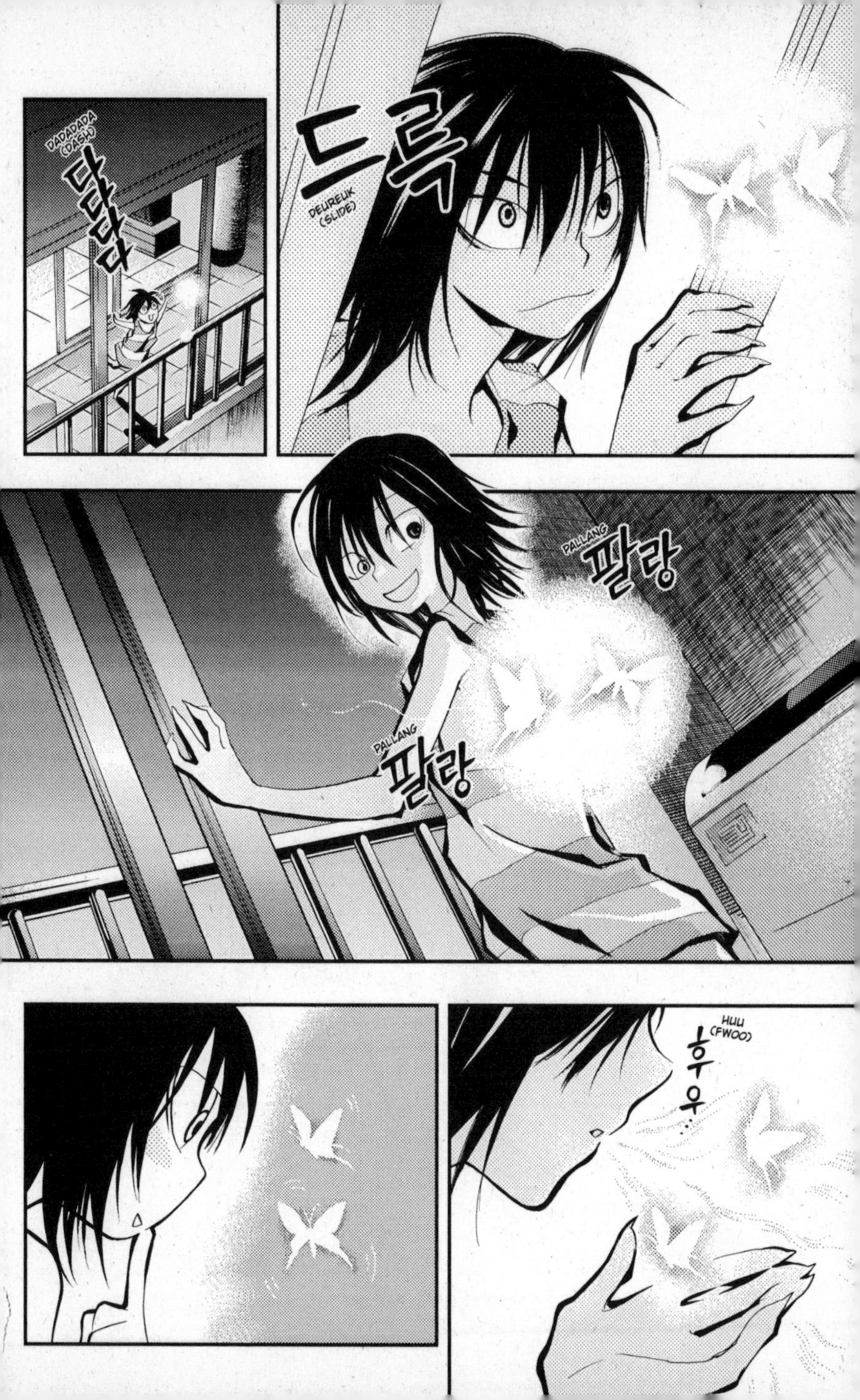
DADADADA (DASH)
다다다다
드륵
DEUREUK (SLIDE)
PALLANG
팔랑
PALLANG
팔랑
HUU (FWOO)
후우…

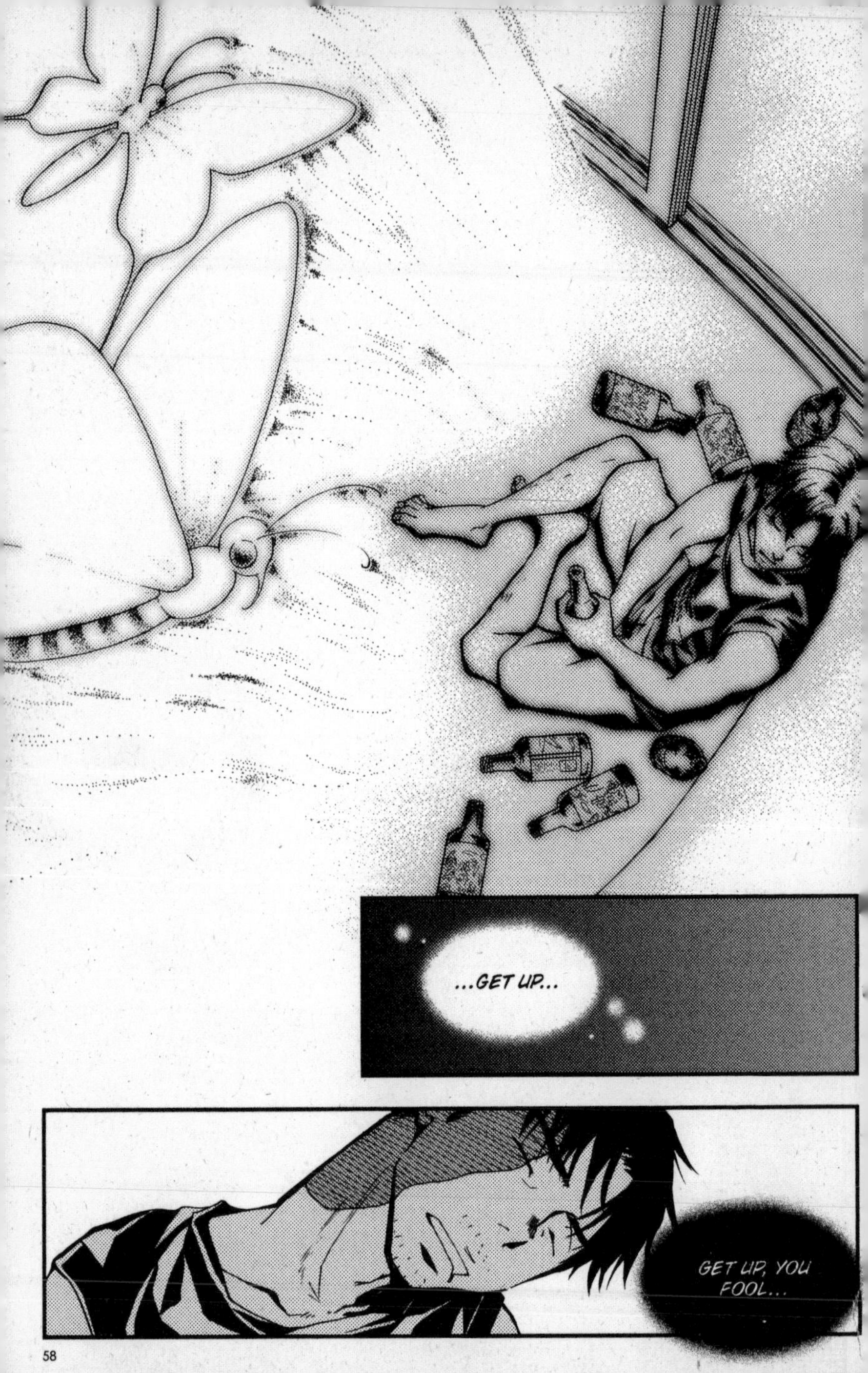
...GET UP...
GET UP, YOU FOOL...

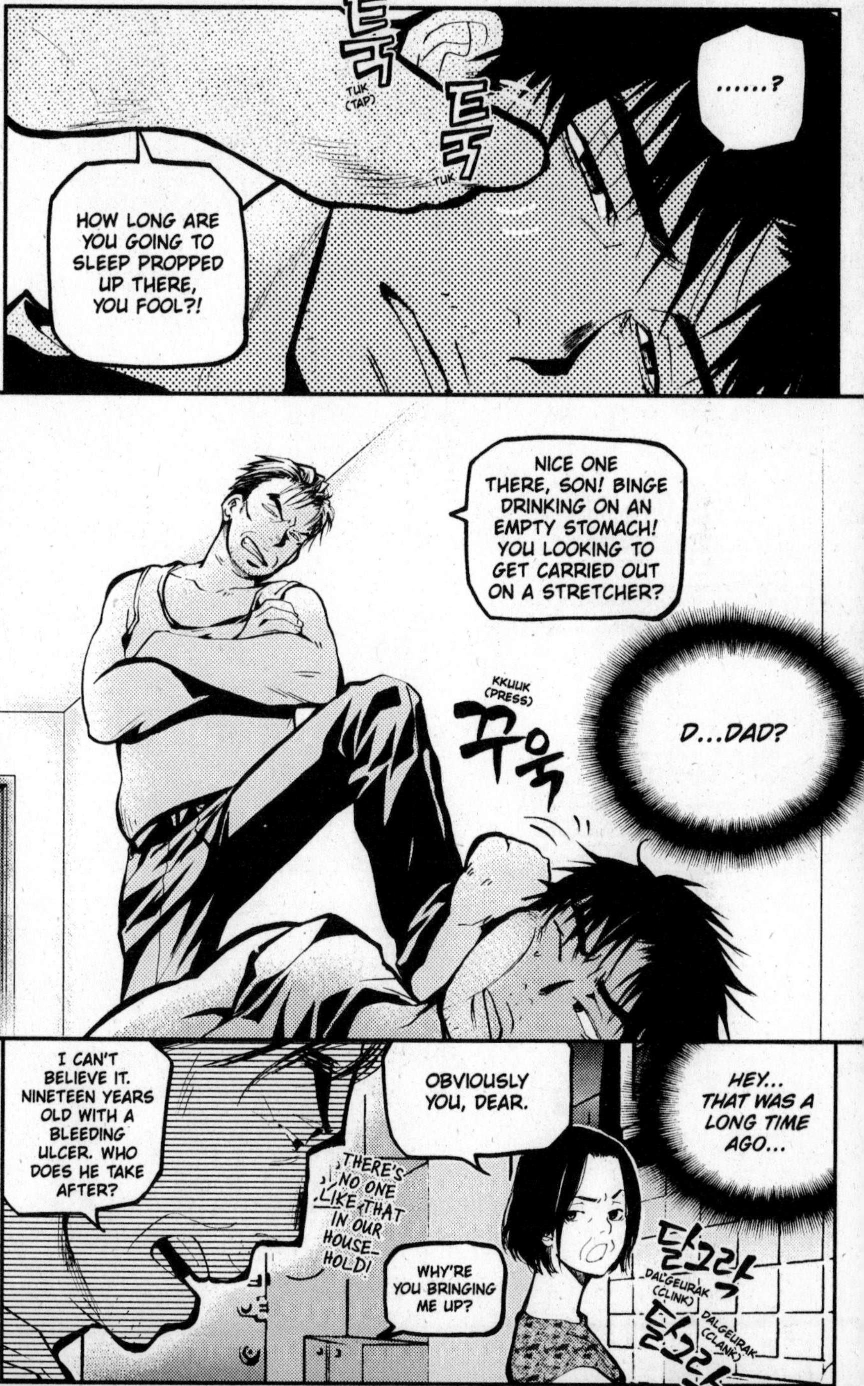
톡
TUK (TAP)
톡
TUK
HOW LONG ARE YOU GOING TO SLEEP PROPPED UP THERE, YOU FOOL?!
......?
NICE ONE THERE, SON! BINGE DRINKING ON AN EMPTY STOMACH! YOU LOOKING TO GET CARRIED OUT ON A STRETCHER?
꾸욱
KKUUK (PRESS)
D...DAD?
I CAN'T BELIEVE IT. NINETEEN YEARS OLD WITH A BLEEDING ULCER. WHO DOES HE TAKE AFTER?
THERE'S NO ONE LIKE THAT IN OUR HOUSEHOLD!
OBVIOUSLY YOU, DEAR.
WHY'RE YOU BRINGING ME UP?
HEY... THAT WAS A LONG TIME AGO...
달그락
DALGEURAK (CLINK)
달그락
DALGEURAK (CLANK)

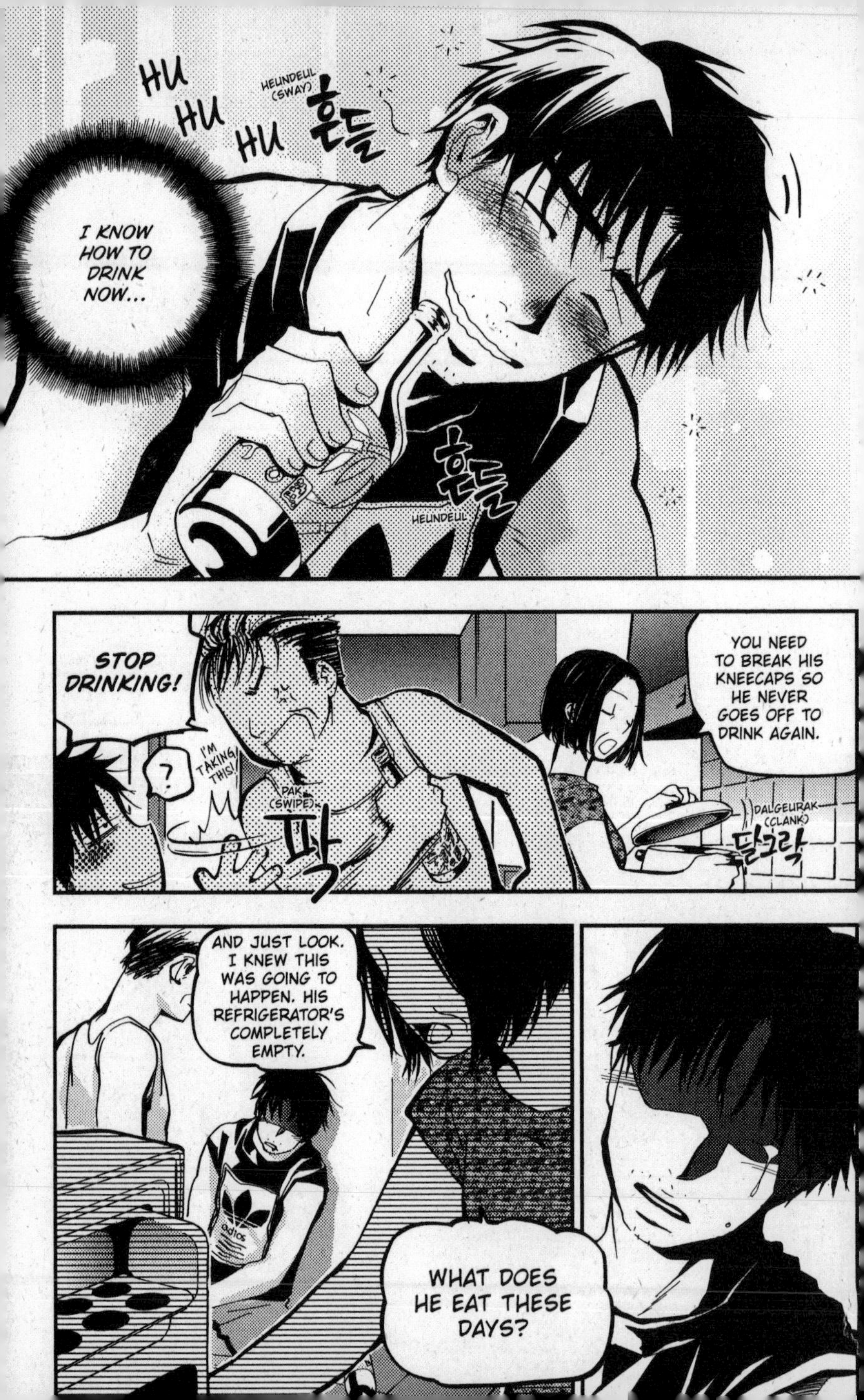
HU
HU
HU
HEUNDEUL (SWAY)
흔들
I KNOW HOW TO DRINK NOW...
흔들
HEUNDEUL
STOP DRINKING!
?
I'M TAKING THIS!
PAK (SWIPE)
팍
YOU NEED TO BREAK HIS KNEECAPS SO HE NEVER GOES OFF TO DRINK AGAIN.
DALGEURAK (CLANK)
달그락
AND JUST LOOK. I KNEW THIS WAS GOING TO HAPPEN. HIS REFRIGERATOR'S COMPLETELY EMPTY.
WHAT DOES HE EAT THESE DAYS?

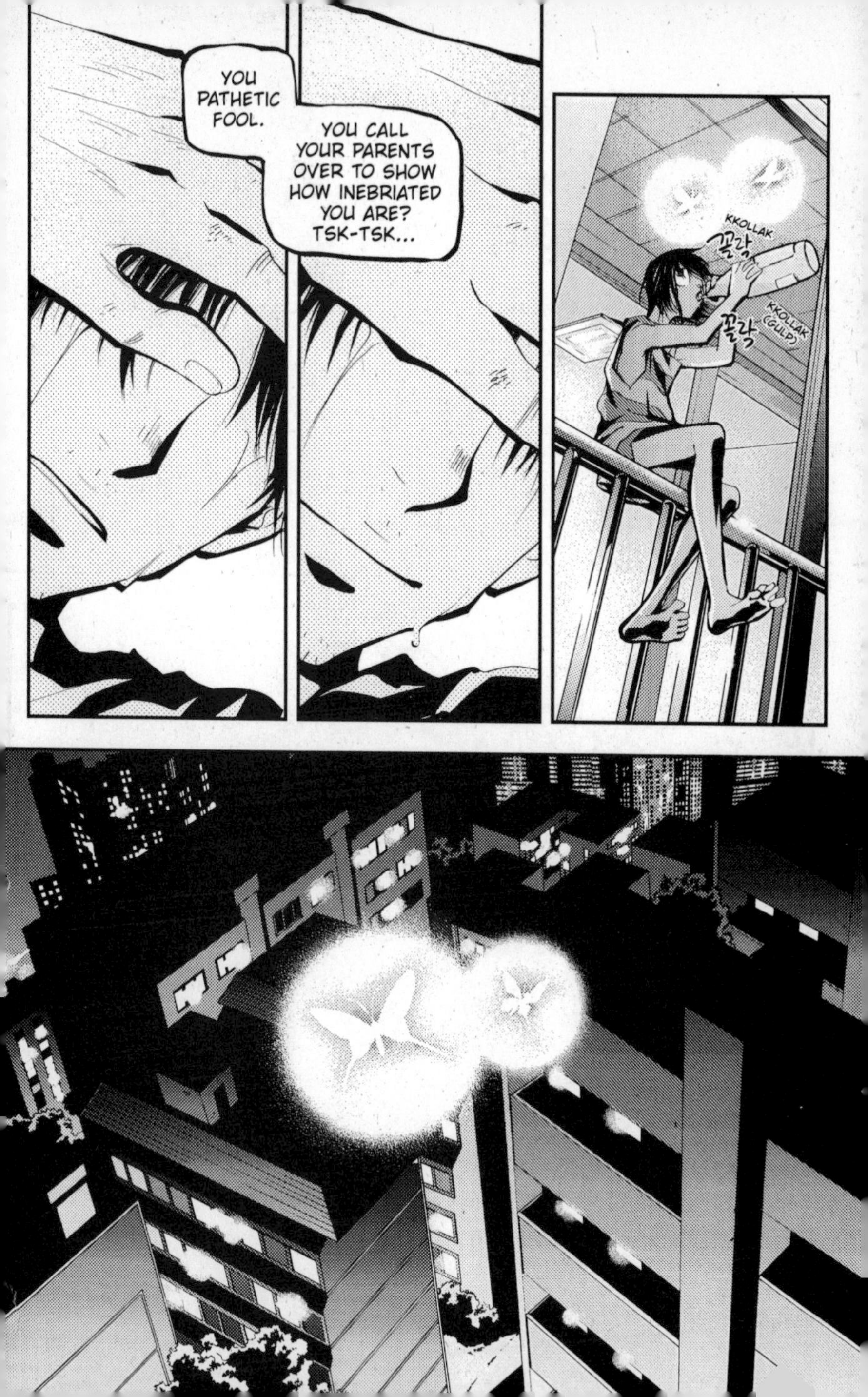
YOU PATHETIC FOOL.
YOU CALL YOUR PARENTS OVER TO SHOW HOW INEBRIATED YOU ARE? TSK-TSK...
KKOLLAK
꼴깍
KKOLLAK (GULP)
꼴깍

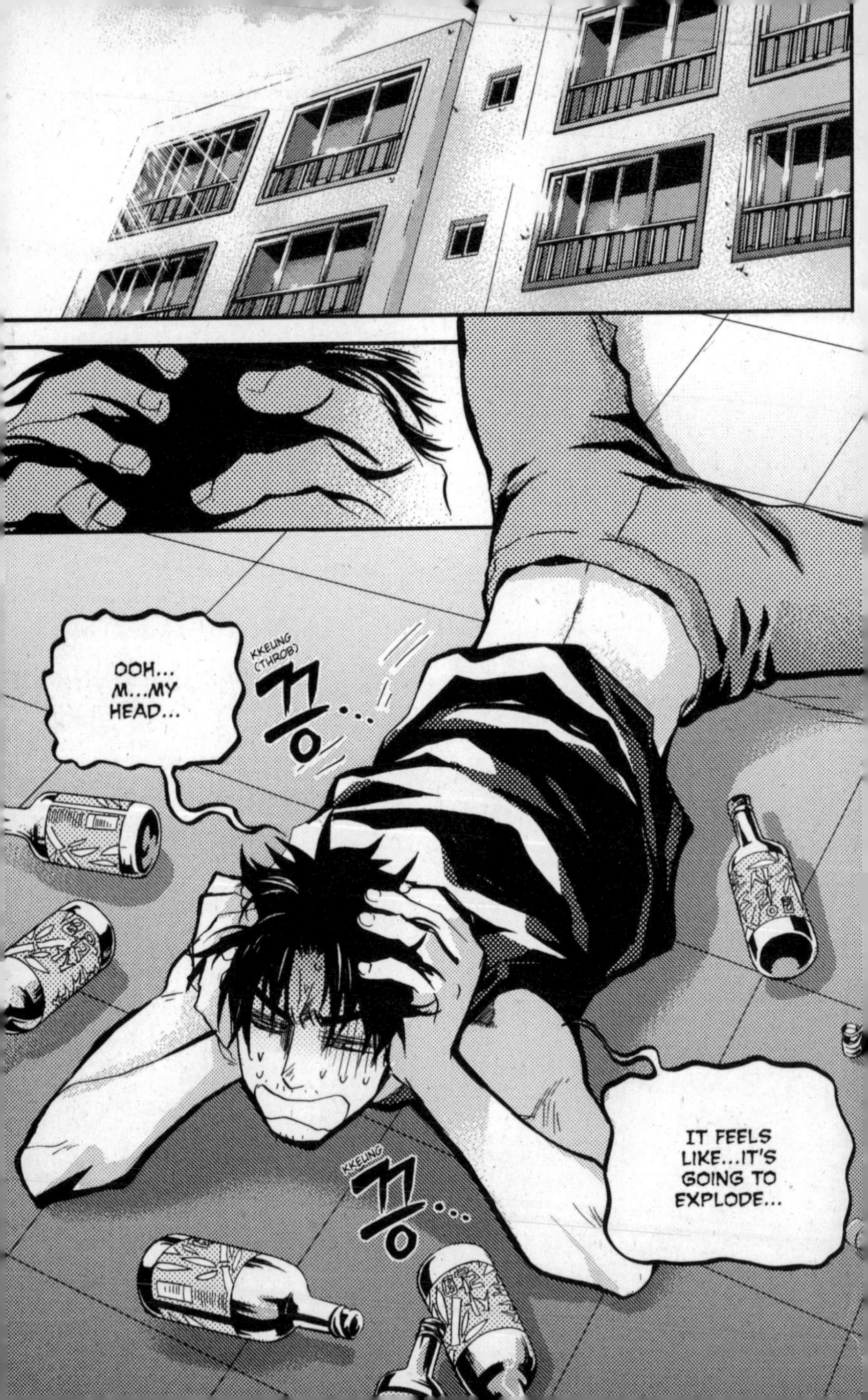
OOH... M...MY HEAD...
KKEUNG (THROB)
IT FEELS LIKE...IT'S GOING TO EXPLODE...
KKEUNG

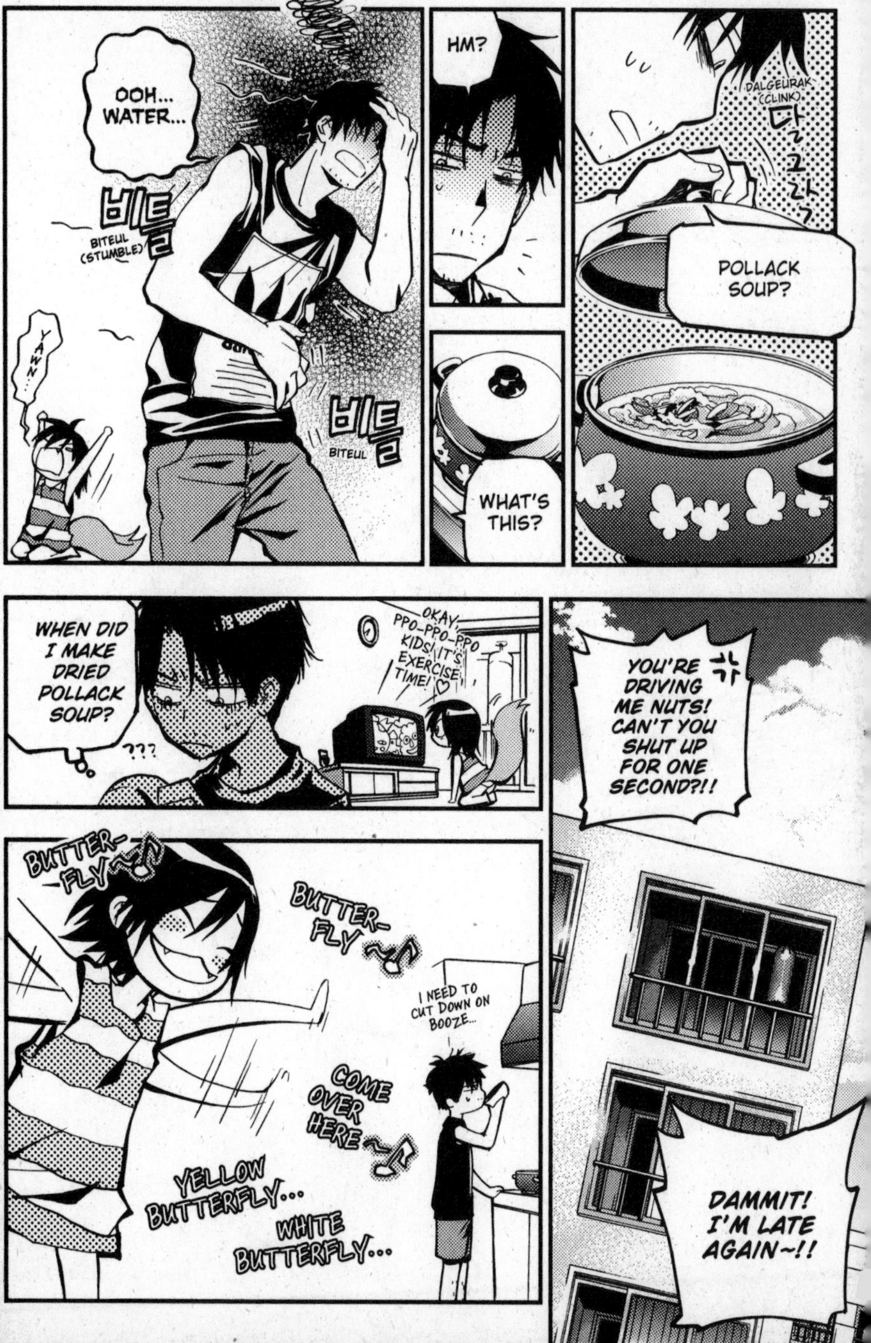
OOH... WATER...
비틀
BITEUL (STUMBLE)
YAWN...
비틀
BITEUL
HM?
WHAT'S THIS?
DALGEURAK (CLINK)
달그락
POLLACK SOUP?
WHEN DID I MAKE DRIED POLLACK SOUP?
???
OKAY, PPO-PPO-PPO KIDS! IT'S EXERCISE TIME! ♡
BUTTER-FLY~♪
BUTTER-FLY~♪
I NEED TO CUT DOWN ON BOOZE...
COME OVER HERE~♪
YELLOW BUTTERFLY...
WHITE BUTTERFLY...
YOU'RE DRIVING ME NUTS! CAN'T YOU SHUT UP FOR ONE SECOND?!!
DAMMIT! I'M LATE AGAIN~!!

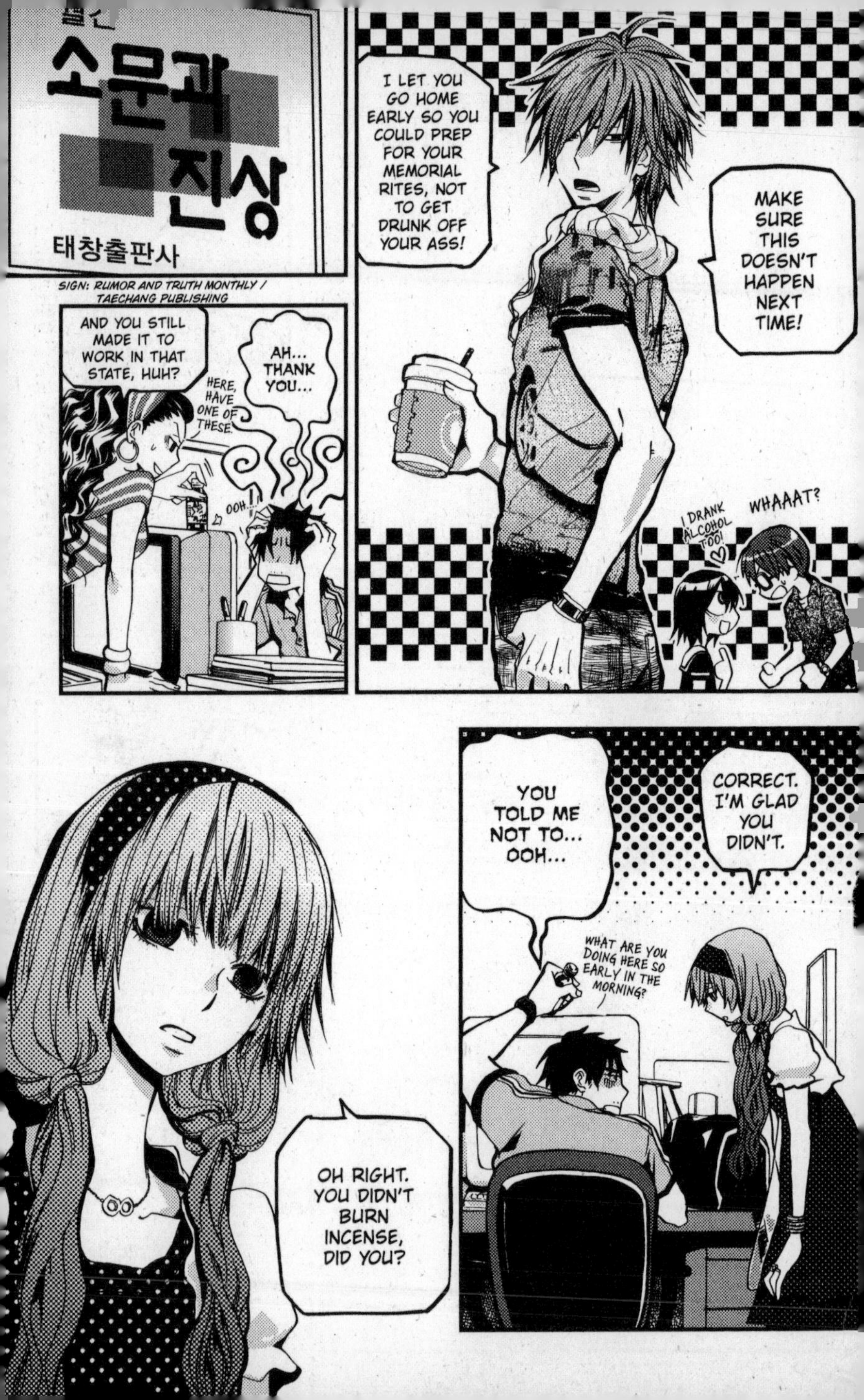
소문과 진상
태창출판사
SIGN: RUMOR AND TRUTH MONTHLY / TAECHANG PUBLISHING
AND YOU STILL MADE IT TO WORK IN THAT STATE, HUH?
HERE, HAVE ONE OF THESE.
AH... THANK YOU...
OOH...!
I LET YOU GO HOME EARLY SO YOU COULD PREP FOR YOUR MEMORIAL RITES, NOT TO GET DRUNK OFF YOUR ASS!
MAKE SURE THIS DOESN'T HAPPEN NEXT TIME!
I DRANK ALCOHOL TOO!
WHAAAT?
OH RIGHT. YOU DIDN'T BURN INCENSE, DID YOU?
YOU TOLD ME NOT TO... OOH...
CORRECT. I'M GLAD YOU DIDN'T.
WHAT ARE YOU DOING HERE SO EARLY IN THE MORNING?

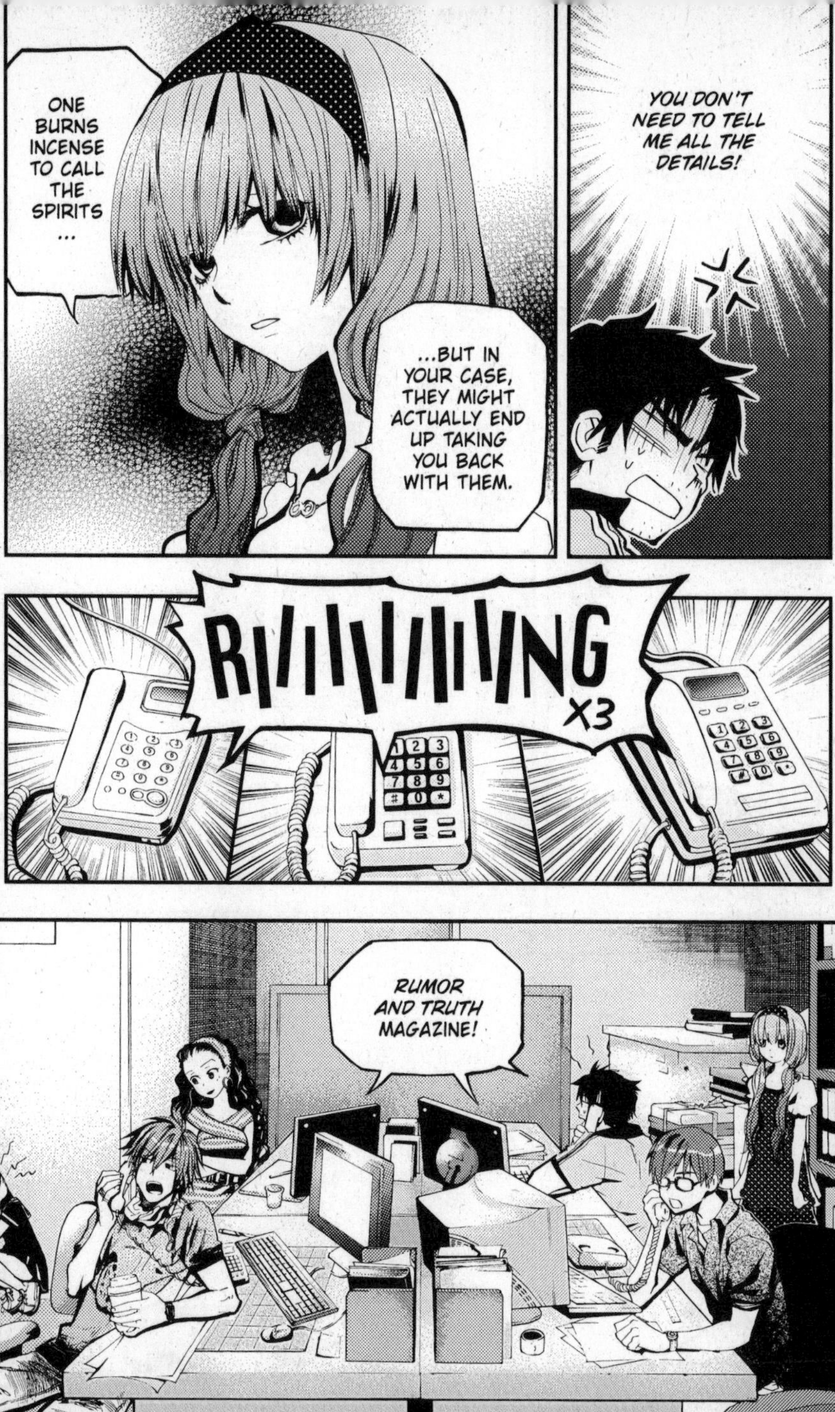
ONE BURNS INCENSE TO CALL THE SPIRITS ...
...BUT IN YOUR CASE, THEY MIGHT ACTUALLY END UP TAKING YOU BACK WITH THEM.
YOU DON'T NEED TO TELL ME ALL THE DETAILS!
RIIIIIIIIIING
X3
RUMOR AND TRUTH MAGAZINE!

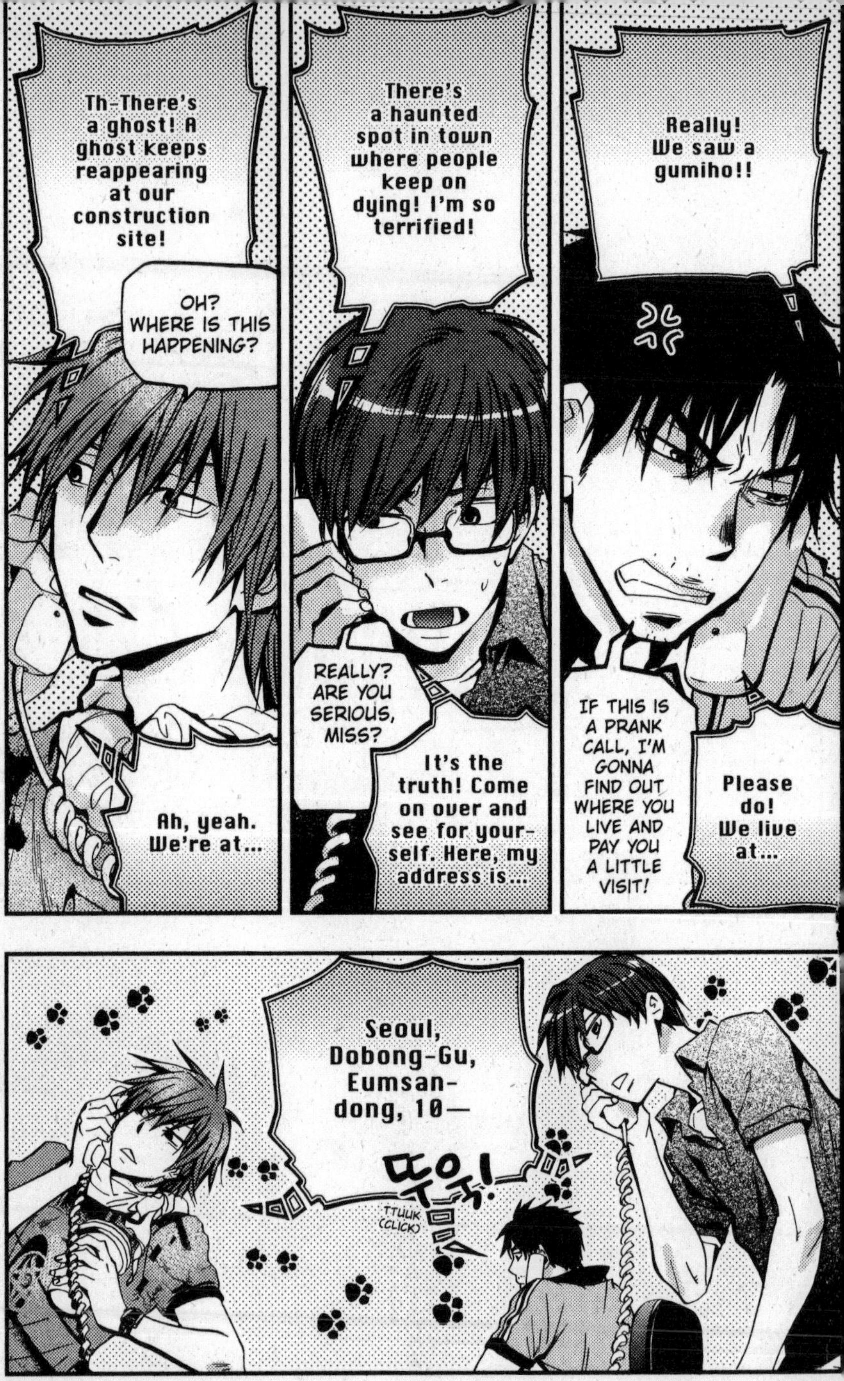

Th-There's a ghost! A ghost keeps reappearing at our construction site!
OH? WHERE IS THIS HAPPENING?
Ah, yeah. We're at...
There's a haunted spot in town where people keep on dying! I'm so terrified!
REALLY? ARE YOU SERIOUS, MISS?
It's the truth! Come on over and see for your-self. Here, my address is...
Really! We saw a gumiho!!
IF THIS IS A PRANK CALL, I'M GONNA FIND OUT WHERE YOU LIVE AND PAY YOU A LITTLE VISIT!
Please do! We live at...
Seoul, Dobong-Gu, Eumsan-dong, 10—
TTUUK (CLICK)

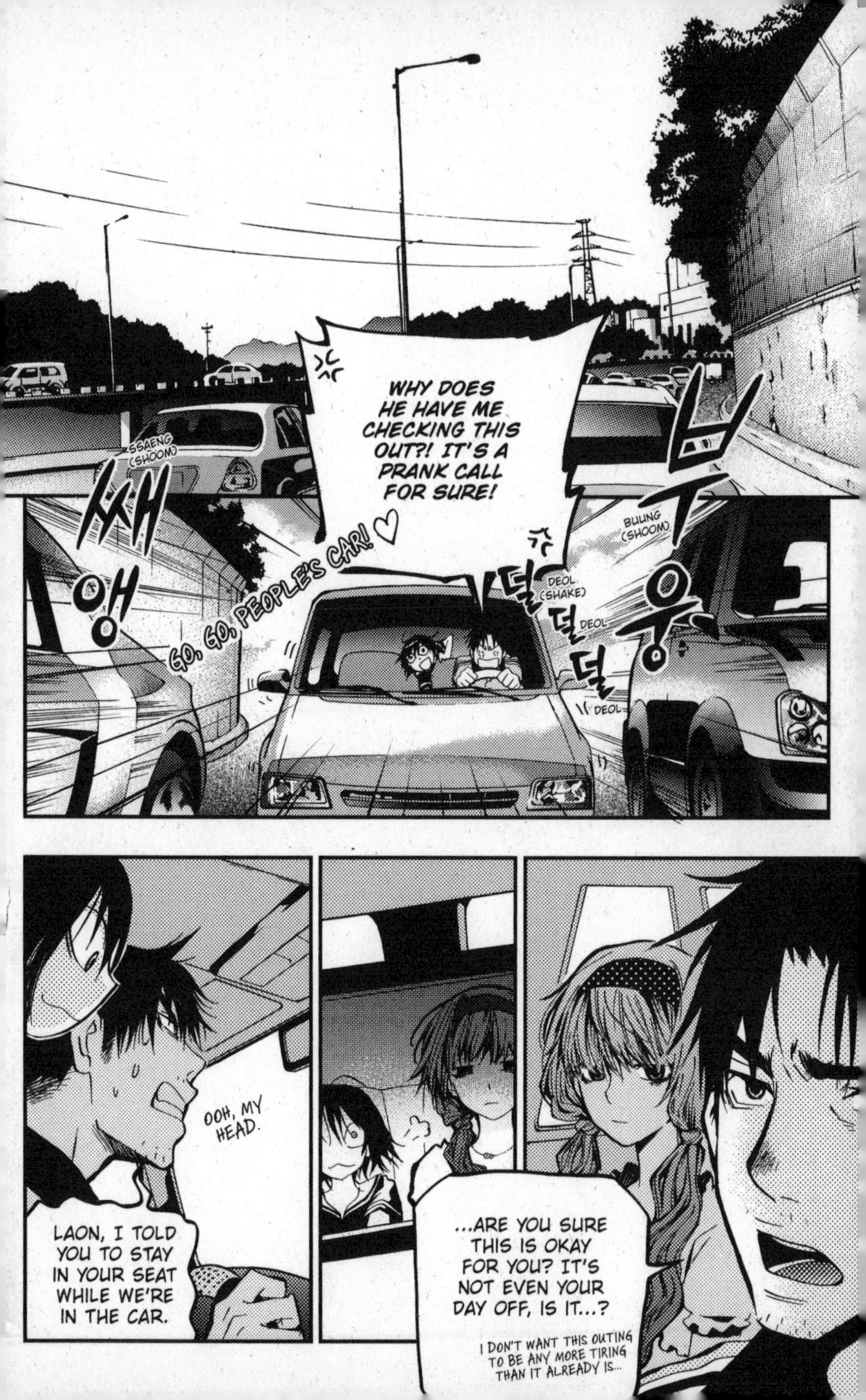
쌔앵
SSAENG (SHOOM)
WHY DOES HE HAVE ME CHECKING THIS OUT?! IT'S A PRANK CALL FOR SURE!
부웅
BUUNG (SHOOM)
GO, GO, PEOPLE'S CAR! ♡
덜덜덜
DEOL (SHAKE)
DEOL
DEOL
OOH, MY HEAD.
LAON, I TOLD YOU TO STAY IN YOUR SEAT WHILE WE'RE IN THE CAR.
...ARE YOU SURE THIS IS OKAY FOR YOU? IT'S NOT EVEN YOUR DAY OFF, IS IT...?
I DON'T WANT THIS OUTING TO BE ANY MORE TIRING THAN IT ALREADY IS...

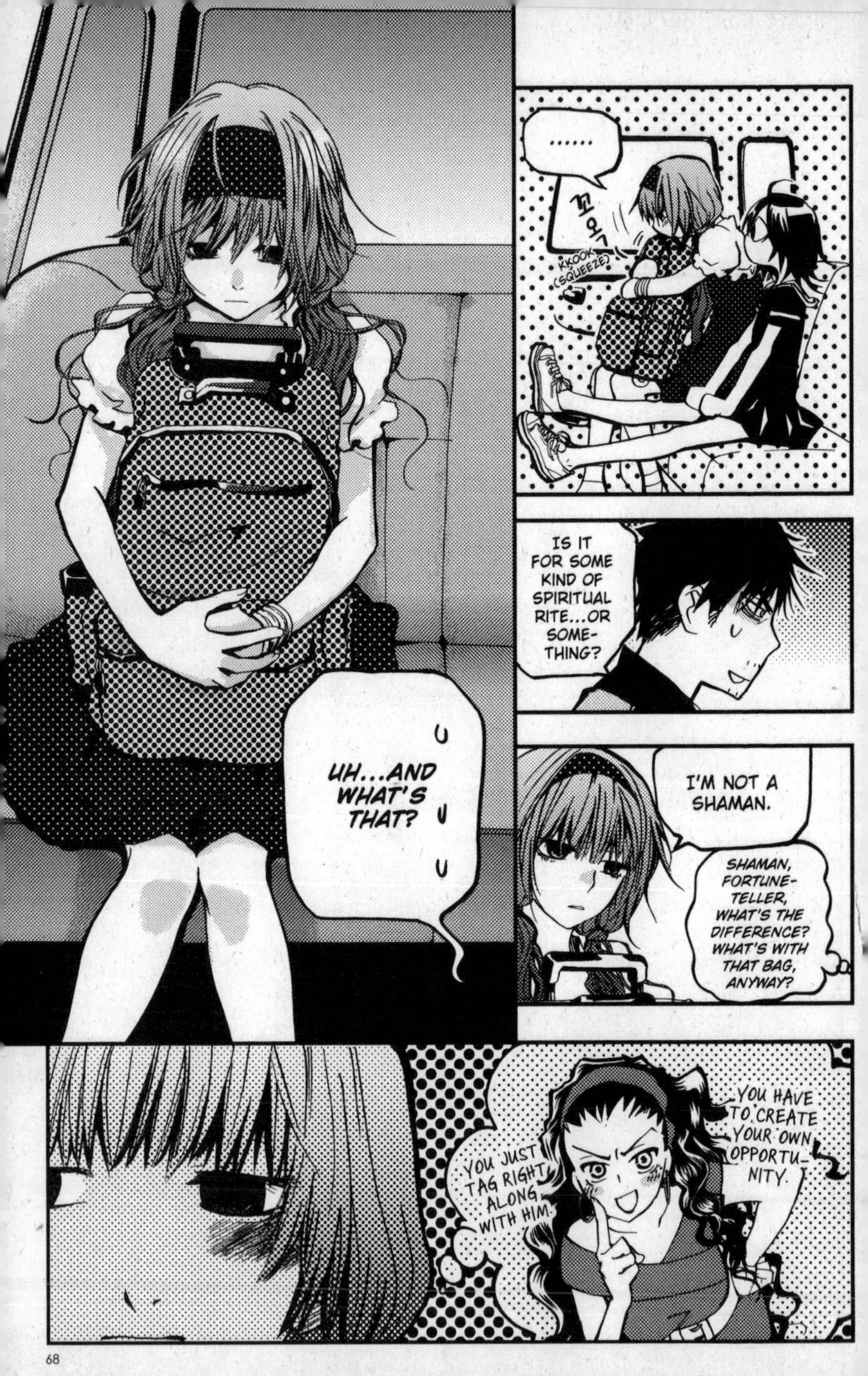
UH...AND WHAT'S THAT?
......
꼬옥
KKOOK (SQUEEZE)
IS IT FOR SOME KIND OF SPIRITUAL RITE...OR SOMETHING?
I'M NOT A SHAMAN.
SHAMAN, FORTUNE-TELLER, WHAT'S THE DIFFERENCE? WHAT'S WITH THAT BAG, ANYWAY?
YOU JUST TAG RIGHT ALONG WITH HIM.
YOU HAVE TO CREATE YOUR OWN OPPORTUNITY.

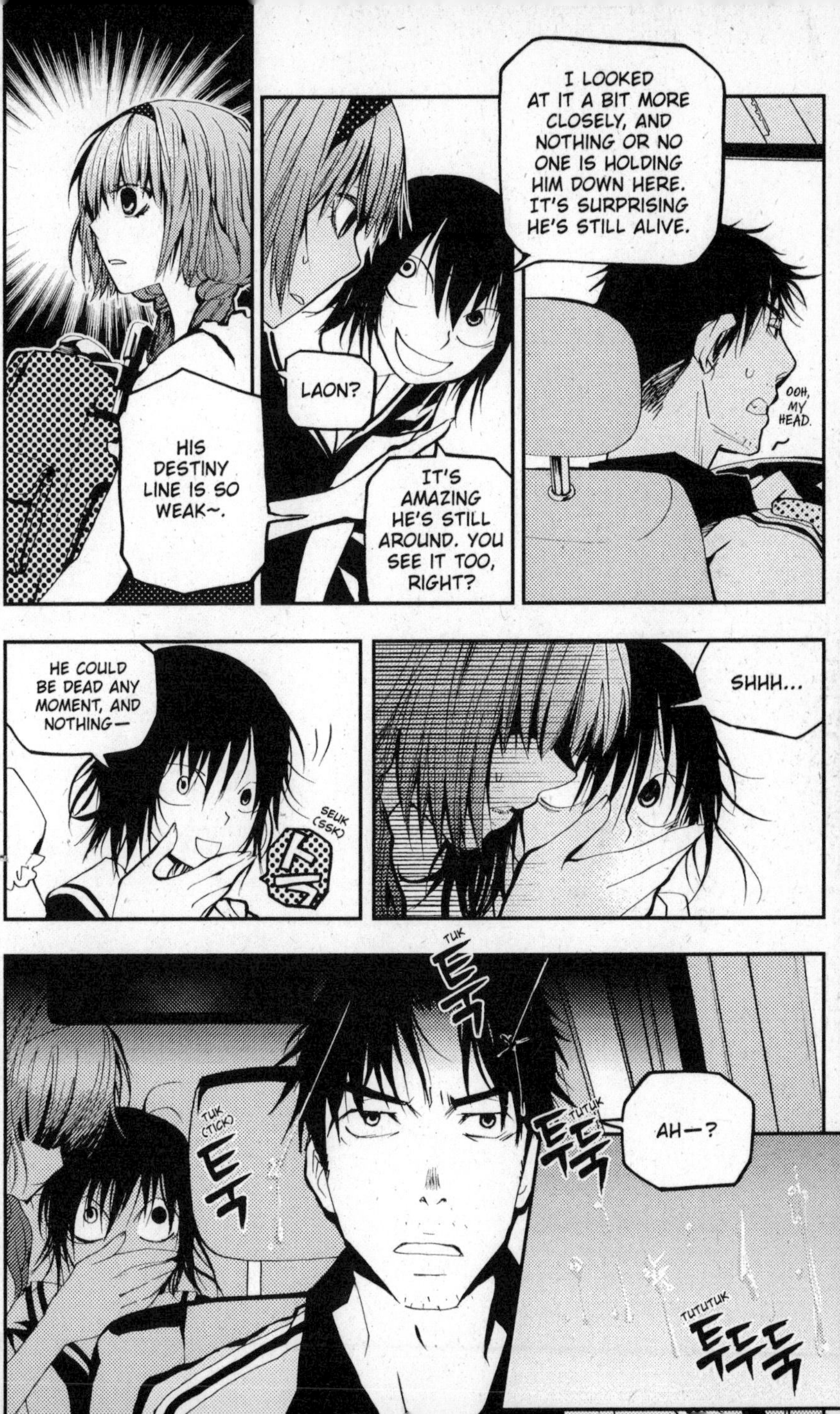
HIS DESTINY LINE IS SO WEAK~.
LAON?
IT'S AMAZING HE'S STILL AROUND. YOU SEE IT TOO, RIGHT?
I LOOKED AT IT A BIT MORE CLOSELY, AND NOTHING OR NO ONE IS HOLDING HIM DOWN HERE. IT'S SURPRISING HE'S STILL ALIVE.
OOH, MY HEAD.
HE COULD BE DEAD ANY MOMENT, AND NOTHING—
SEUK (SSK)
SHHH...
TUK
툭
TUK (TICK)
툭
TUTUK
투둑
AH—?
TUTUTUK
투두둑

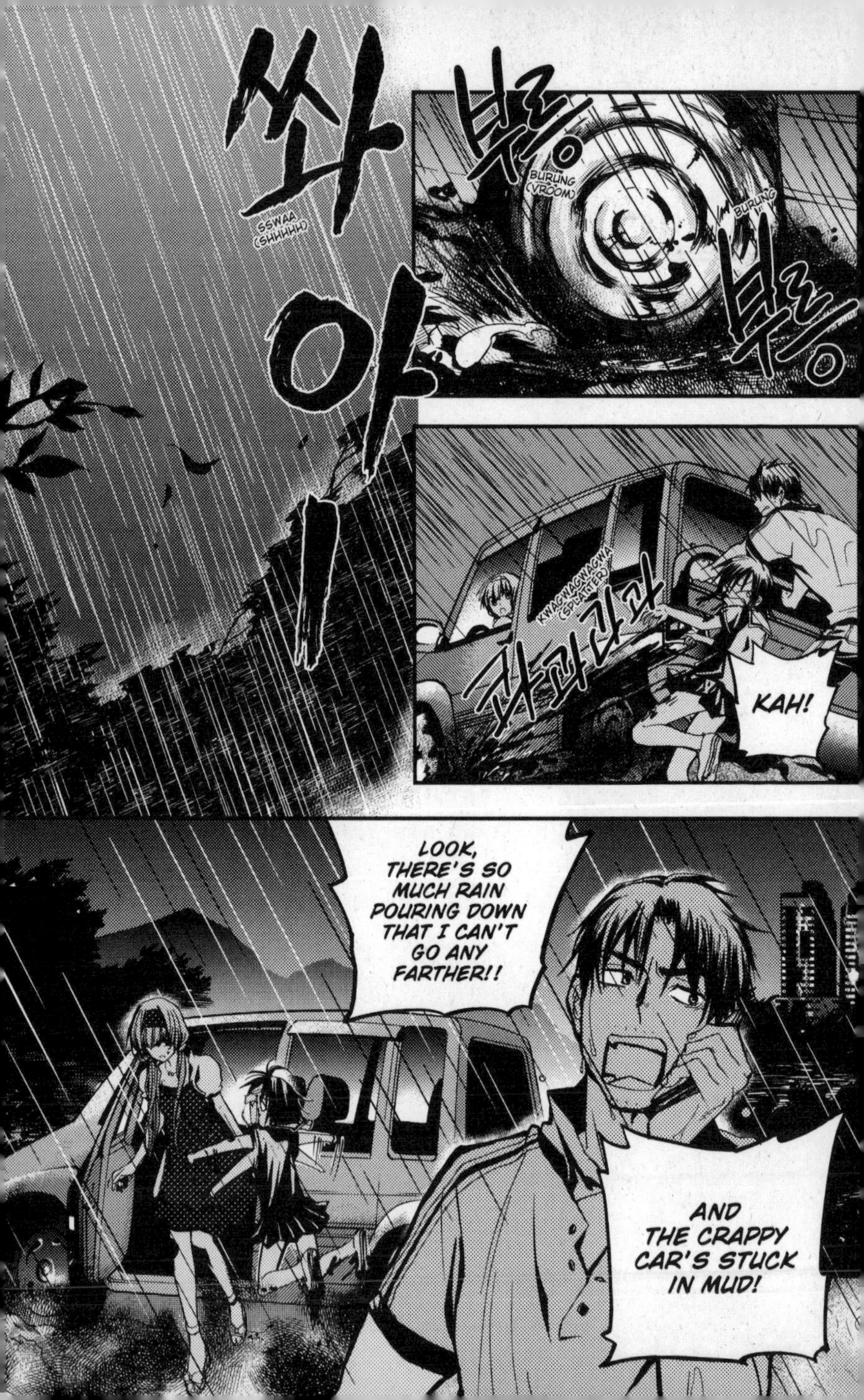

쏴아!
SSWAA (SHHHHHH)
부릉
BURUNG (VROOM)
부릉
BURUNG
KWAGWAGWAGWA (SPLATTER)
KAH!
LOOK, THERE'S SO MUCH RAIN POURING DOWN THAT I CAN'T GO ANY FARTHER!!
AND THE CRAPPY CAR'S STUCK IN MUD!

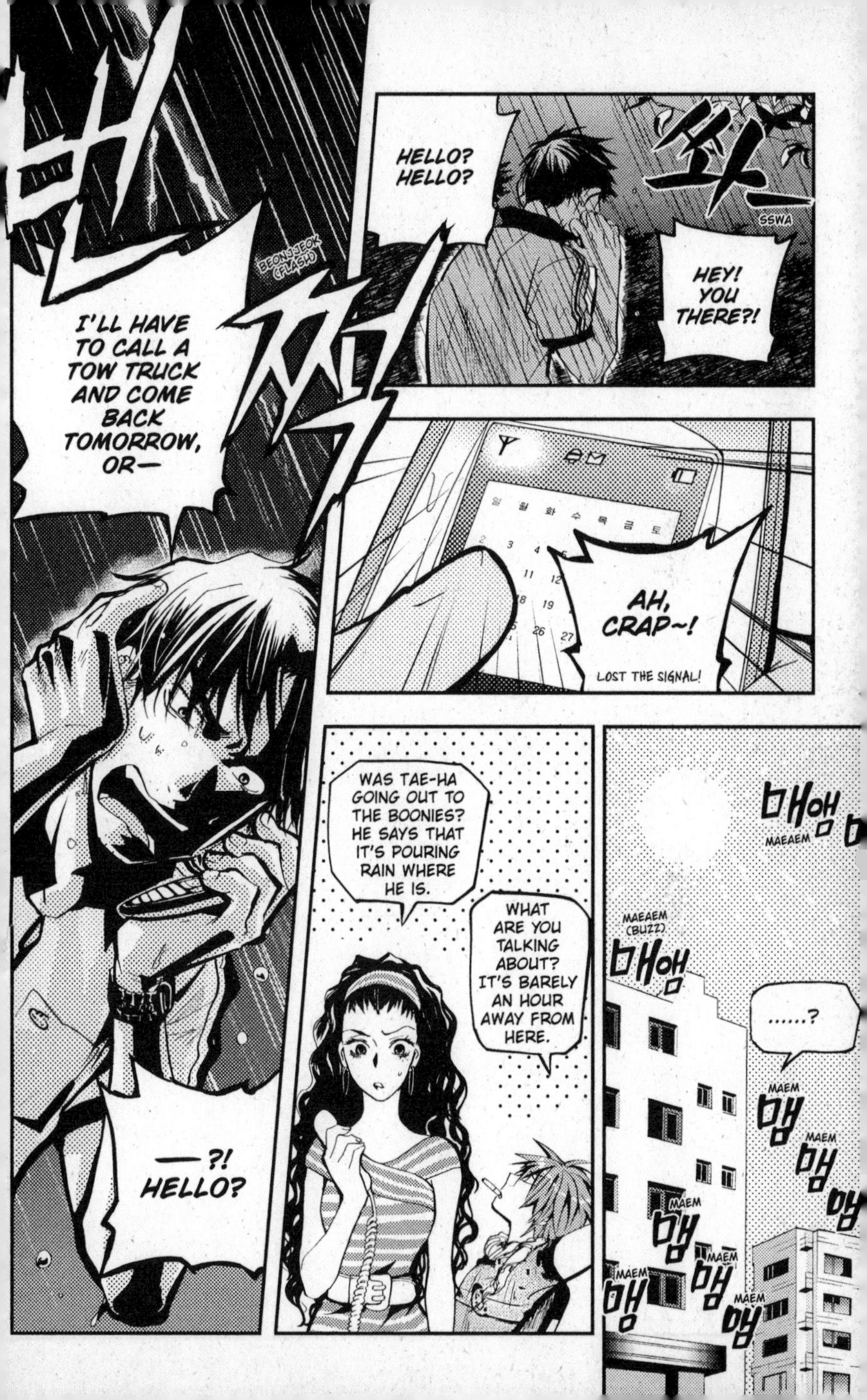
BEONJJEOK (FLASH)
I'LL HAVE TO CALL A TOW TRUCK AND COME BACK TOMORROW, OR—
—?! HELLO?
HELLO? HELLO?
SSWA
HEY! YOU THERE?!
AH, CRAP~!
LOST THE SIGNAL!
WAS TAE-HA GOING OUT TO THE BOONIES? HE SAYS THAT IT'S POURING RAIN WHERE HE IS.
WHAT ARE YOU TALKING ABOUT? IT'S BARELY AN HOUR AWAY FROM HERE.
MAEAEM
MAEAEM (BUZZ)
......?
MAEM
MAEM
MAEM
MAEM
MAEM
MAEM

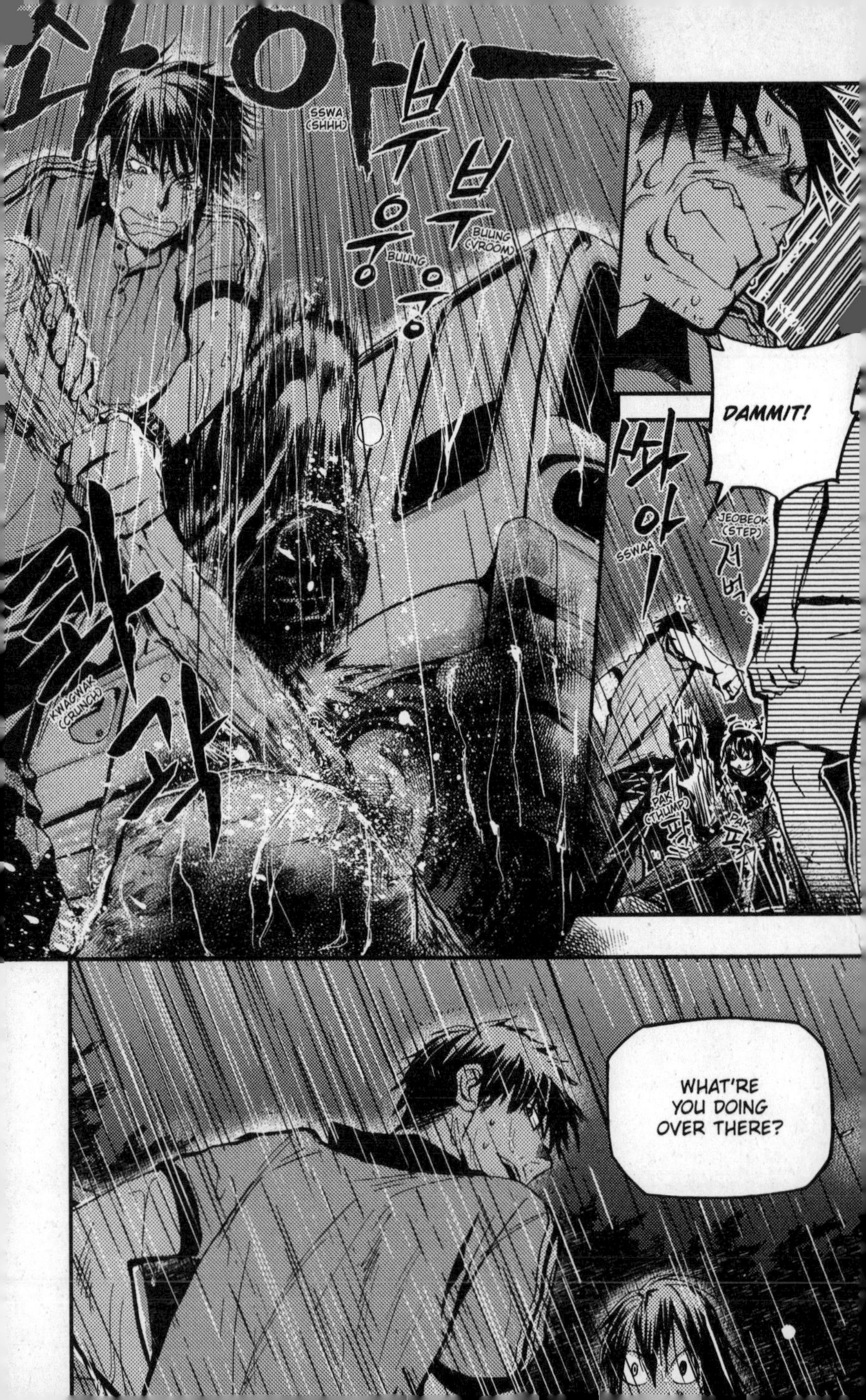

솨아—
SSWA (SHHH)
부웅
BUUNG (VROOM)
부웅
BUUNG
콰각
KWAGWAK (CRUNCH)
DAMMIT!
쏴아—!
SSWAA
저벅
JEOBEOK (STEP)
PAK (THUMP)
PAK
WHAT'RE YOU DOING OVER THERE?

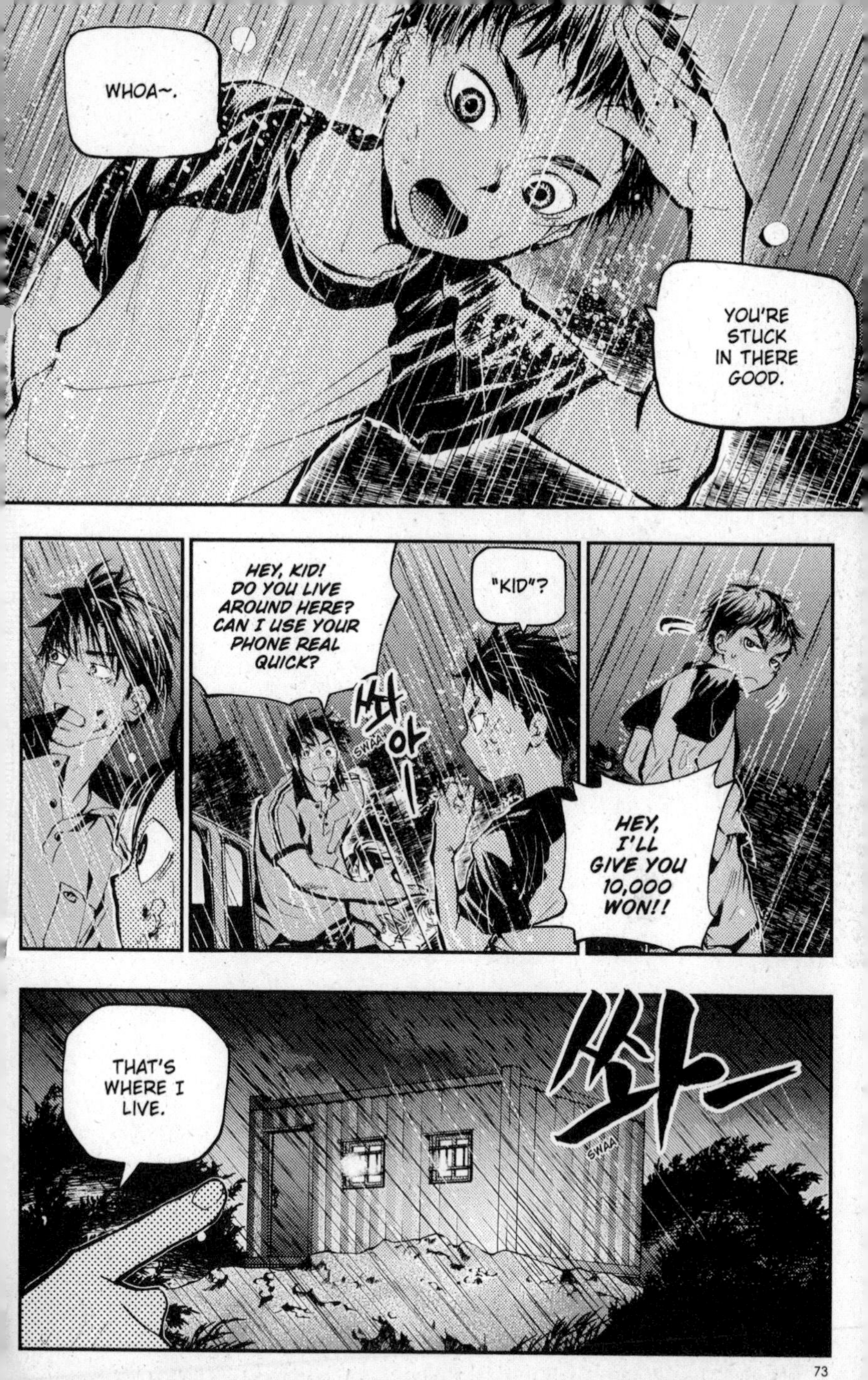
WHOA~.
YOU'RE STUCK IN THERE GOOD.
HEY, KID! DO YOU LIVE AROUND HERE? CAN I USE YOUR PHONE REAL QUICK?
"KID"?
쏴아
SWAA
HEY, I'LL GIVE YOU 10,000 WON!!
THAT'S WHERE I LIVE.
쏴
SWAA

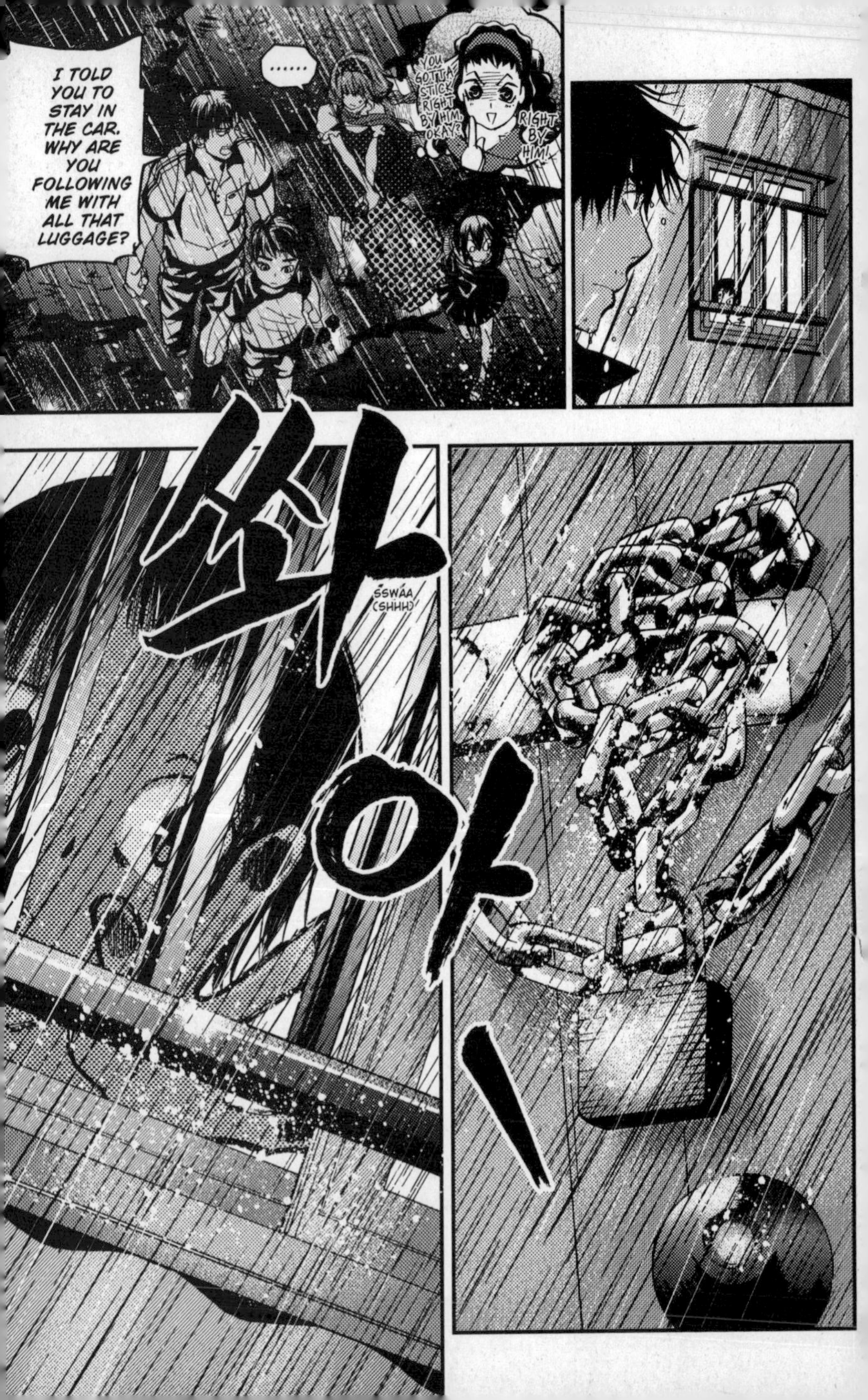
I TOLD YOU TO STAY IN THE CAR. WHY ARE YOU FOLLOWING ME WITH ALL THAT LUGGAGE?
......
YOU GOTTA STICK RIGHT BY HIM, OKAY?
RIGHT BY HIM!
쏴아!
SSWAA (SHHH)

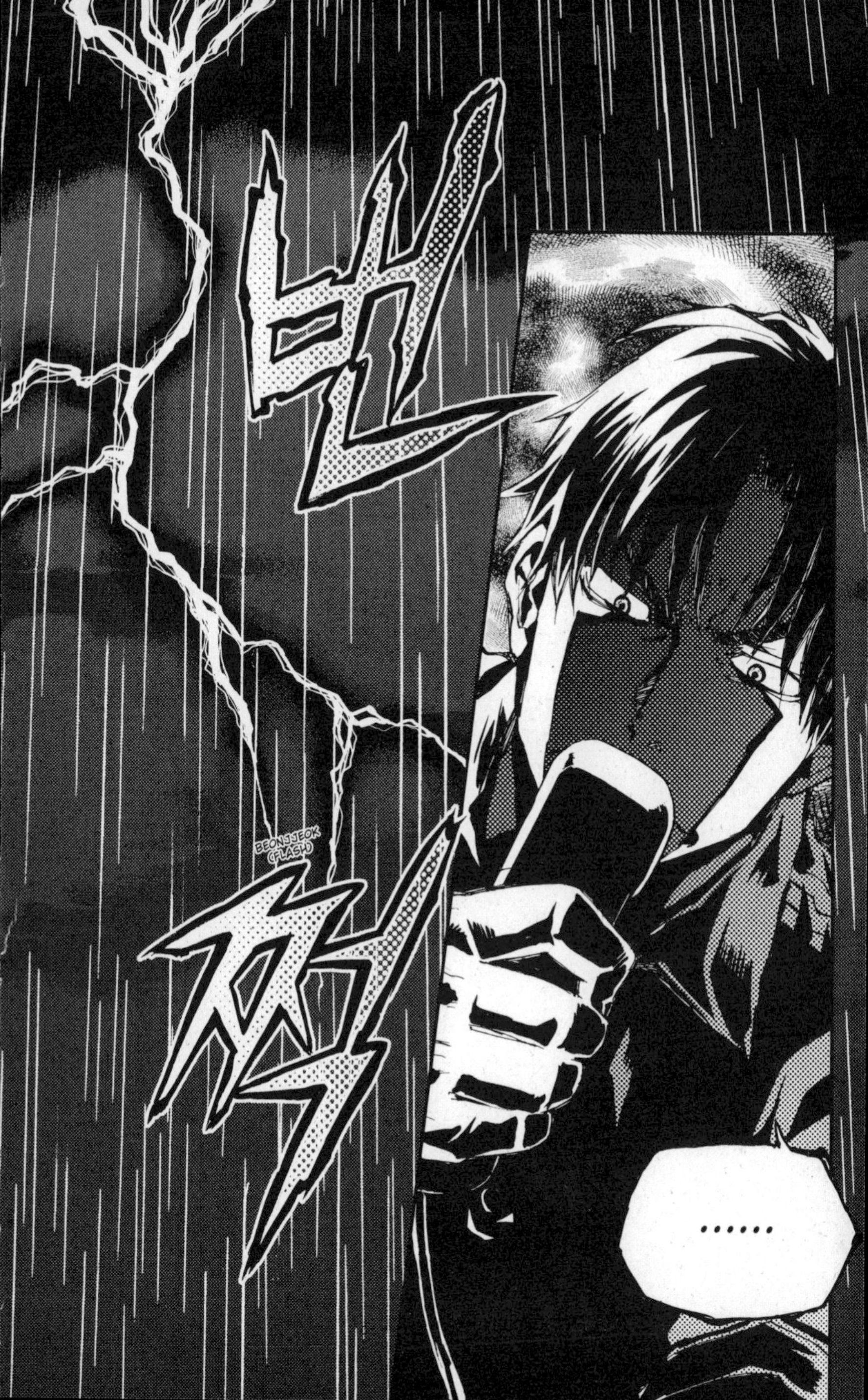

BEONJJEOK
(FLASH)
......

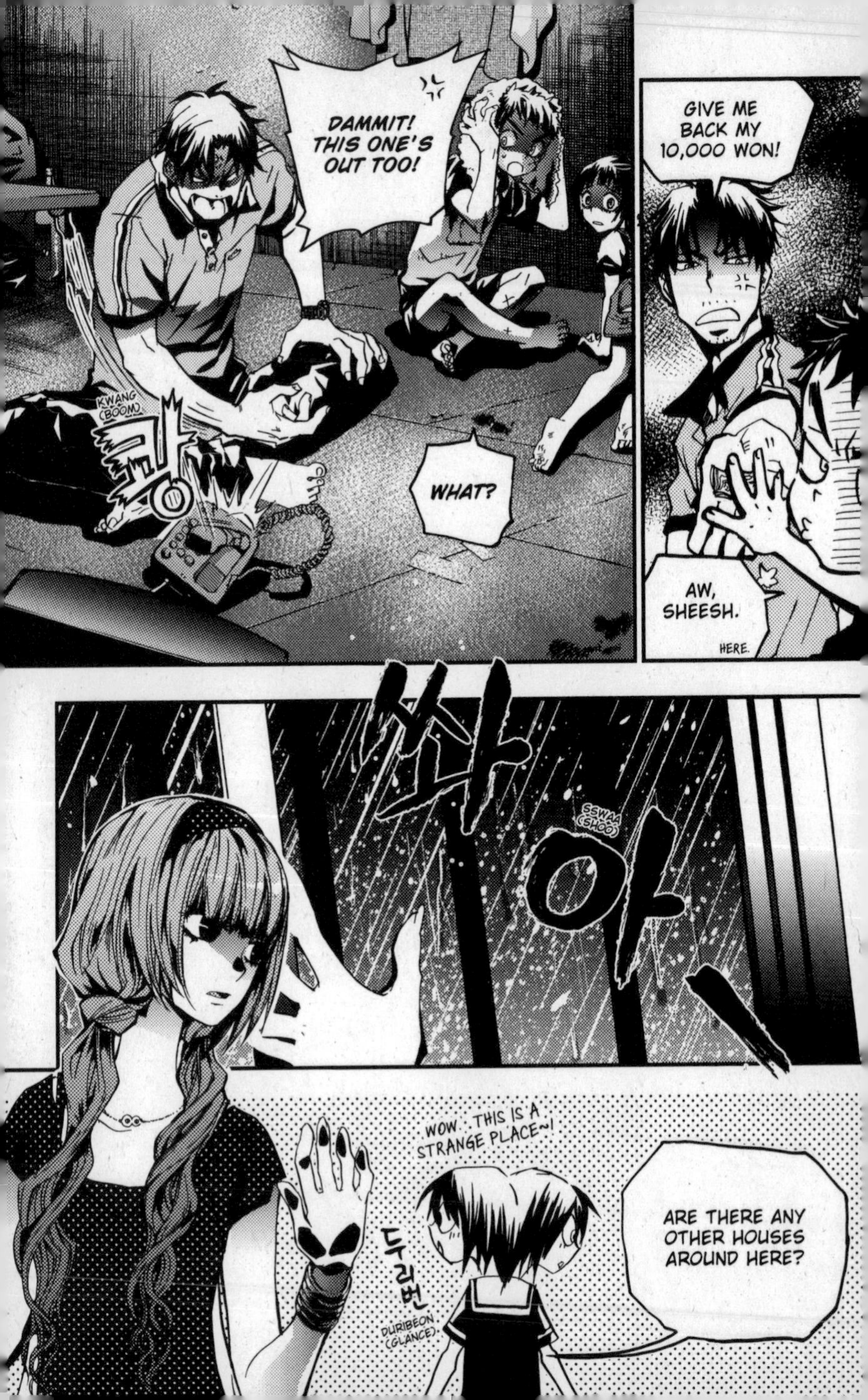
DAMMIT! THIS ONE'S OUT TOO!
KWANG (BOOM)
WHAT?
GIVE ME BACK MY 10,000 WON!
AW, SHEESH.
HERE.
SSWAA (SHOO)
WOW, THIS IS A STRANGE PLACE~!
ARE THERE ANY OTHER HOUSES AROUND HERE?
두리번
DURIBEON (GLANCE)

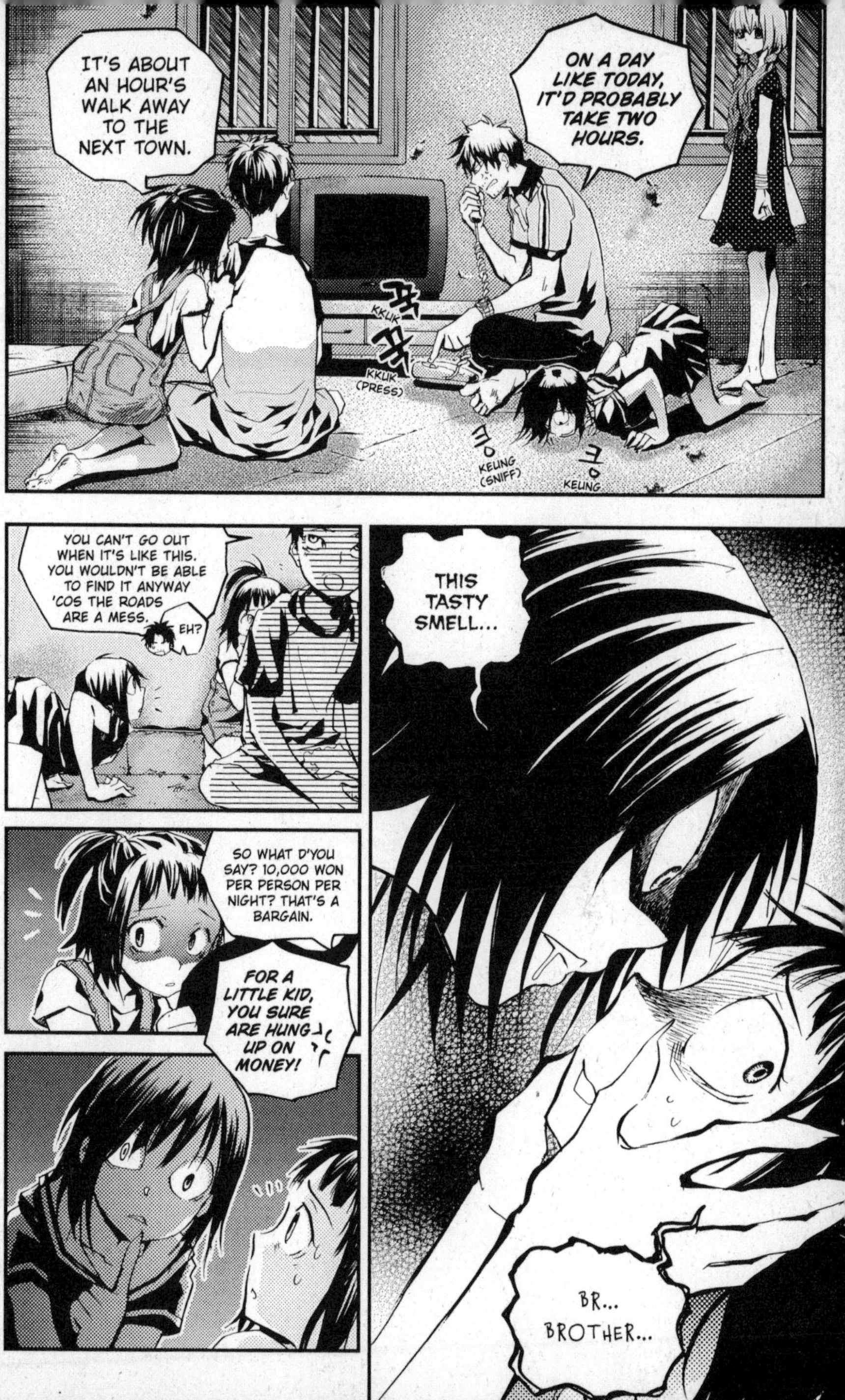
IT'S ABOUT AN HOUR'S WALK AWAY TO THE NEXT TOWN.
ON A DAY LIKE TODAY, IT'D PROBABLY TAKE TWO HOURS.
KKUK
KKUK (PRESS)
KEUNG (SNIFF)
KEUNG
YOU CAN'T GO OUT WHEN IT'S LIKE THIS. YOU WOULDN'T BE ABLE TO FIND IT ANYWAY 'COS THE ROADS ARE A MESS.
EH?
SO WHAT D'YOU SAY? 10,000 WON PER PERSON PER NIGHT? THAT'S A BARGAIN.
FOR A LITTLE KID, YOU SURE ARE HUNG UP ON MONEY!
THIS TASTY SMELL...
BR... BROTHER...

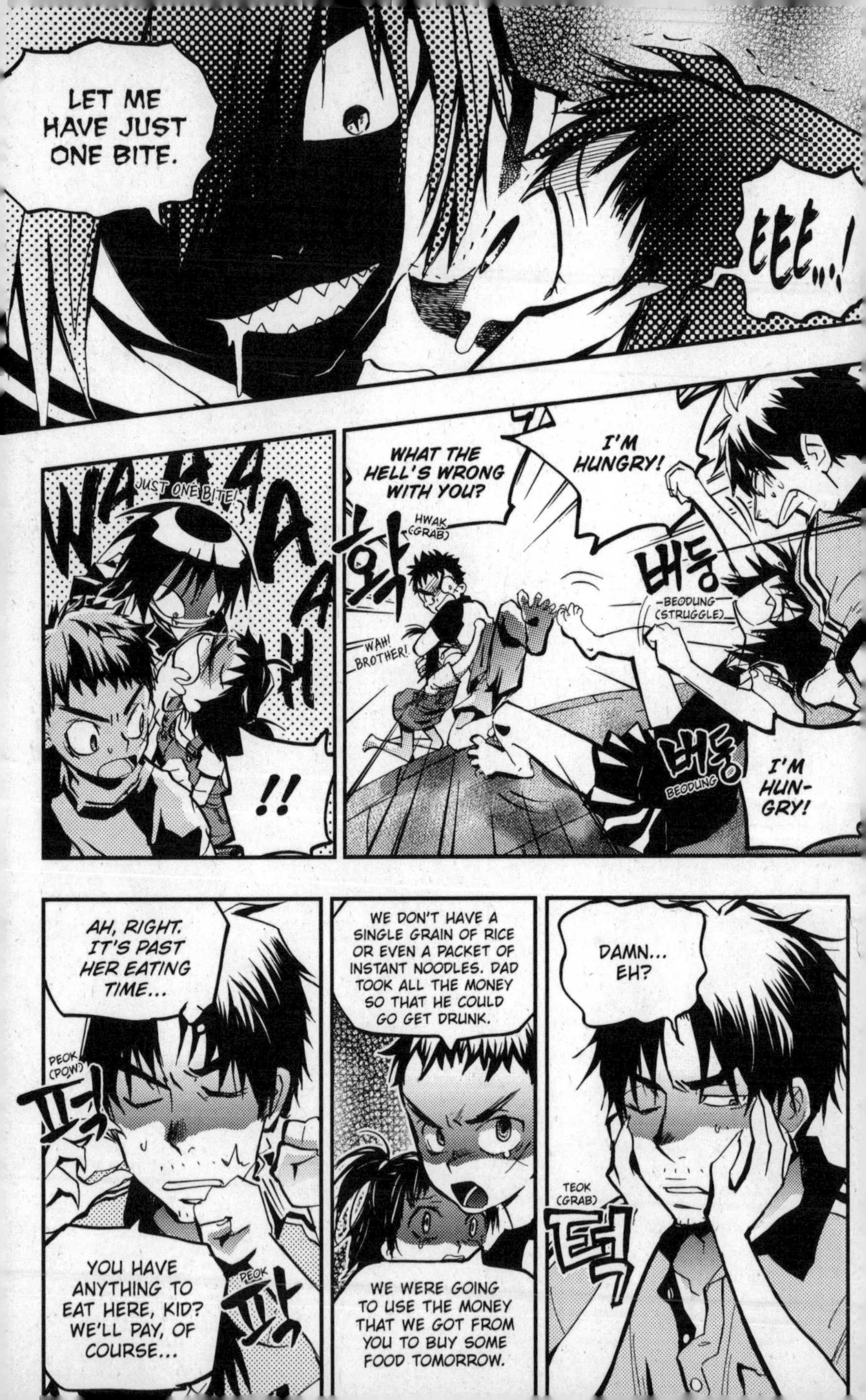
LET ME HAVE JUST ONE BITE.
EEE...!
WAAAAAH
JUST ONE BITE!
!!
WHAT THE HELL'S WRONG WITH YOU?
HWAK (GRAB)
확
WAH! BROTHER!
I'M HUNGRY!
버둥
BEODUNG (STRUGGLE)
버둥
BEODUNG
I'M HUN-GRY!
AH, RIGHT. IT'S PAST HER EATING TIME...
PEOK (POW)
퍽
YOU HAVE ANYTHING TO EAT HERE, KID? WE'LL PAY, OF COURSE...
PEOK
퍽
WE DON'T HAVE A SINGLE GRAIN OF RICE OR EVEN A PACKET OF INSTANT NOODLES. DAD TOOK ALL THE MONEY SO THAT HE COULD GO GET DRUNK.
WE WERE GOING TO USE THE MONEY THAT WE GOT FROM YOU TO BUY SOME FOOD TOMORROW.
DAMN... EH?
TEOK (GRAB)
턱

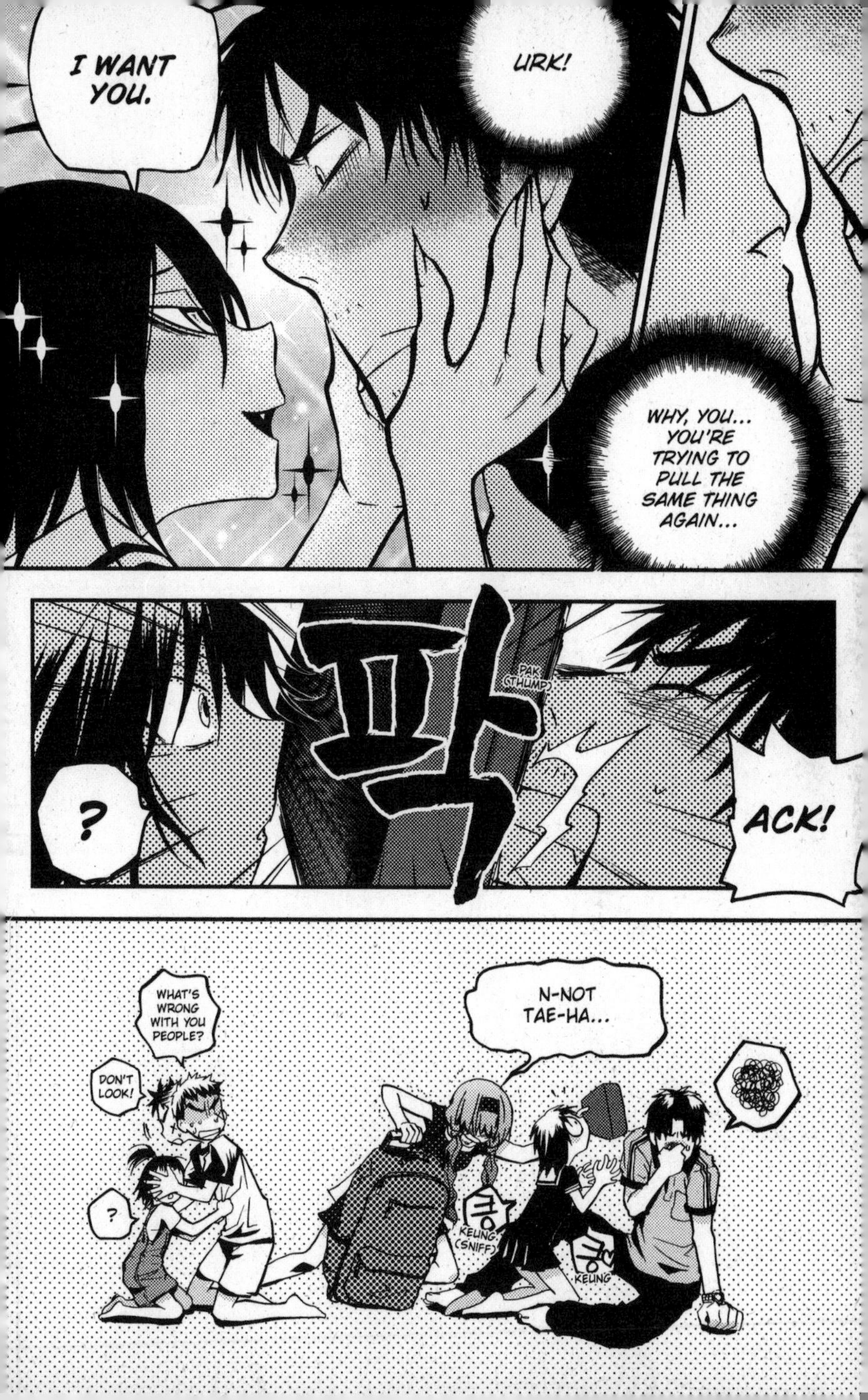
I WANT YOU.
URK!
WHY, YOU... YOU'RE TRYING TO PULL THE SAME THING AGAIN...
?
파
PAK (THUMP)
ACK!
WHAT'S WRONG WITH YOU PEOPLE?
DON'T LOOK!
?
N-NOT TAE-HA...
킁
KEUNG (SNIFF)
킁
KEUNG

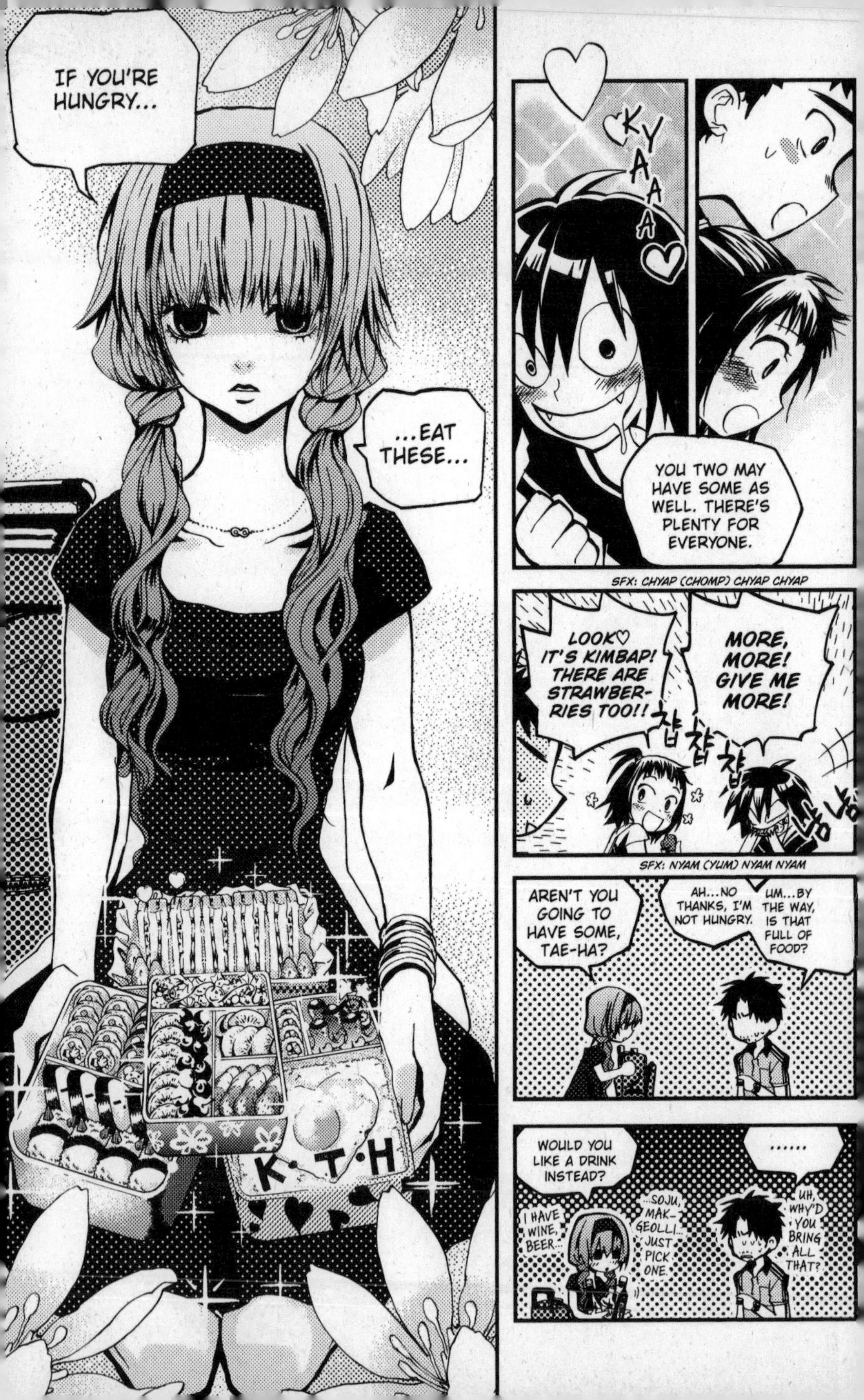
IF YOU'RE HUNGRY...
...EAT THESE...
K·T·H
KYAAAA
YOU TWO MAY HAVE SOME AS WELL. THERE'S PLENTY FOR EVERYONE.
SFX: CHYAP (CHOMP) CHYAP CHYAP
LOOK♡ IT'S KIMBAP! THERE ARE STRAWBER-RIES TOO!!
MORE, MORE! GIVE ME MORE!
찹 찹 찹
SFX: NYAM (YUM) NYAM NYAM
AREN'T YOU GOING TO HAVE SOME, TAE-HA?
AH...NO THANKS, I'M NOT HUNGRY.
UM...BY THE WAY, IS THAT FULL OF FOOD?
WOULD YOU LIKE A DRINK INSTEAD?
......
I HAVE WINE, BEER...
...SOJU, MAK-GEOLLI... JUST PICK ONE.
UH, WHY'D YOU BRING ALL THAT?

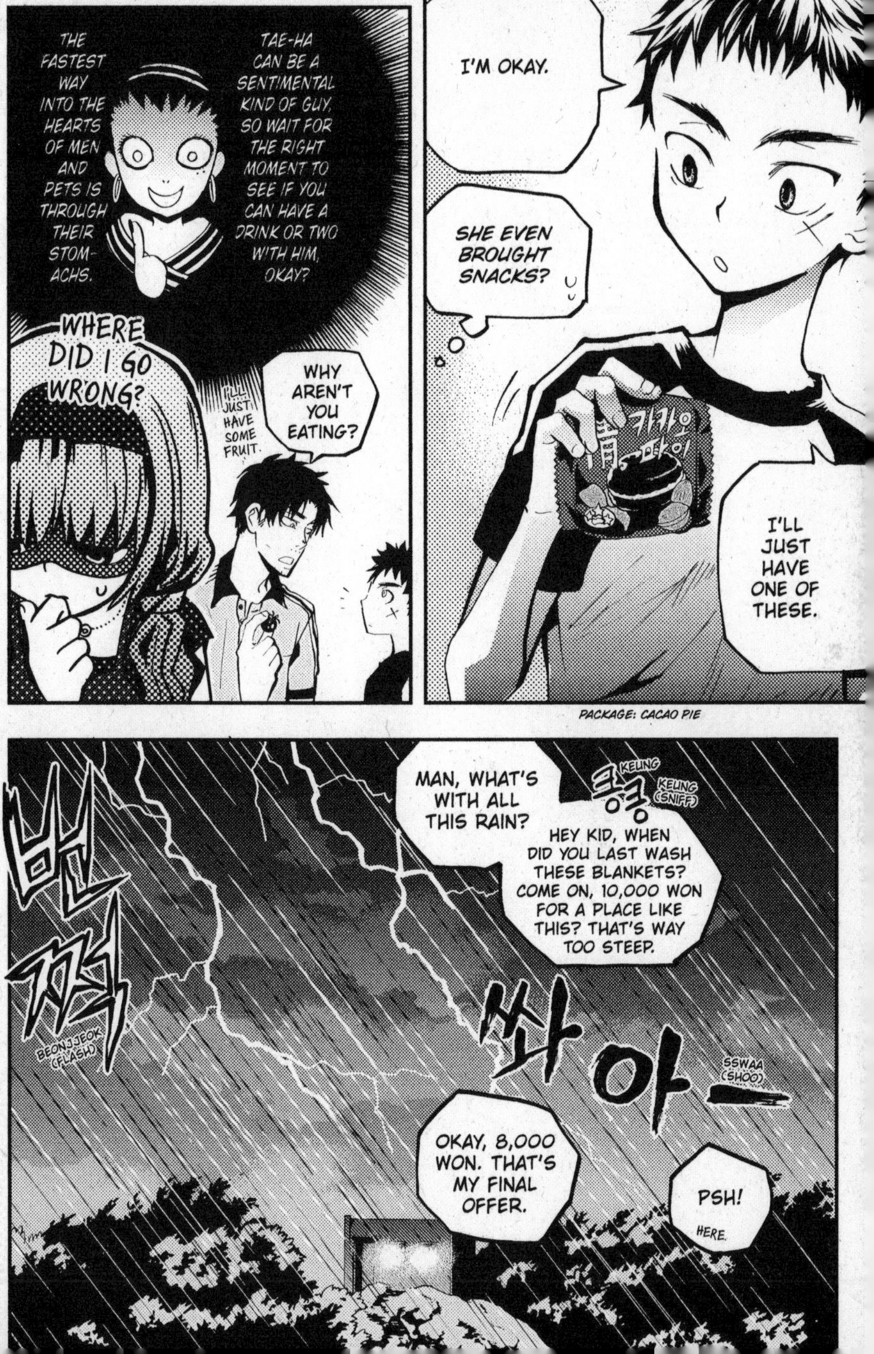
THE FASTEST WAY INTO THE HEARTS OF MEN AND PETS IS THROUGH THEIR STOM-ACHS.
TAE-HA CAN BE A SENTIMENTAL KIND OF GUY, SO WAIT FOR THE RIGHT MOMENT TO SEE IF YOU CAN HAVE A DRINK OR TWO WITH HIM, OKAY?
WHERE DID I GO WRONG?
WHY AREN'T YOU EATING?
I'LL JUST HAVE SOME FRUIT.
I'M OKAY.
SHE EVEN BROUGHT SNACKS?
I'LL JUST HAVE ONE OF THESE.
PACKAGE: CACAO PIE
번쩍
BEONJJEOK (FLASH)
MAN, WHAT'S WITH ALL THIS RAIN?
KEUNG KEUNG (SNIFF)
HEY KID, WHEN DID YOU LAST WASH THESE BLANKETS? COME ON, 10,000 WON FOR A PLACE LIKE THIS? THAT'S WAY TOO STEEP.
쏴아
SSWAA (SHOO)
OKAY, 8,000 WON. THAT'S MY FINAL OFFER.
PSH!
HERE.

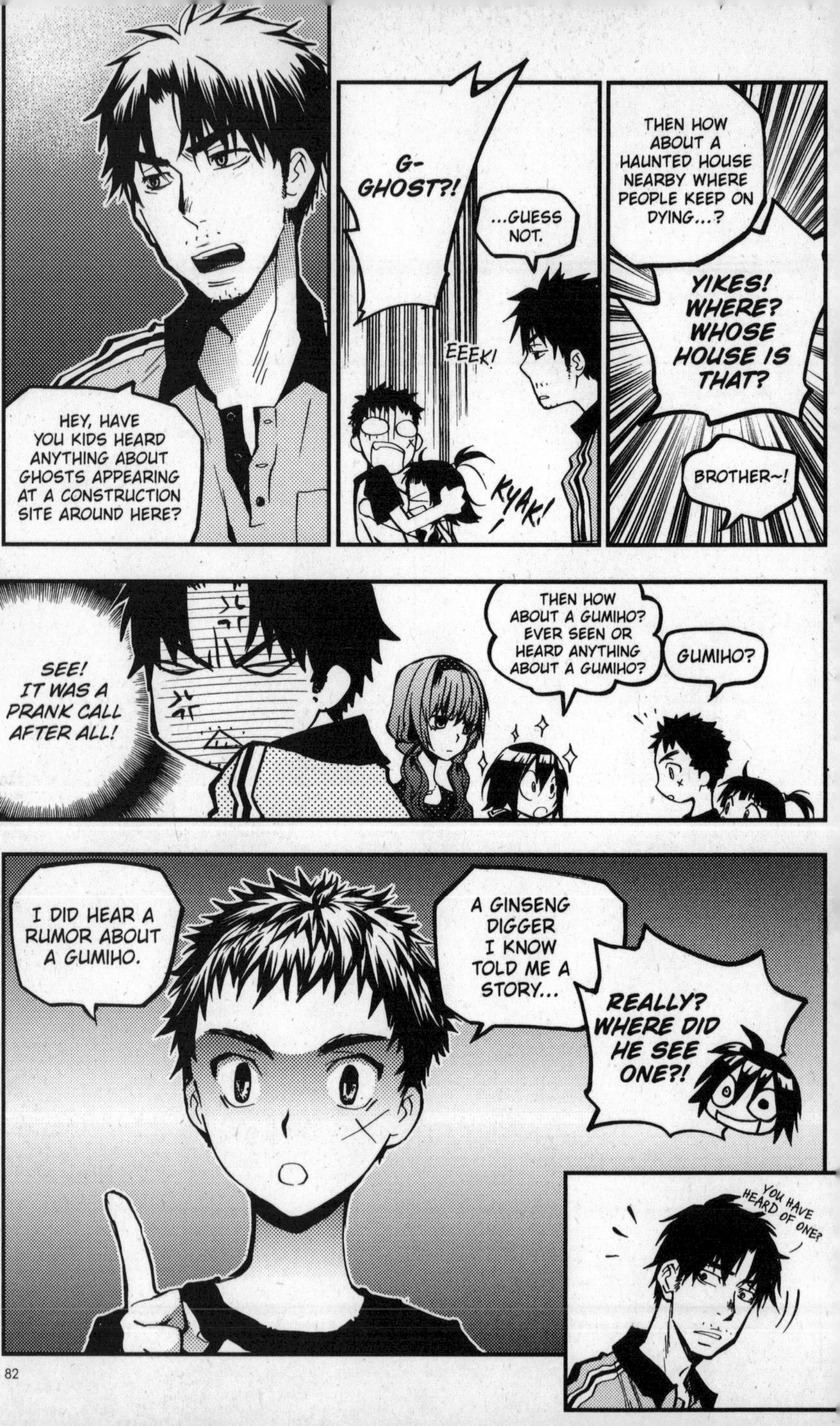
HEY, HAVE YOU KIDS HEARD ANYTHING ABOUT GHOSTS APPEARING AT A CONSTRUCTION SITE AROUND HERE?
G-GHOST?!
EEEK!
KYAK!
...GUESS NOT.
THEN HOW ABOUT A HAUNTED HOUSE NEARBY WHERE PEOPLE KEEP ON DYING...?
YIKES! WHERE? WHOSE HOUSE IS THAT?
BROTHER~!
SEE! IT WAS A PRANK CALL AFTER ALL!
THEN HOW ABOUT A GUMIHO? EVER SEEN OR HEARD ANYTHING ABOUT A GUMIHO?
GUMIHO?
I DID HEAR A RUMOR ABOUT A GUMIHO.
A GINSENG DIGGER I KNOW TOLD ME A STORY...
REALLY? WHERE DID HE SEE ONE?!
YOU HAVE HEARD OF ONE?

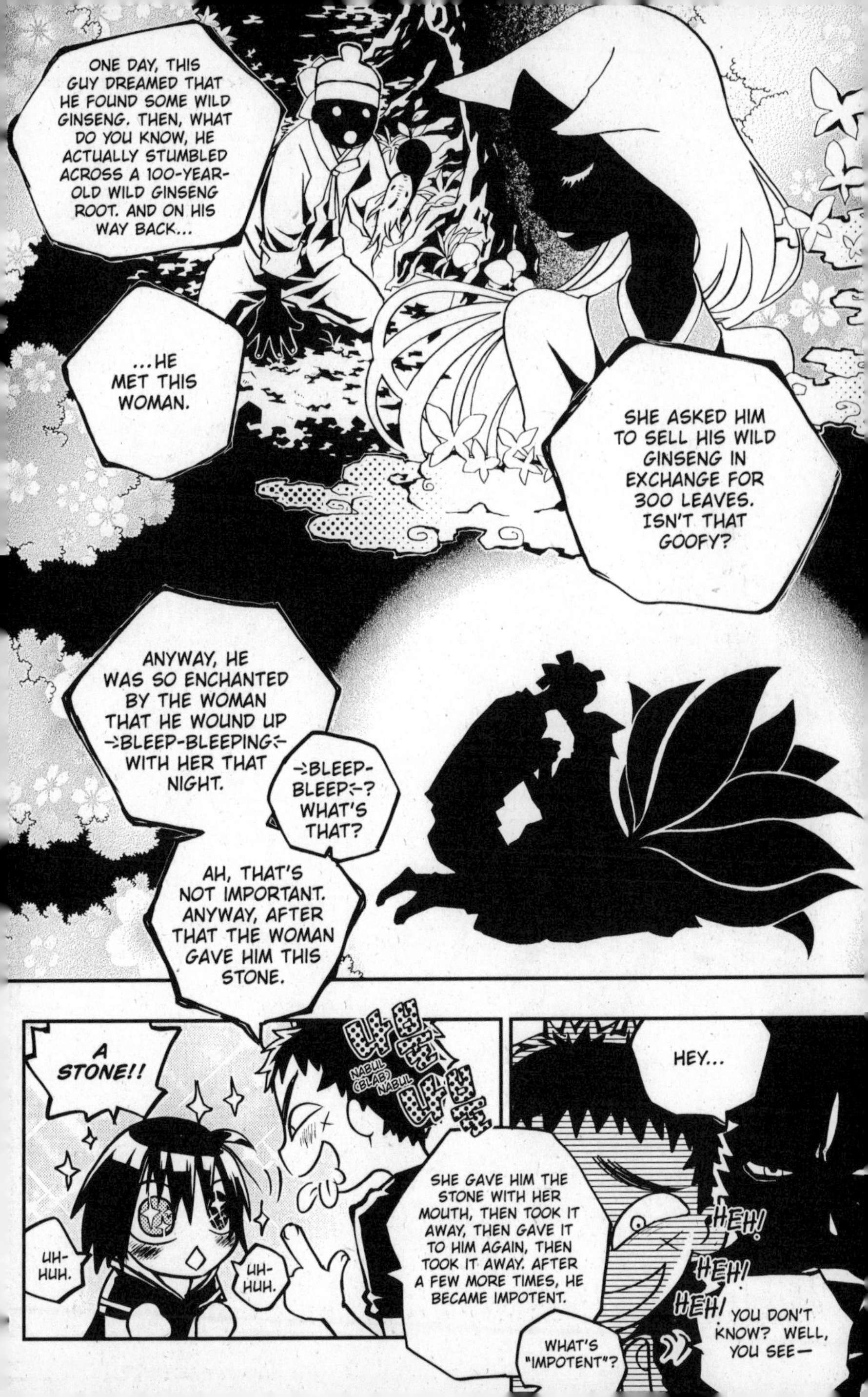
ONE DAY, THIS GUY DREAMED THAT HE FOUND SOME WILD GINSENG. THEN, WHAT DO YOU KNOW, HE ACTUALLY STUMBLED ACROSS A 100-YEAR-OLD WILD GINSENG ROOT. AND ON HIS WAY BACK...
...HE MET THIS WOMAN.
SHE ASKED HIM TO SELL HIS WILD GINSENG IN EXCHANGE FOR 300 LEAVES. ISN'T THAT GOOFY?
ANYWAY, HE WAS SO ENCHANTED BY THE WOMAN THAT HE WOUND UP BLEEP-BLEEPING WITH HER THAT NIGHT.
BLEEP-BLEEP? WHAT'S THAT?
AH, THAT'S NOT IMPORTANT. ANYWAY, AFTER THAT THE WOMAN GAVE HIM THIS STONE.
A STONE!!
NABUL (BLAB) NABUL
UH-HUH.
UH-HUH.
SHE GAVE HIM THE STONE WITH HER MOUTH, THEN TOOK IT AWAY, THEN GAVE IT TO HIM AGAIN, THEN TOOK IT AWAY. AFTER A FEW MORE TIMES, HE BECAME IMPOTENT.
WHAT'S "IMPOTENT"?
HEY...
HEH! HEH! HEH!
YOU DON'T KNOW? WELL, YOU SEE—

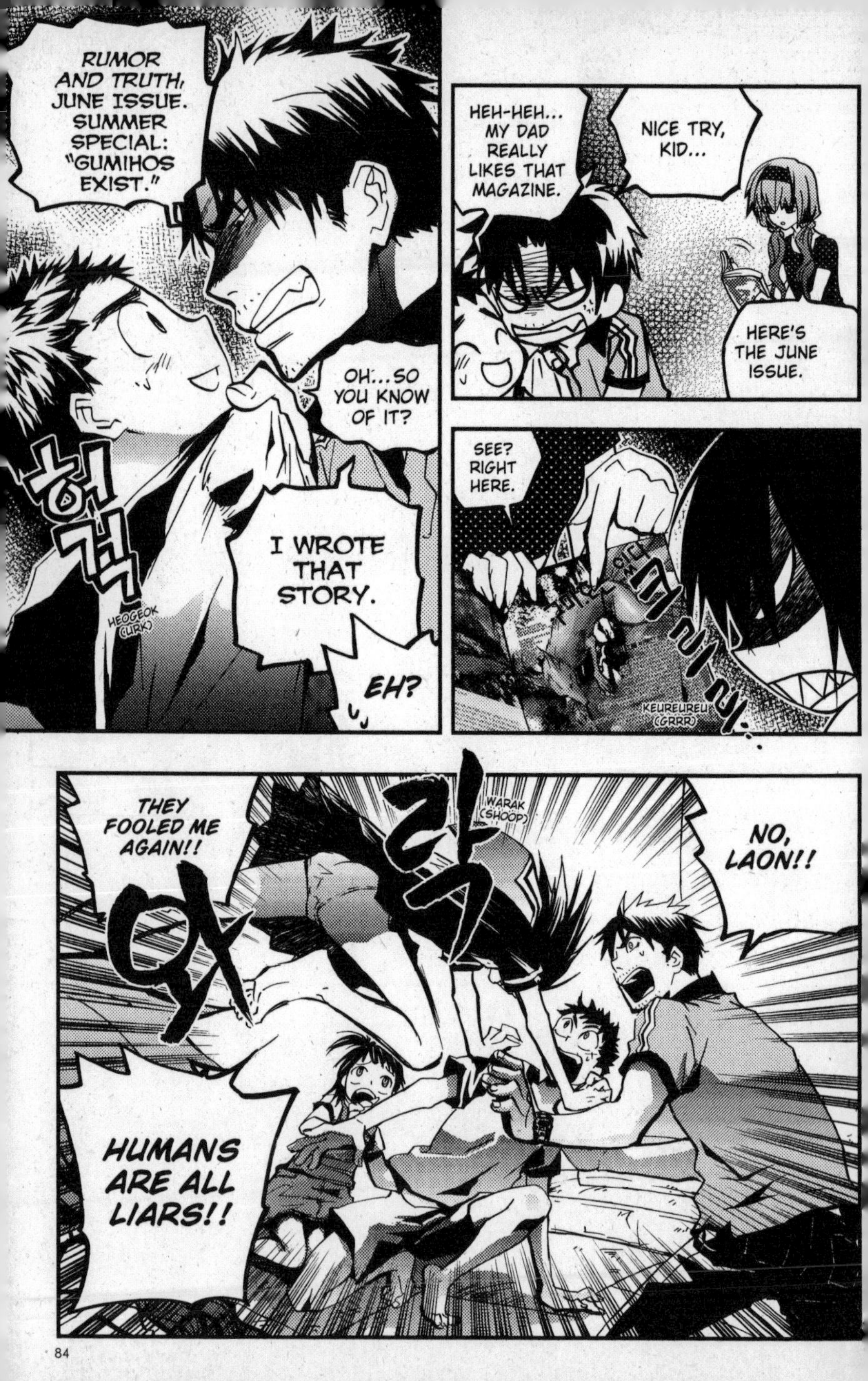
RUMOR AND TRUTH, JUNE ISSUE. SUMMER SPECIAL: "GUMIHOS EXIST."
OH...SO YOU KNOW OF IT?
HEOGEOK (URK)
I WROTE THAT STORY.
EH?
HEH-HEH... MY DAD REALLY LIKES THAT MAGAZINE.
NICE TRY, KID...
HERE'S THE JUNE ISSUE.
SEE? RIGHT HERE.
KEUREUREU (GRRR)
THEY FOOLED ME AGAIN!!
WARAK (SHOOP)
NO, LAON!!
HUMANS ARE ALL LIARS!!

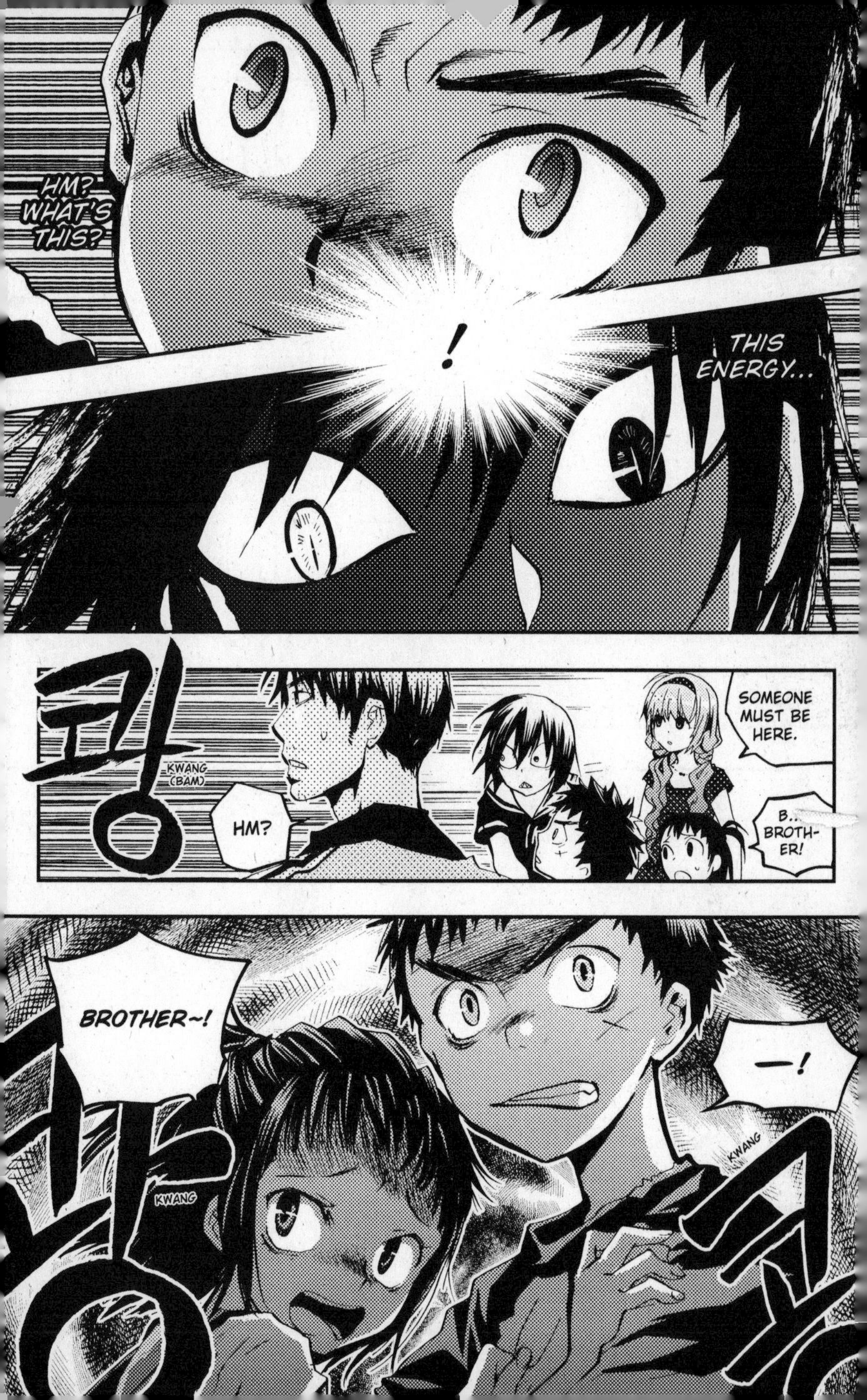
HM? WHAT'S THIS?
!
THIS ENERGY...
쾅
KWANG (BAM)
HM?
SOMEONE MUST BE HERE.
B... BROTHER!
BROTHER~!
KWANG
—!
KWANG

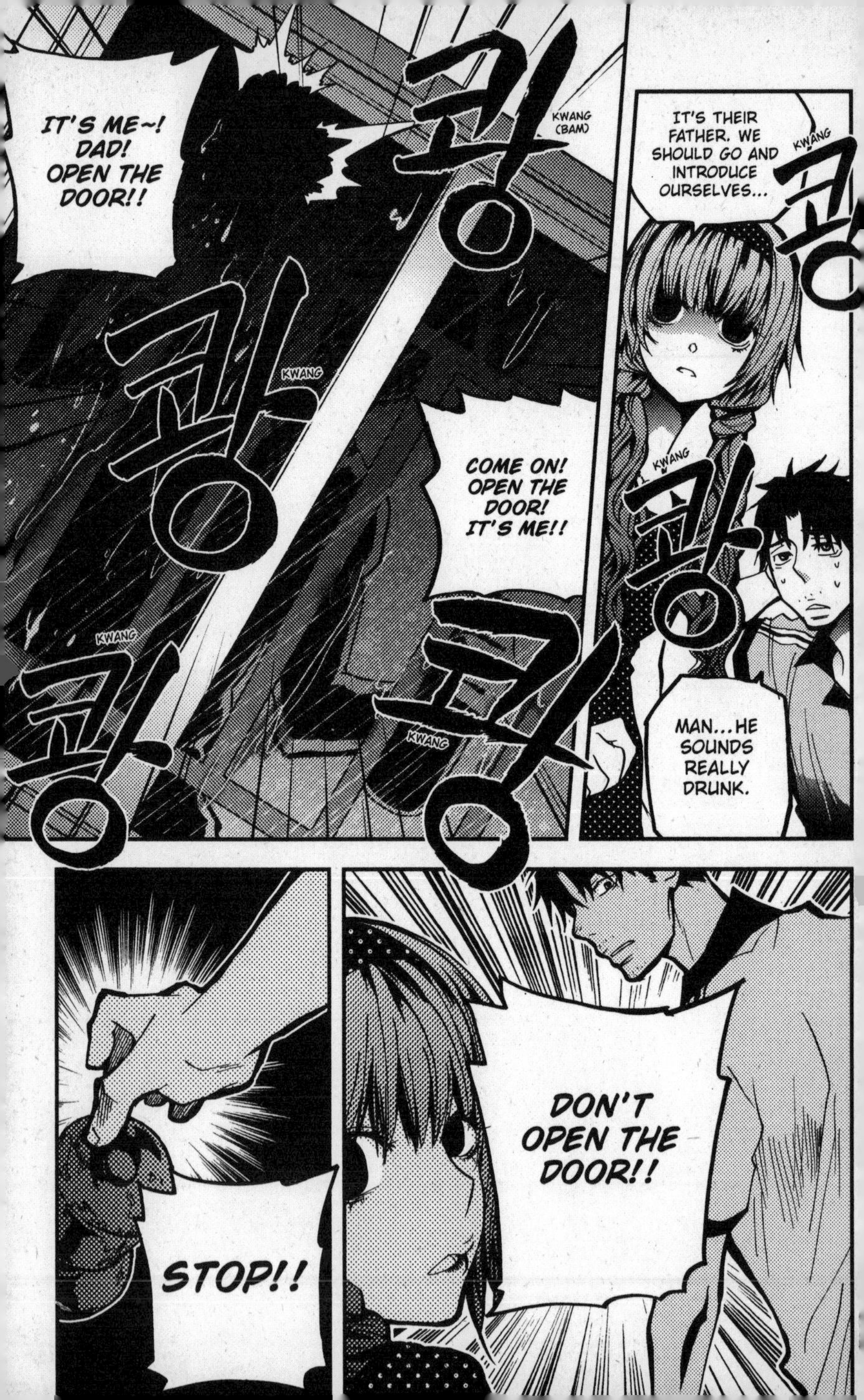
IT'S ME~! DAD! OPEN THE DOOR!!
쾅
KWANG (BAM)
쾅
KWANG
COME ON! OPEN THE DOOR! IT'S ME!!
쾅
KWANG
쾅
KWANG
IT'S THEIR FATHER. WE SHOULD GO AND INTRODUCE OURSELVES...
쾅
KWANG
쾅
KWANG
MAN...HE SOUNDS REALLY DRUNK.
STOP!!
DON'T OPEN THE DOOR!!

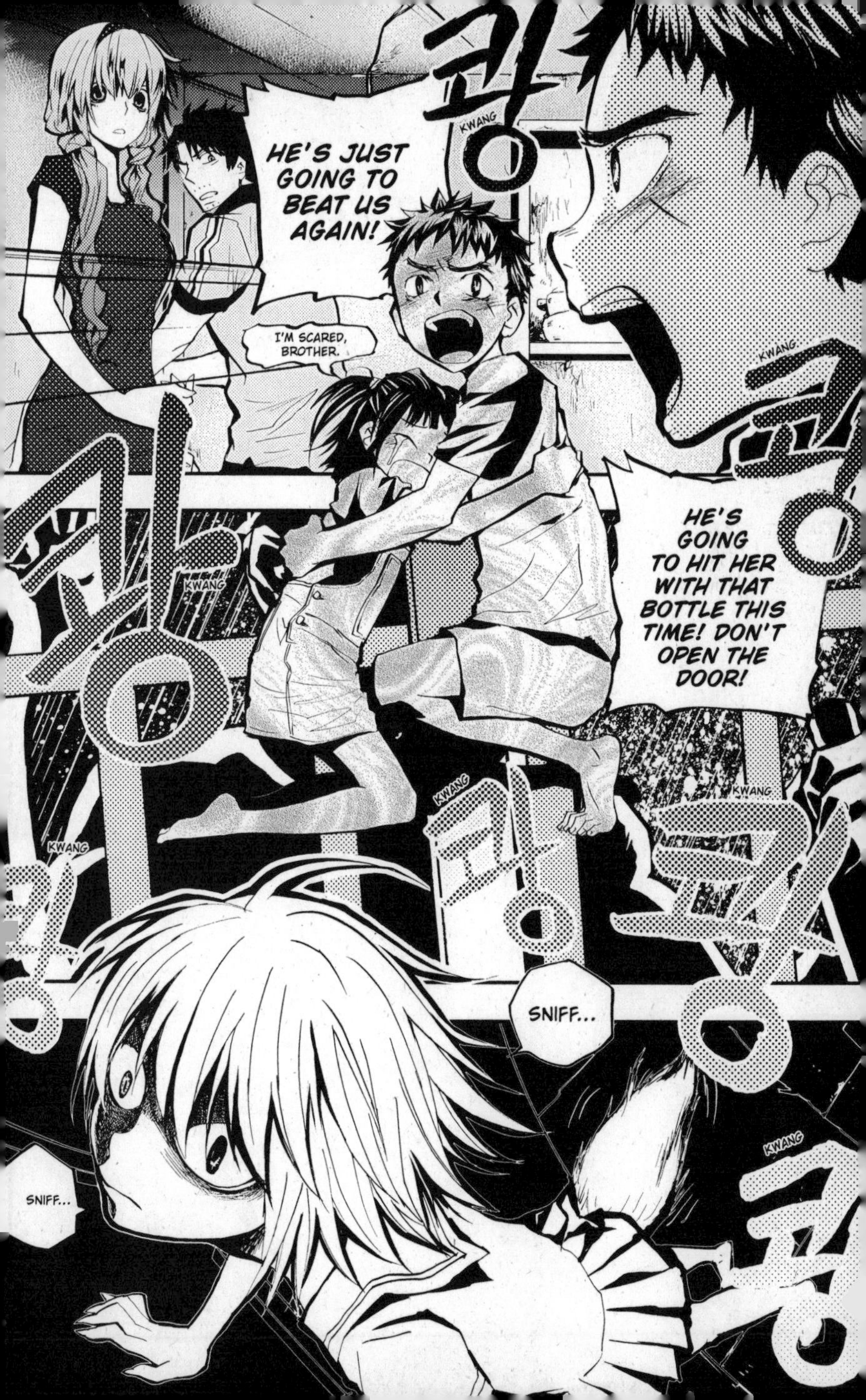
KWANG
HE'S JUST GOING TO BEAT US AGAIN!
I'M SCARED, BROTHER.
KWANG
KWANG
HE'S GOING TO HIT HER WITH THAT BOTTLE THIS TIME! DON'T OPEN THE DOOR!
KWANG
KWANG
KWANG
SNIFF...
SNIFF...
KWANG

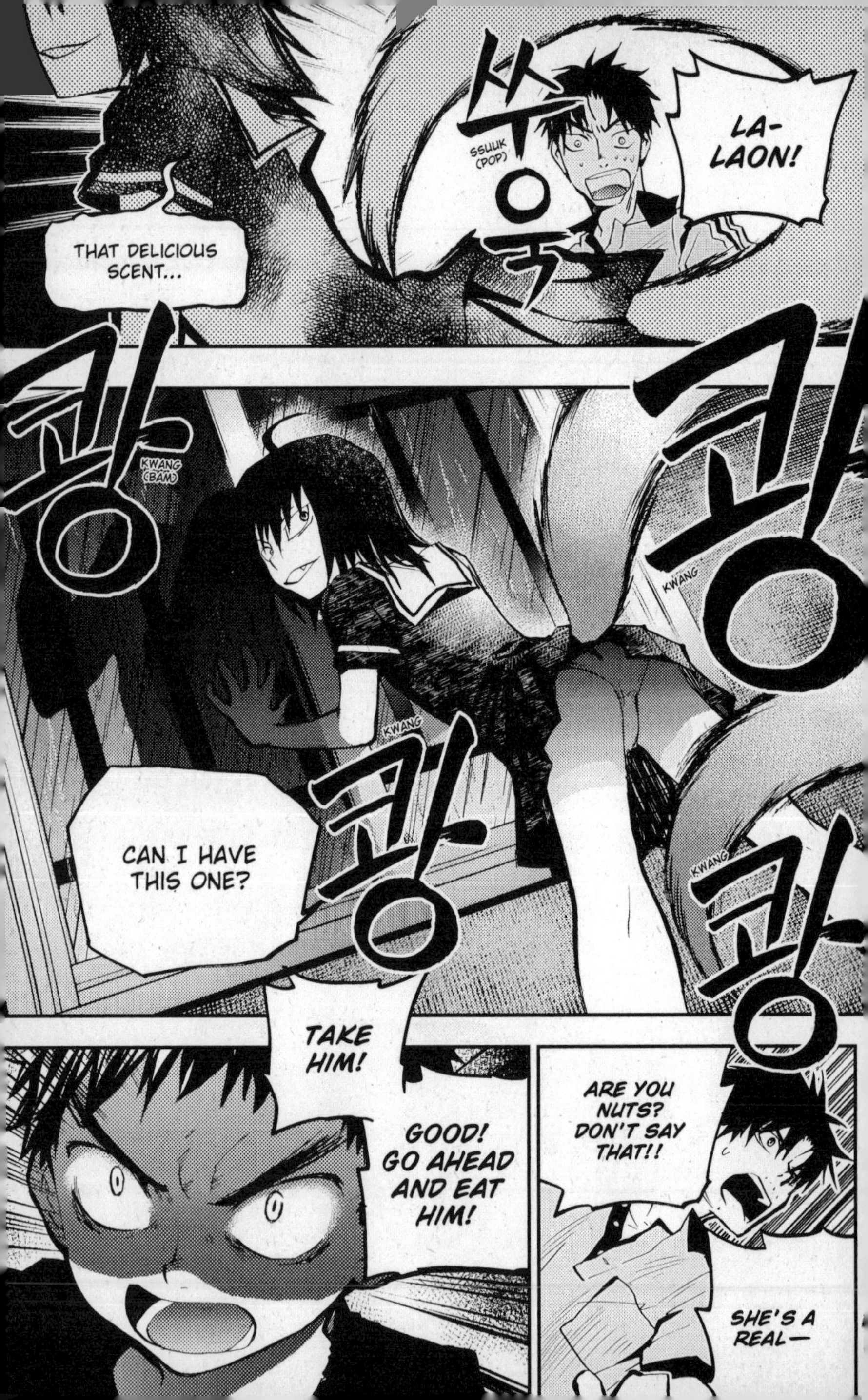

THAT DELICIOUS SCENT...
쑤욱
SSUUK (POP)
LA-LAON!
쾅
KWANG (BAM)
CAN I HAVE THIS ONE?
쾅
KWANG
쾅
KWANG
쾅
KWANG
TAKE HIM!
GOOD! GO AHEAD AND EAT HIM!
ARE YOU NUTS? DON'T SAY THAT!!
SHE'S A REAL—

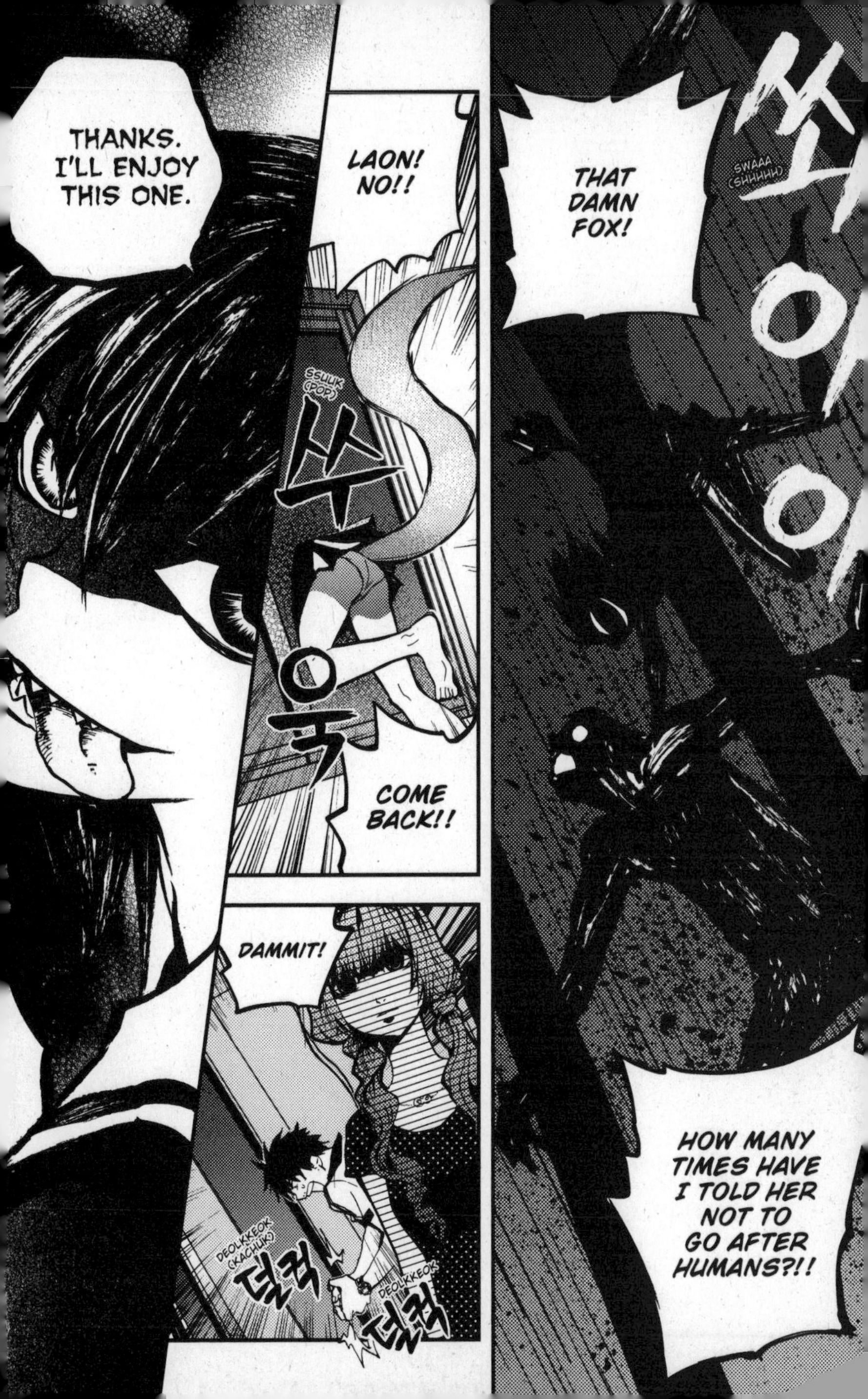
THANKS. I'LL ENJOY THIS ONE.
LAON! NO!!
SSUUK (POP)
COME BACK!!
DAMMIT!
DEOLKKEOK (KACHUK)
덜컥
DEOLKKEOK
덜컥
THAT DAMN FOX!
SWAAA (SHHHHH)
HOW MANY TIMES HAVE I TOLD HER NOT TO GO AFTER HUMANS?!!

FUCK! WHY WON'T THIS THING OPEN?!
철컥
CHEOLKEOK
철컥
CHEOLKEOK (KACHUK)
HEY, GET OVER HERE AND OPEN THIS! HURRY!!
IT WON'T OPEN. DAD LOCKED IT BEFORE HE WENT OUT.
CHEOLKEOK
CHEOLKEOK
WHAT THE HELL? DIDN'T YOU OPEN IT BEFORE?!
SWAAA (SHHHH)
HURRY! OPEN IT!!
SWAAA
OR ELSE SHE'S REALLY GOING TO END UP EATING YOUR DAD!

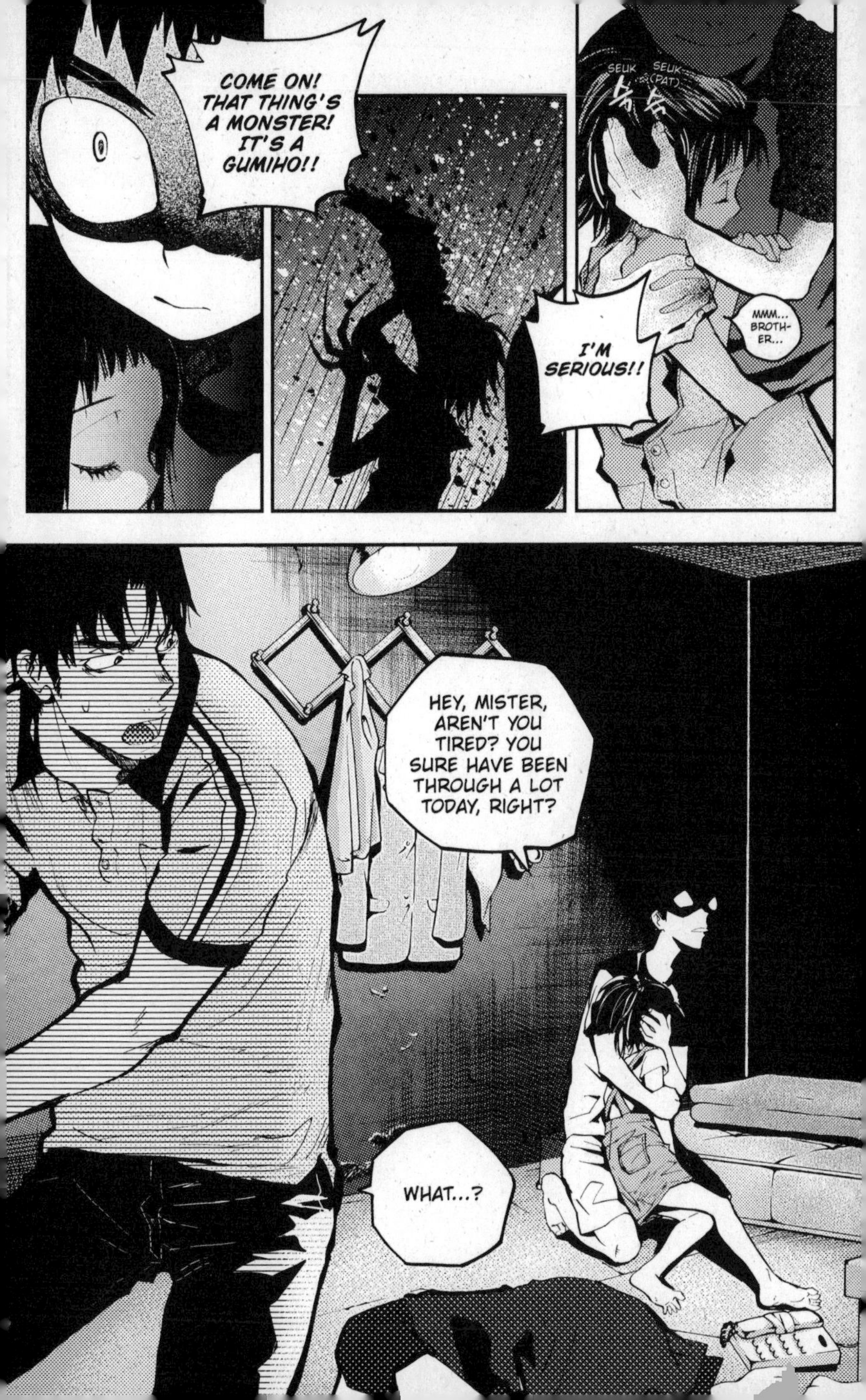
COME ON! THAT THING'S A MONSTER! IT'S A GUMIHO!!
SEUK SEUK (PAT)
I'M SERIOUS!!
MMM... BROTH-ER...
HEY, MISTER, AREN'T YOU TIRED? YOU SURE HAVE BEEN THROUGH A LOT TODAY, RIGHT?
WHAT...?

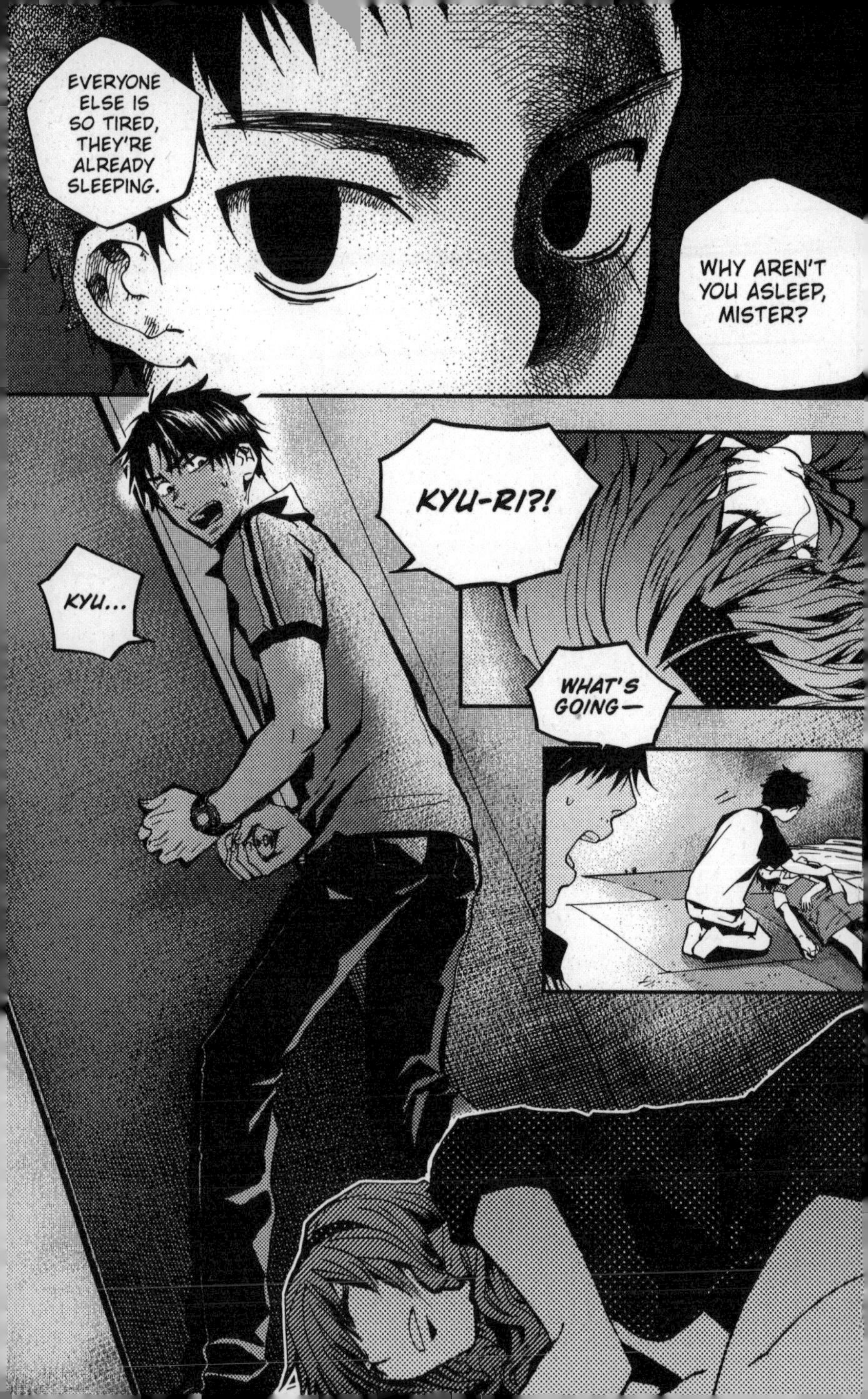
EVERYONE ELSE IS SO TIRED, THEY'RE ALREADY SLEEPING.
WHY AREN'T YOU ASLEEP, MISTER?
KYU...
KYU-RI?!
WHAT'S GOING—

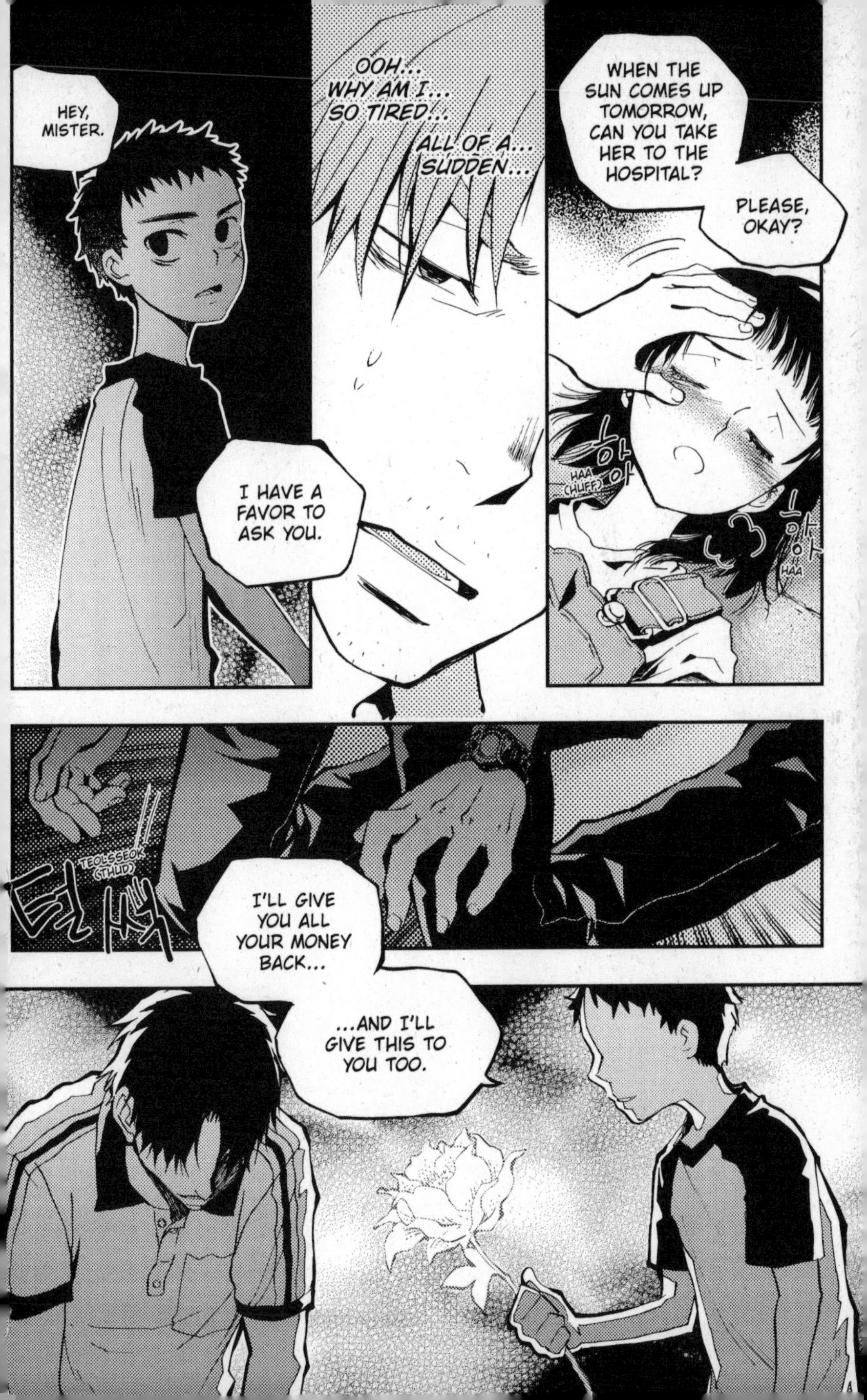
HEY, MISTER.
I HAVE A FAVOR TO ASK YOU.
OOH... WHY AM I... SO TIRED...
ALL OF A... SUDDEN...
WHEN THE SUN COMES UP TOMORROW, CAN YOU TAKE HER TO THE HOSPITAL?
PLEASE, OKAY?
하아
HAA (HUFF)
하아
HAA
털썩
TEOLSSEOK (THUD)
I'LL GIVE YOU ALL YOUR MONEY BACK...
...AND I'LL GIVE THIS TO YOU TOO.

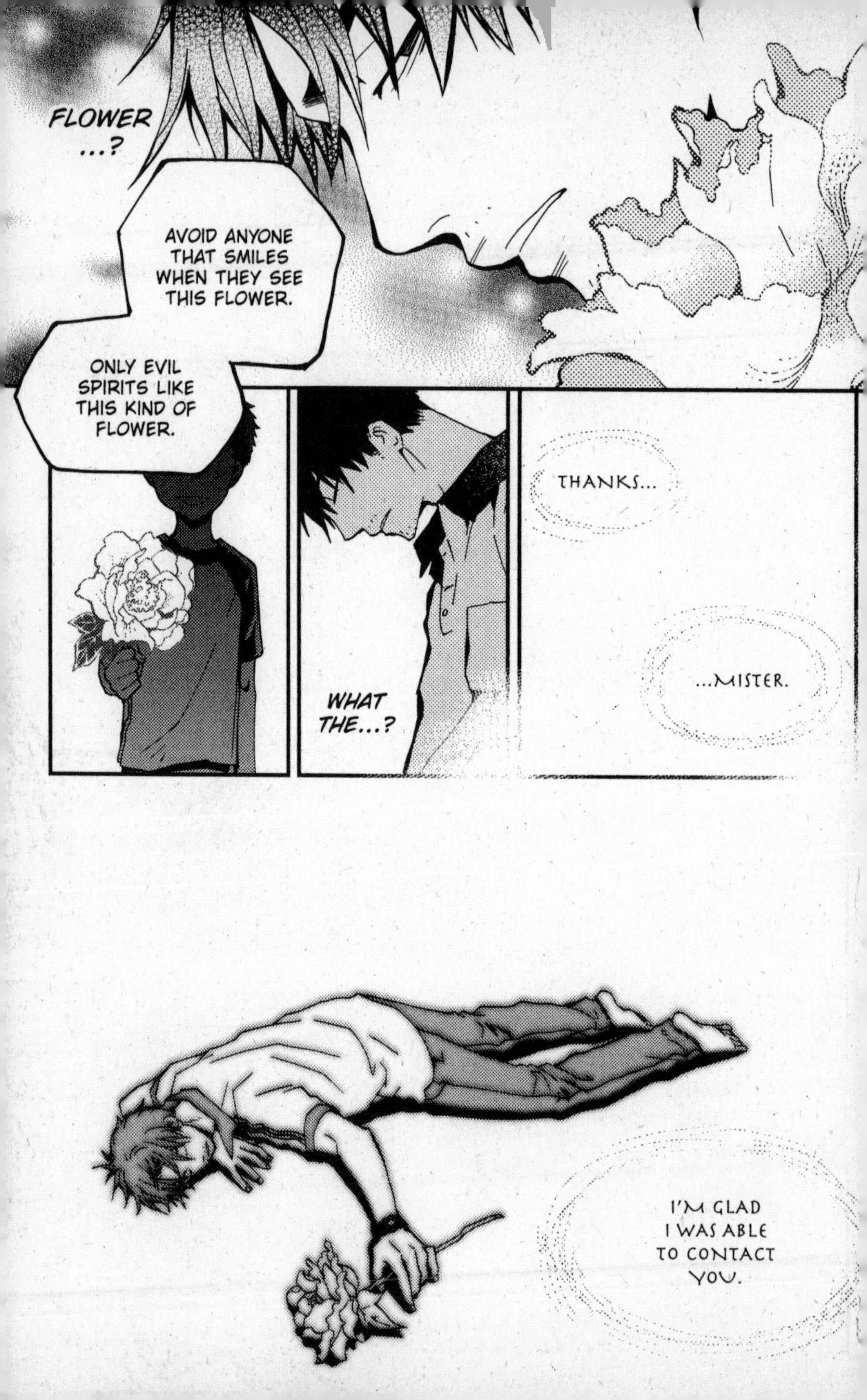
FLOWER ...?
AVOID ANYONE THAT SMILES WHEN THEY SEE THIS FLOWER.
ONLY EVIL SPIRITS LIKE THIS KIND OF FLOWER.
WHAT THE...?
THANKS...
...MISTER.
I'M GLAD I WAS ABLE TO CONTACT YOU.

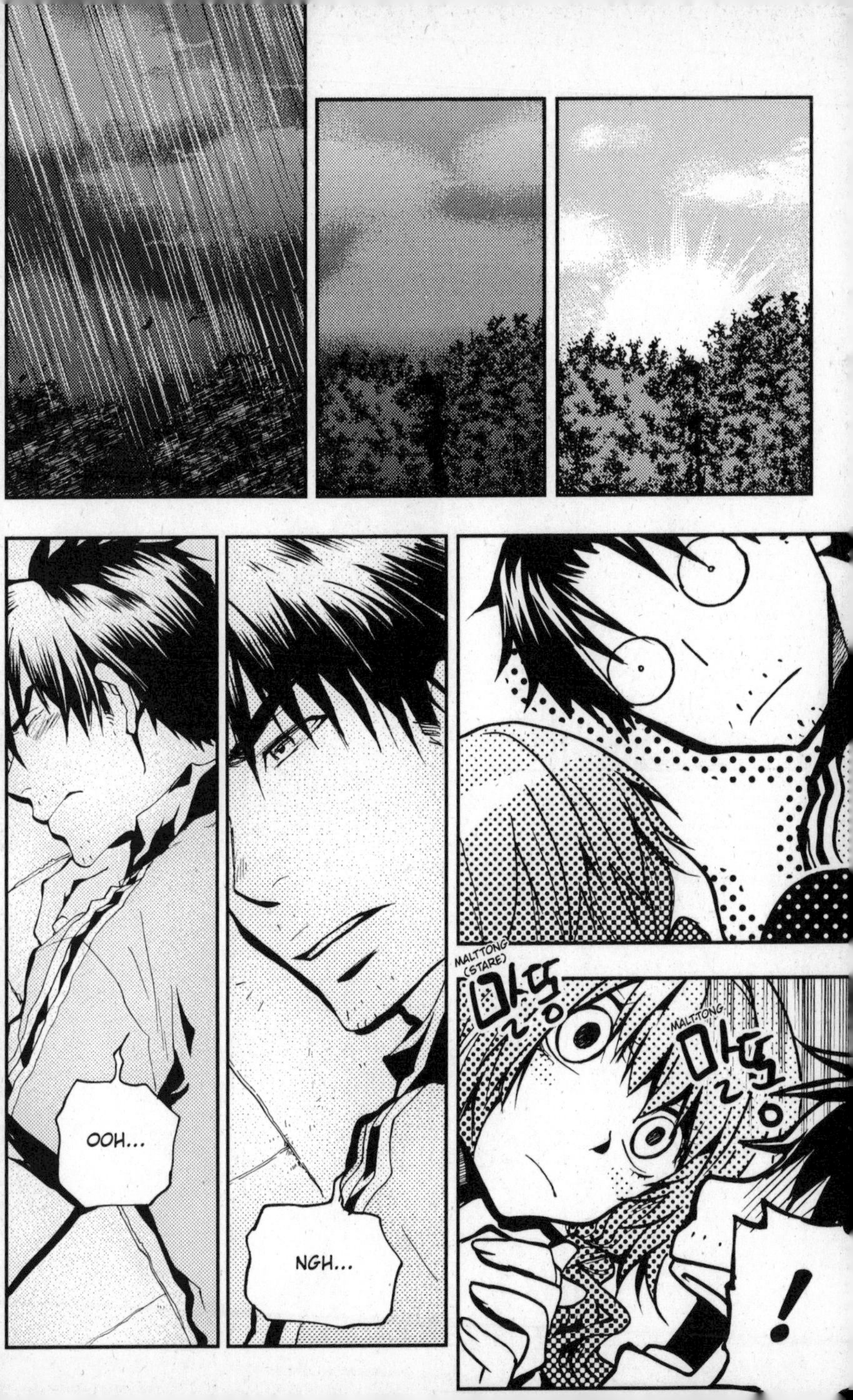
OOH...
NGH...
MALTTONG (STARE)
말똥
MALTTONG
말똥
!

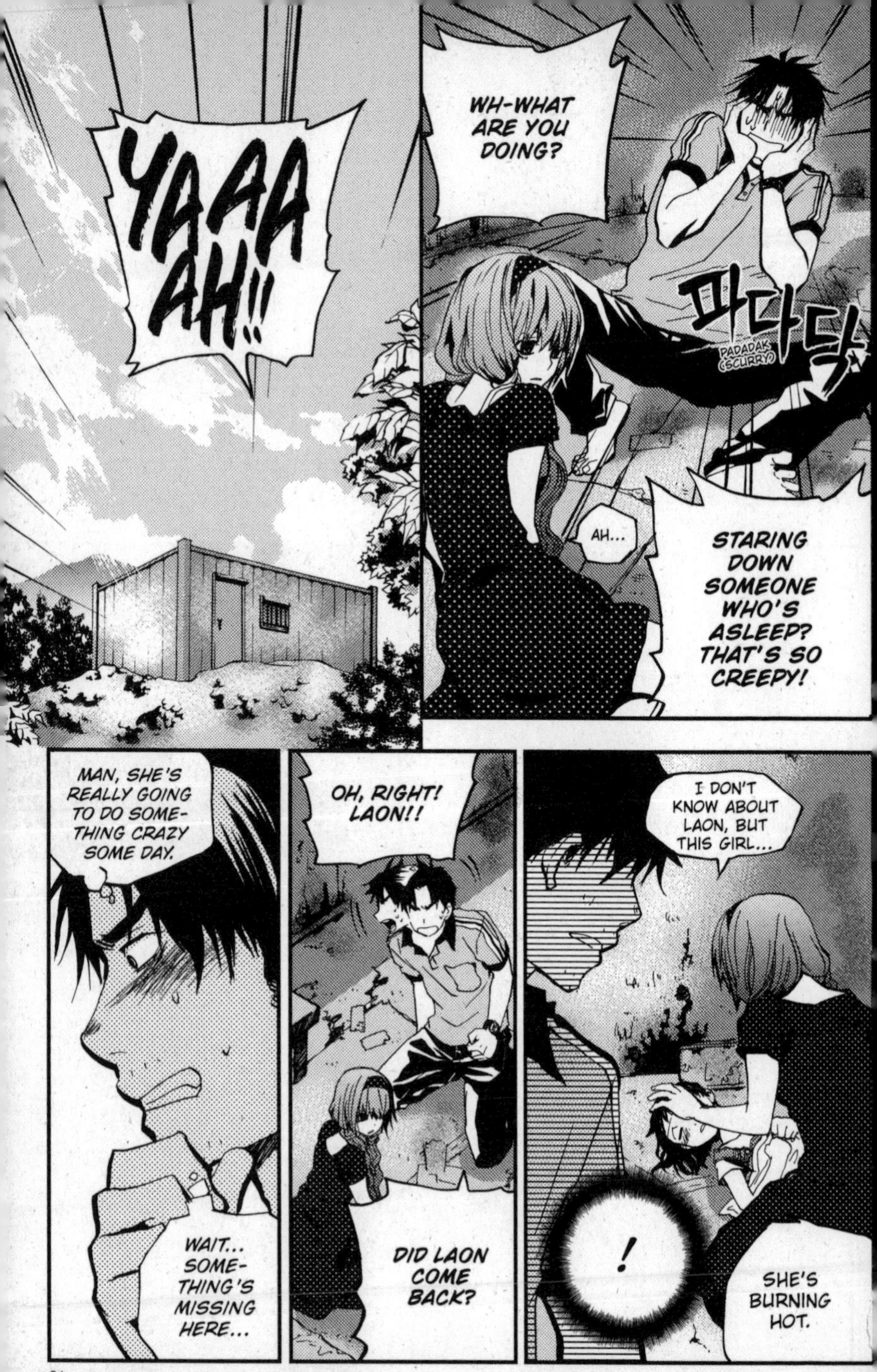
YAAAAH!!
WH-WHAT ARE YOU DOING?
파다닥
PADADAK (SCURRY)
AH...
STARING DOWN SOMEONE WHO'S ASLEEP? THAT'S SO CREEPY!
MAN, SHE'S REALLY GOING TO DO SOME-THING CRAZY SOME DAY.
WAIT... SOME-THING'S MISSING HERE...
OH, RIGHT! LAON!!
DID LAON COME BACK?
I DON'T KNOW ABOUT LAON, BUT THIS GIRL...
!
SHE'S BURNING HOT.

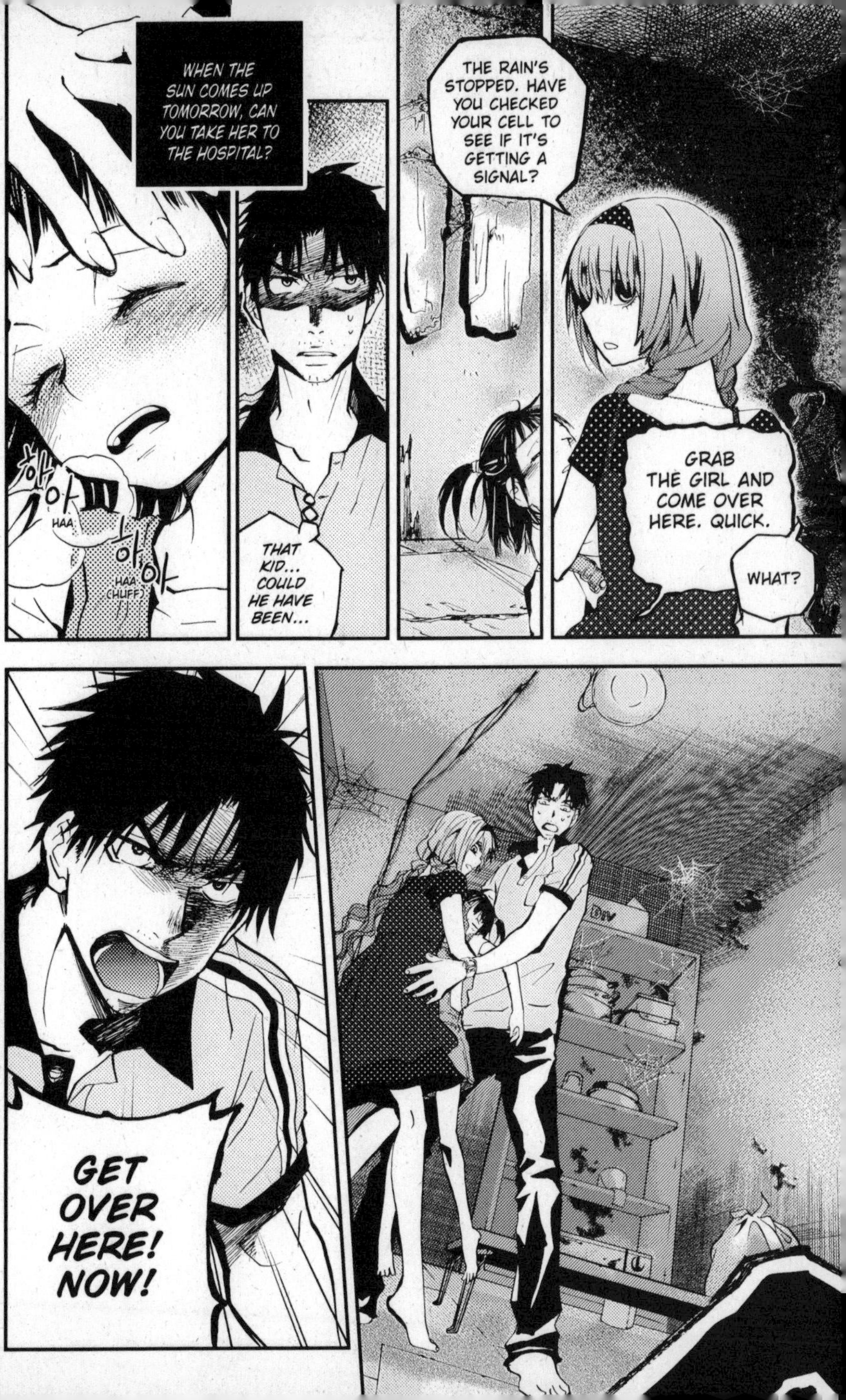
WHEN THE SUN COMES UP TOMORROW, CAN YOU TAKE HER TO THE HOSPITAL?
하아
HAA
하아
HAA (HUFF)
THAT KID... COULD HE HAVE BEEN...
THE RAIN'S STOPPED. HAVE YOU CHECKED YOUR CELL TO SEE IF IT'S GETTING A SIGNAL?
GRAB THE GIRL AND COME OVER HERE. QUICK.
WHAT?
GET OVER HERE! NOW!

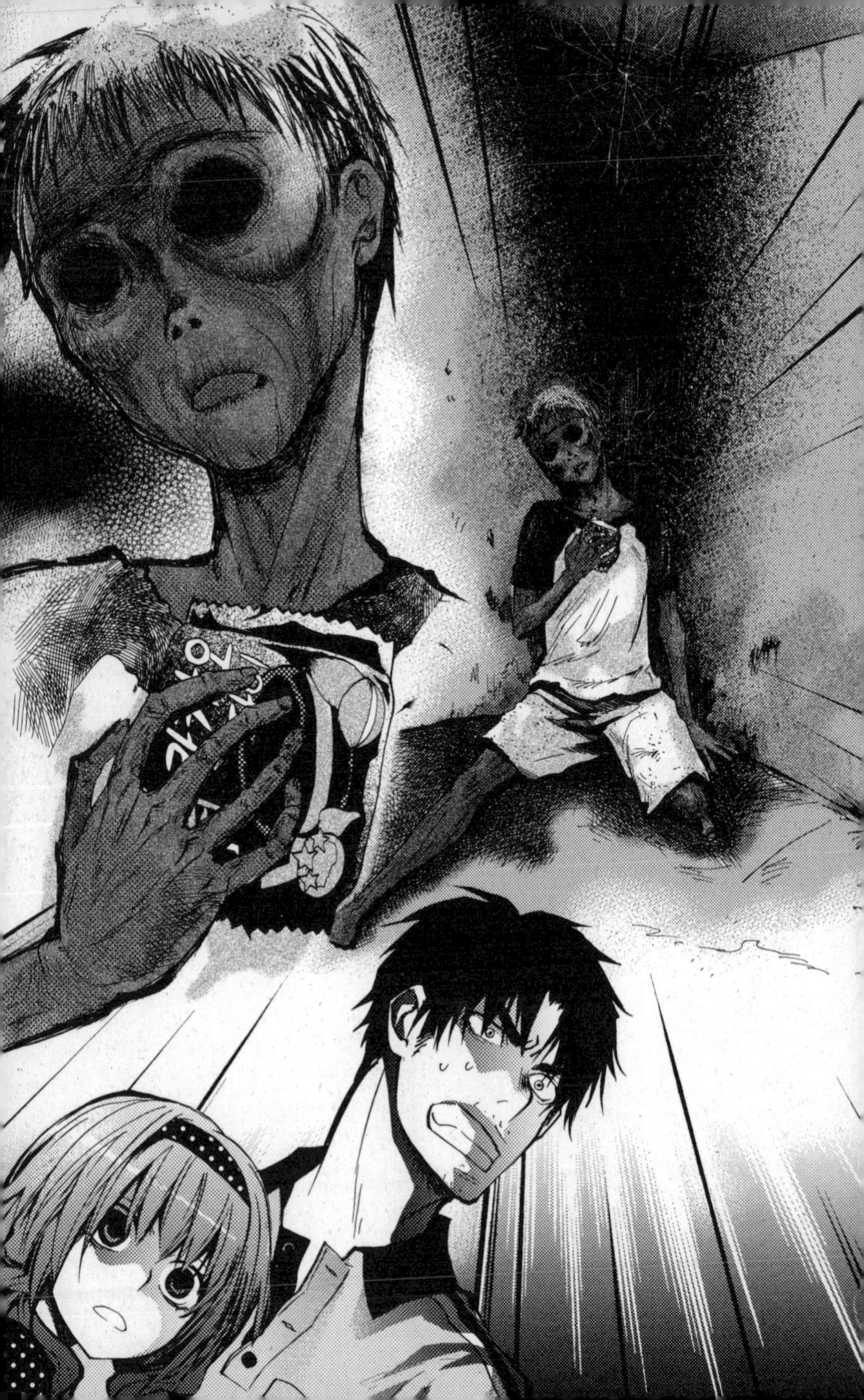

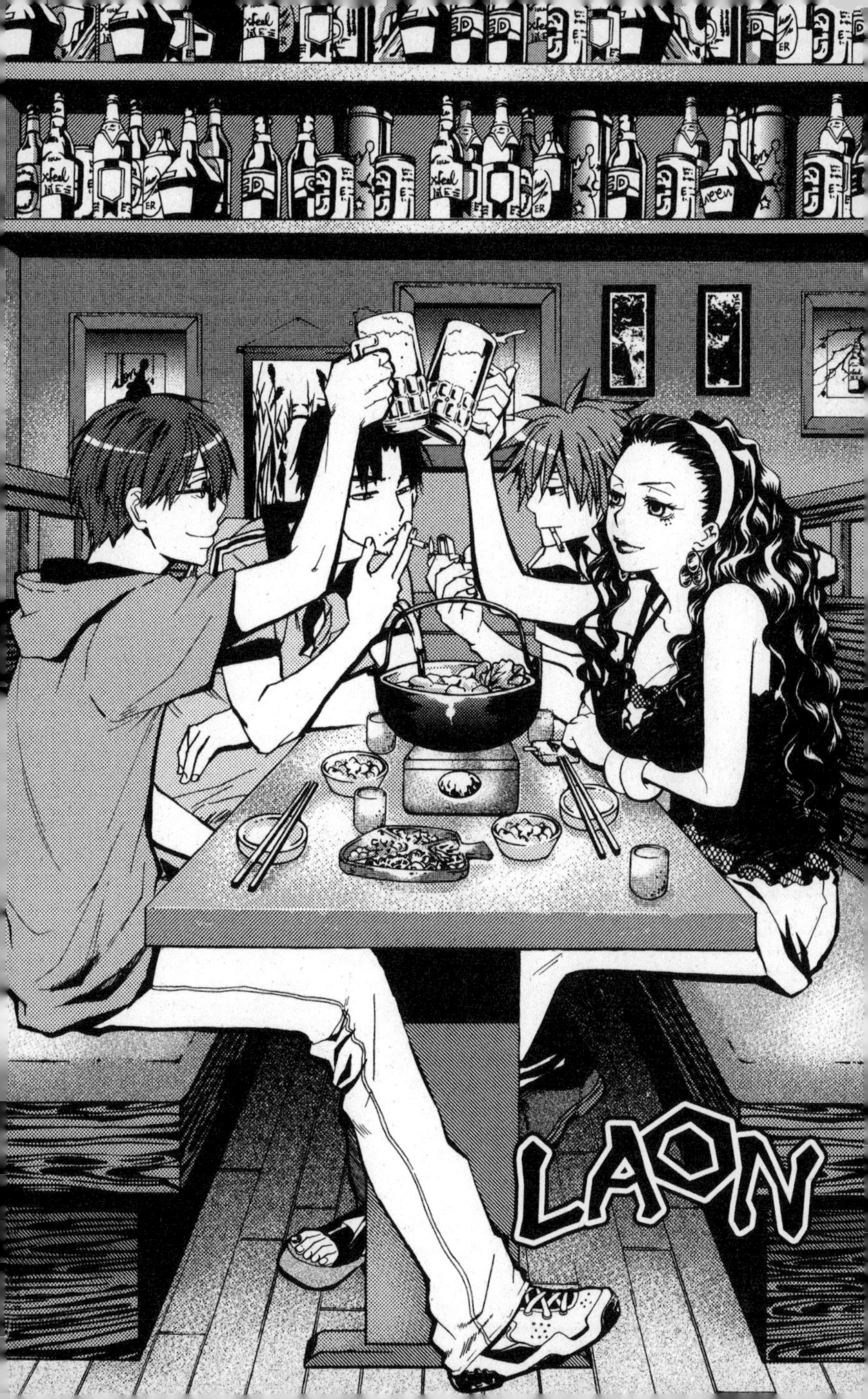
LAON

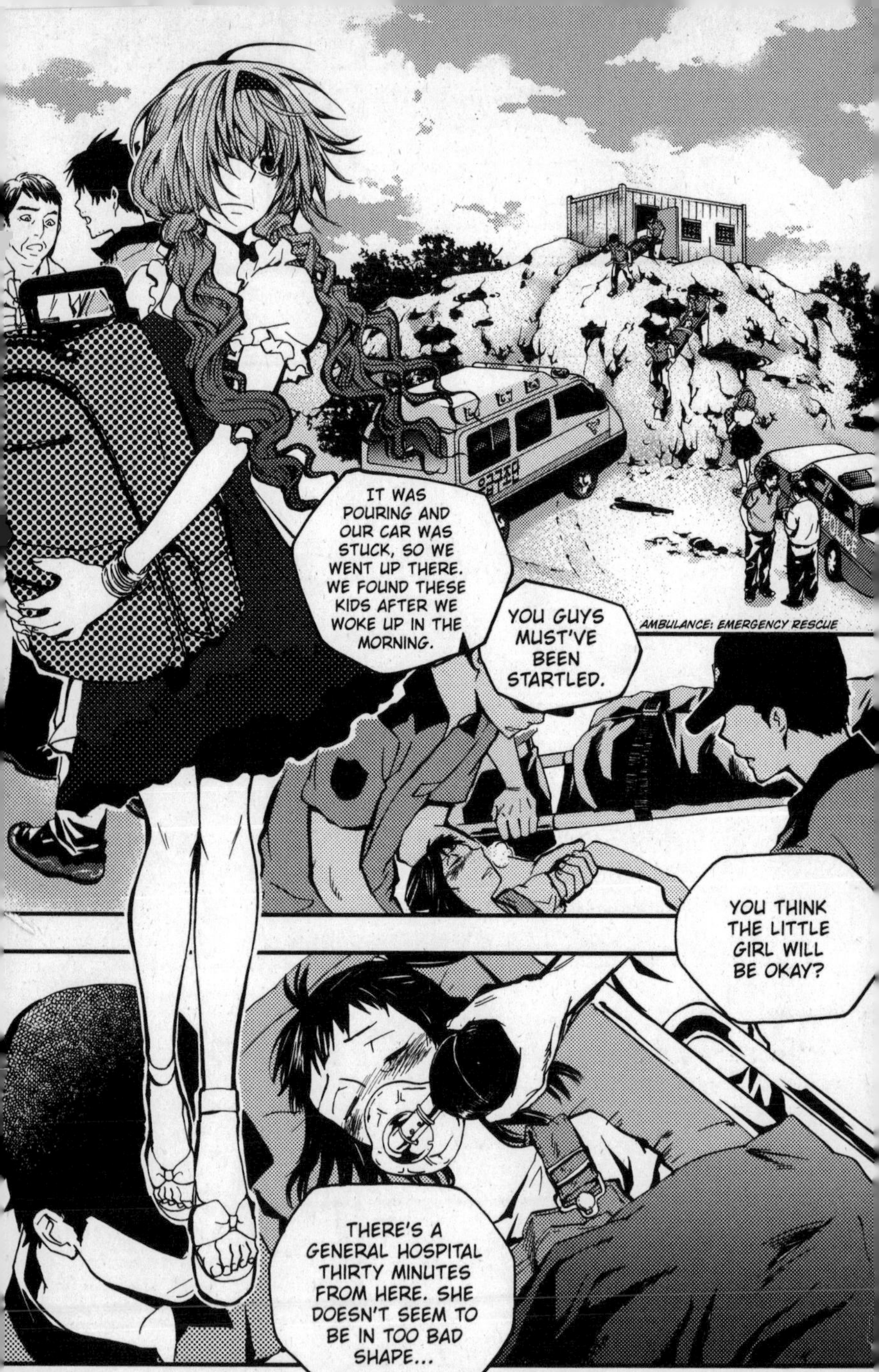
AMBULANCE: EMERGENCY RESCUE
IT WAS POURING AND OUR CAR WAS STUCK, SO WE WENT UP THERE. WE FOUND THESE KIDS AFTER WE WOKE UP IN THE MORNING.
YOU GUYS MUST'VE BEEN STARTLED.
YOU THINK THE LITTLE GIRL WILL BE OKAY?
THERE'S A GENERAL HOSPITAL THIRTY MINUTES FROM HERE. SHE DOESN'T SEEM TO BE IN TOO BAD SHAPE...

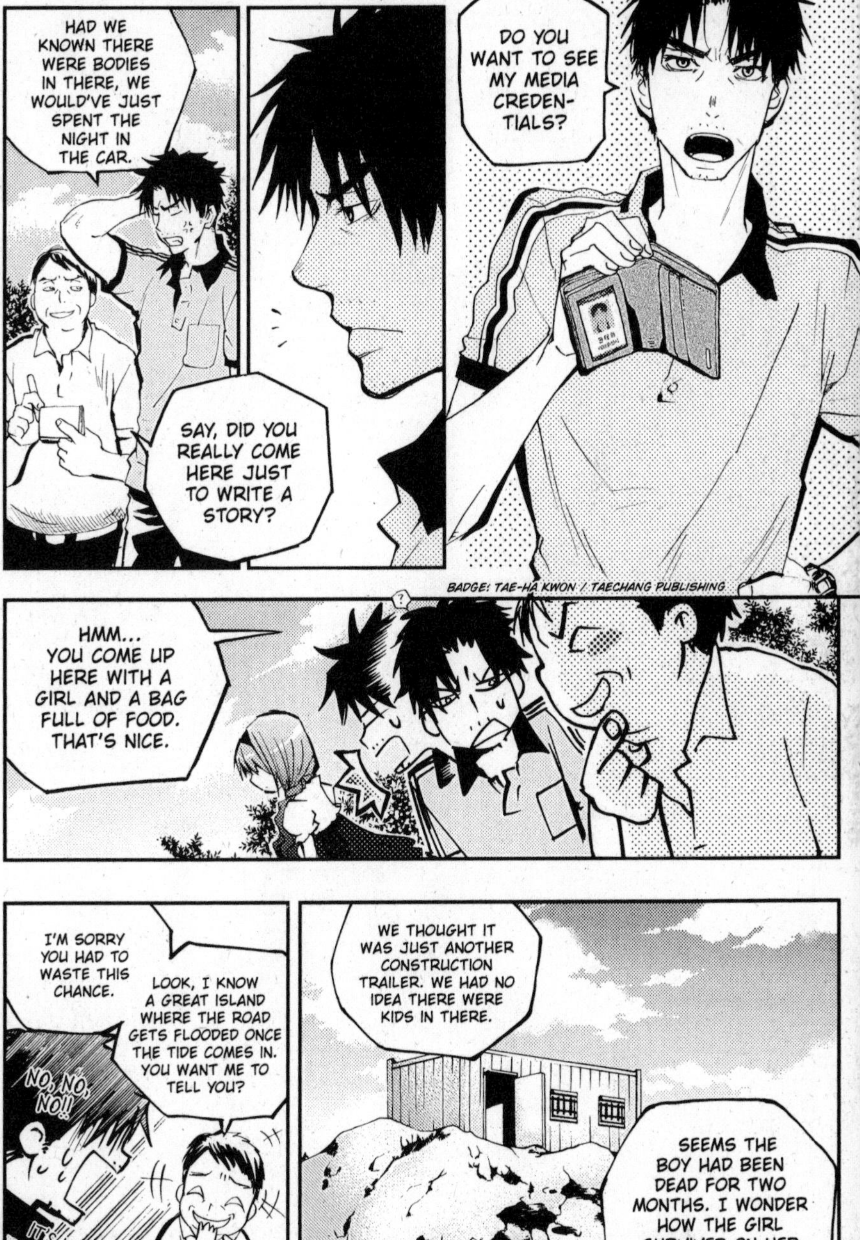
HAD WE KNOWN THERE WERE BODIES IN THERE, WE WOULD'VE JUST SPENT THE NIGHT IN THE CAR.
SAY, DID YOU REALLY COME HERE JUST TO WRITE A STORY?
DO YOU WANT TO SEE MY MEDIA CREDEN-TIALS?
BADGE: TAE-HA KWON / TAECHANG PUBLISHING
HMM... YOU COME UP HERE WITH A GIRL AND A BAG FULL OF FOOD. THAT'S NICE.
I'M SORRY YOU HAD TO WASTE THIS CHANCE.
LOOK, I KNOW A GREAT ISLAND WHERE THE ROAD GETS FLOODED ONCE THE TIDE COMES IN. YOU WANT ME TO TELL YOU?
NO, NO, NO!!
IT'S NOT WHAT YOU THINK!
WE THOUGHT IT WAS JUST ANOTHER CONSTRUCTION TRAILER. WE HAD NO IDEA THERE WERE KIDS IN THERE.
SEEMS THE BOY HAD BEEN DEAD FOR TWO MONTHS. I WONDER HOW THE GIRL SURVIVED ON HER OWN ALL THAT TIME...GEEZ...

TWO MONTHS...
FORTUNATELY, THE BODY JUST DRIED UP INSTEAD OF ROTTING AWAY. CAN YOU IMAGINE WHAT THAT TRAILER WOULD'VE BEEN LIKE IF THE BODY HAD DECOMPOSED?
CAUSE OF DEATH MIGHT BE RELATED TO THE DEPRESSION WE FOUND ON THE BACK OF HIS HEAD. HE'S MISSING A LEG TOO, SO IF WE DO A SEARCH ON THE DISABLED PERSONS LIST, WE SHOULD BE ABLE TO I.D. HIM.
HM? HIS LEGS SEEMED FINE TO ME...
HE'S GOING TO HIT HER WITH THAT BOTTLE THIS TIME!
ANY-WAY...

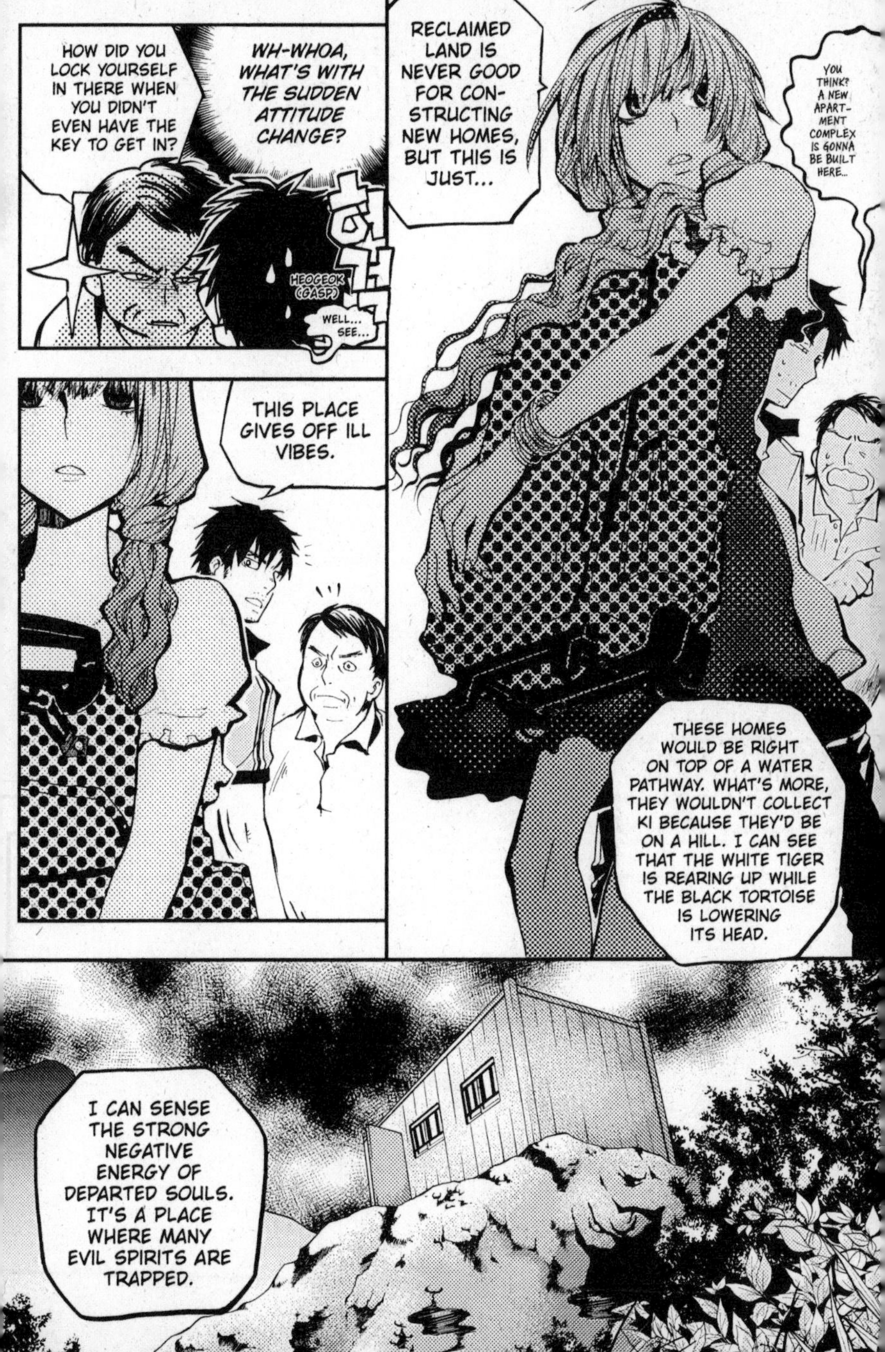
HOW DID YOU LOCK YOURSELF IN THERE WHEN YOU DIDN'T EVEN HAVE THE KEY TO GET IN?
WH-WHOA, WHAT'S WITH THE SUDDEN ATTITUDE CHANGE?
HEOGEOK (GASP)
WELL... SEE...
THIS PLACE GIVES OFF ILL VIBES.
RECLAIMED LAND IS NEVER GOOD FOR CON-STRUCTING NEW HOMES, BUT THIS IS JUST...
YOU THINK? A NEW APART-MENT COMPLEX IS GONNA BE BUILT HERE...
THESE HOMES WOULD BE RIGHT ON TOP OF A WATER PATHWAY. WHAT'S MORE, THEY WOULDN'T COLLECT KI BECAUSE THEY'D BE ON A HILL. I CAN SEE THAT THE WHITE TIGER IS REARING UP WHILE THE BLACK TORTOISE IS LOWERING ITS HEAD.
I CAN SENSE THE STRONG NEGATIVE ENERGY OF DEPARTED SOULS. IT'S A PLACE WHERE MANY EVIL SPIRITS ARE TRAPPED.

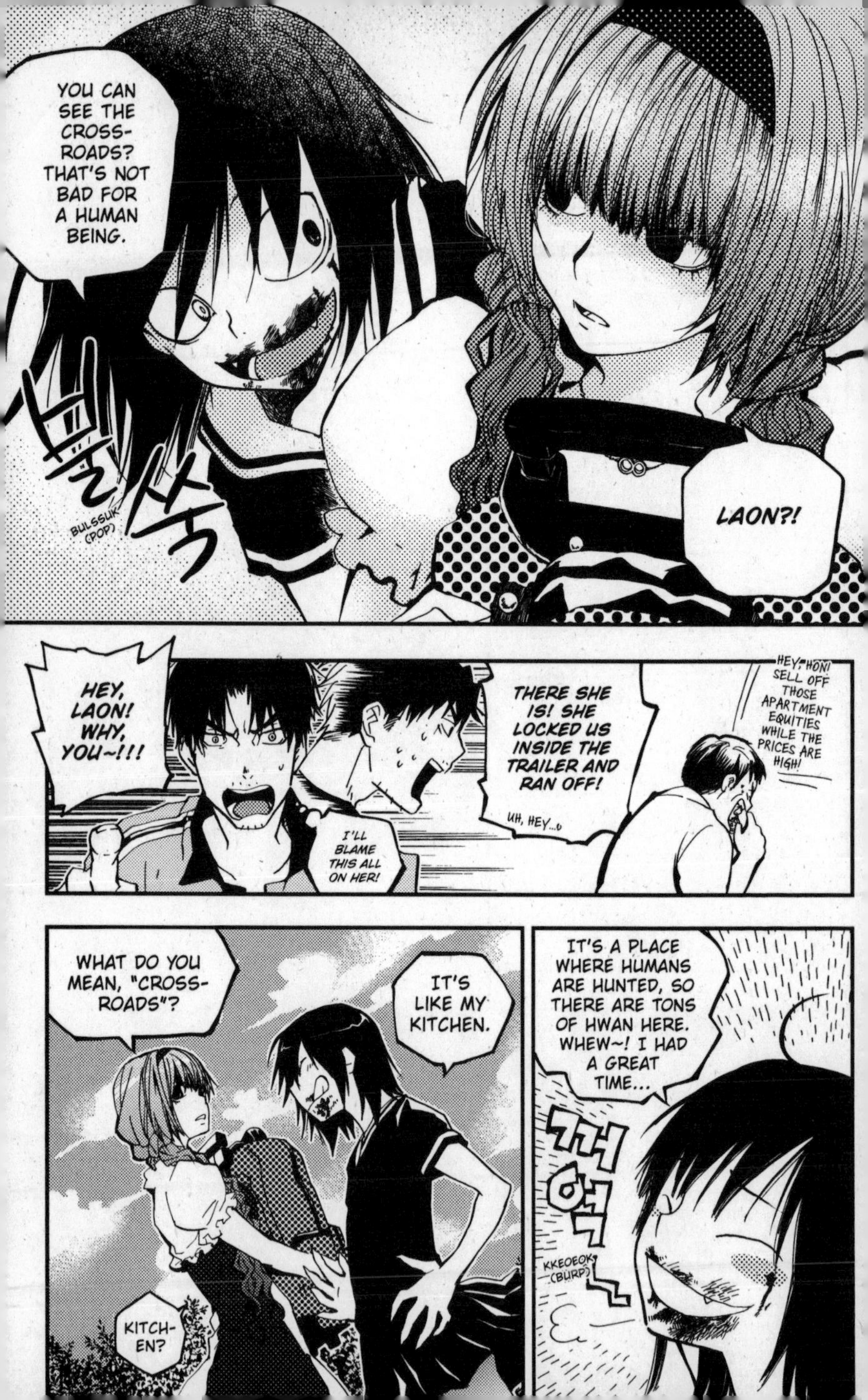
YOU CAN SEE THE CROSS-ROADS? THAT'S NOT BAD FOR A HUMAN BEING.
BULSSUK (POP)
LAON?!
HEY, LAON! WHY, YOU~!!!
I'LL BLAME THIS ALL ON HER!
THERE SHE IS! SHE LOCKED US INSIDE THE TRAILER AND RAN OFF!
UH, HEY...
HEY, HON! SELL OFF THOSE APARTMENT EQUITIES WHILE THE PRICES ARE HIGH!
WHAT DO YOU MEAN, "CROSS-ROADS"?
IT'S LIKE MY KITCHEN.
KITCH-EN?
IT'S A PLACE WHERE HUMANS ARE HUNTED, SO THERE ARE TONS OF HWAN HERE. WHEW~! I HAD A GREAT TIME...
KKEOEOK (BURP)

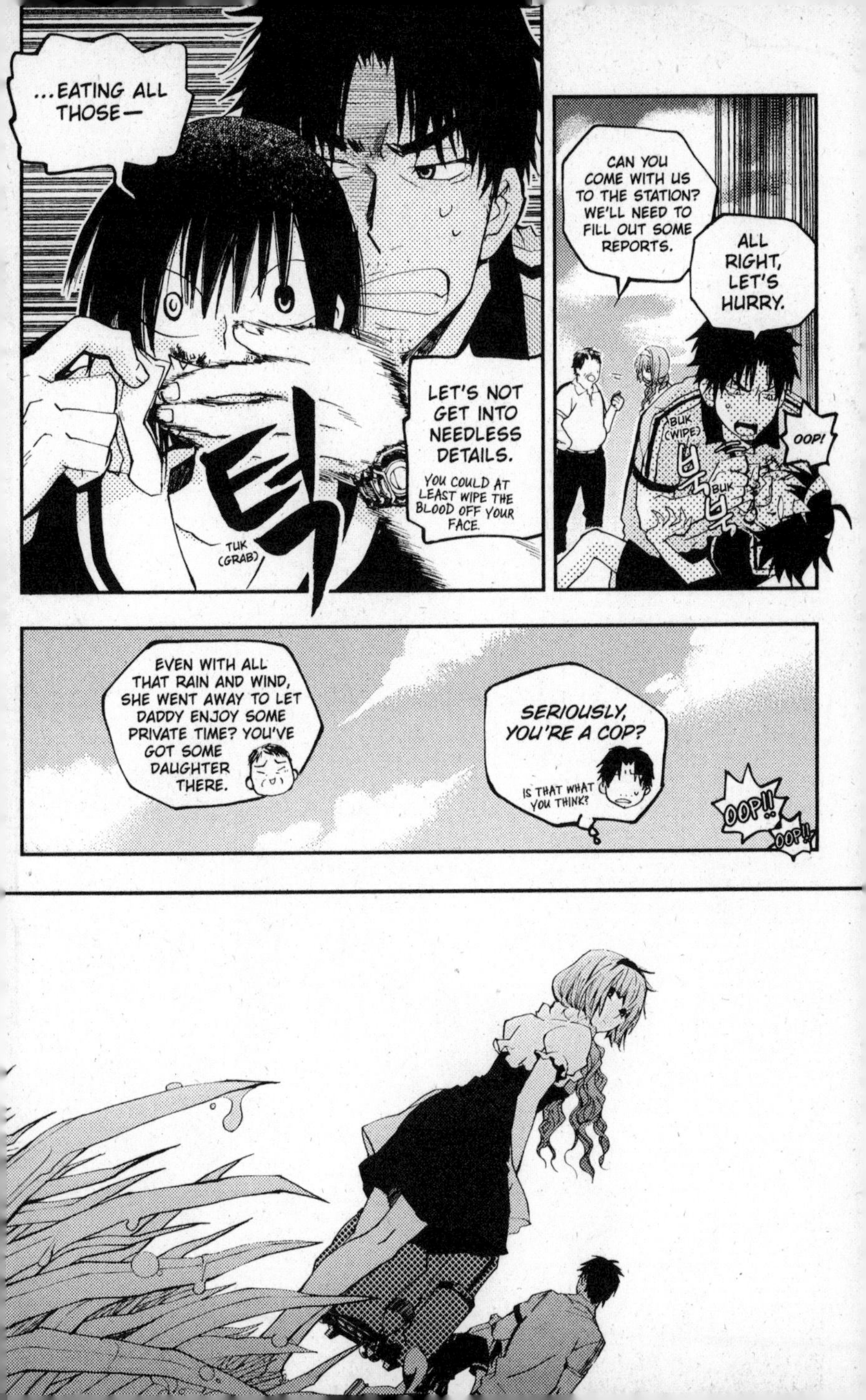
...EATING ALL THOSE—
LET'S NOT GET INTO NEEDLESS DETAILS.
YOU COULD AT LEAST WIPE THE BLOOD OFF YOUR FACE.
TUK (GRAB)
CAN YOU COME WITH US TO THE STATION? WE'LL NEED TO FILL OUT SOME REPORTS.
ALL RIGHT, LET'S HURRY.
BUK (WIPE)
BUK
OOP!
EVEN WITH ALL THAT RAIN AND WIND, SHE WENT AWAY TO LET DADDY ENJOY SOME PRIVATE TIME? YOU'VE GOT SOME DAUGHTER THERE.
SERIOUSLY, YOU'RE A COP?
IS THAT WHAT YOU THINK?
OOP!!
OOP!!

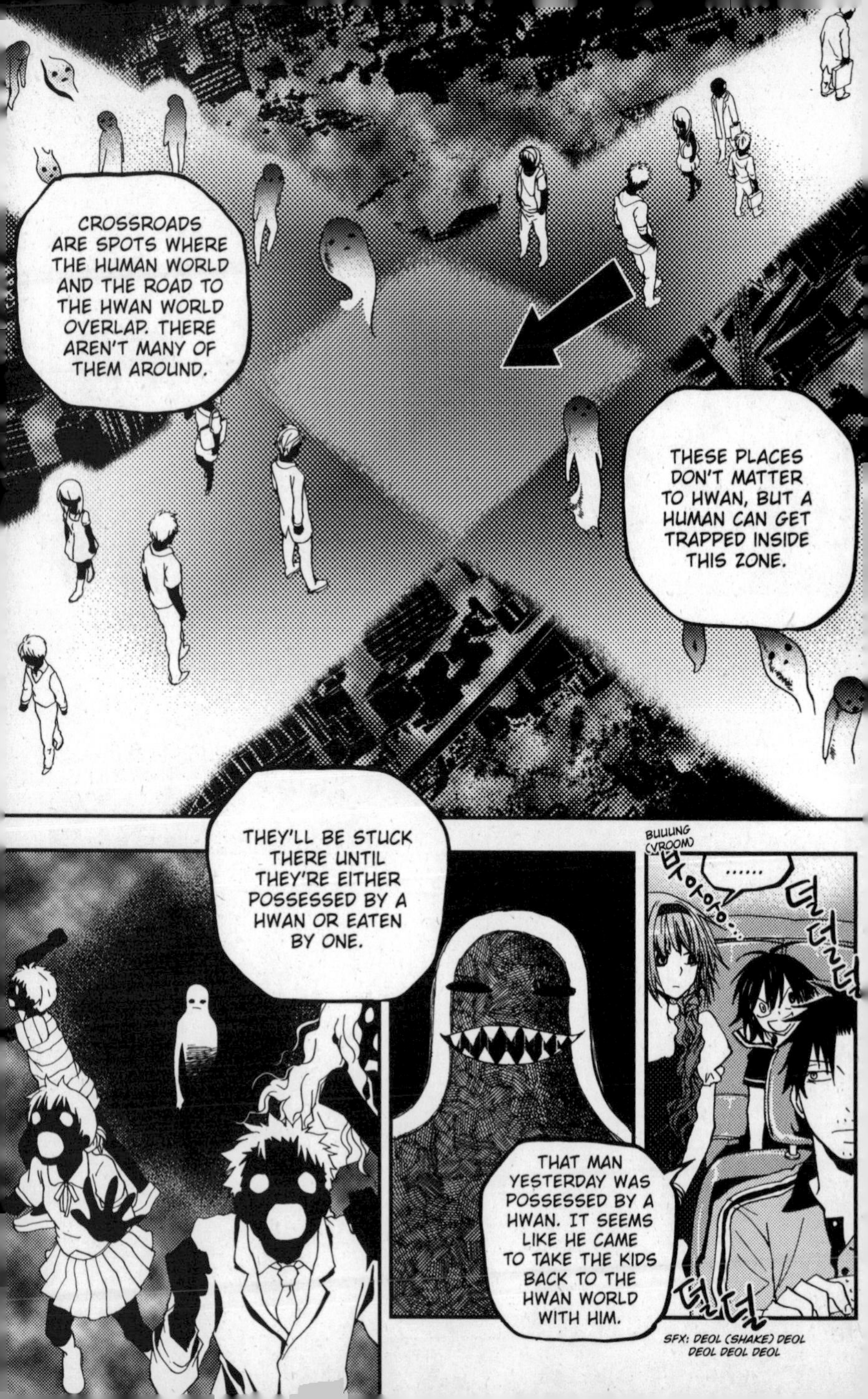
CROSSROADS ARE SPOTS WHERE THE HUMAN WORLD AND THE ROAD TO THE HWAN WORLD OVERLAP. THERE AREN'T MANY OF THEM AROUND.
THESE PLACES DON'T MATTER TO HWAN, BUT A HUMAN CAN GET TRAPPED INSIDE THIS ZONE.
THEY'LL BE STUCK THERE UNTIL THEY'RE EITHER POSSESSED BY A HWAN OR EATEN BY ONE.
THAT MAN YESTERDAY WAS POSSESSED BY A HWAN. IT SEEMS LIKE HE CAME TO TAKE THE KIDS BACK TO THE HWAN WORLD WITH HIM.
BUUUNG (VROOM)
......
SFX: DEOL (SHAKE) DEOL DEOL DEOL DEOL

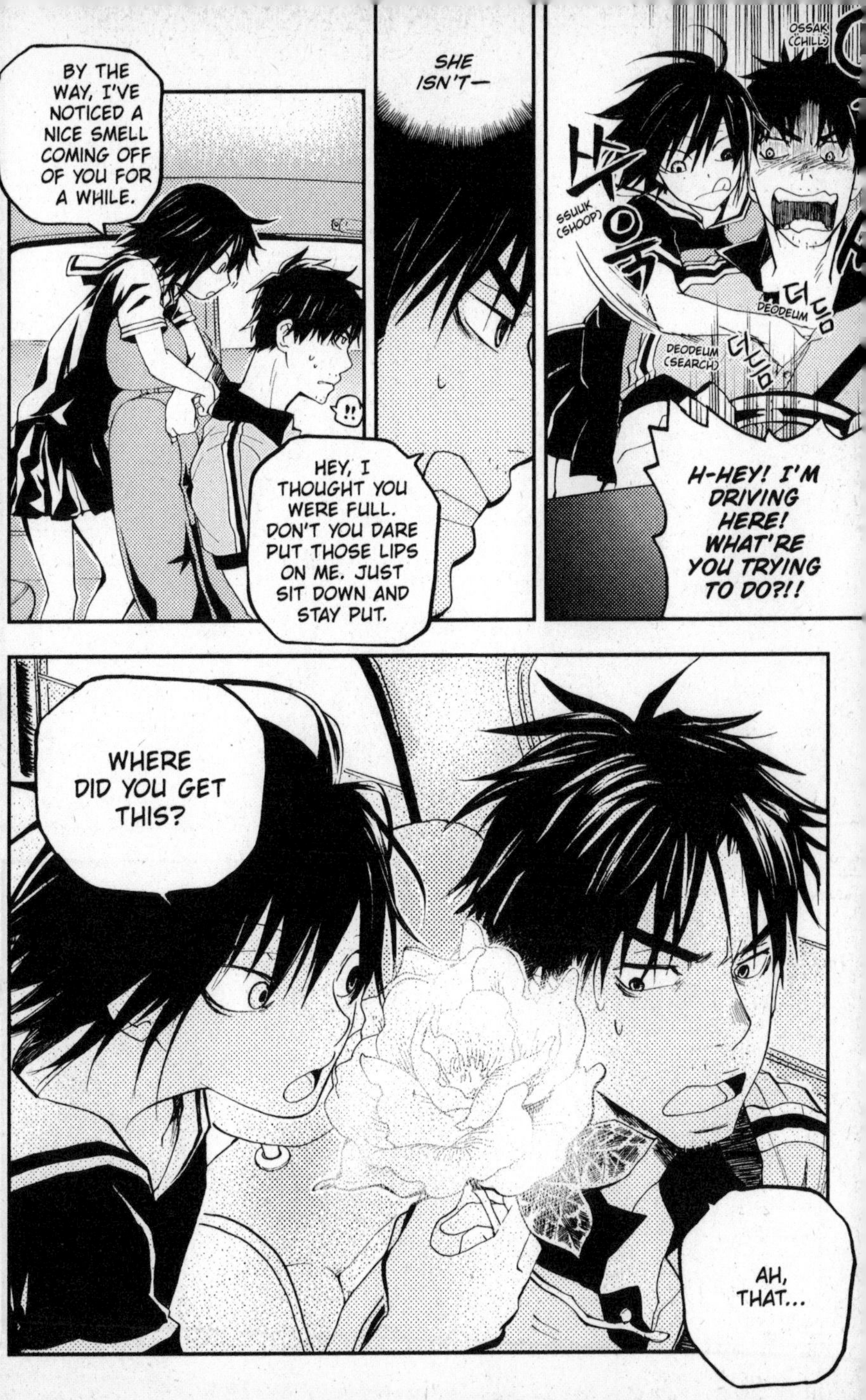
BY THE WAY, I'VE NOTICED A NICE SMELL COMING OFF OF YOU FOR A WHILE.
!!
SHE ISN'T—
HEY, I THOUGHT YOU WERE FULL. DON'T YOU DARE PUT THOSE LIPS ON ME. JUST SIT DOWN AND STAY PUT.
OSSAK (CHILL)
SSUUK (SHOOP)
DEODEUM
DEODEUM (SEARCH)
H-HEY! I'M DRIVING HERE! WHAT'RE YOU TRYING TO DO?!!
WHERE DID YOU GET THIS?
AH, THAT...

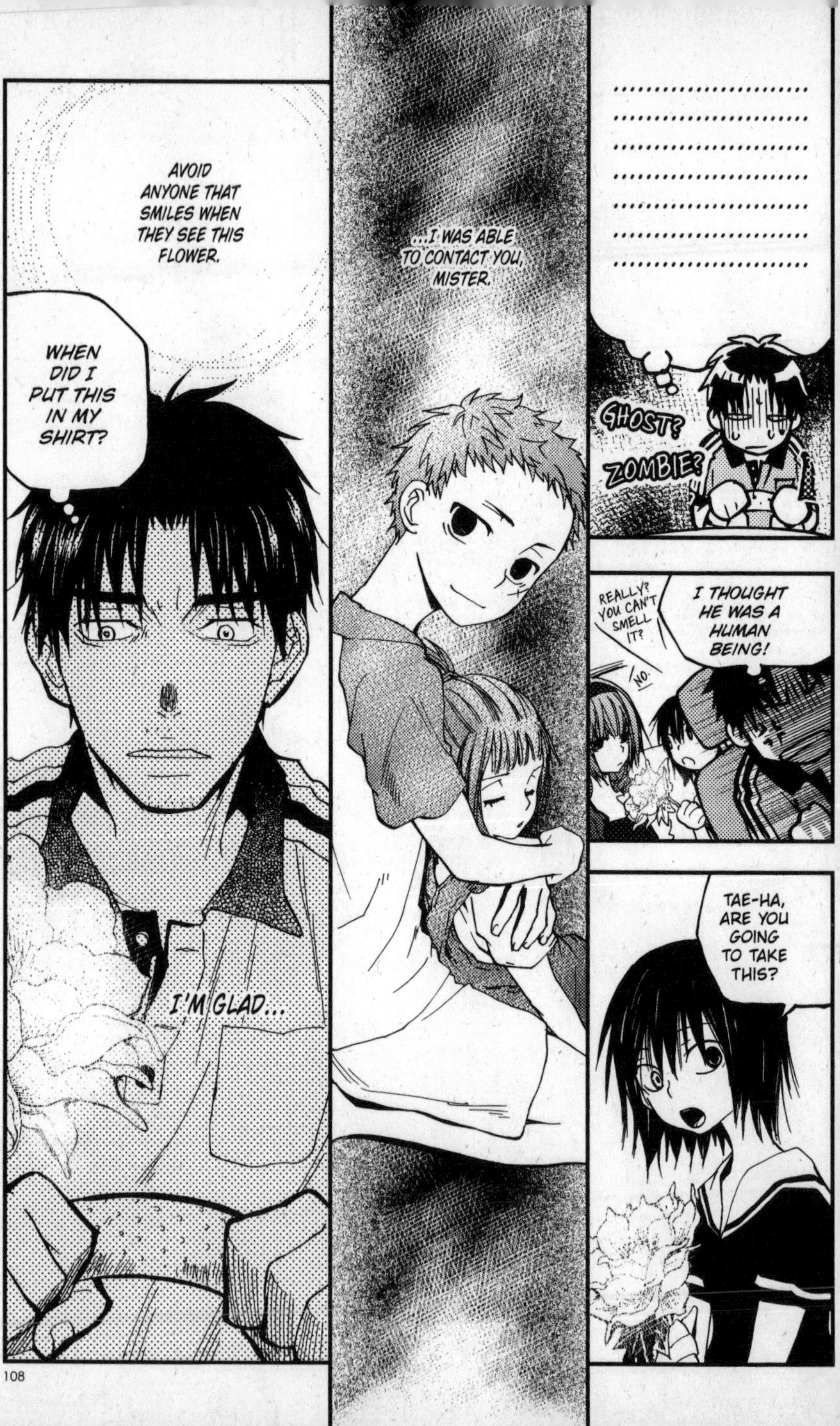

AVOID ANYONE THAT SMILES WHEN THEY SEE THIS FLOWER.
WHEN DID I PUT THIS IN MY SHIRT?
I'M GLAD...
...I WAS ABLE TO CONTACT YOU, MISTER.
....
GHOST?
ZOMBIE?
REALLY? YOU CAN'T SMELL IT?
I THOUGHT HE WAS A HUMAN BEING!
NO.
TAE-HA, ARE YOU GOING TO TAKE THIS?

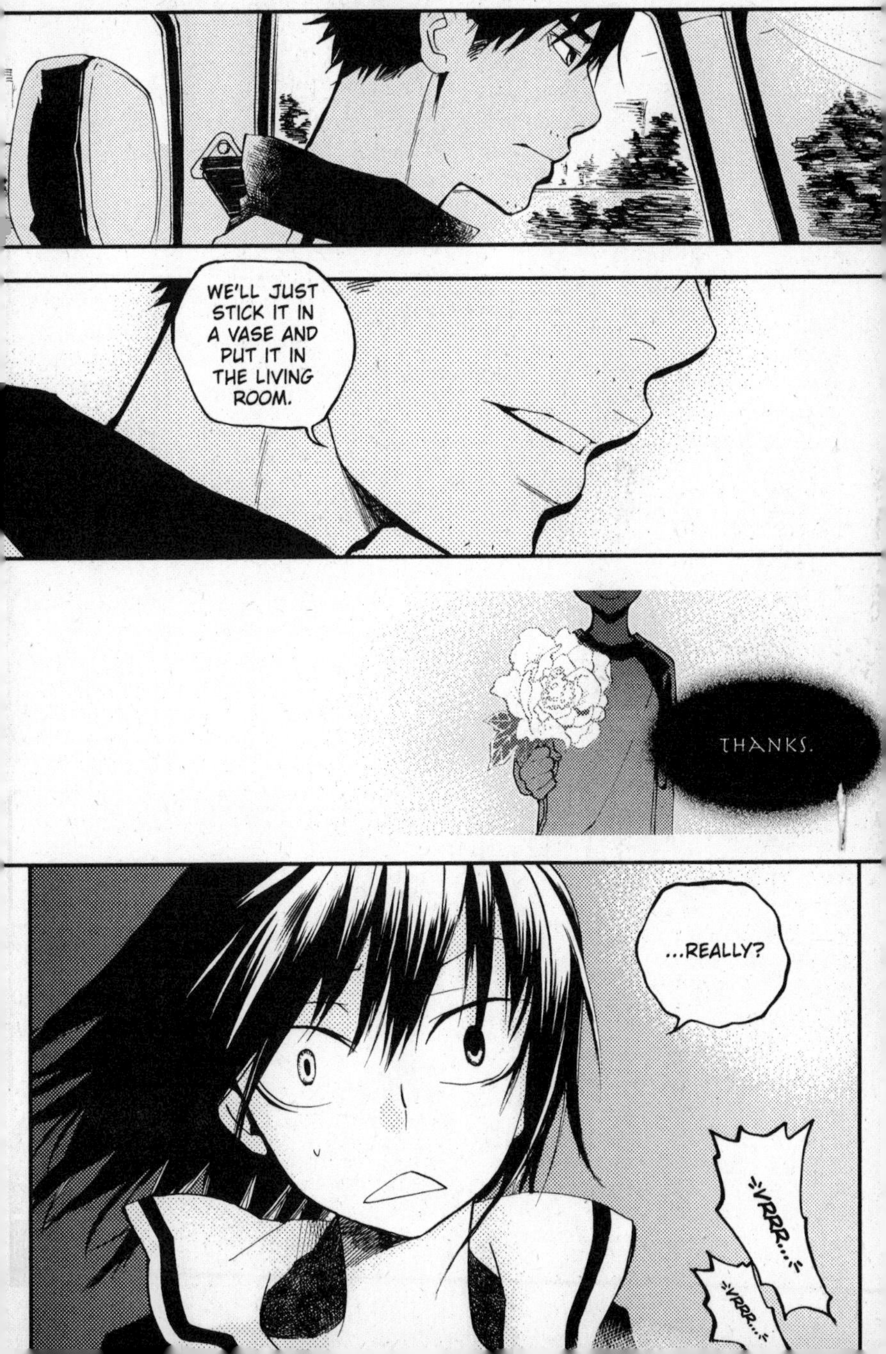
WE'LL JUST STICK IT IN A VASE AND PUT IT IN THE LIVING ROOM.
THANKS.
...REALLY?
VRRR...
VRRR...

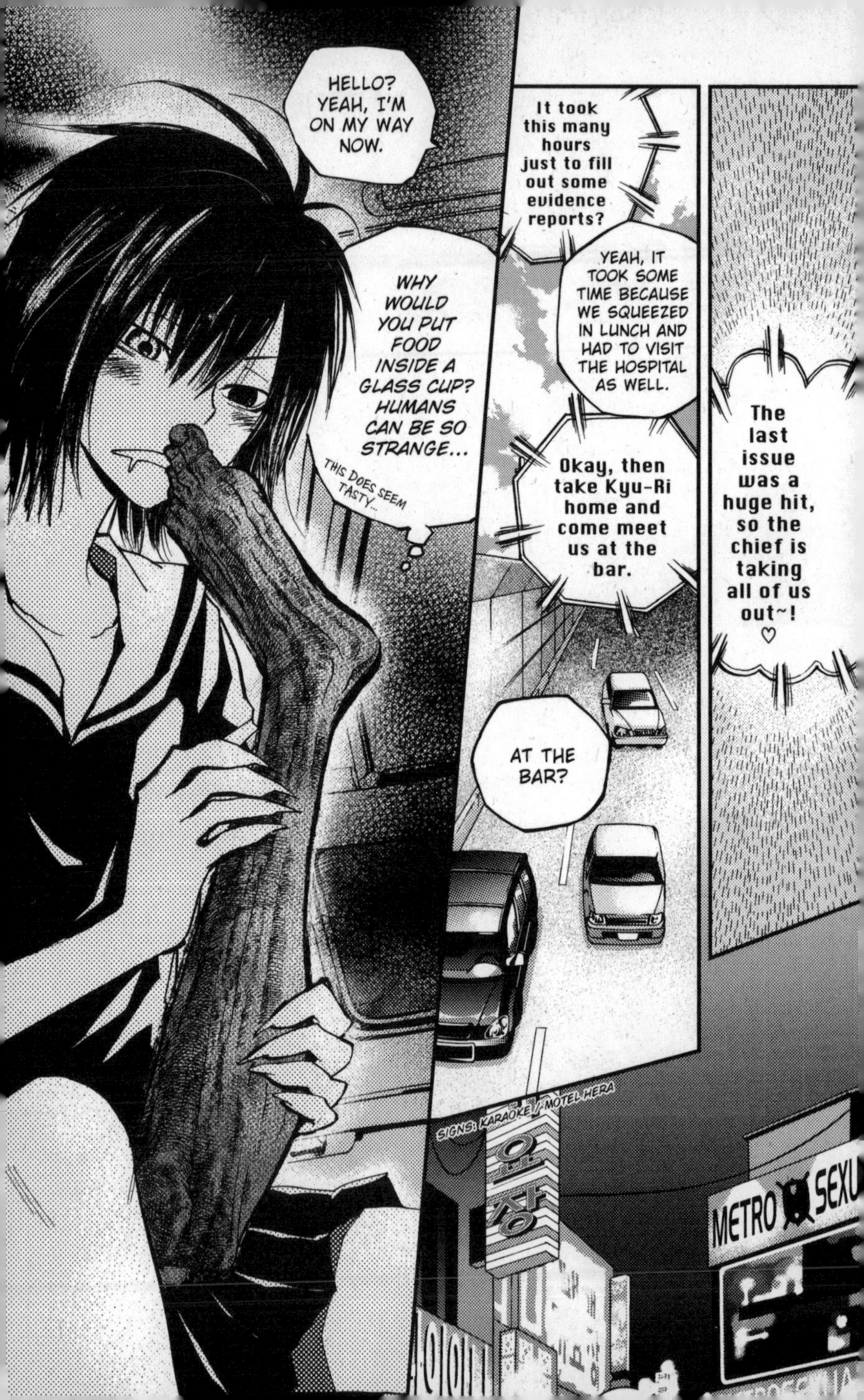
HELLO? YEAH, I'M ON MY WAY NOW.
WHY WOULD YOU PUT FOOD INSIDE A GLASS CUP? HUMANS CAN BE SO STRANGE...
THIS DOES SEEM TASTY...
It took this many hours just to fill out some evidence reports?
YEAH, IT TOOK SOME TIME BECAUSE WE SQUEEZED IN LUNCH AND HAD TO VISIT THE HOSPITAL AS WELL.
Okay, then take Kyu-Ri home and come meet us at the bar.
AT THE BAR?
The last issue was a huge hit, so the chief is taking all of us out~! ♡
SIGNS: KARAOKE / MOTEL HERA
METRO

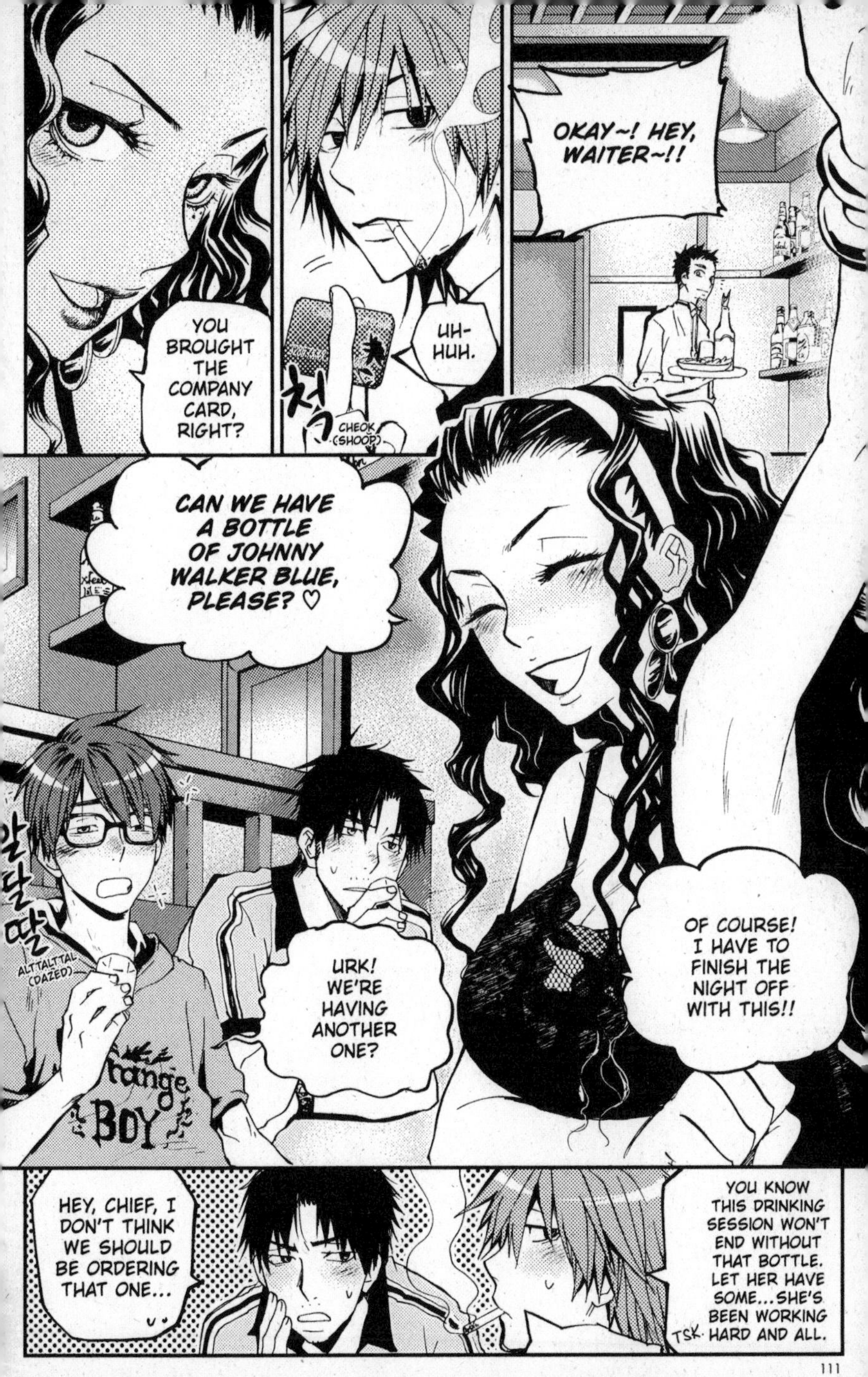
YOU BROUGHT THE COMPANY CARD, RIGHT?
UH-HUH.
척
CHEOK (SHOOP)
OKAY~! HEY, WAITER~!!
CAN WE HAVE A BOTTLE OF JOHNNY WALKER BLUE, PLEASE? ♡
알딸딸
ALTTALTTAL (DAZED)
URK! WE'RE HAVING ANOTHER ONE?
OF COURSE! I HAVE TO FINISH THE NIGHT OFF WITH THIS!!
HEY, CHIEF, I DON'T THINK WE SHOULD BE ORDERING THAT ONE...
TSK.
YOU KNOW THIS DRINKING SESSION WON'T END WITHOUT THAT BOTTLE. LET HER HAVE SOME...SHE'S BEEN WORKING HARD AND ALL.

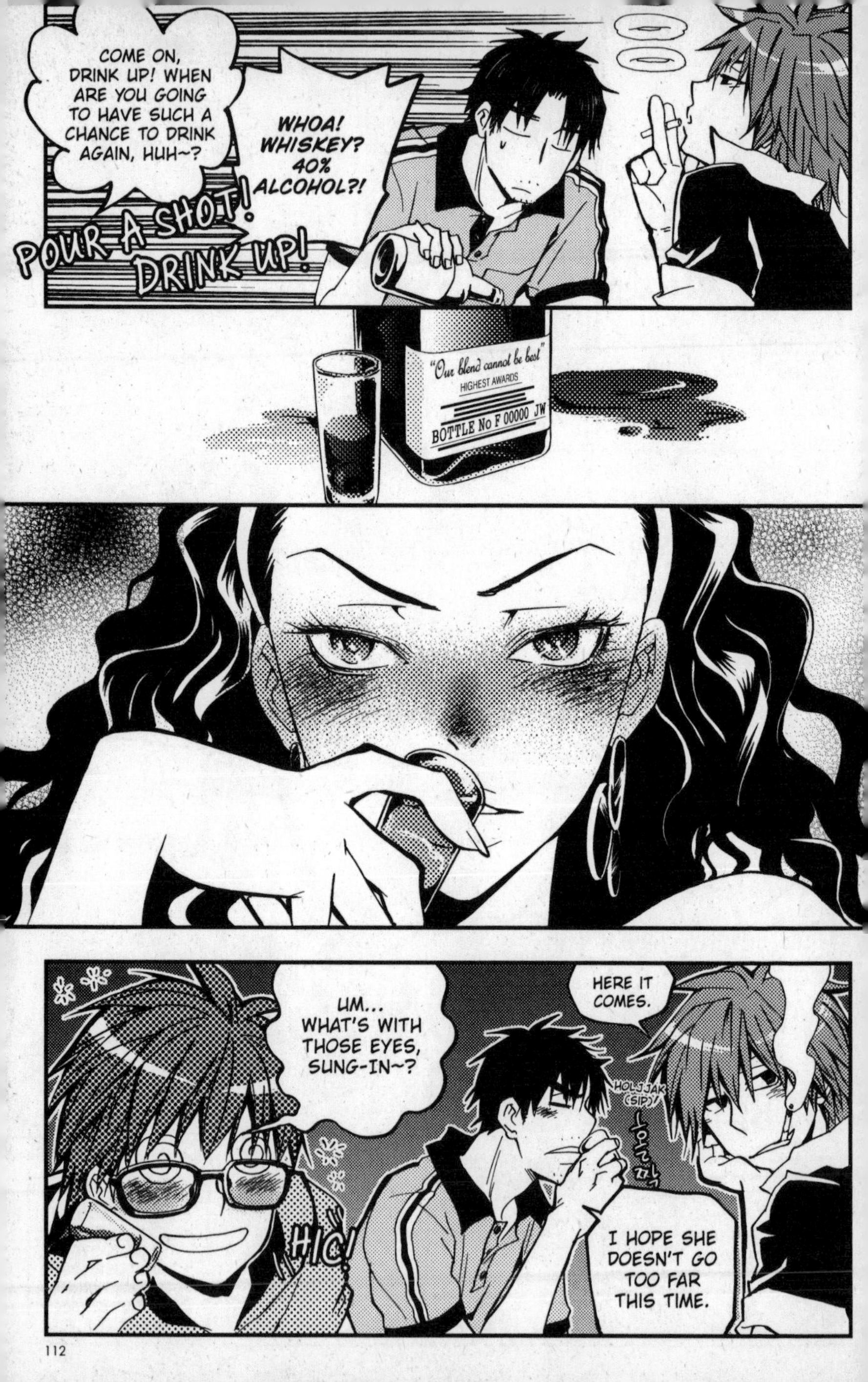
COME ON, DRINK UP! WHEN ARE YOU GOING TO HAVE SUCH A CHANCE TO DRINK AGAIN, HUH~?
WHOA! WHISKEY? 40% ALCOHOL?!
POUR A SHOT! DRINK UP!
"Our blend cannot be best"
HIGHEST AWARDS
BOTTLE No F 00000 JW
UM... WHAT'S WITH THOSE EYES, SUNG-IN~?
HIC!
HERE IT COMES.
HOLJJAK (SIP)
I HOPE SHE DOESN'T GO TOO FAR THIS TIME.

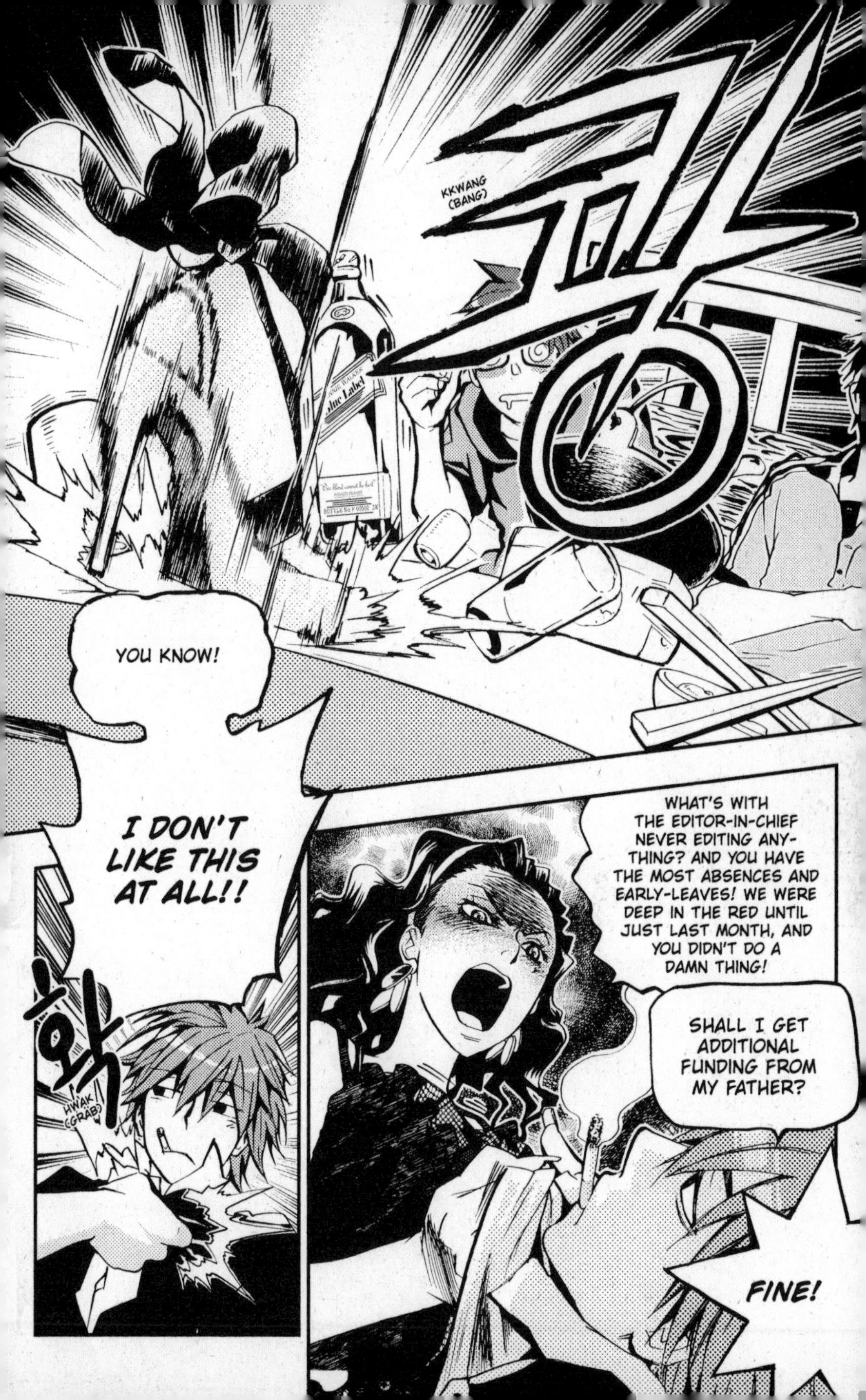
KKWANG (BANG)
YOU KNOW!
I DON'T LIKE THIS AT ALL!!
HWAK (GRAB)
WHAT'S WITH THE EDITOR-IN-CHIEF NEVER EDITING ANY-THING? AND YOU HAVE THE MOST ABSENCES AND EARLY-LEAVES! WE WERE DEEP IN THE RED UNTIL JUST LAST MONTH, AND YOU DIDN'T DO A DAMN THING!
SHALL I GET ADDITIONAL FUNDING FROM MY FATHER?
FINE!

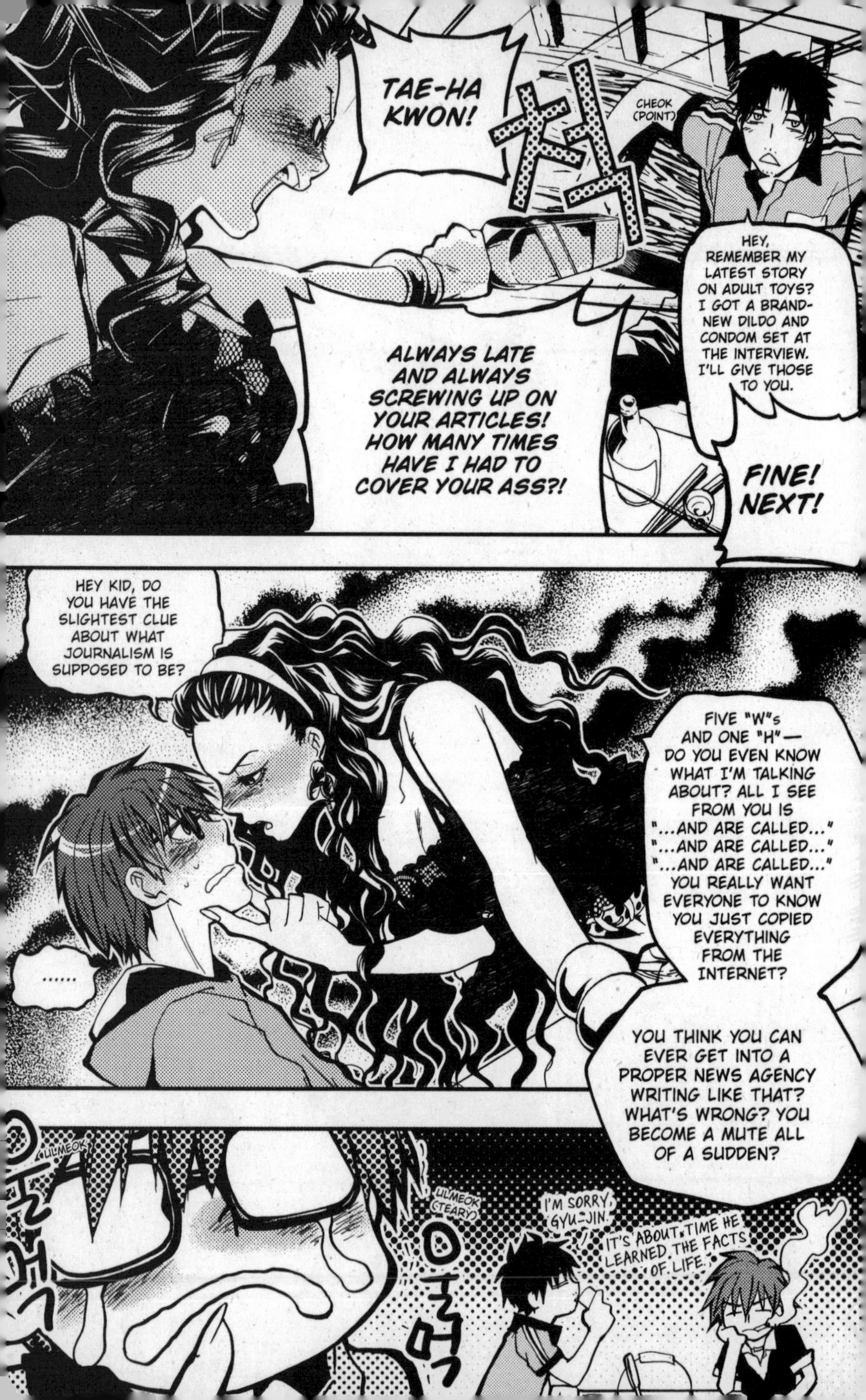
TAE-HA KWON!
CHEOK (POINT)
ALWAYS LATE AND ALWAYS SCREWING UP ON YOUR ARTICLES! HOW MANY TIMES HAVE I HAD TO COVER YOUR ASS?!
HEY, REMEMBER MY LATEST STORY ON ADULT TOYS? I GOT A BRAND-NEW DILDO AND CONDOM SET AT THE INTERVIEW. I'LL GIVE THOSE TO YOU.
FINE! NEXT!
HEY KID, DO YOU HAVE THE SLIGHTEST CLUE ABOUT WHAT JOURNALISM IS SUPPOSED TO BE?
FIVE "W"s AND ONE "H"— DO YOU EVEN KNOW WHAT I'M TALKING ABOUT? ALL I SEE FROM YOU IS "...AND ARE CALLED..." "...AND ARE CALLED..." "...AND ARE CALLED..." YOU REALLY WANT EVERYONE TO KNOW YOU JUST COPIED EVERYTHING FROM THE INTERNET?
......
YOU THINK YOU CAN EVER GET INTO A PROPER NEWS AGENCY WRITING LIKE THAT? WHAT'S WRONG? YOU BECOME A MUTE ALL OF A SUDDEN?
GULMEOK
GULMEOK (TEARY)
I'M SORRY, GYU-JIN.
IT'S ABOUT TIME HE LEARNED THE FACTS OF LIFE.

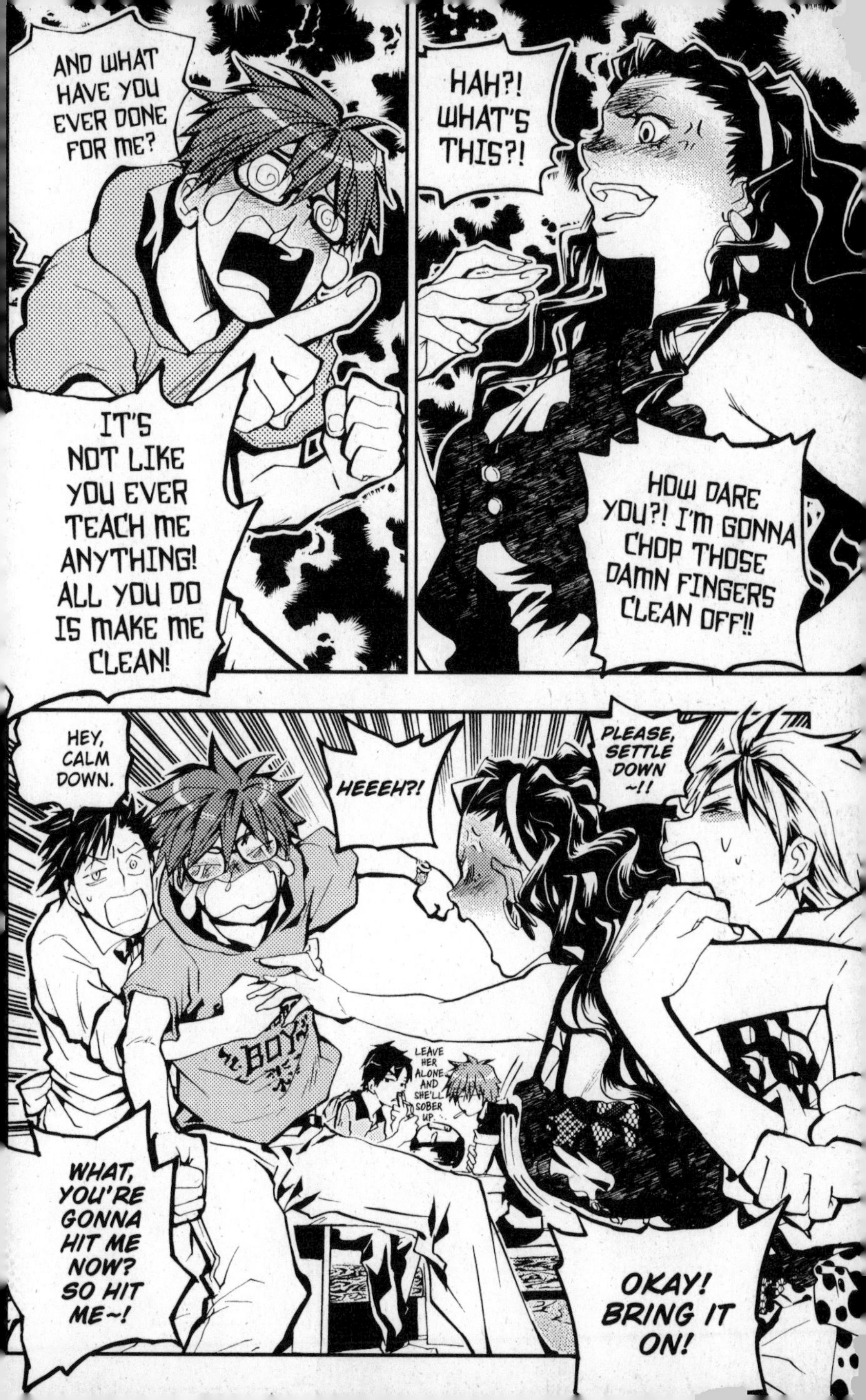
AND WHAT HAVE YOU EVER DONE FOR ME?
IT'S NOT LIKE YOU EVER TEACH ME ANYTHING! ALL YOU DO IS MAKE ME CLEAN!
HAH?! WHAT'S THIS?!
HOW DARE YOU?! I'M GONNA CHOP THOSE DAMN FINGERS CLEAN OFF!!
HEY, CALM DOWN.
HEEEH?!
PLEASE, SETTLE DOWN ~!!
LEAVE HER ALONE AND SHE'LL SOBER UP.
BOY
WHAT, YOU'RE GONNA HIT ME NOW? SO HIT ME~!
OKAY! BRING IT ON!

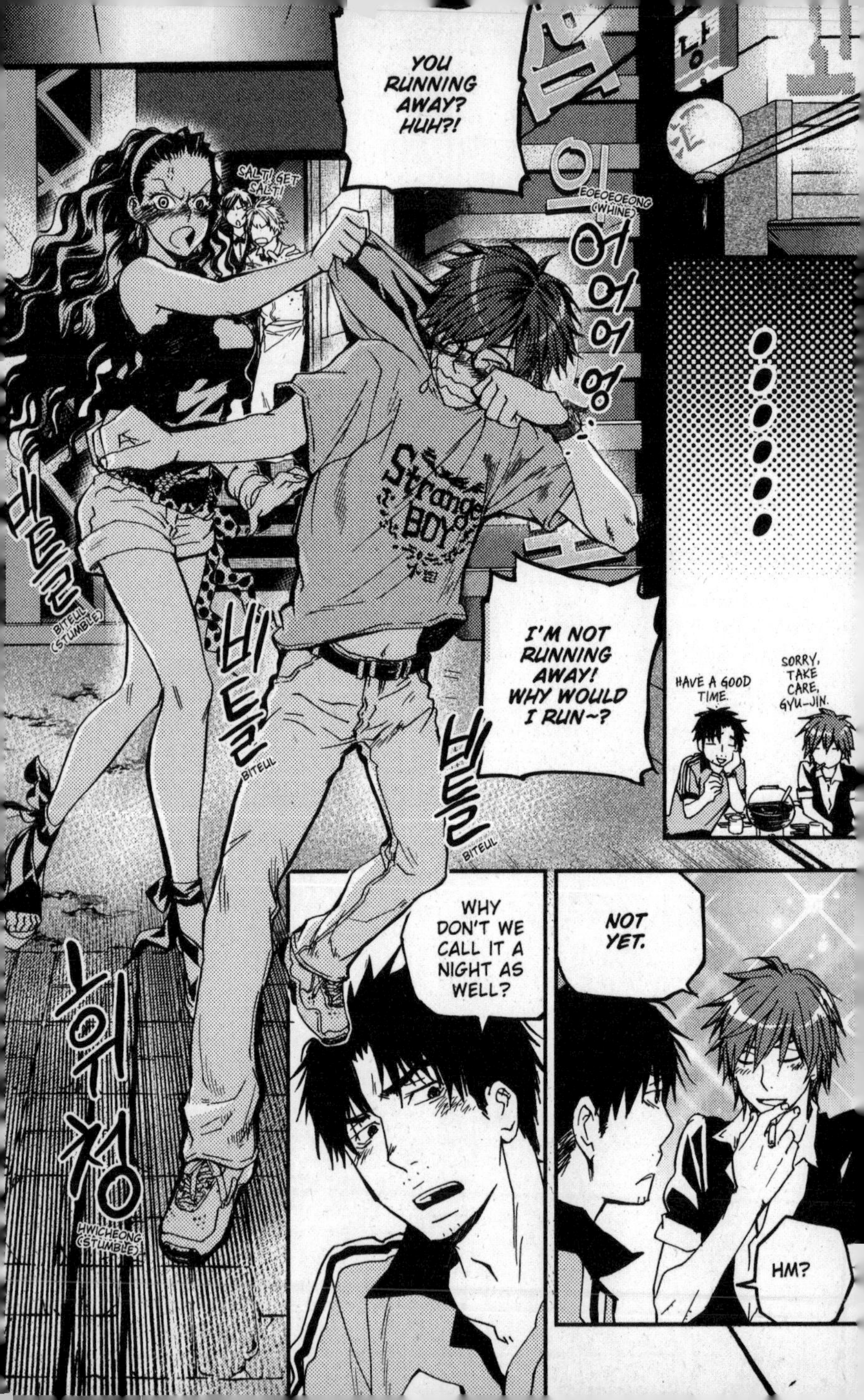
YOU RUNNING AWAY? HUH?!
SALT! GET SALT!
EOEOEOEOENG (WHINE)
비틀
BITEUL (STUMBLE)
비틀
BITEUL
비틀
BITEUL
휘청
HWICHEONG (STUMBLE)
I'M NOT RUNNING AWAY! WHY WOULD I RUN~?
......
HAVE A GOOD TIME.
SORRY, TAKE CARE, GYU-JIN.
WHY DON'T WE CALL IT A NIGHT AS WELL?
NOT YET.
HM?

IT'S BEEN A WHILE FOR YOU, RIGHT?

A WHILE SINCE WHAT?

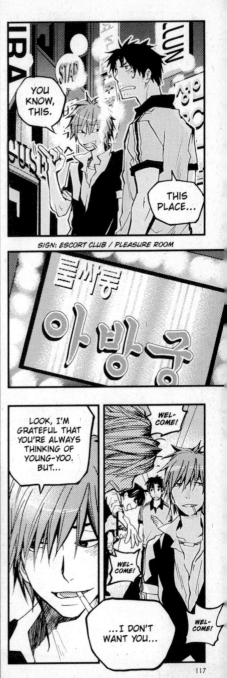

YOU KNOW, THIS.

THIS PLACE...

SIGN: ESCORT CLUB / PLEASURE ROOM

LOOK, I'M GRATEFUL THAT YOU'RE ALWAYS THINKING OF YOUNG-YOO. BUT...

WEL- COME!

WEL- COME!

...I DON'T WANT YOU...

WEL- COME!

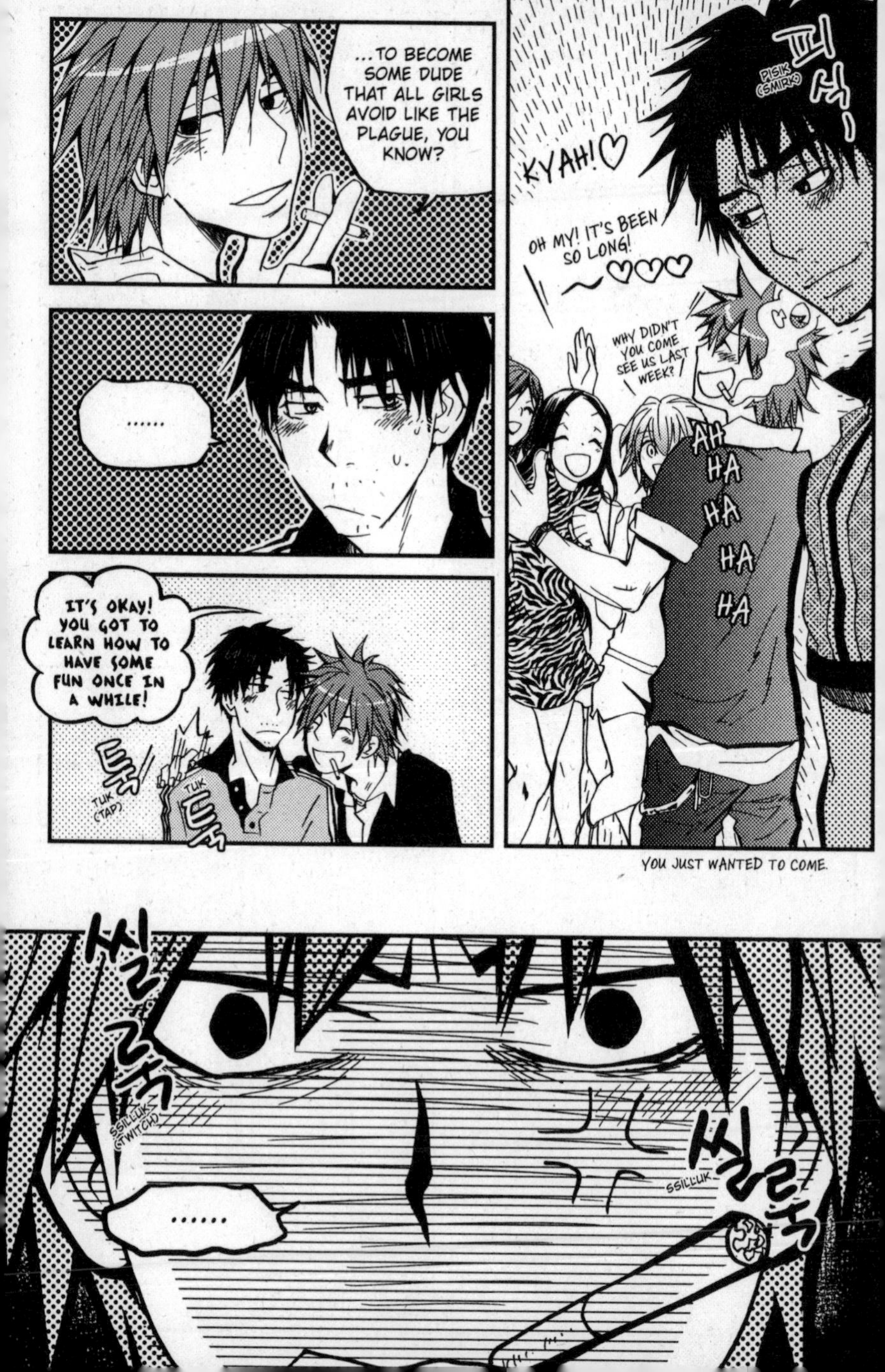
...TO BECOME SOME DUDE THAT ALL GIRLS AVOID LIKE THE PLAGUE, YOU KNOW?
......
IT'S OKAY! YOU GOT TO LEARN HOW TO HAVE SOME FUN ONCE IN A WHILE!
툭
TUK (TAP)
툭
TUK
피식
PISIK (SMIRK)
KYAH!♡
OH MY! IT'S BEEN SO LONG!
~♡♡♡
WHY DIDN'T YOU COME SEE US LAST WEEK?
AH HA HA HA HA HA
YOU JUST WANTED TO COME.
씰룩
SSILLUK (TWITCH)
......
씰룩
SSILLUK

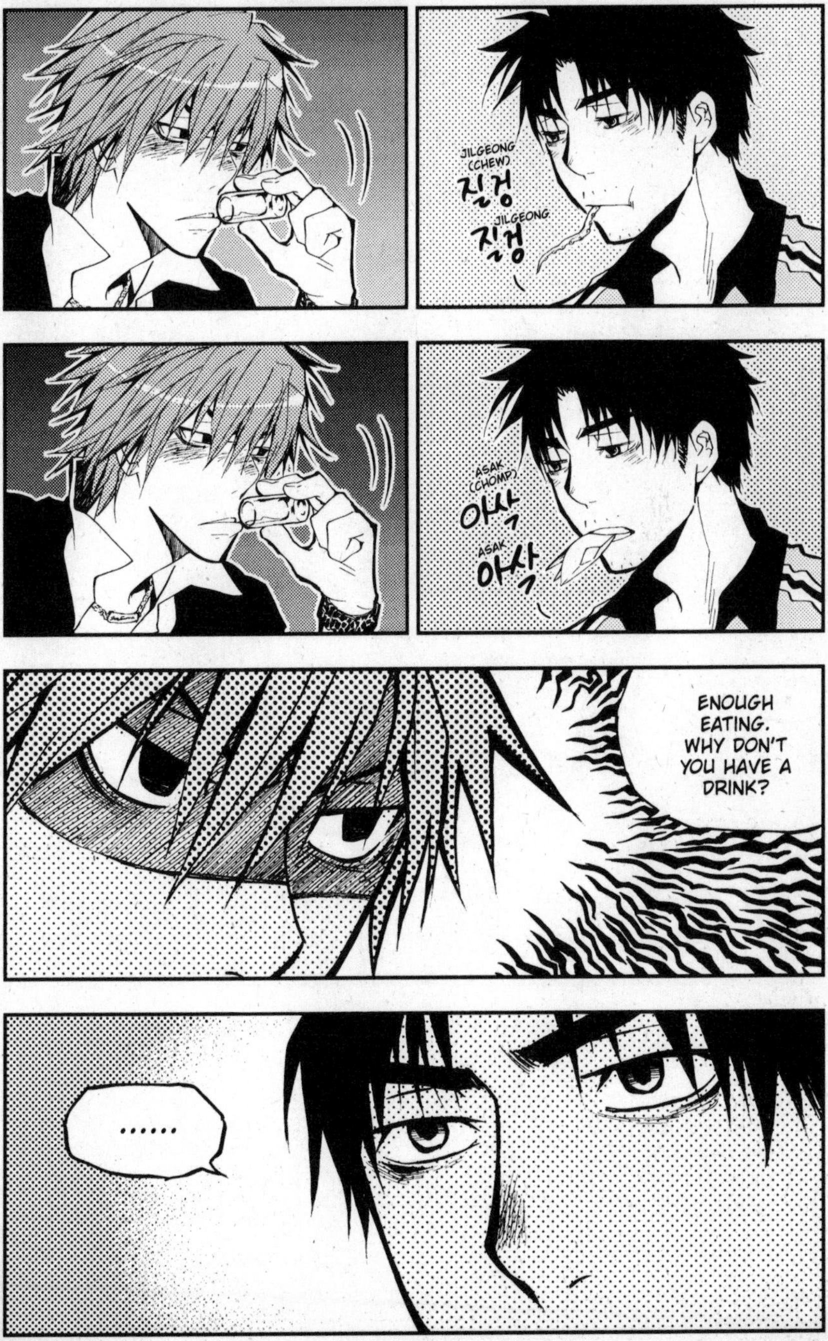
JILGEONG (CHEW)
질겅
JILGEONG
질겅
ASAK (CHOMP)
아삭
ASAK
아삭
ENOUGH EATING. WHY DON'T YOU HAVE A DRINK?
......

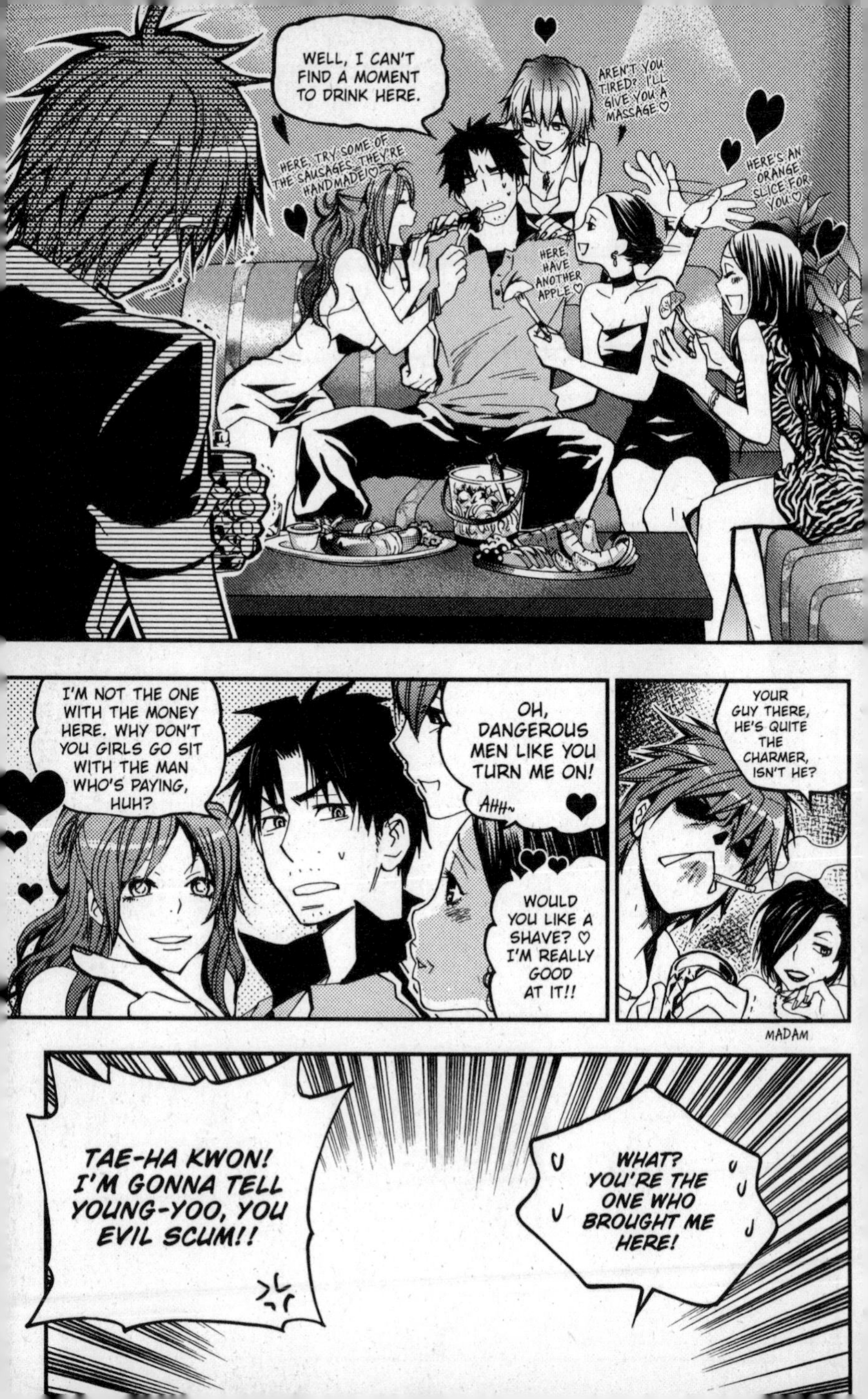
WELL, I CAN'T FIND A MOMENT TO DRINK HERE.
AREN'T YOU TIRED? I'LL GIVE YOU A MASSAGE♡
HERE, TRY SOME OF THE SAUSAGES. THEY'RE HANDMADE!♡
HERE'S AN ORANGE SLICE FOR YOU♡
HERE, HAVE ANOTHER APPLE♡
I'M NOT THE ONE WITH THE MONEY HERE. WHY DON'T YOU GIRLS GO SIT WITH THE MAN WHO'S PAYING, HUH?
OH, DANGEROUS MEN LIKE YOU TURN ME ON!
AHH~
WOULD YOU LIKE A SHAVE? ♡ I'M REALLY GOOD AT IT!!
YOUR GUY THERE, HE'S QUITE THE CHARMER, ISN'T HE?
MADAM
TAE-HA KWON! I'M GONNA TELL YOUNG-YOO, YOU EVIL SCUM!!
WHAT? YOU'RE THE ONE WHO BROUGHT ME HERE!

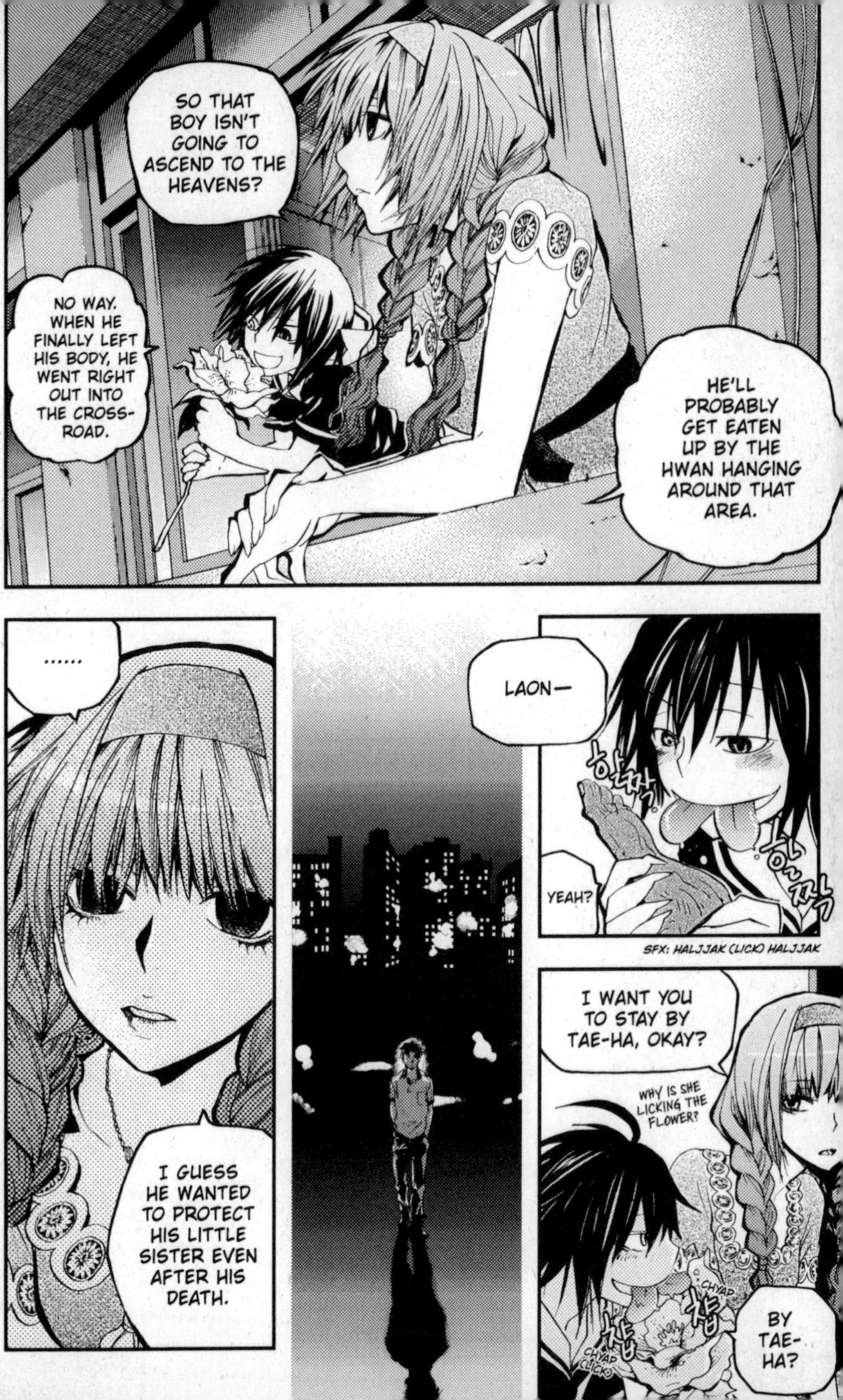
SO THAT BOY ISN'T GOING TO ASCEND TO THE HEAVENS?
NO WAY. WHEN HE FINALLY LEFT HIS BODY, HE WENT RIGHT OUT INTO THE CROSS-ROAD.
HE'LL PROBABLY GET EATEN UP BY THE HWAN HANGING AROUND THAT AREA.
......
I GUESS HE WANTED TO PROTECT HIS LITTLE SISTER EVEN AFTER HIS DEATH.
LAON—
할짝
할짝
YEAH?
SFX: HALJJAK (LICK) HALJJAK
I WANT YOU TO STAY BY TAE-HA, OKAY?
WHY IS SHE LICKING THE FLOWER?
챱
CHYAP
챱
CHYAP (LICK)
BY TAE-HA?

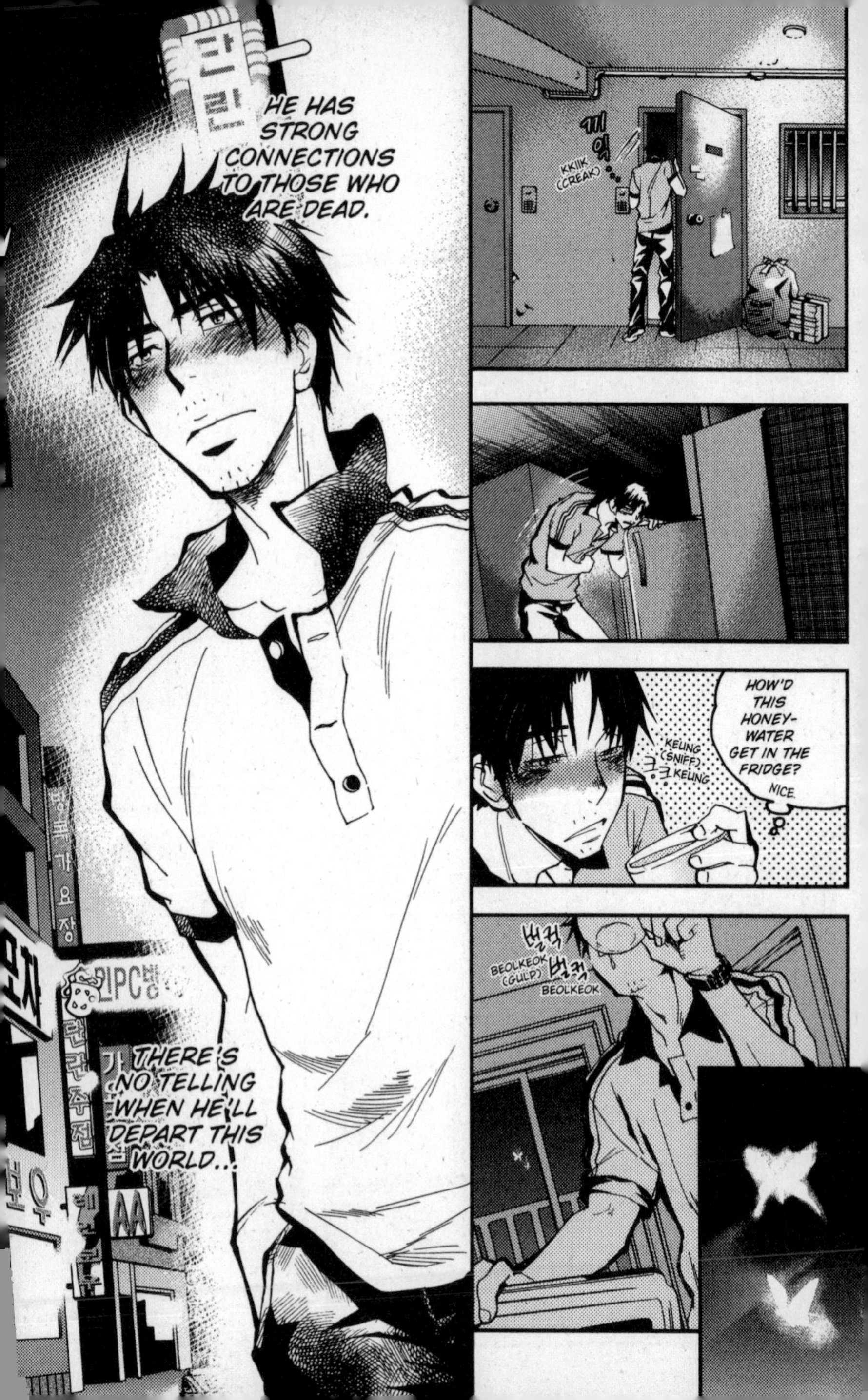
HE HAS STRONG CONNECTIONS TO THOSE WHO ARE DEAD.
THERE'S NO TELLING WHEN HE'LL DEPART THIS WORLD...
끼익
KKIIK (CREAK)
킁킁
KEUNG (SNIFF) KEUNG
HOW'D THIS HONEY-WATER GET IN THE FRIDGE?
NICE.
벌컥 벌컥
BEOLKEOK (GULP) BEOLKEOK

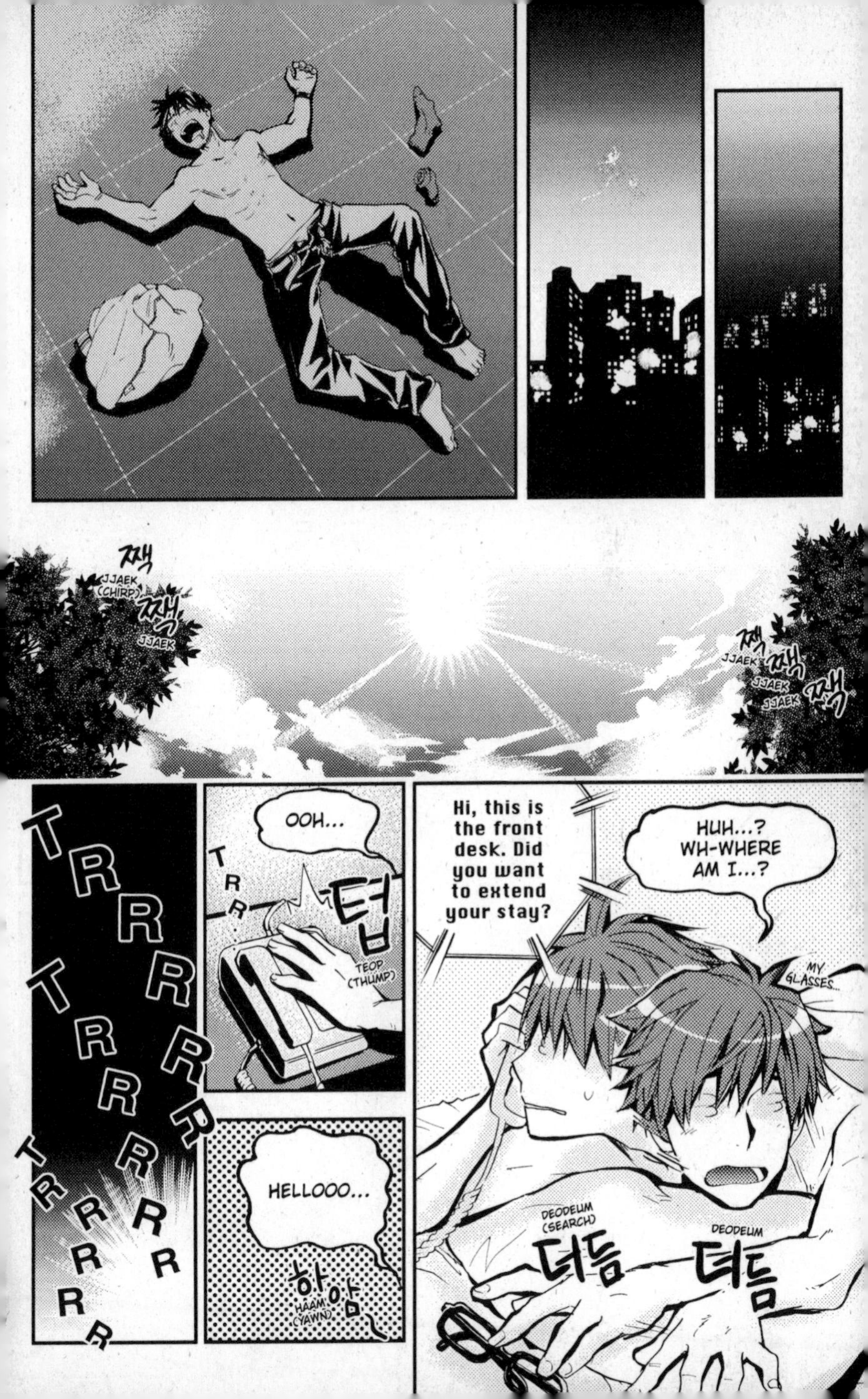

짹
JJAEK (CHIRP)
짹
JJAEK
짹
JJAEK
짹
JJAEK
짹
JJAEK
TRRTRRRRRTRRRRRTRRRRR
OOH...
TRR...
텁
TEOP (THUMP)
HELLOOO...
하암
HAAM (YAWN)
Hi, this is the front desk. Did you want to extend your stay?
HUH...? WH-WHERE AM I...?
MY GLASSES...
더듬
DEODEUM (SEARCH)
더듬
DEODEUM

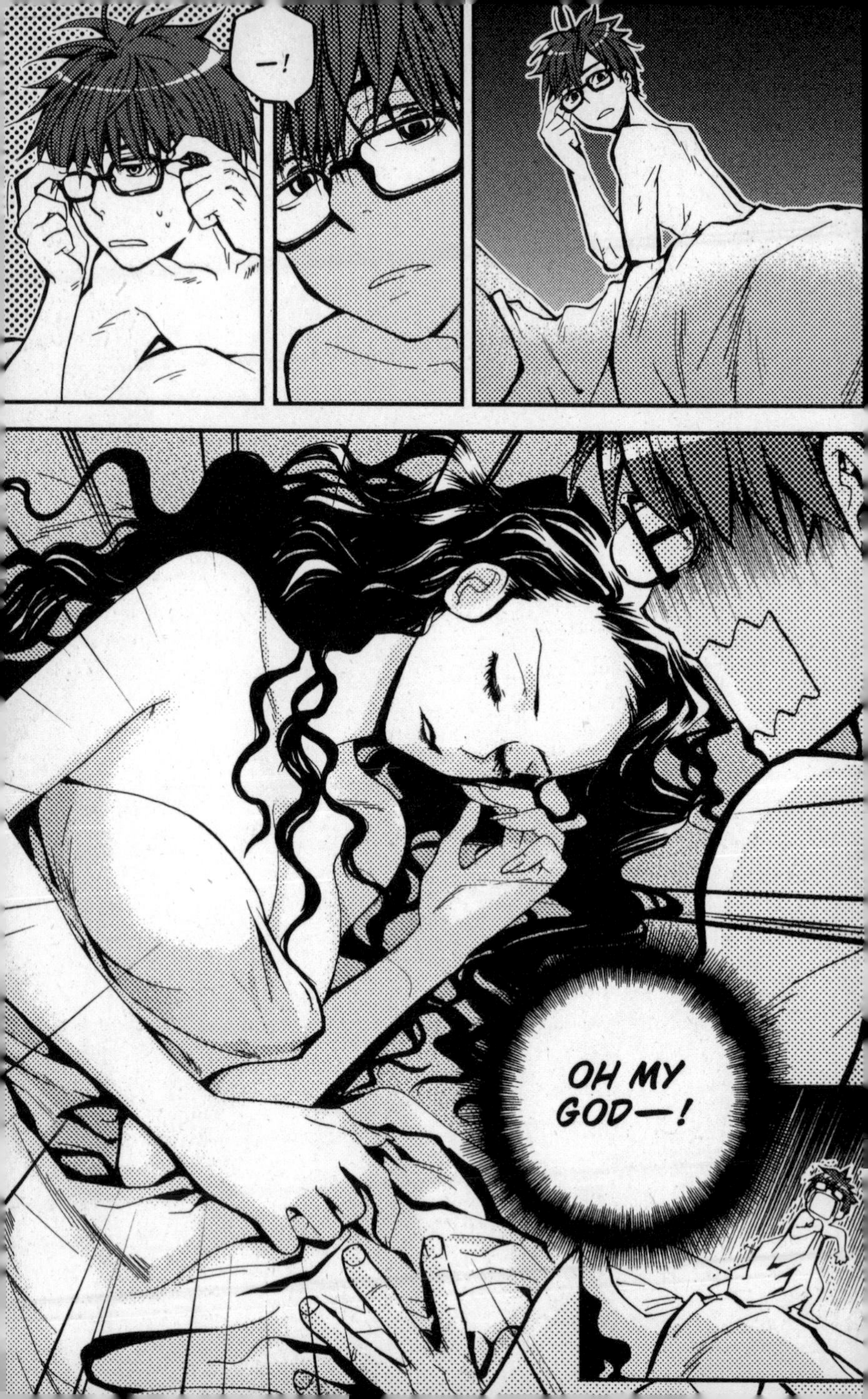
—!
OH MY GOD—!

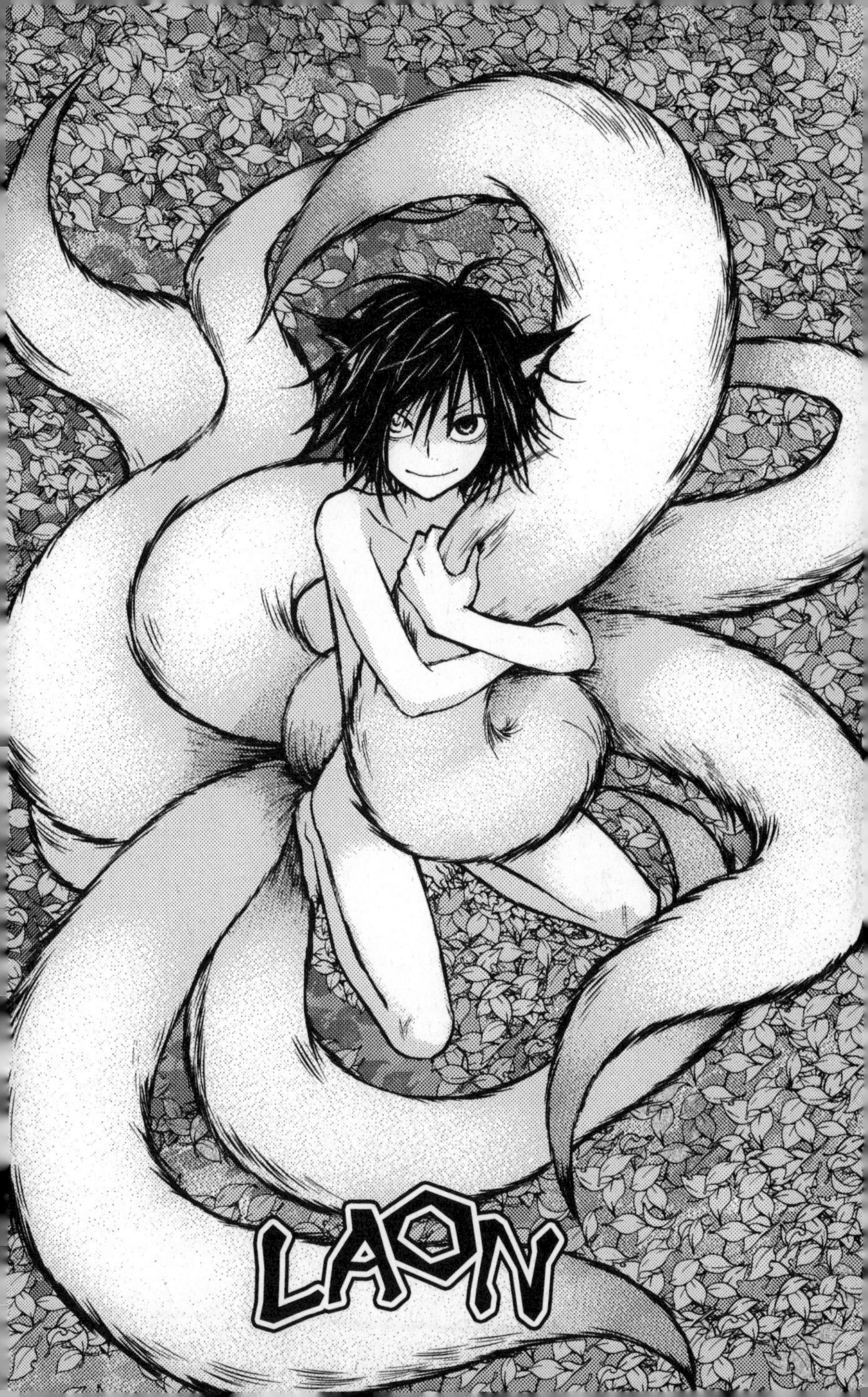
LAON

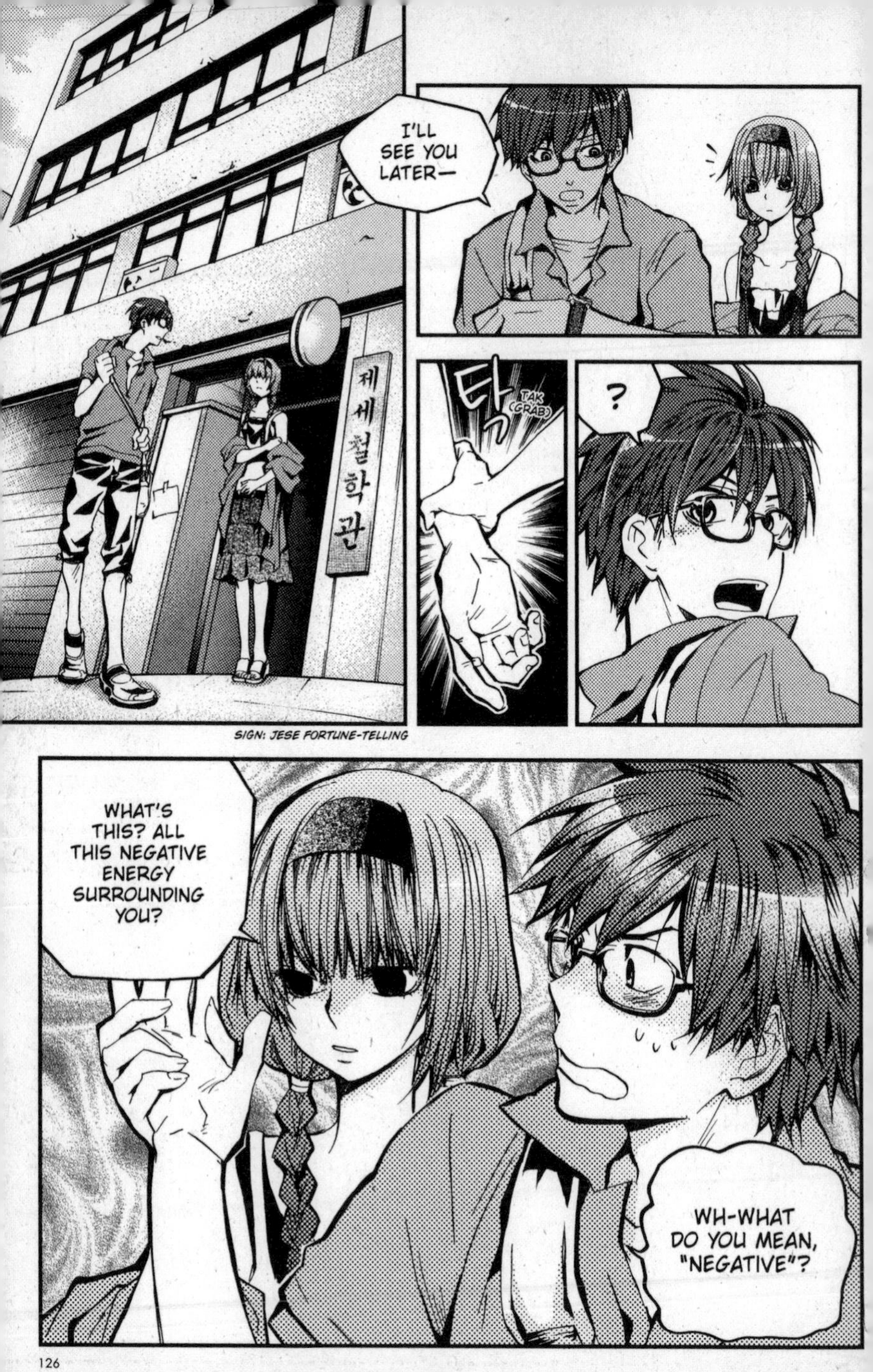
제세철학관
SIGN: JESE FORTUNE-TELLING
I'LL SEE YOU LATER—
탁
TAK (GRAB)
?
WHAT'S THIS? ALL THIS NEGATIVE ENERGY SURROUNDING YOU?
WH-WHAT DO YOU MEAN, "NEGATIVE"?

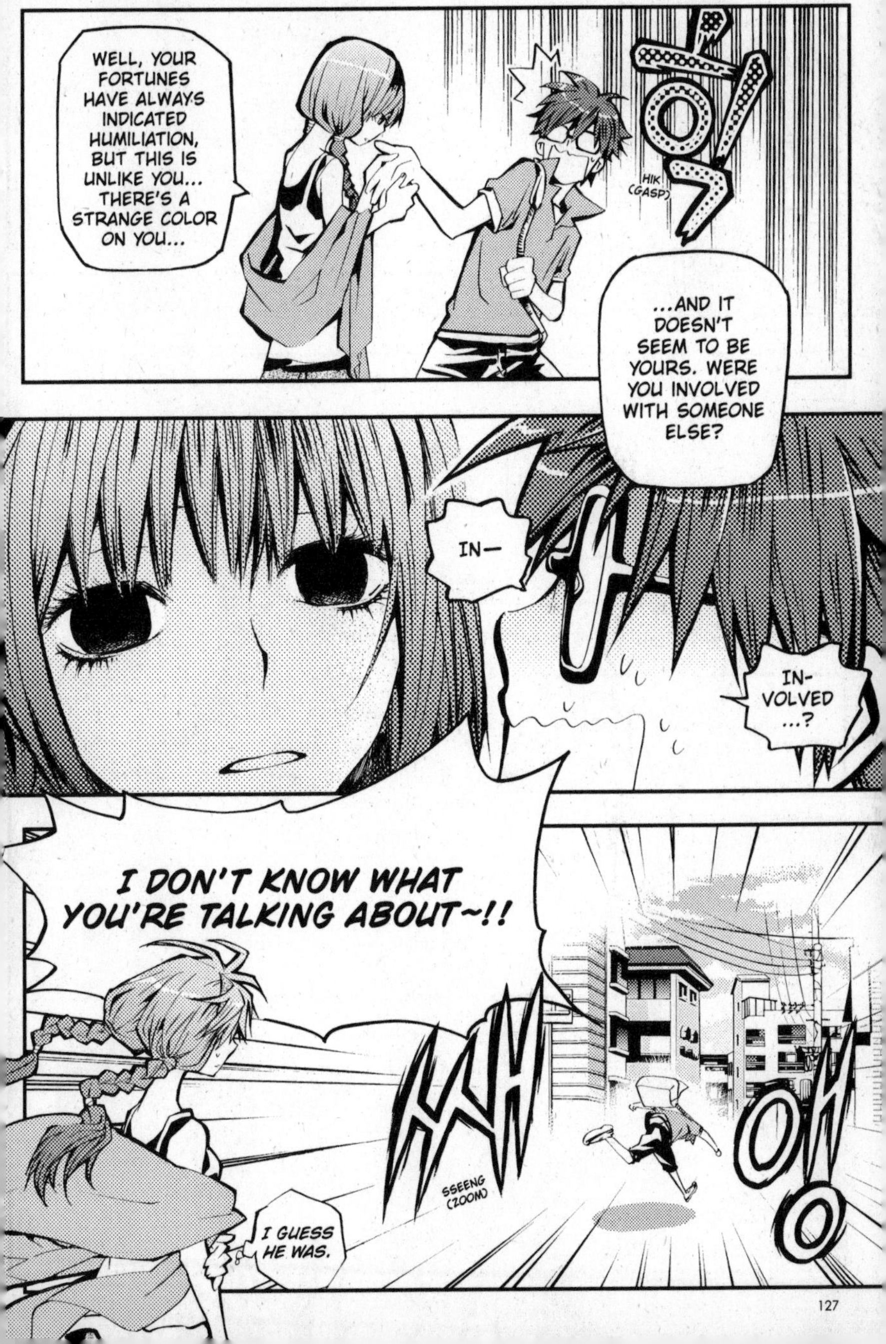
WELL, YOUR FORTUNES HAVE ALWAYS INDICATED HUMILIATION, BUT THIS IS UNLIKE YOU... THERE'S A STRANGE COLOR ON YOU...
HIK (GASP)
...AND IT DOESN'T SEEM TO BE YOURS. WERE YOU INVOLVED WITH SOMEONE ELSE?
IN—
IN-VOLVED ...?
I DON'T KNOW WHAT YOU'RE TALKING ABOUT~!!
SSEENG (ZOOM)
I GUESS HE WAS.

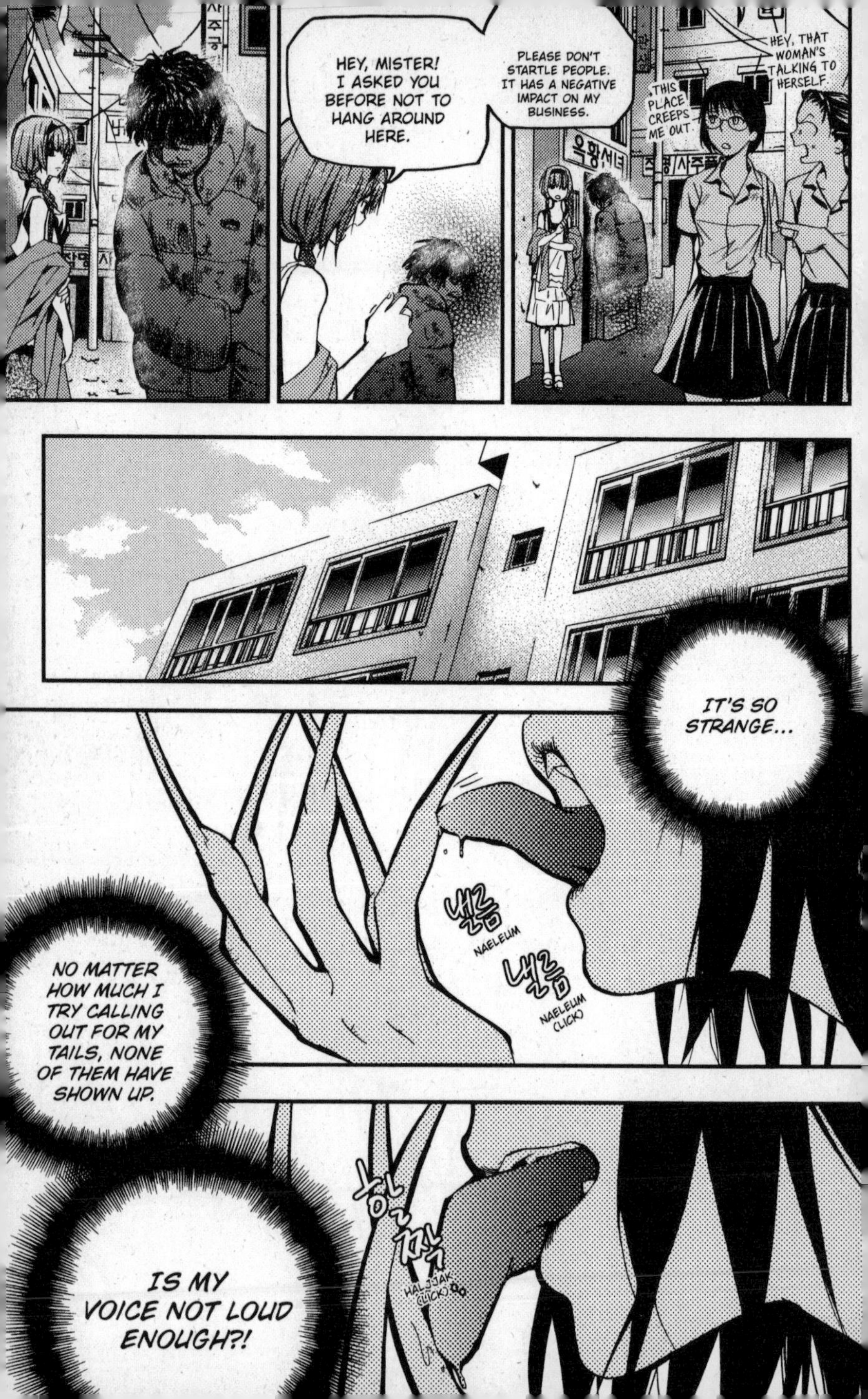
HEY, MISTER! I ASKED YOU BEFORE NOT TO HANG AROUND HERE.
PLEASE DON'T STARTLE PEOPLE. IT HAS A NEGATIVE IMPACT ON MY BUSINESS.
THIS PLACE CREEPS ME OUT
HEY, THAT WOMAN'S TALKING TO HERSELF.
IT'S SO STRANGE...
낼름
NAELEUM
낼름
NAELEUM (LICK)
NO MATTER HOW MUCH I TRY CALLING OUT FOR MY TAILS, NONE OF THEM HAVE SHOWN UP.
할짝
HALJJAK (LICK)
IS MY VOICE NOT LOUD ENOUGH?!

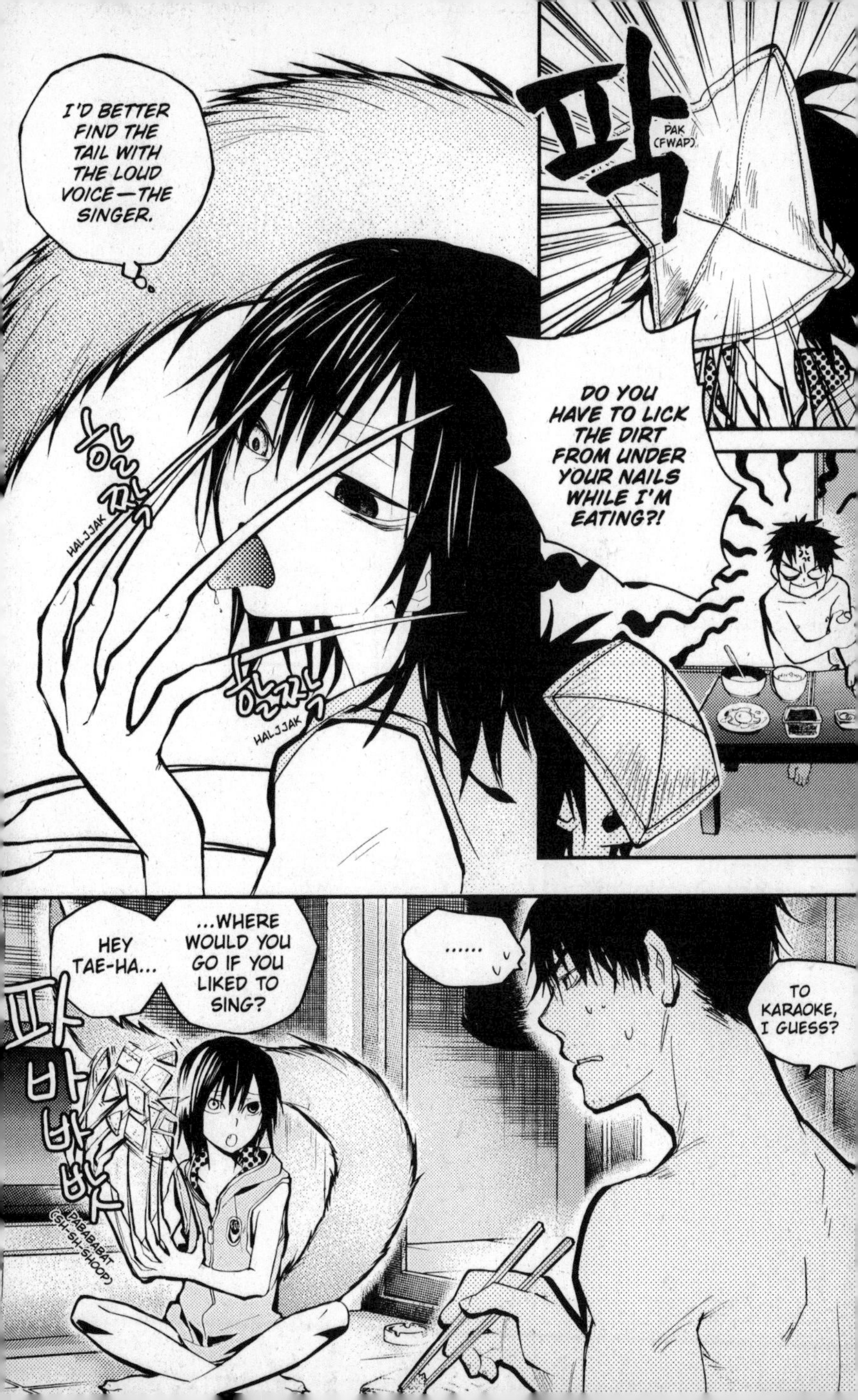

I'D BETTER FIND THE TAIL WITH THE LOUD VOICE—THE SINGER.
할짝
HALJJAK
할짝
HALJJAK
팍
PAK (FWAP)
DO YOU HAVE TO LICK THE DIRT FROM UNDER YOUR NAILS WHILE I'M EATING?!
HEY TAE-HA...
...WHERE WOULD YOU GO IF YOU LIKED TO SING?
파바바밧
PABABABAT (SH-SH-SHOOP)
......
TO KARAOKE, I GUESS?

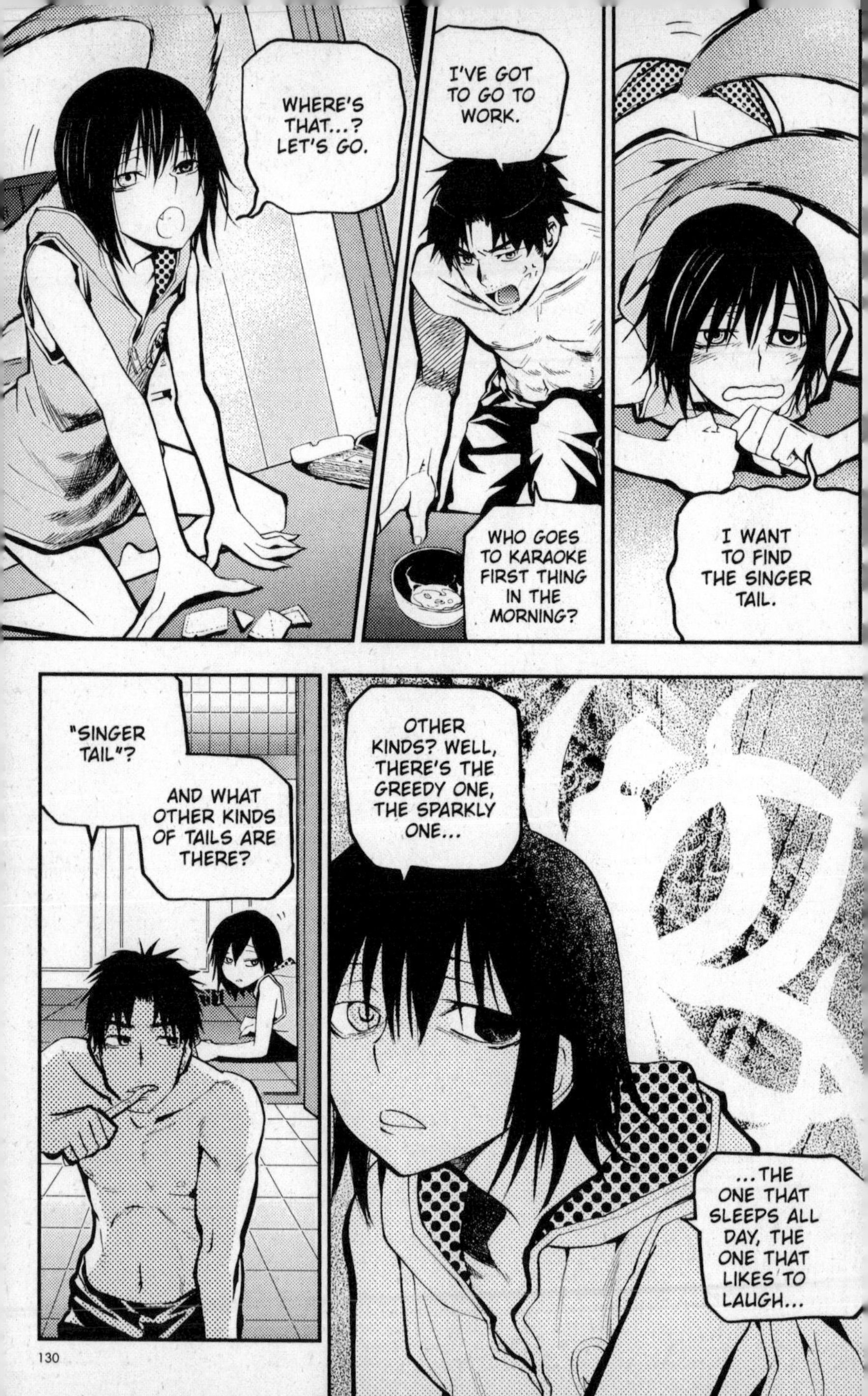
WHERE'S THAT...? LET'S GO.
I'VE GOT TO GO TO WORK.
WHO GOES TO KARAOKE FIRST THING IN THE MORNING?
I WANT TO FIND THE SINGER TAIL.
"SINGER TAIL"?
AND WHAT OTHER KINDS OF TAILS ARE THERE?
OTHER KINDS? WELL, THERE'S THE GREEDY ONE, THE SPARKLY ONE...
...THE ONE THAT SLEEPS ALL DAY, THE ONE THAT LIKES TO LAUGH...

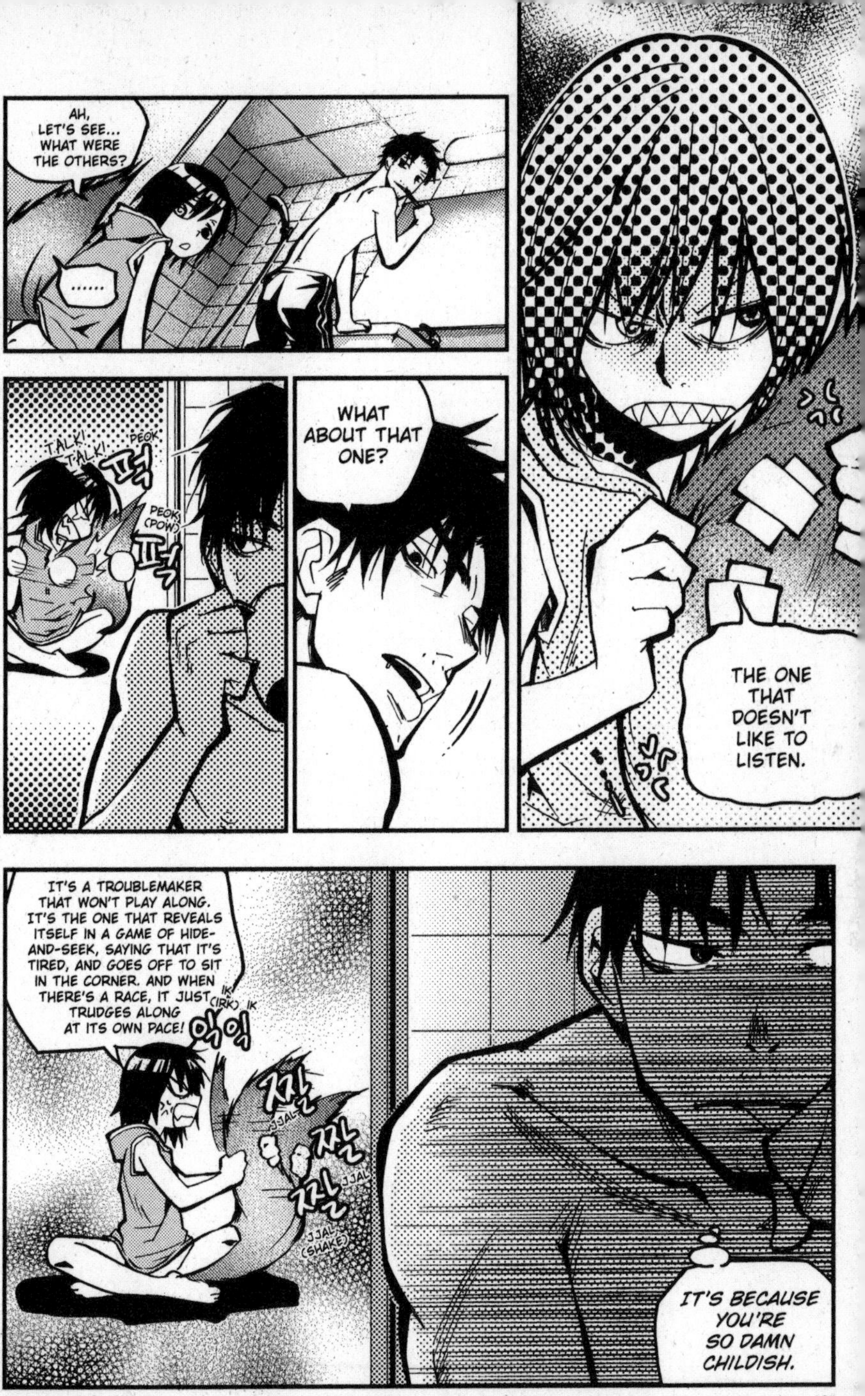
AH, LET'S SEE... WHAT WERE THE OTHERS?
....
TALK! TALK!
PEOK
퍽
PEOK (POW)
퍽
WHAT ABOUT THAT ONE?
THE ONE THAT DOESN'T LIKE TO LISTEN.
IT'S A TROUBLEMAKER THAT WON'T PLAY ALONG. IT'S THE ONE THAT REVEALS ITSELF IN A GAME OF HIDE-AND-SEEK, SAYING THAT IT'S TIRED, AND GOES OFF TO SIT IN THE CORNER. AND WHEN THERE'S A RACE, IT JUST TRUDGES ALONG AT ITS OWN PACE!
IK (IRK) IK
JJAL
JJAL
JJAL (SHAKE)
IT'S BECAUSE YOU'RE SO DAMN CHILDISH.

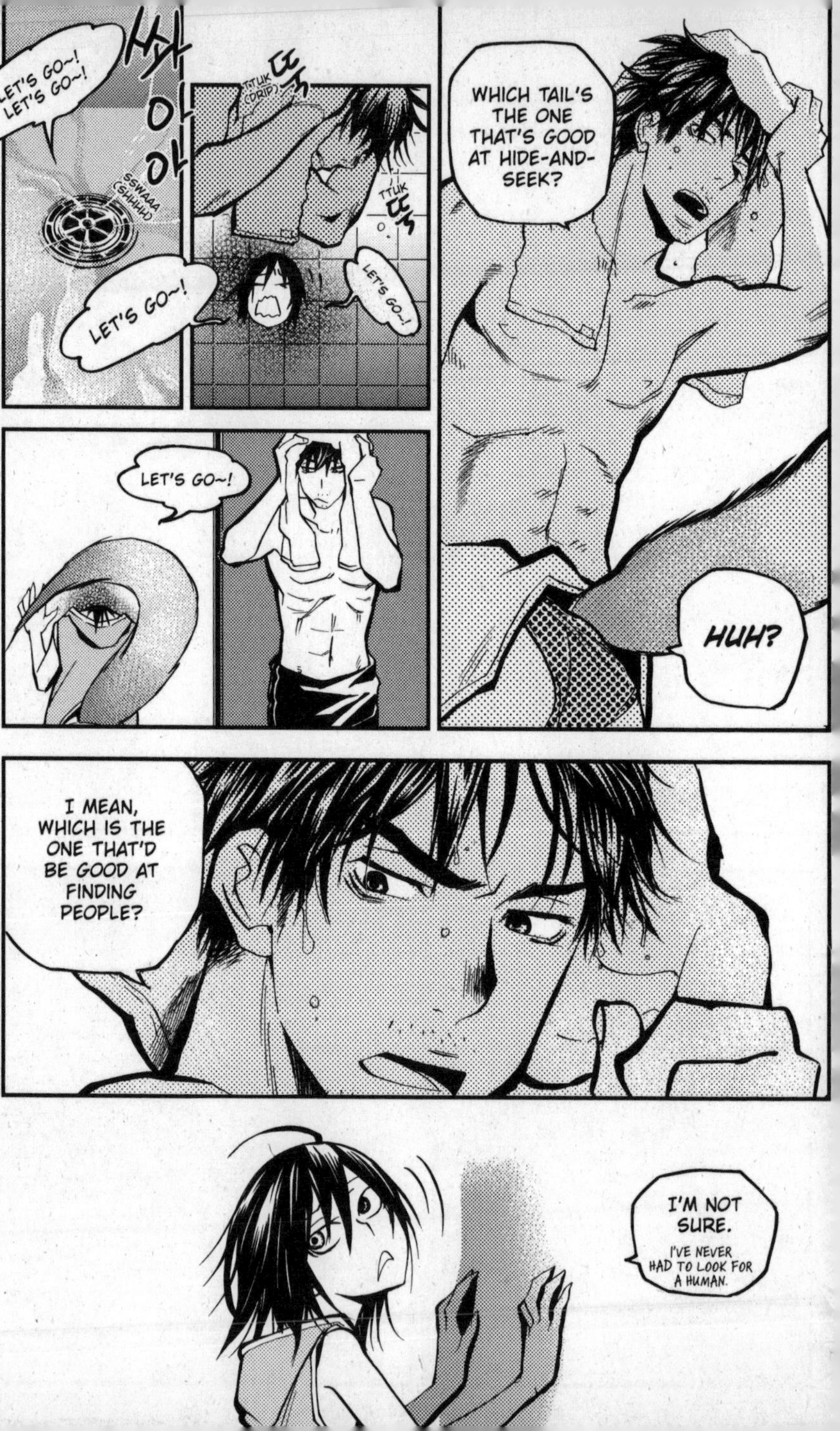
LET'S GO~! LET'S GO~!
싸아아
SSWAAA (SHHHH)
LET'S GO~!
TTUK (DRIP)
뚝
TTUK
뚝
LET'S GO~!
LET'S GO~!
WHICH TAIL'S THE ONE THAT'S GOOD AT HIDE-AND-SEEK?
HUH?
I MEAN, WHICH IS THE ONE THAT'D BE GOOD AT FINDING PEOPLE?
I'M NOT SURE.
I'VE NEVER HAD TO LOOK FOR A HUMAN.

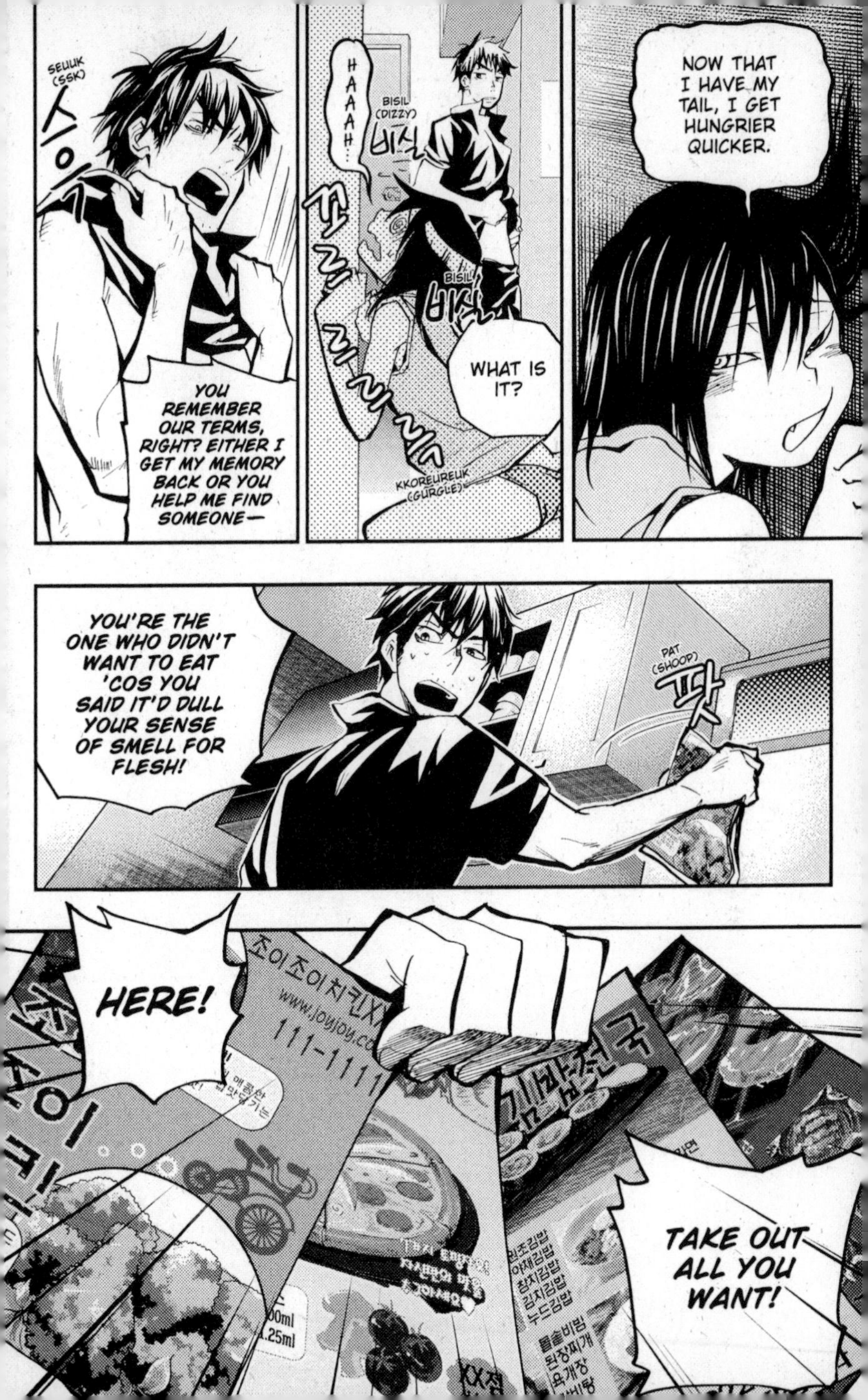

SEUUK (SSK)
YOU REMEMBER OUR TERMS, RIGHT? EITHER I GET MY MEMORY BACK OR YOU HELP ME FIND SOMEONE—
HAAAAH...
BISIL (DIZZY)
비실
BISIL
비실
WHAT IS IT?
KKOREUREUK (GURGLE)
NOW THAT I HAVE MY TAIL, I GET HUNGRIER QUICKER.
YOU'RE THE ONE WHO DIDN'T WANT TO EAT 'COS YOU SAID IT'D DULL YOUR SENSE OF SMELL FOR FLESH!
PAT (SHOOP)
팍
HERE!
TAKE OUT ALL YOU WANT!

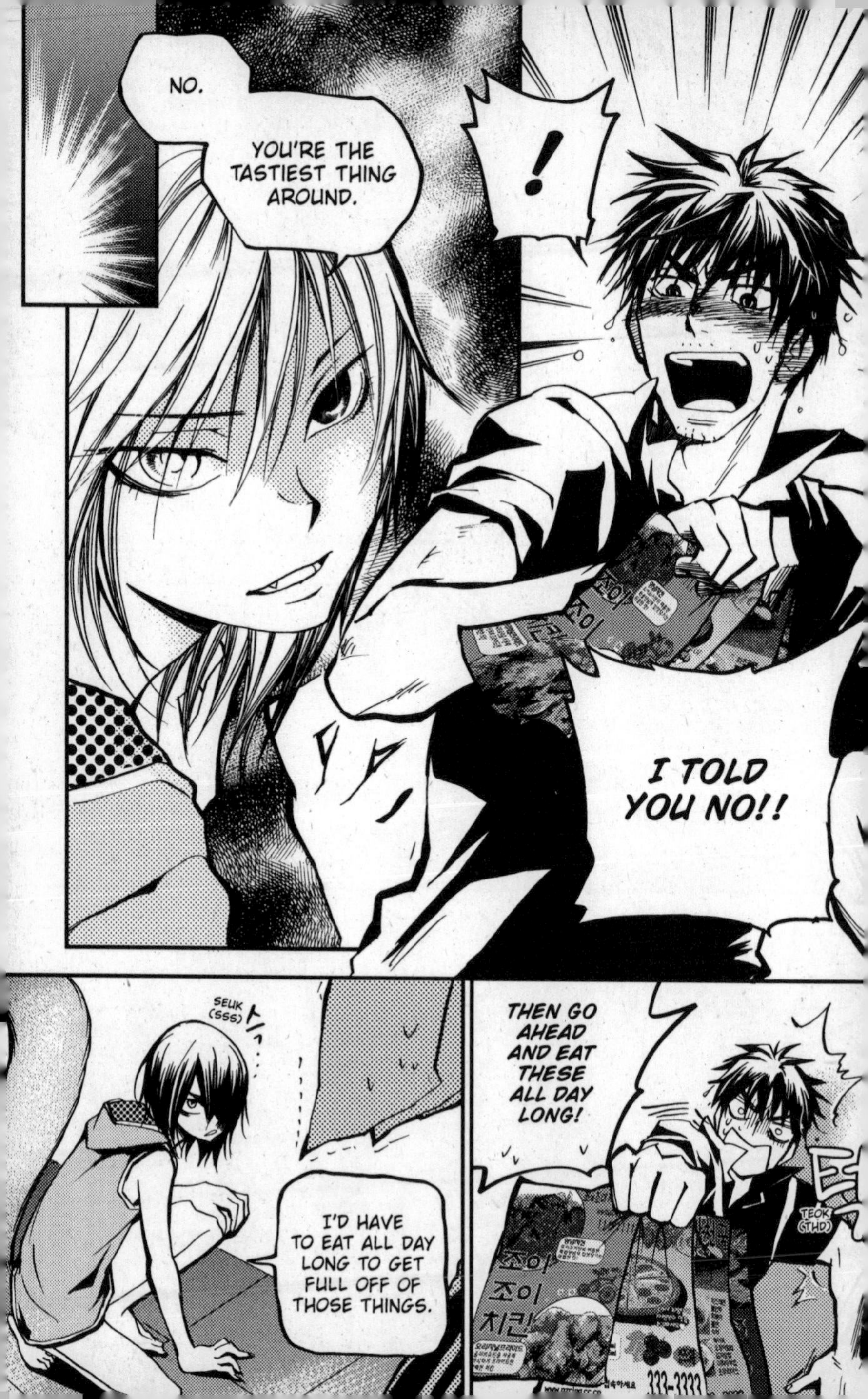
NO.
YOU'RE THE TASTIEST THING AROUND.
!
I TOLD YOU NO!!
SEUK (SSS)
I'D HAVE TO EAT ALL DAY LONG TO GET FULL OFF OF THOSE THINGS.
THEN GO AHEAD AND EAT THESE ALL DAY LONG!
TEOK (THD)
조이
조이
치킨
333-3333

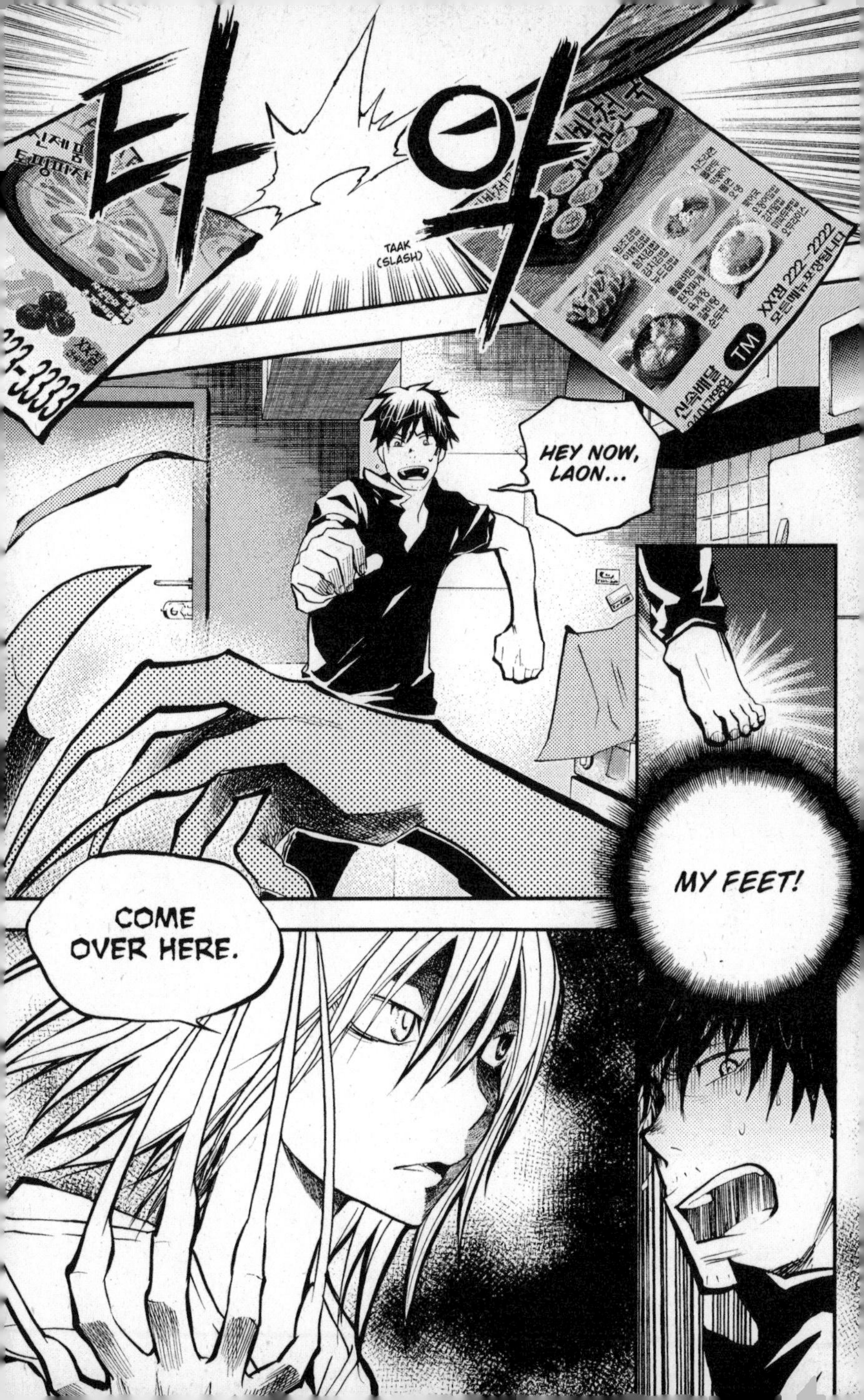

TAAK (SLASH)
HEY NOW, LAON...
MY FEET!
COME OVER HERE.

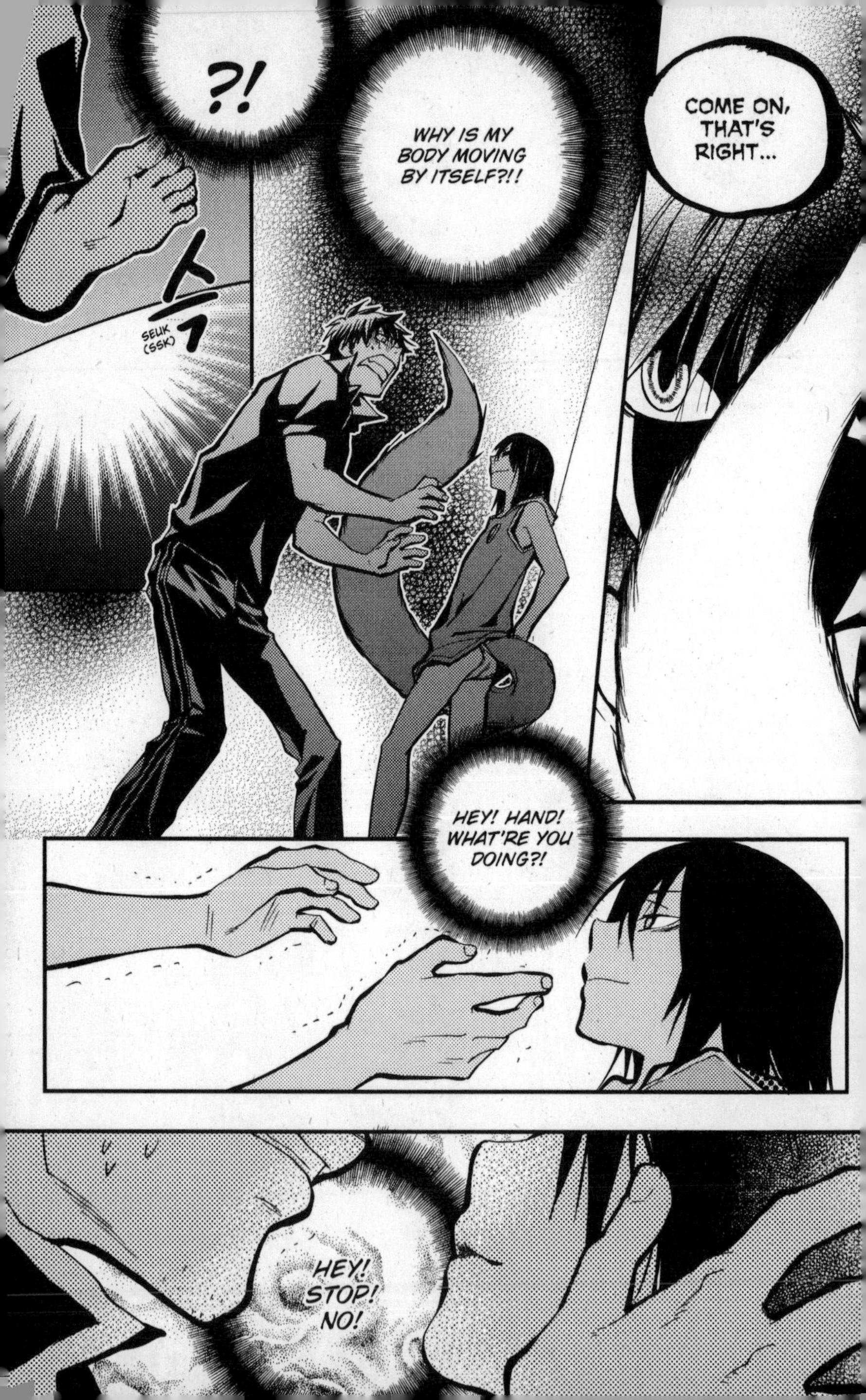
?!
WHY IS MY BODY MOVING BY ITSELF?!!
SEUK (SSK)
COME ON, THAT'S RIGHT...
HEY! HAND! WHAT'RE YOU DOING?!
HEY! STOP! NO!

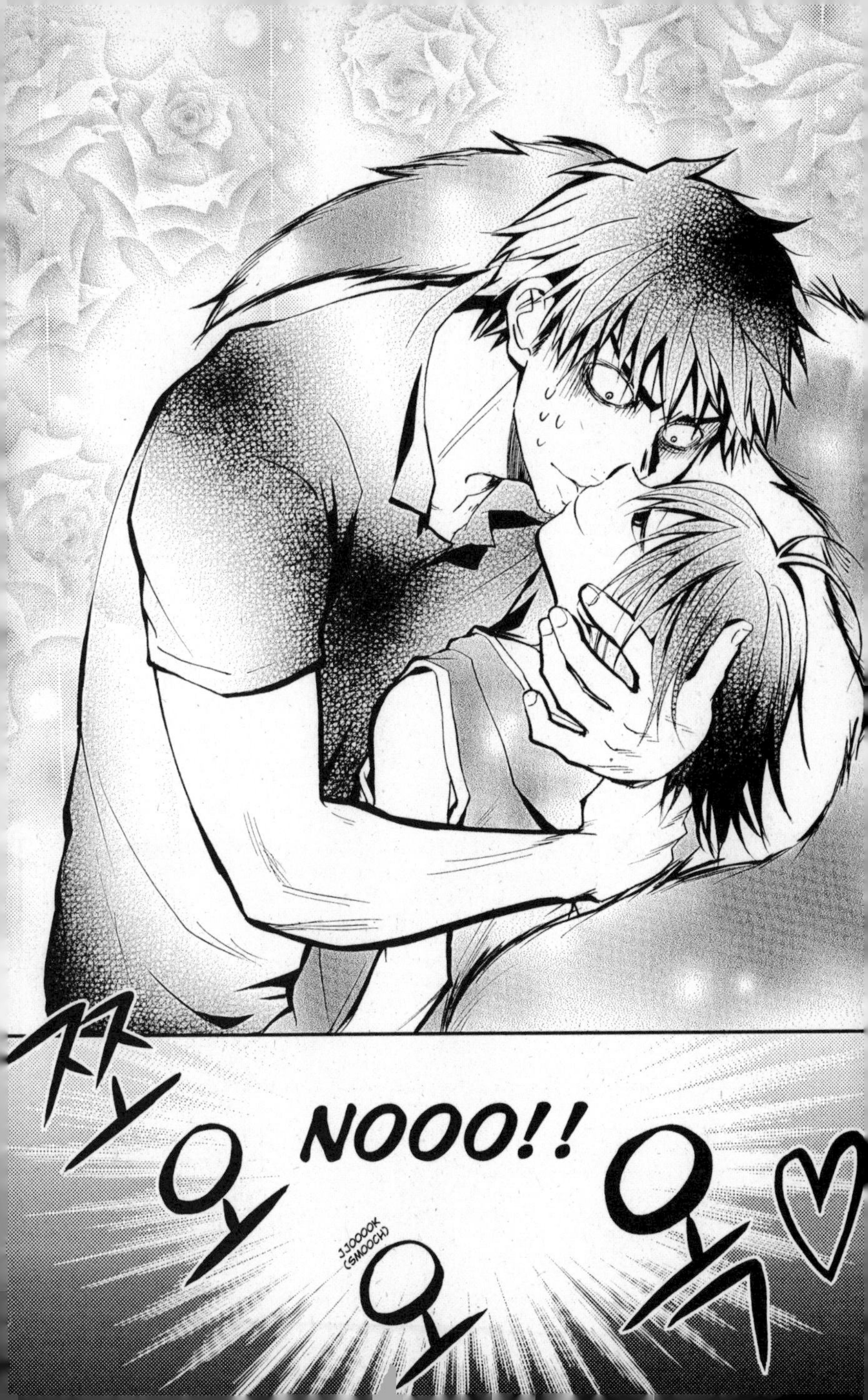
NOOO!!
JJOOOOK
(SMOOCH)

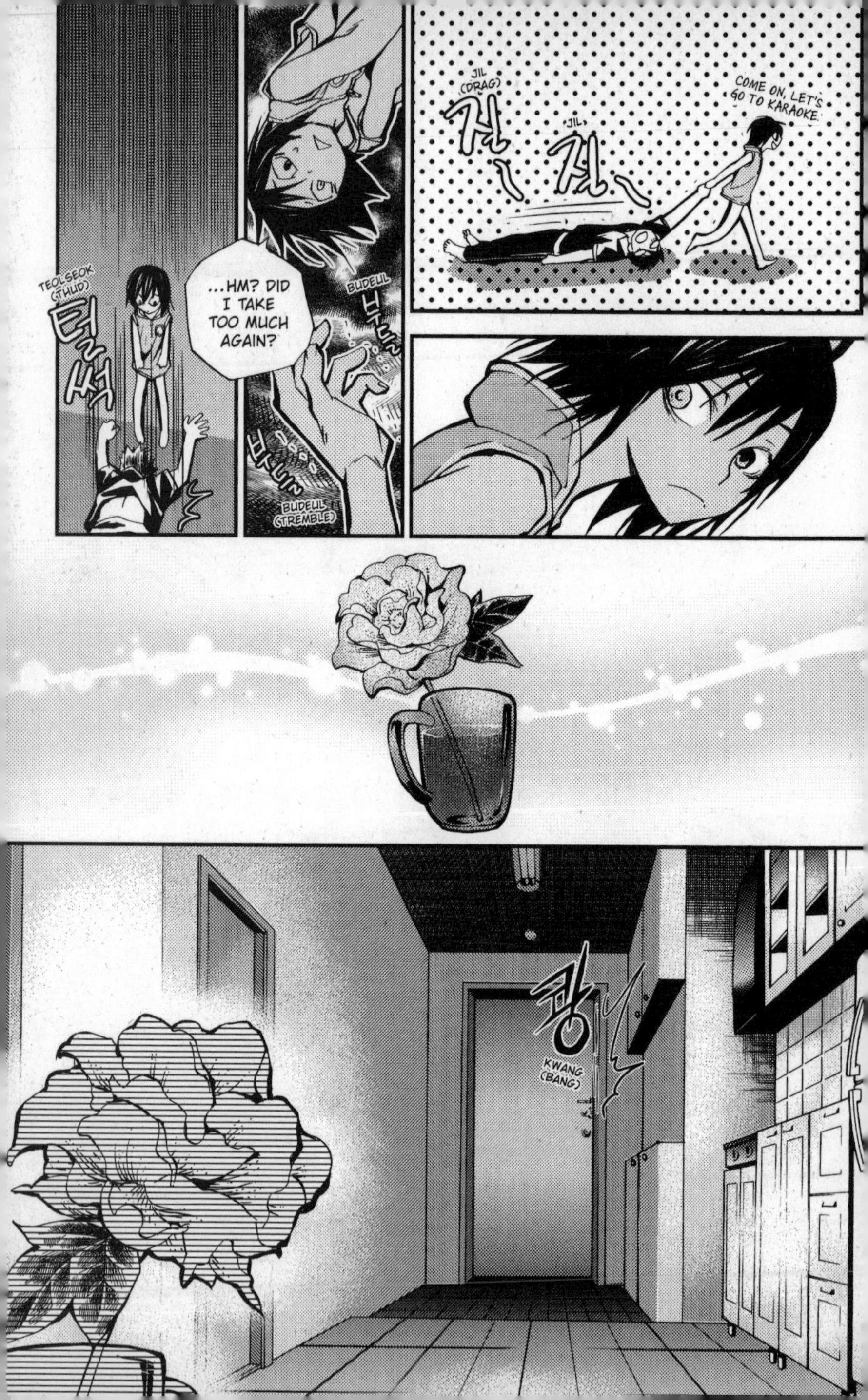
TEOLSEOK (THUD)
털썩
...HM? DID I TAKE TOO MUCH AGAIN?
BUDEUL
BUDEUL (TREMBLE)
JIL (DRAG)
JIL
COME ON, LET'S GO TO KARAOKE.
광
KWANG (BANG)

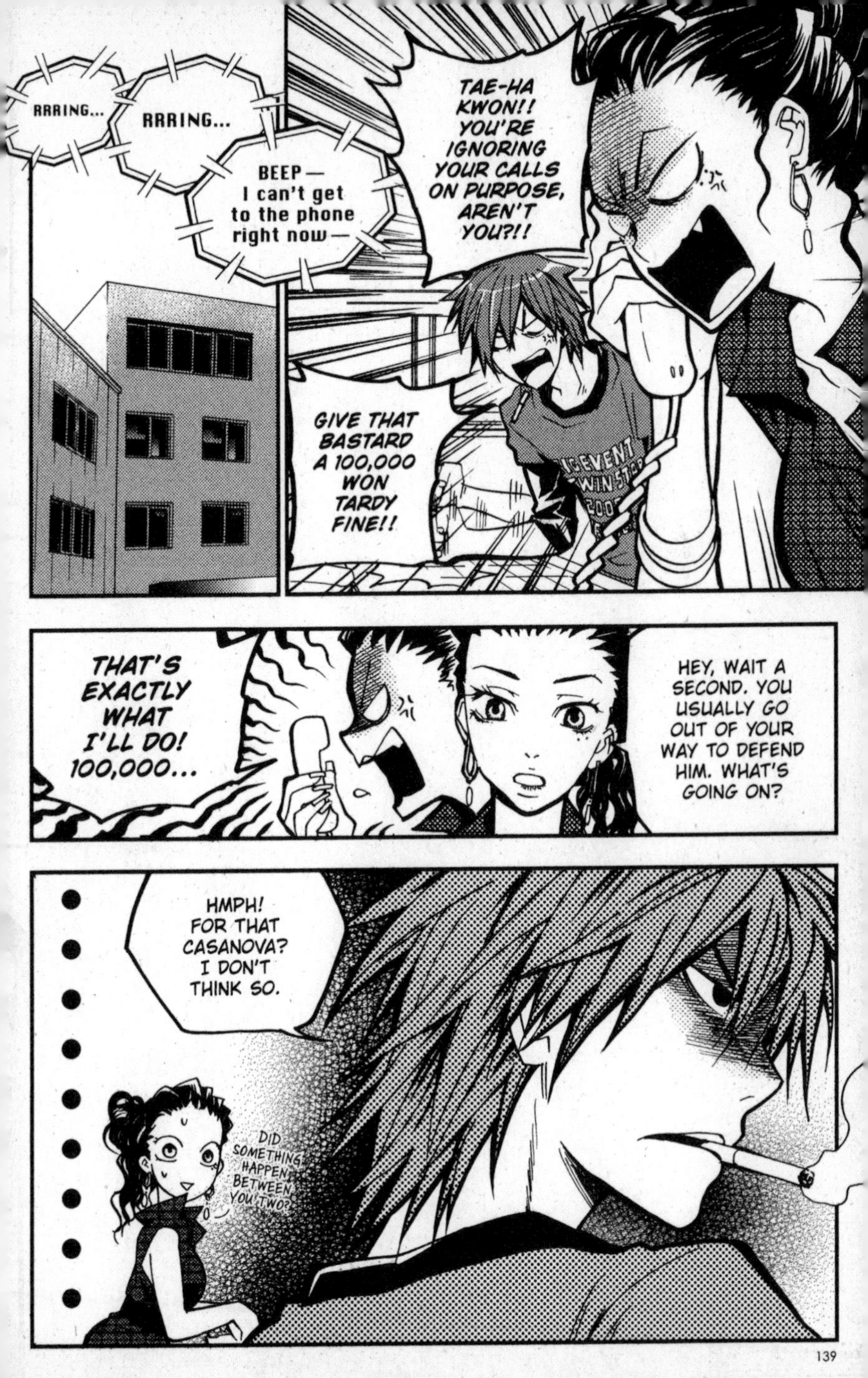
RRRING...
RRRING...
BEEP— I can't get to the phone right now—
TAE-HA KWON!! YOU'RE IGNORING YOUR CALLS ON PURPOSE, AREN'T YOU?!!
GIVE THAT BASTARD A 100,000 WON TARDY FINE!!
THAT'S EXACTLY WHAT I'LL DO! 100,000...
HEY, WAIT A SECOND. YOU USUALLY GO OUT OF YOUR WAY TO DEFEND HIM. WHAT'S GOING ON?
HMPH! FOR THAT CASANOVA? I DON'T THINK SO.
DID SOMETHING HAPPEN BETWEEN YOU TWO?

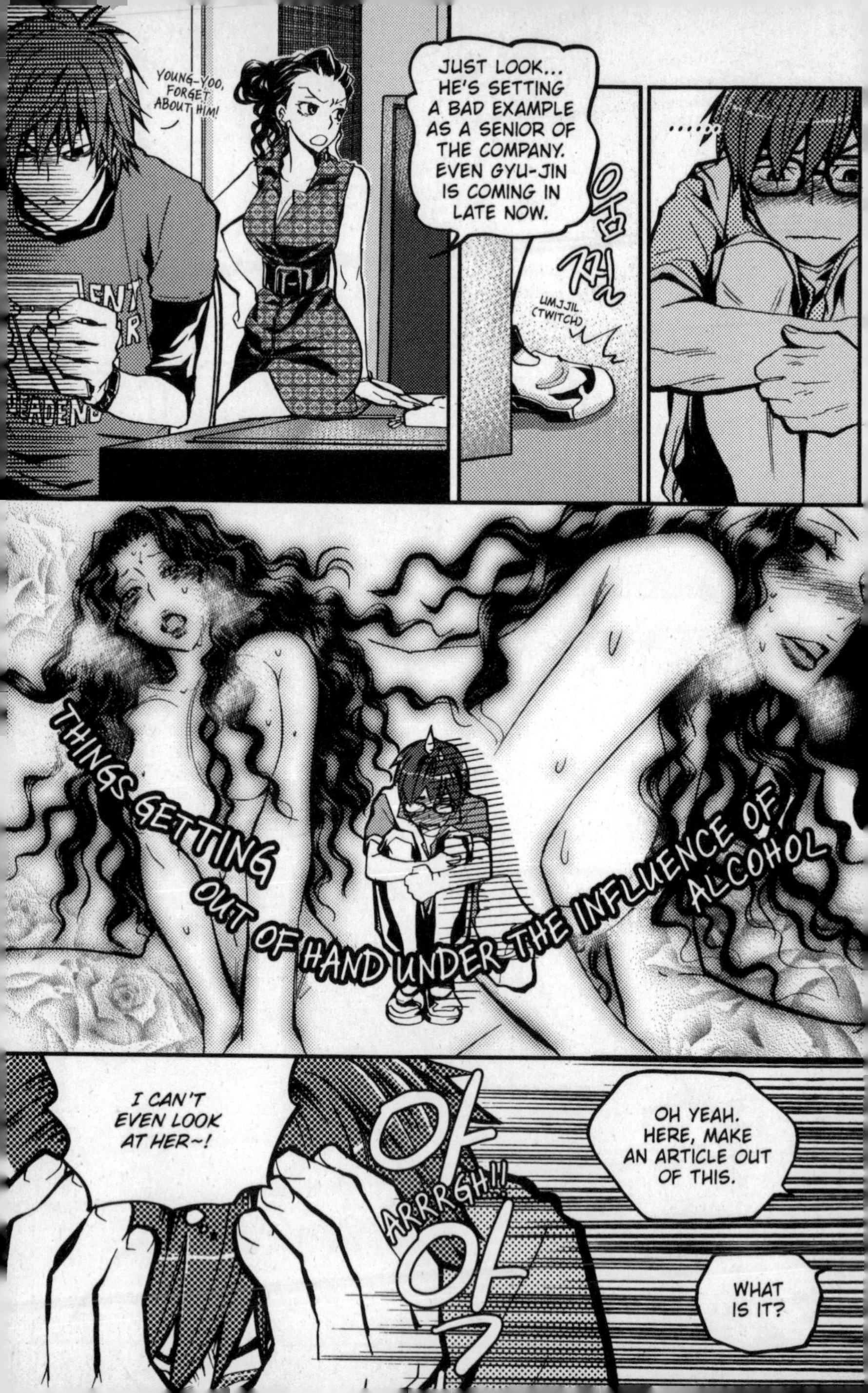
YOUNG-YOO, FORGET ABOUT HIM!
JUST LOOK... HE'S SETTING A BAD EXAMPLE AS A SENIOR OF THE COMPANY. EVEN GYU-JIN IS COMING IN LATE NOW.
움찔
UMJJIL (TWITCH)
......?
THINGS GETTING OUT OF HAND UNDER THE INFLUENCE OF ALCOHOL
I CAN'T EVEN LOOK AT HER~!
ARRRGH!!
OH YEAH. HERE, MAKE AN ARTICLE OUT OF THIS.
WHAT IS IT?

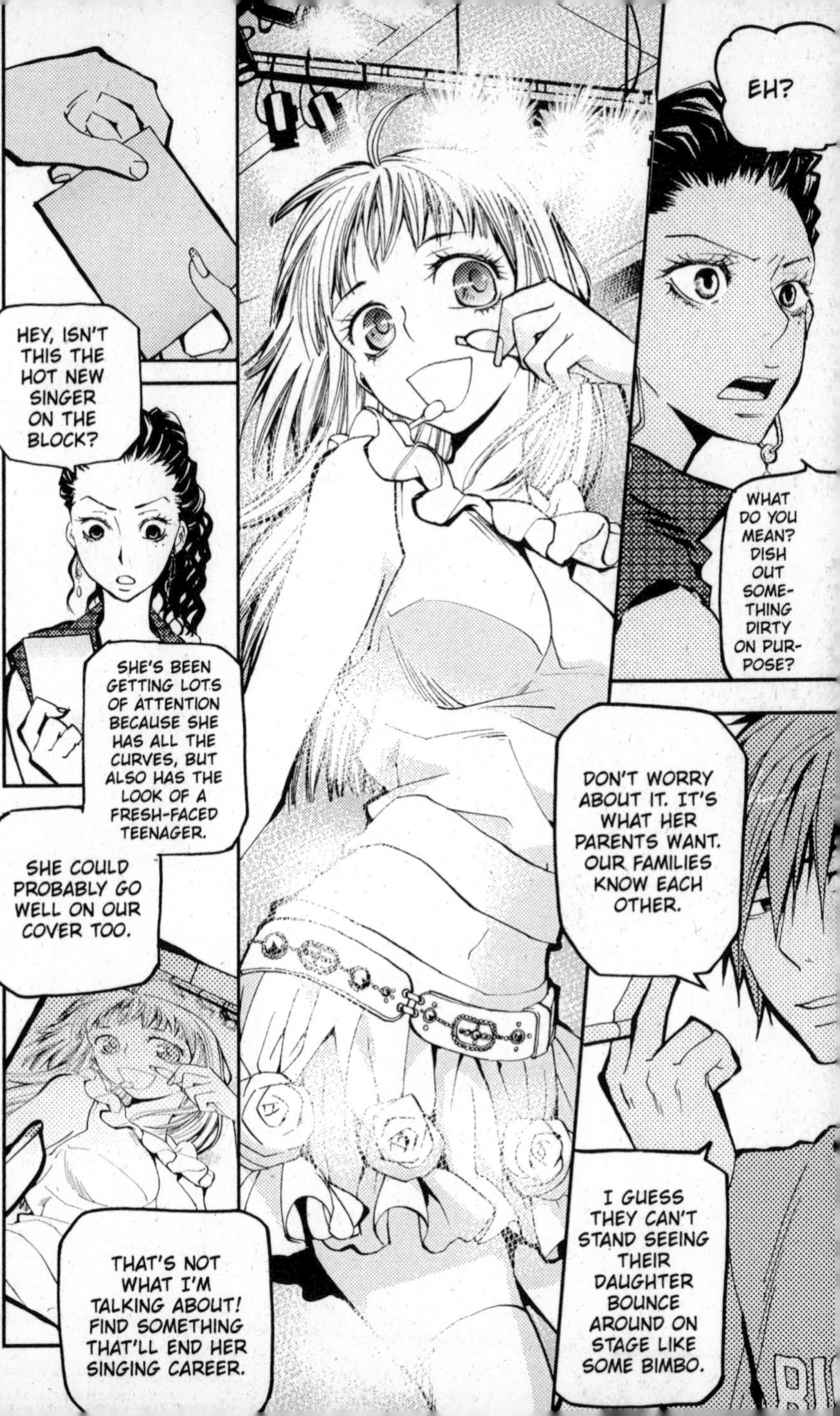
HEY, ISN'T THIS THE HOT NEW SINGER ON THE BLOCK?
SHE'S BEEN GETTING LOTS OF ATTENTION BECAUSE SHE HAS ALL THE CURVES, BUT ALSO HAS THE LOOK OF A FRESH-FACED TEENAGER.
SHE COULD PROBABLY GO WELL ON OUR COVER TOO.
THAT'S NOT WHAT I'M TALKING ABOUT! FIND SOMETHING THAT'LL END HER SINGING CAREER.
EH?
WHAT DO YOU MEAN? DISH OUT SOME-THING DIRTY ON PUR-POSE?
DON'T WORRY ABOUT IT. IT'S WHAT HER PARENTS WANT. OUR FAMILIES KNOW EACH OTHER.
I GUESS THEY CAN'T STAND SEEING THEIR DAUGHTER BOUNCE AROUND ON STAGE LIKE SOME BIMBO.

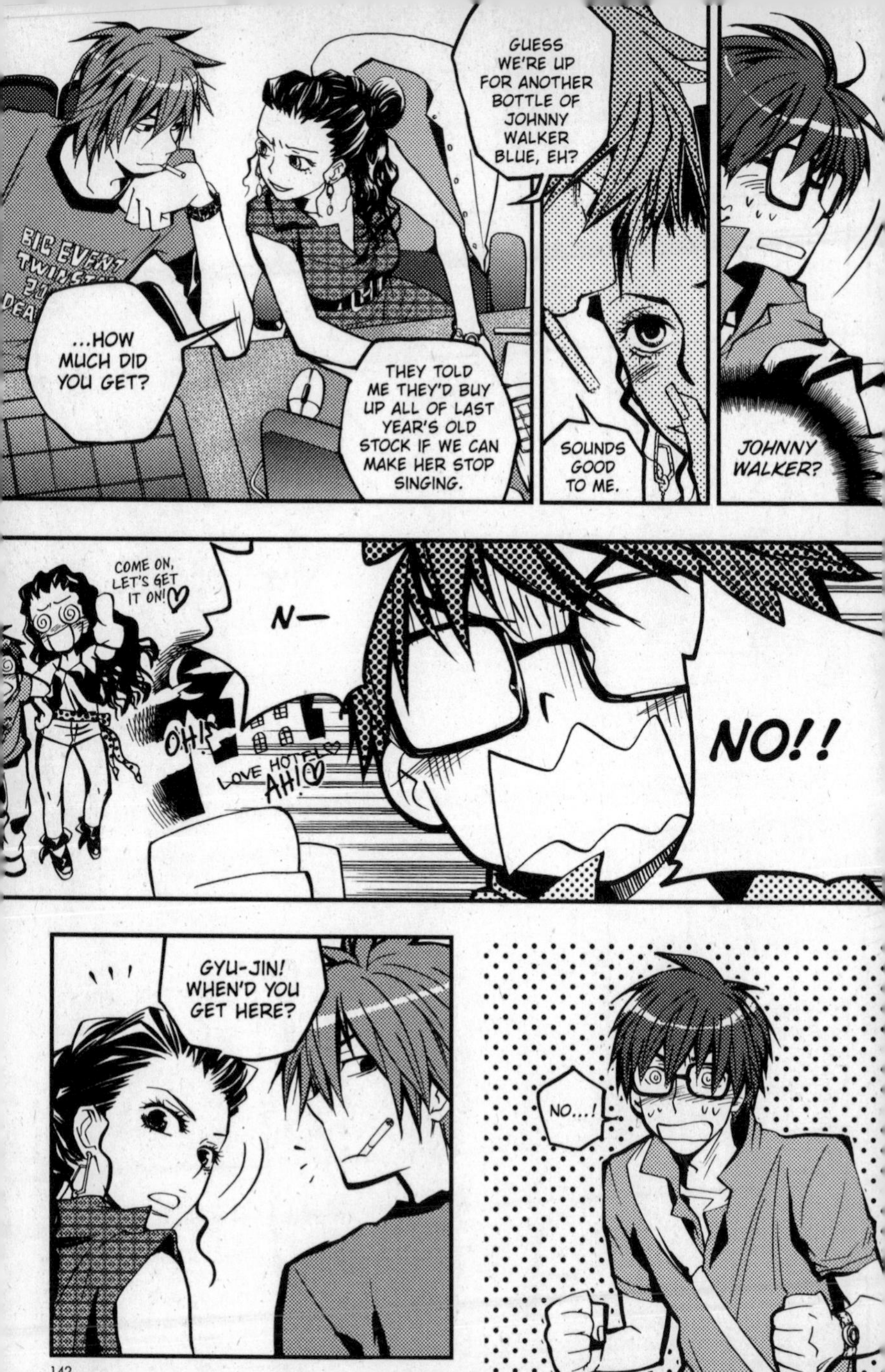

...HOW MUCH DID YOU GET?
THEY TOLD ME THEY'D BUY UP ALL OF LAST YEAR'S OLD STOCK IF WE CAN MAKE HER STOP SINGING.
GUESS WE'RE UP FOR ANOTHER BOTTLE OF JOHNNY WALKER BLUE, EH?
SOUNDS GOOD TO ME.
JOHNNY WALKER?
COME ON, LET'S GET IT ON!♡
OH!
LOVE HOTEL♡
AH!♡
N—
NO!!
GYU-JIN! WHEN'D YOU GET HERE?
NO...!

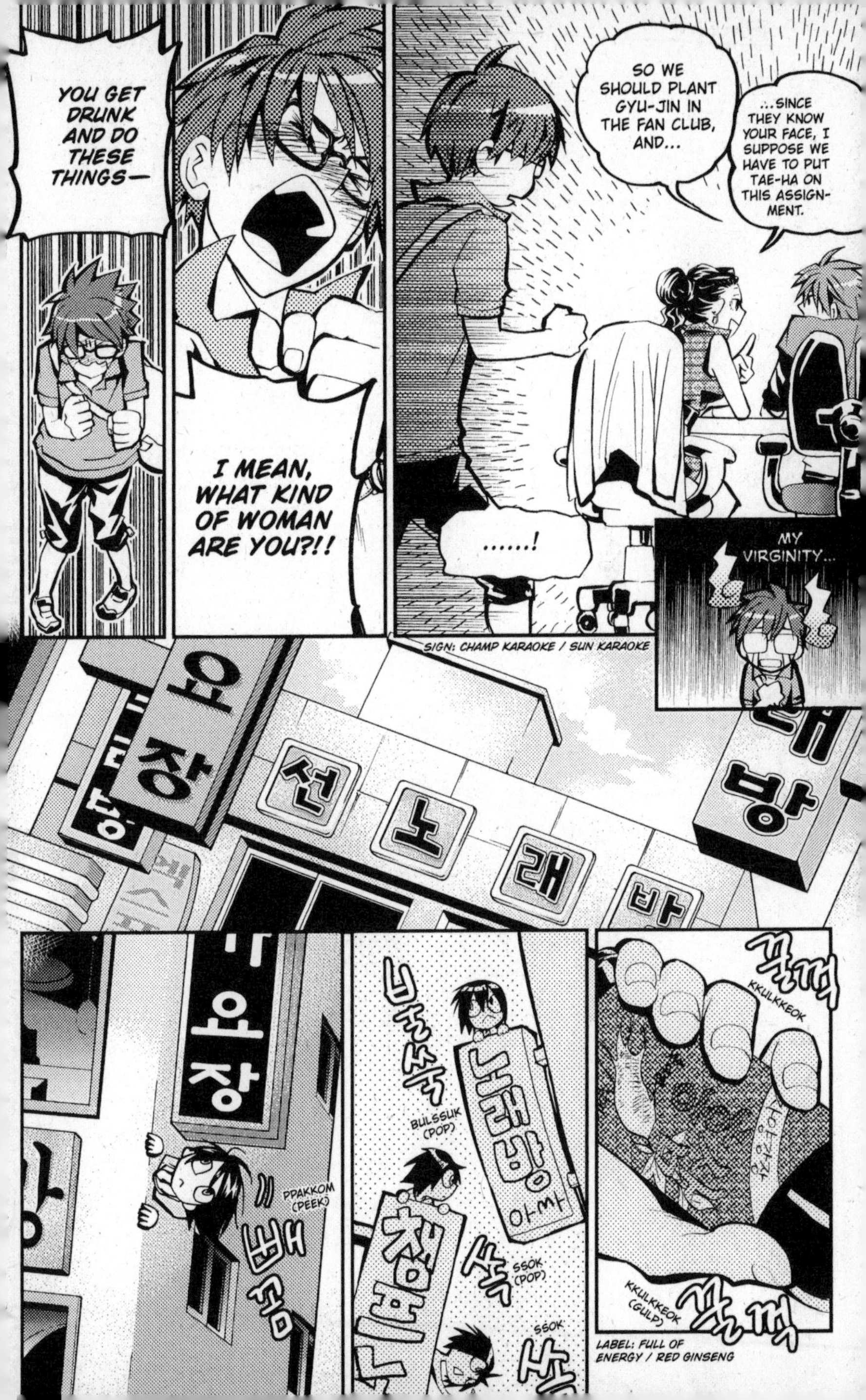
YOU GET DRUNK AND DO THESE THINGS—
I MEAN, WHAT KIND OF WOMAN ARE YOU?!!
SO WE SHOULD PLANT GYU-JIN IN THE FAN CLUB, AND...
...SINCE THEY KNOW YOUR FACE, I SUPPOSE WE HAVE TO PUT TAE-HA ON THIS ASSIGN-MENT.
......!
MY VIRGINITY...
SIGN: CHAMP KARAOKE / SUN KARAOKE
PPAKKOM (PEEK)
BULSSUK (POP)
SSOK (POP)
SSOK
KKULKKEOK
KKULKKEOK (GULP)
LABEL: FULL OF ENERGY / RED GINSENG

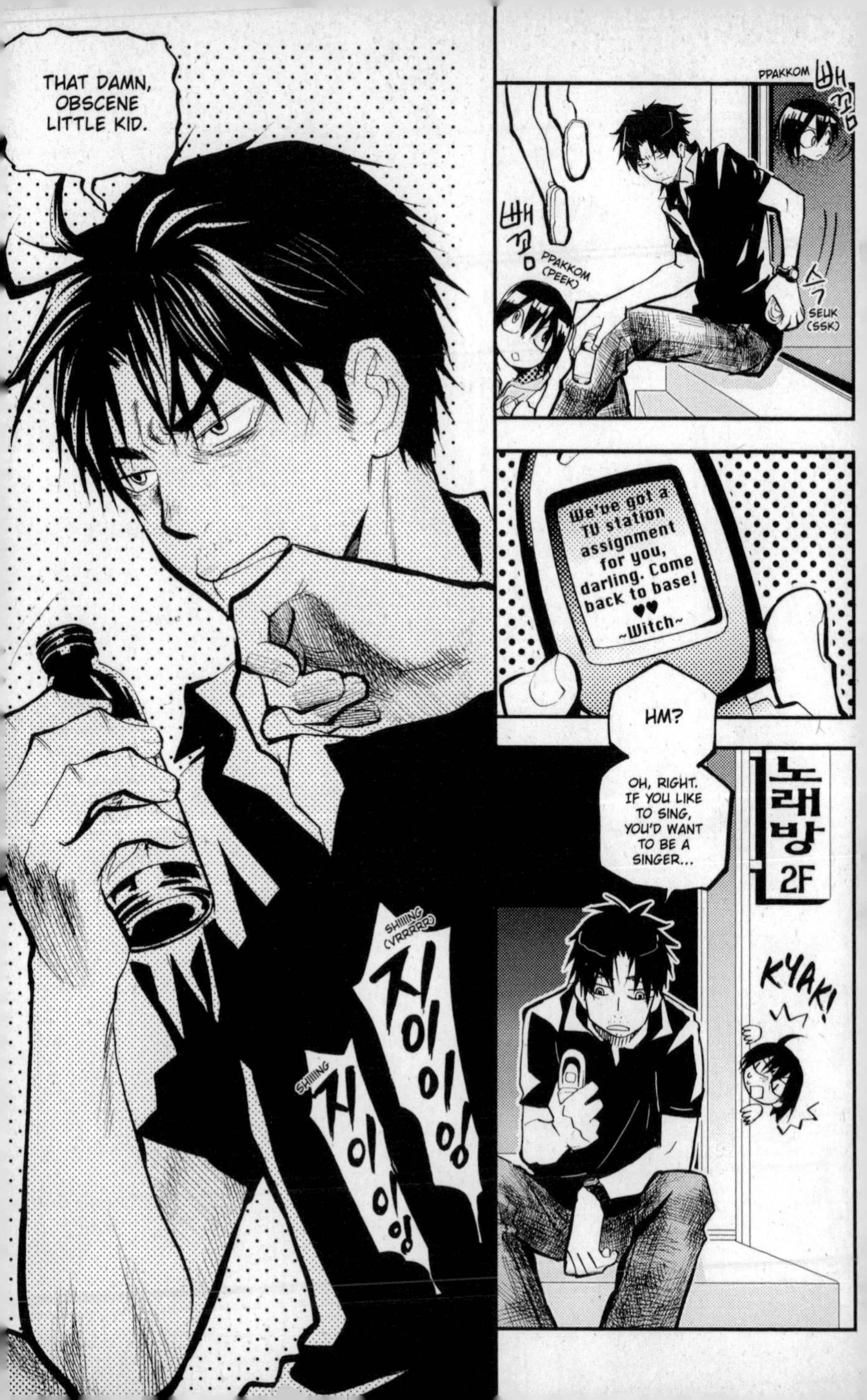
THAT DAMN, OBSCENE LITTLE KID.
SHIIIING (VRRRRR)
지이이잉!
SHIIIING
지이잉
PPAKKOM
빼꼼
빼꼼
PPAKKOM (PEEK)
슥
SEUK (SSK)
We've got a TV station assignment for you, darling. Come back to base! ♥♥ ~Witch~
HM?
OH, RIGHT. IF YOU LIKE TO SING, YOU'D WANT TO BE A SINGER...
노래방
2F
KYAK!

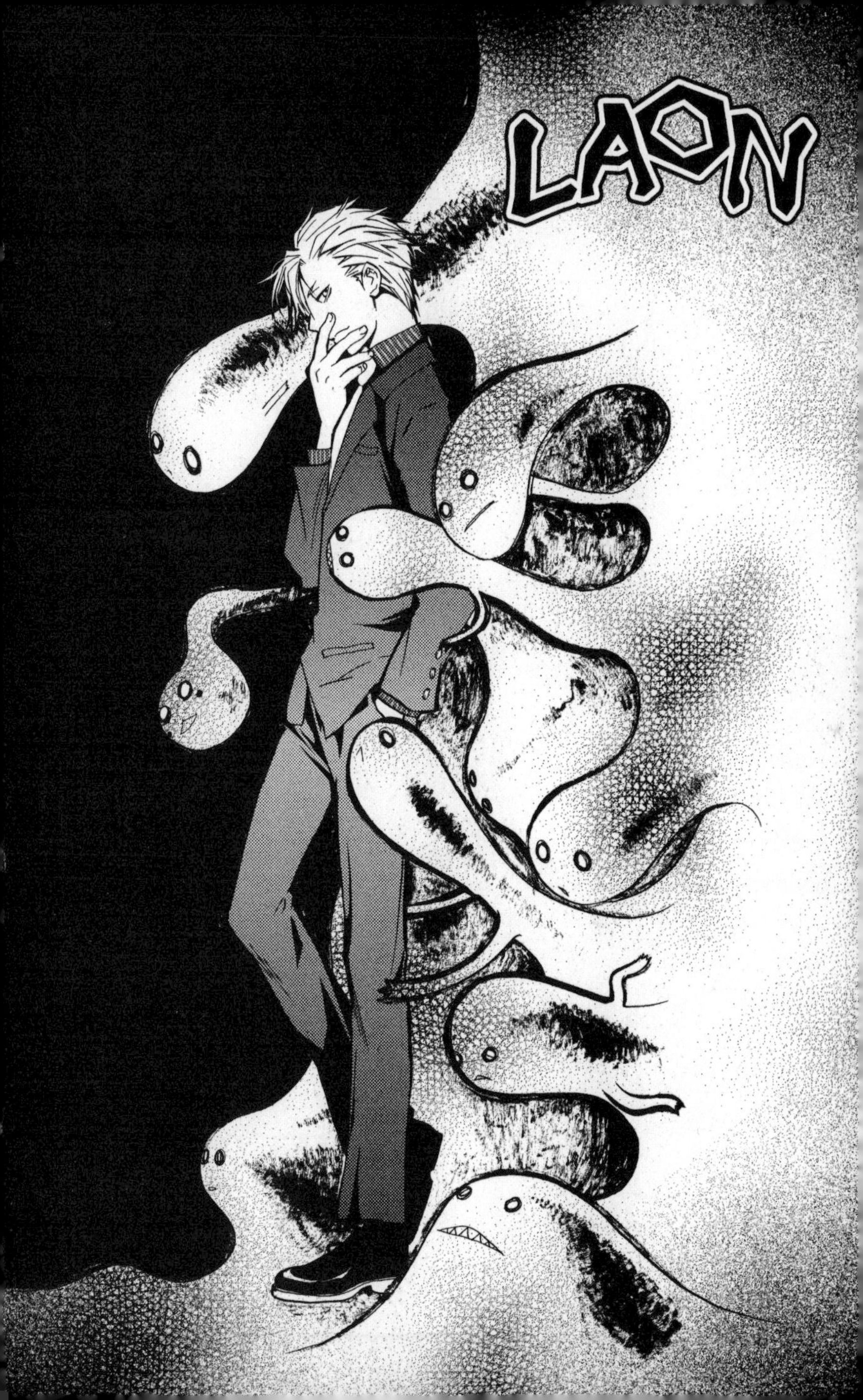
LAON

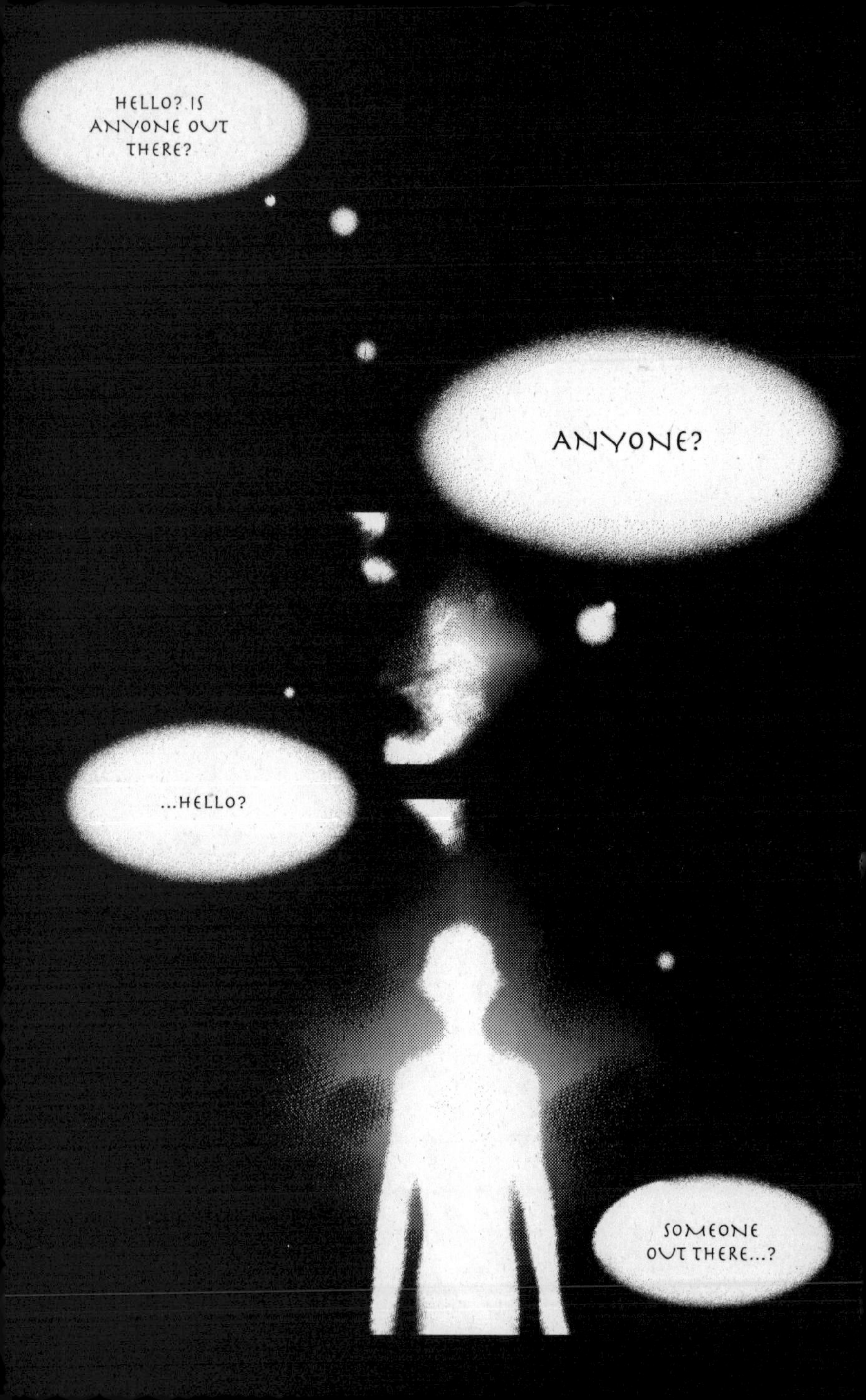
HELLO? IS ANYONE OUT THERE?
ANYONE?
...HELLO?
SOMEONE OUT THERE...?

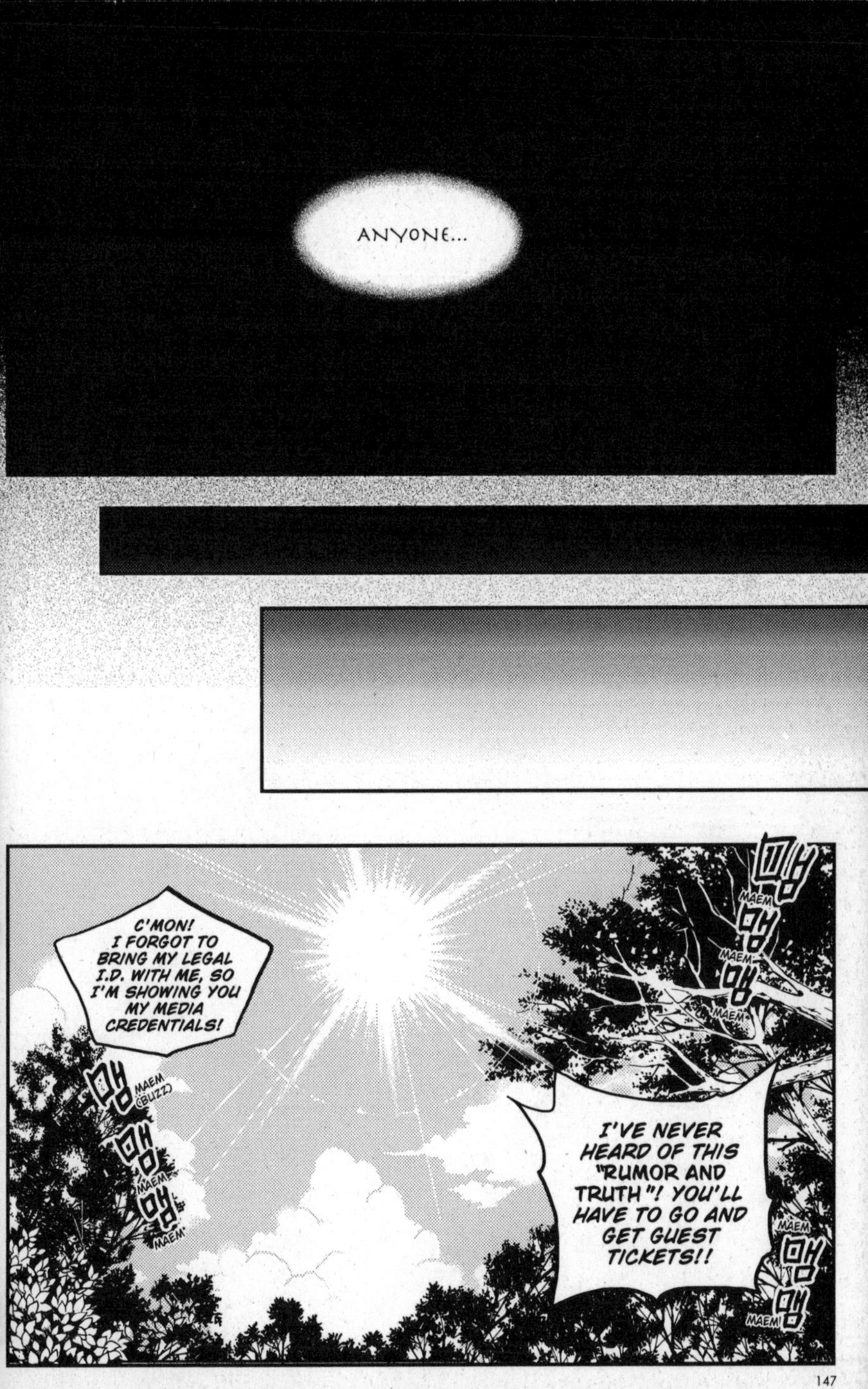
ANYONE...
C'MON! I FORGOT TO BRING MY LEGAL I.D. WITH ME, SO I'M SHOWING YOU MY MEDIA CREDENTIALS!
MAEM
MAEM
MAEM
MAEM (BUZZ)
MAEM
MAEM
I'VE NEVER HEARD OF THIS "RUMOR AND TRUTH"! YOU'LL HAVE TO GO AND GET GUEST TICKETS!!
MAEM
MAEM

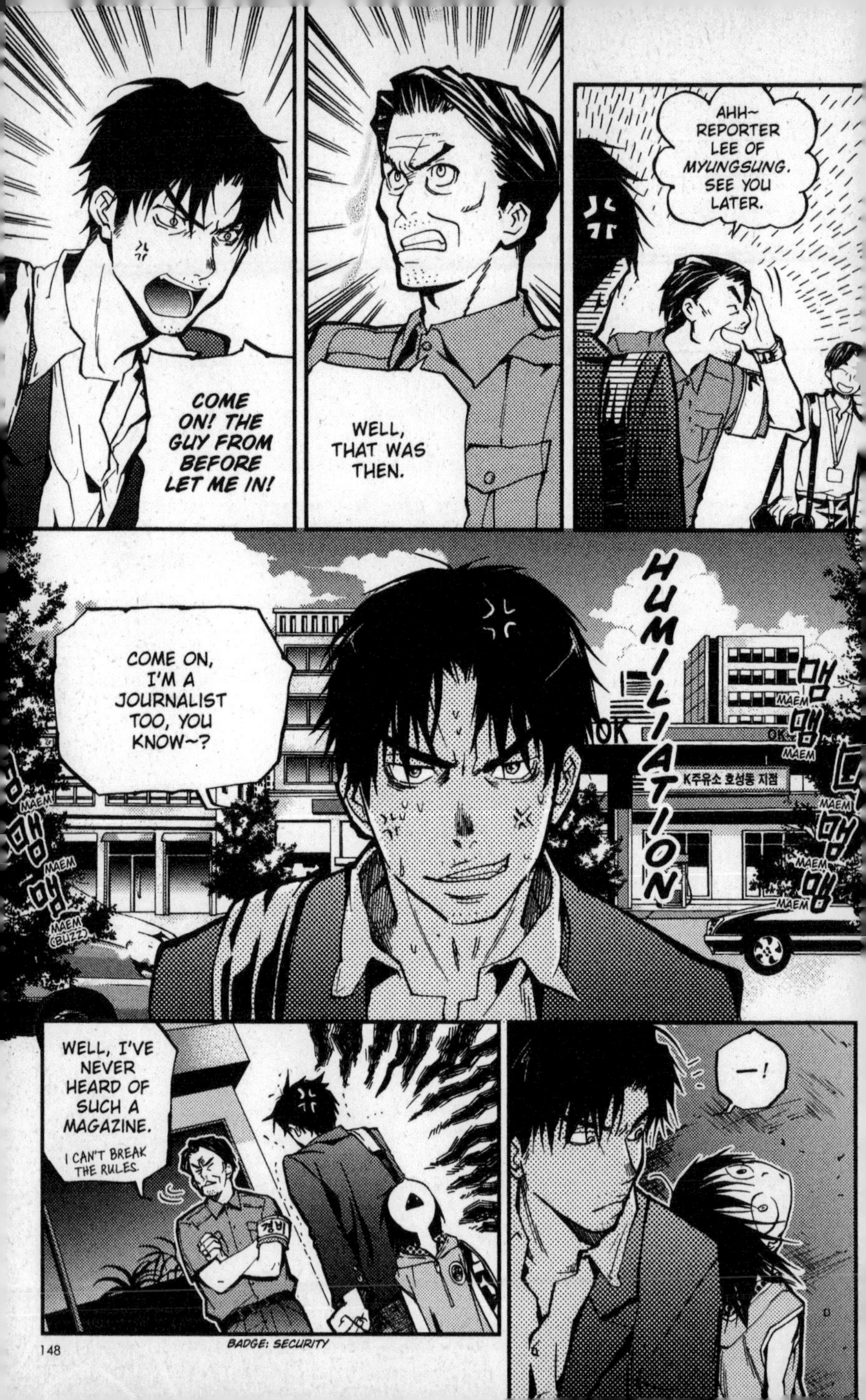

COME ON! THE GUY FROM BEFORE LET ME IN!
WELL, THAT WAS THEN.
AHH~ REPORTER LEE OF MYUNGSUNG. SEE YOU LATER.
COME ON, I'M A JOURNALIST TOO, YOU KNOW~?
맴 MAEM
맴 MAEM
(BUZZ)
HUMILIATION
OK
K주유소 호성동 지점
맴 MAEM
맴 MAEM
맴 MAEM
맴 MAEM
맴 MAEM
WELL, I'VE NEVER HEARD OF SUCH A MAGAZINE.
I CAN'T BREAK THE RULES.
경비
—!

BADGE: SECURITY

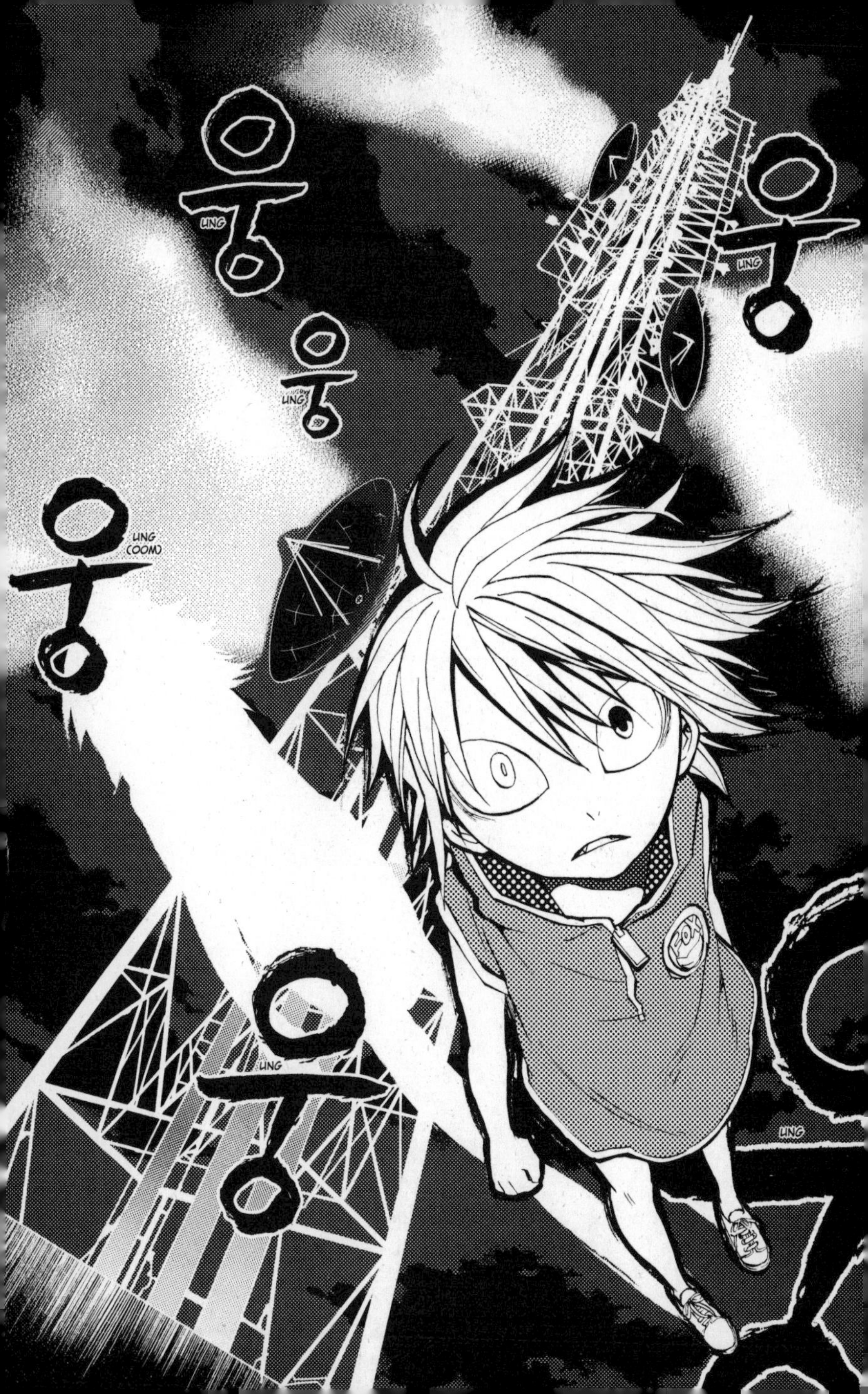

웅
UNG
웅
UNG
웅
UNG
웅
UNG (OOM)
웅
UNG
UNG

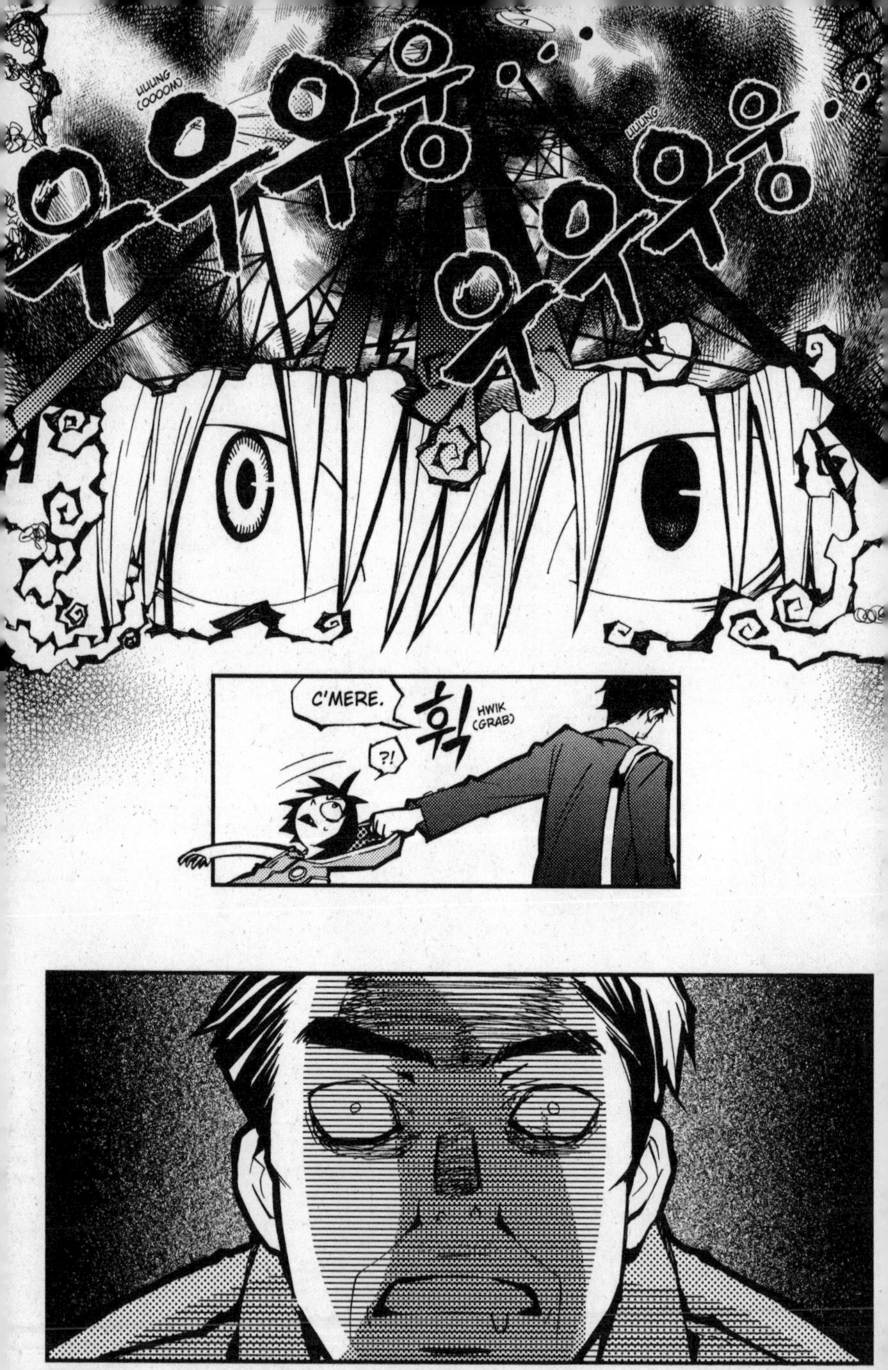
UUUNG (OOOOM)
UUUNG
C'MERE.
휙
HWIK (GRAB)
?!

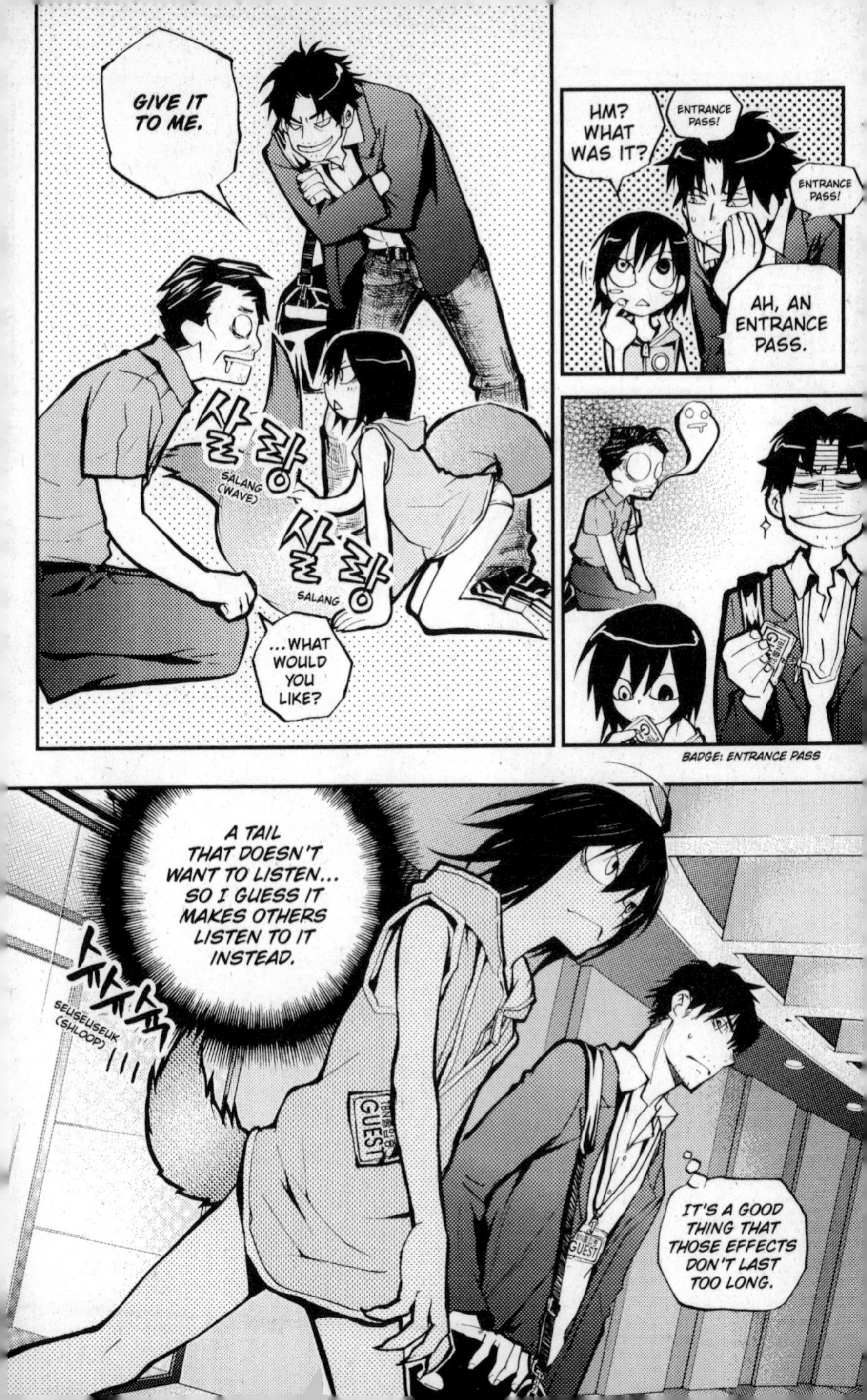

GIVE IT TO ME.
살랑
SALANG (WAVE)
살랑
SALANG
...WHAT WOULD YOU LIKE?
HM? WHAT WAS IT?
ENTRANCE PASS!
ENTRANCE PASS!
AH, AN ENTRANCE PASS.
GUEST
BADGE: ENTRANCE PASS
A TAIL THAT DOESN'T WANT TO LISTEN... SO I GUESS IT MAKES OTHERS LISTEN TO IT INSTEAD.
스스슥
SEUSEUSEUK (SHLOOP)
GUEST
GUEST
IT'S A GOOD THING THAT THOSE EFFECTS DON'T LAST TOO LONG.

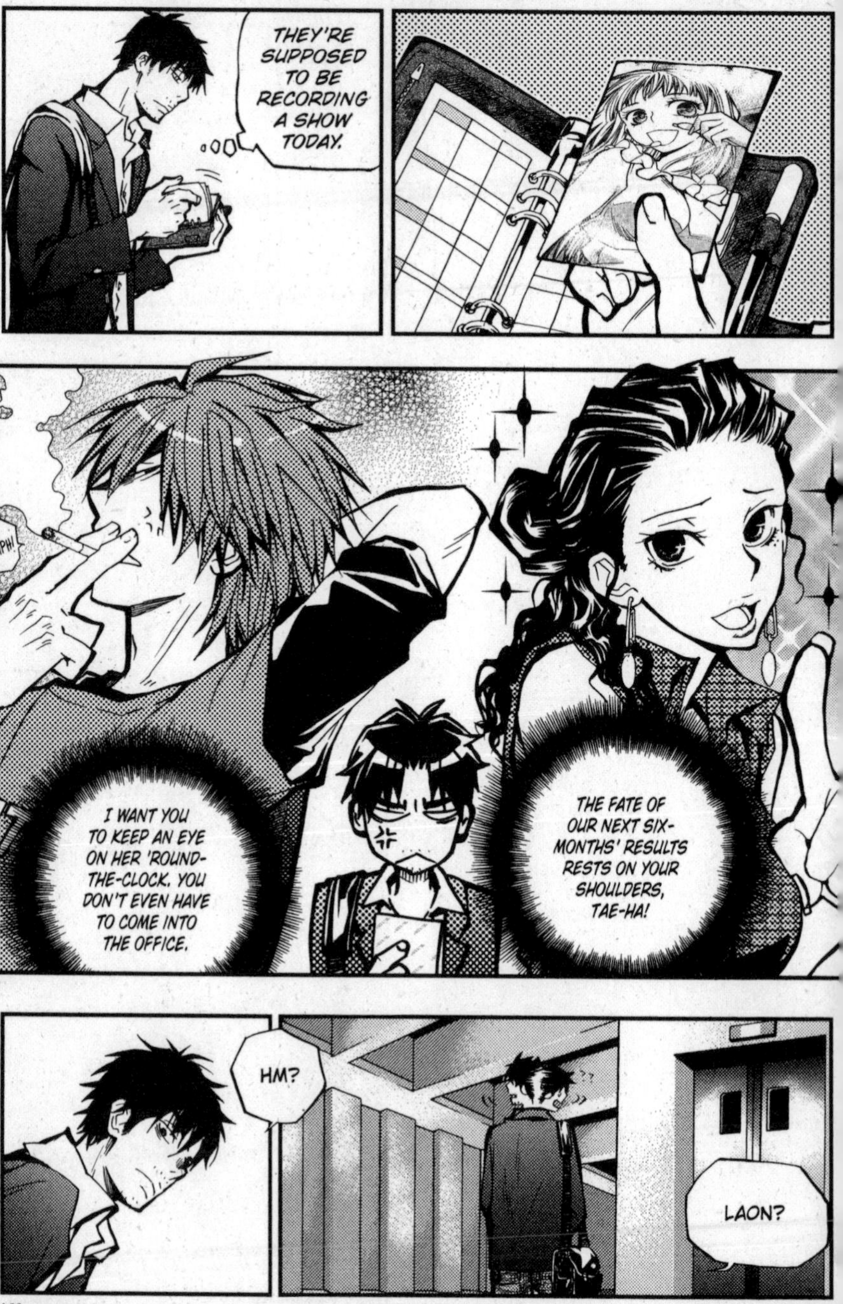
THEY'RE SUPPOSED TO BE RECORDING A SHOW TODAY.
HMPH!
I WANT YOU TO KEEP AN EYE ON HER 'ROUND-THE-CLOCK. YOU DON'T EVEN HAVE TO COME INTO THE OFFICE.
THE FATE OF OUR NEXT SIX-MONTHS' RESULTS RESTS ON YOUR SHOULDERS, TAE-HA!
HM?
LAON?

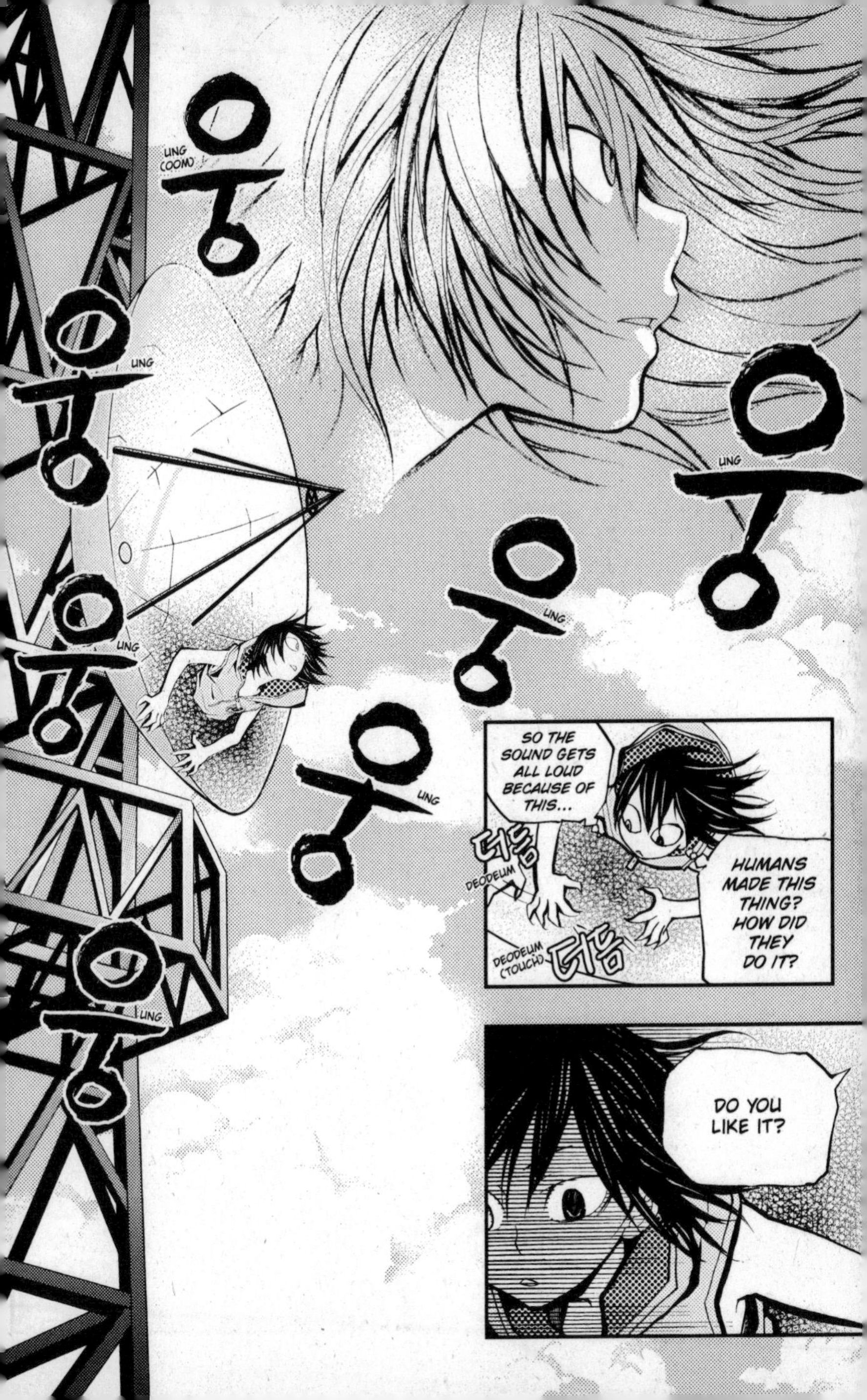
웅
UNG (OOM)
웅
UNG
웅
UNG
웅
UNG
웅
UNG
웅
UNG
웅
UNG
SO THE SOUND GETS ALL LOUD BECAUSE OF THIS...
더듬
DEODEUM
더듬
DEODEUM (TOUCH)
HUMANS MADE THIS THING? HOW DID THEY DO IT?
DO YOU LIKE IT?

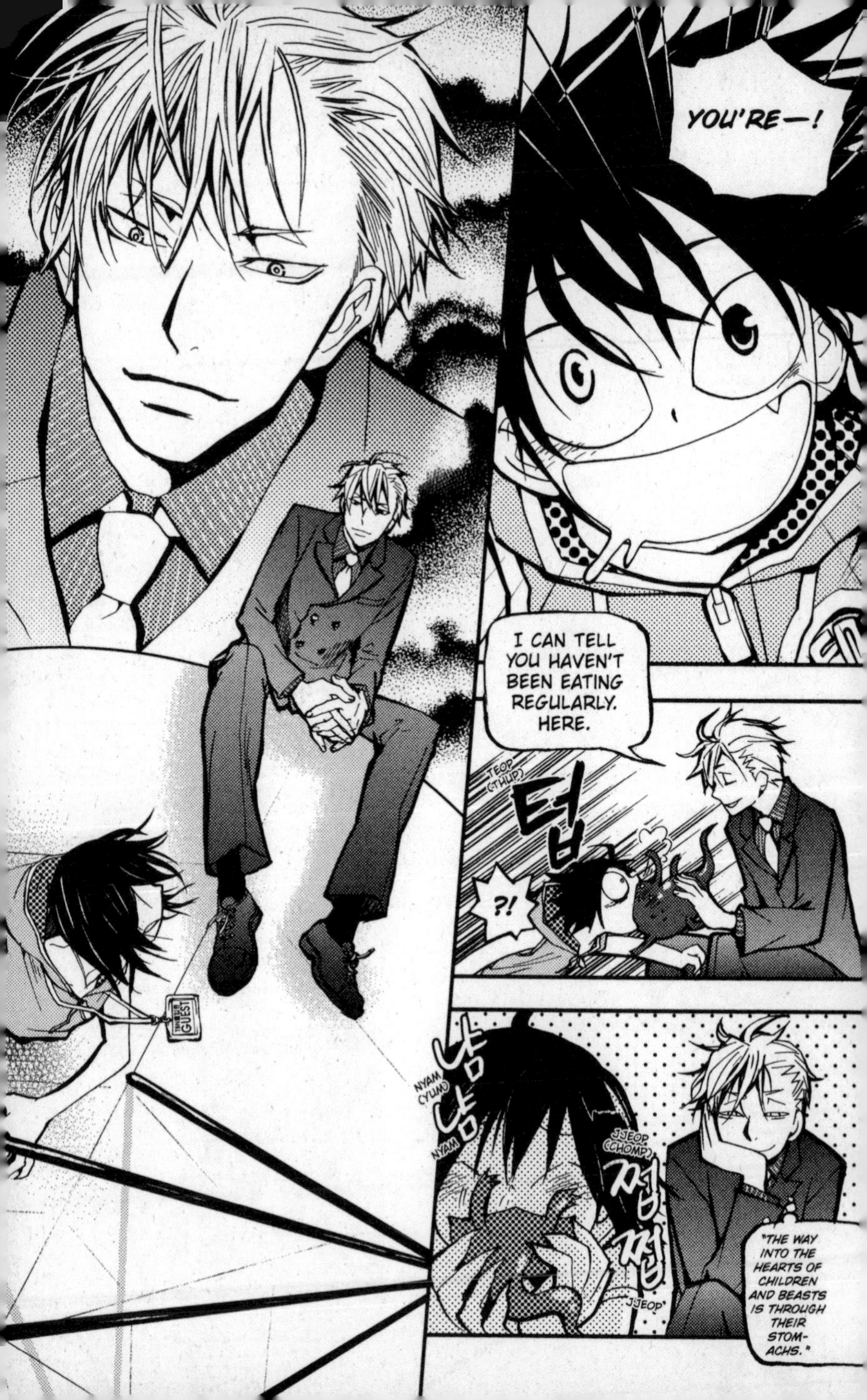
GUEST
YOU'RE—!
I CAN TELL YOU HAVEN'T BEEN EATING REGULARLY. HERE.
TEOP (THUP)
텁
?!
NYAM (YUM)
냠
냠
NYAM
JJEOP (CHOMP)
쩝
쩝
JJEOP
"THE WAY INTO THE HEARTS OF CHILDREN AND BEASTS IS THROUGH THEIR STOM-ACHS."

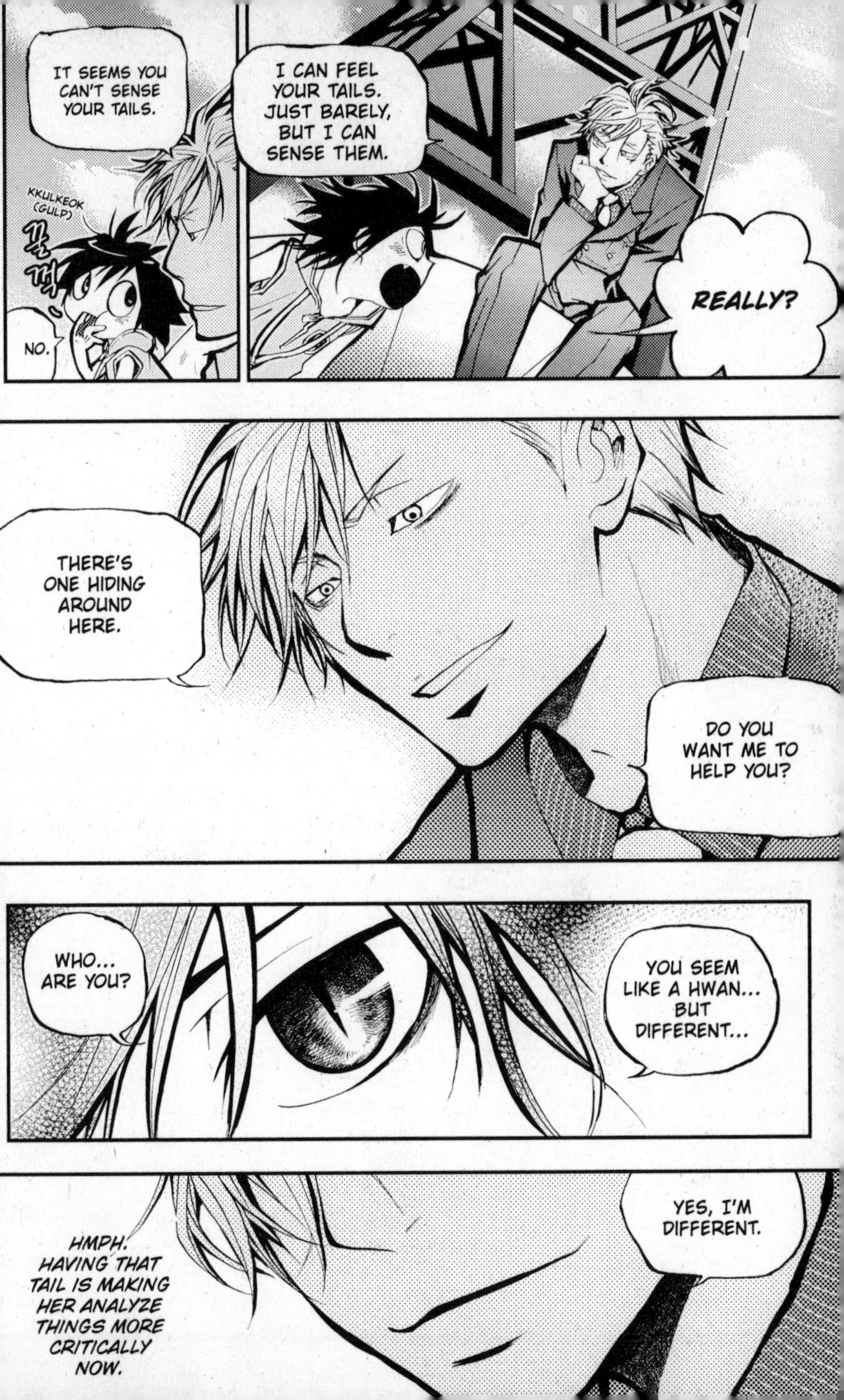
IT SEEMS YOU CAN'T SENSE YOUR TAILS.
KKULKEOK (GULP)
NO.
I CAN FEEL YOUR TAILS. JUST BARELY, BUT I CAN SENSE THEM.
REALLY?
THERE'S ONE HIDING AROUND HERE.
DO YOU WANT ME TO HELP YOU?
WHO... ARE YOU?
YOU SEEM LIKE A HWAN... BUT DIFFERENT...
HMPH. HAVING THAT TAIL IS MAKING HER ANALYZE THINGS MORE CRITICALLY NOW.
YES, I'M DIFFERENT.

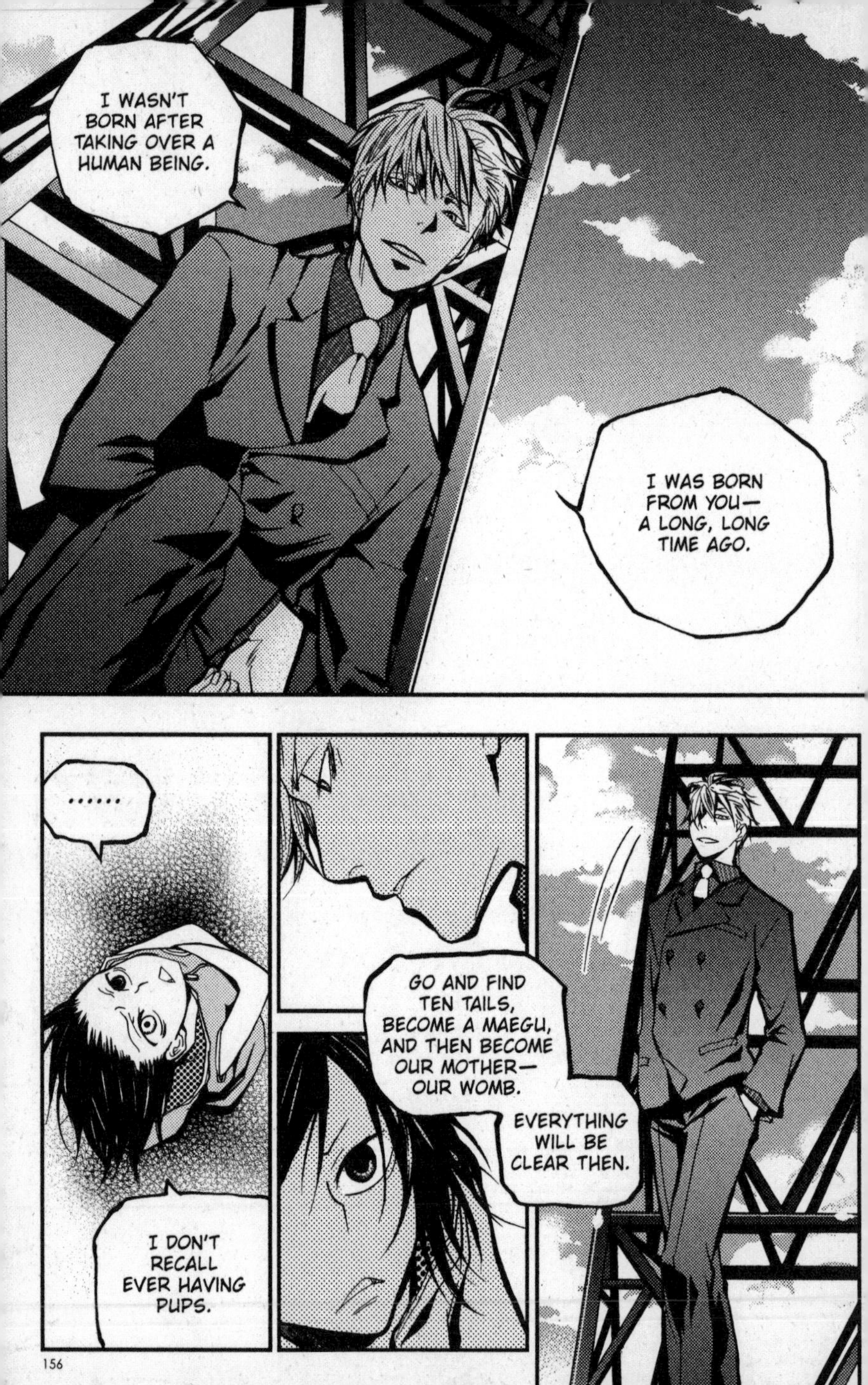
I WASN'T BORN AFTER TAKING OVER A HUMAN BEING.
I WAS BORN FROM YOU— A LONG, LONG TIME AGO.
....
I DON'T RECALL EVER HAVING PUPS.
GO AND FIND TEN TAILS, BECOME A MAEGU, AND THEN BECOME OUR MOTHER— OUR WOMB.
EVERYTHING WILL BE CLEAR THEN.

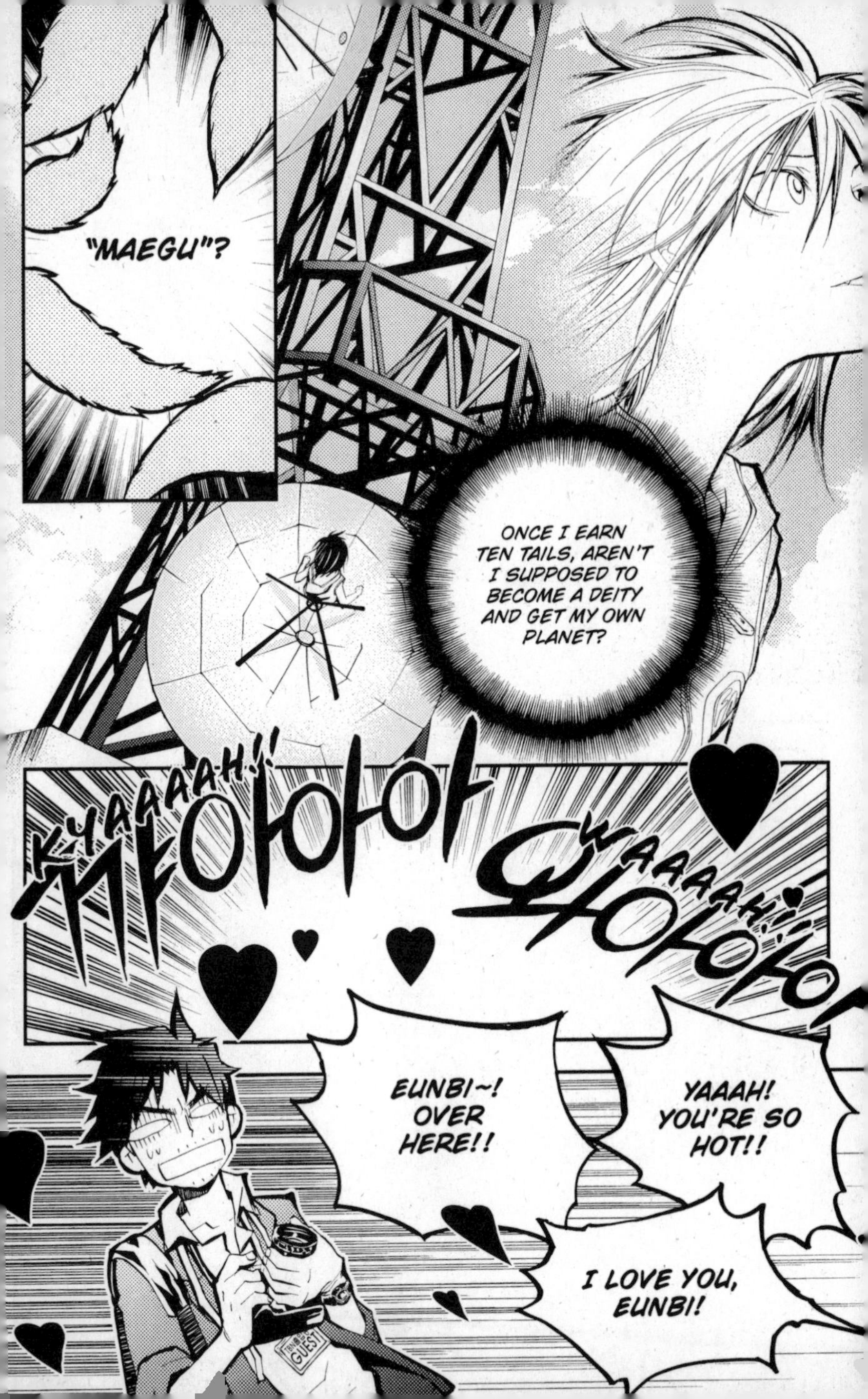
"MAEGU"?
ONCE I EARN TEN TAILS, AREN'T I SUPPOSED TO BECOME A DEITY AND GET MY OWN PLANET?
KYAAAAAH!!
WAAAAAH!!!
EUNBI~! OVER HERE!!
YAAAH! YOU'RE SO HOT!!
I LOVE YOU, EUNBI!
GUEST

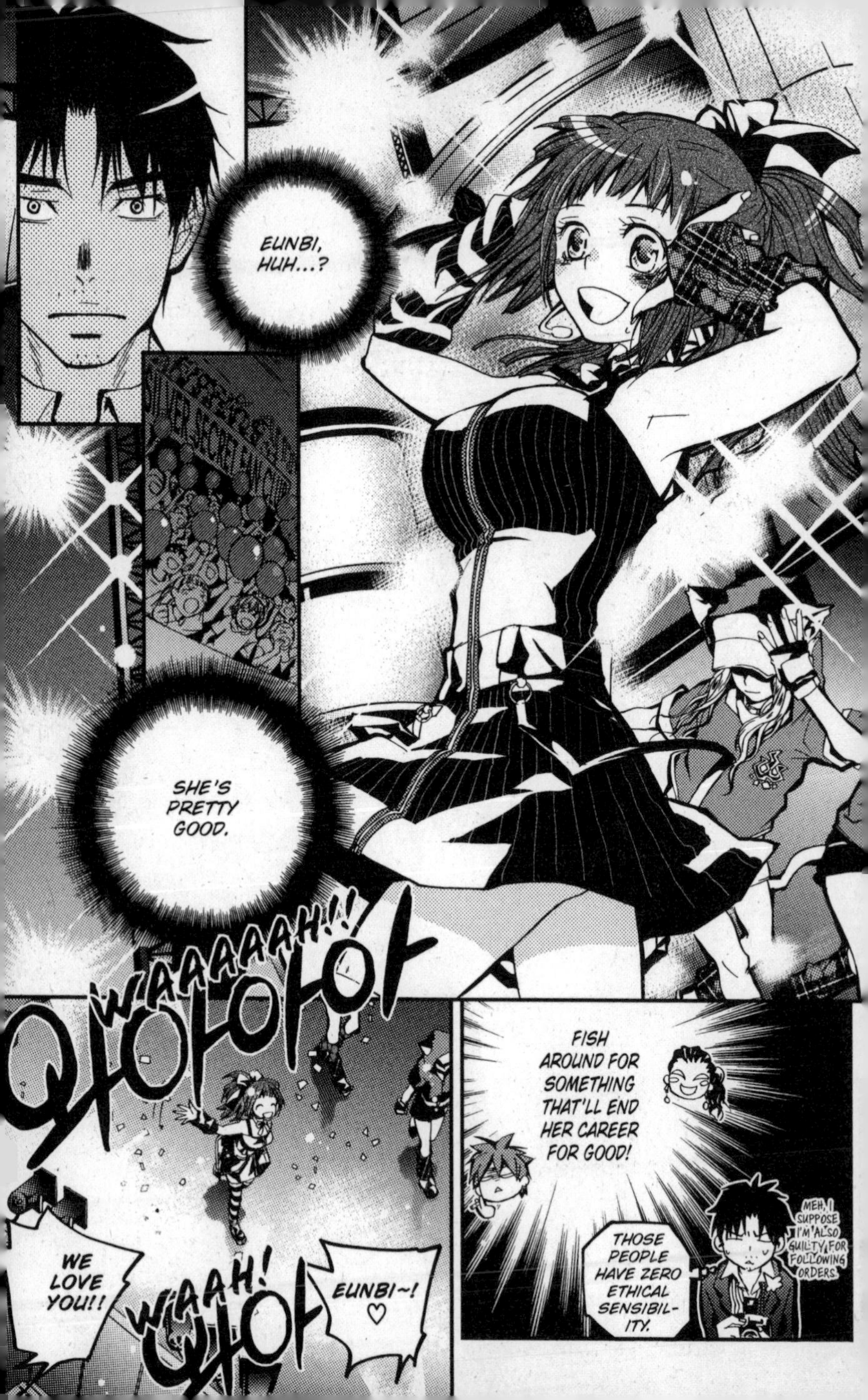
EUNBI, HUH...?
SHE'S PRETTY GOOD.
WAAAAAAH!!!
WE LOVE YOU!!
WAAH!
EUNBI~! ♡
FISH AROUND FOR SOMETHING THAT'LL END HER CAREER FOR GOOD!
THOSE PEOPLE HAVE ZERO ETHICAL SENSIBILITY.
MEH, I SUPPOSE I'M ALSO GUILTY FOR FOLLOWING ORDERS.

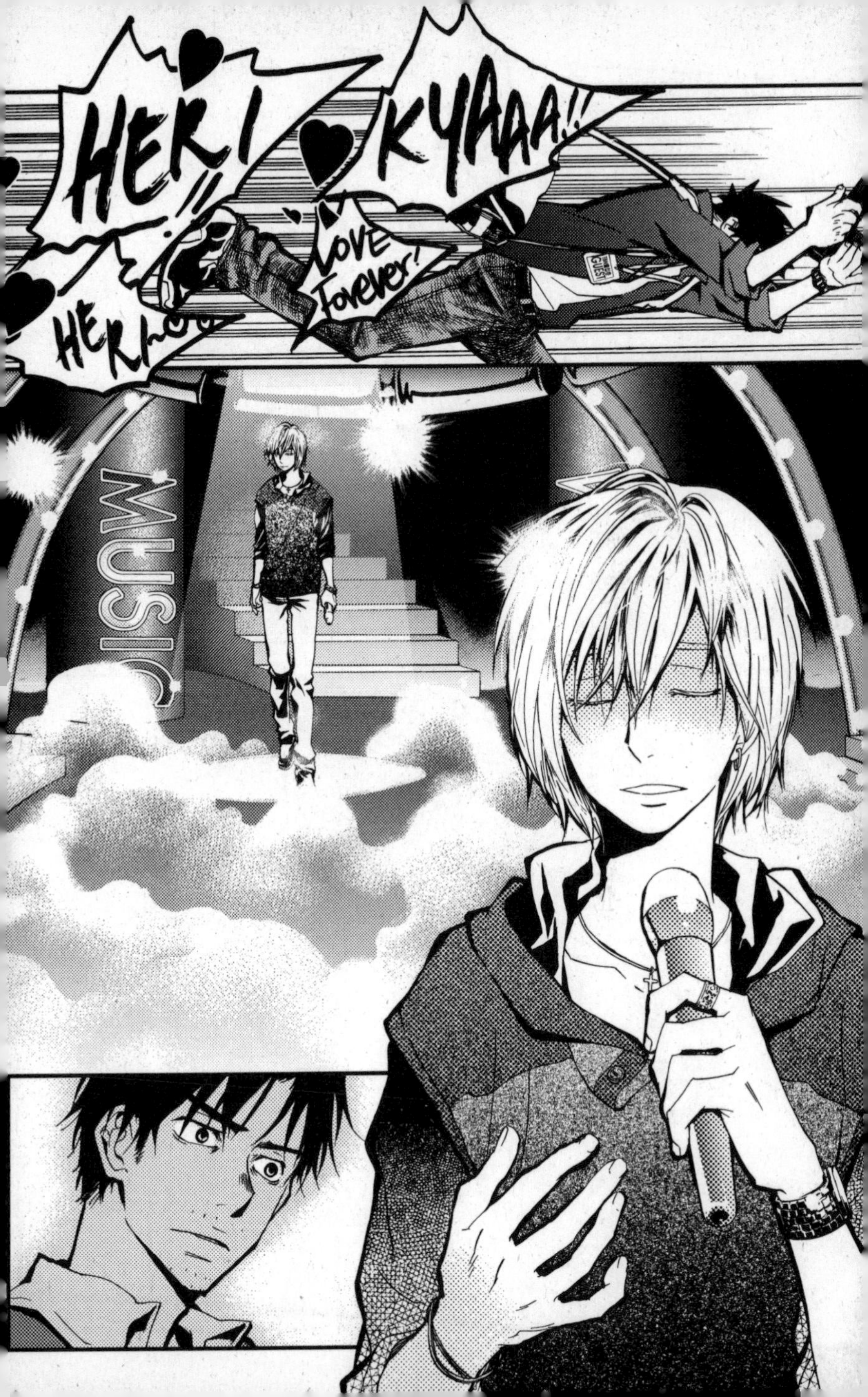
HERI♥
HERI♥♥
KYAAA!!
♥ LOVE Forever!

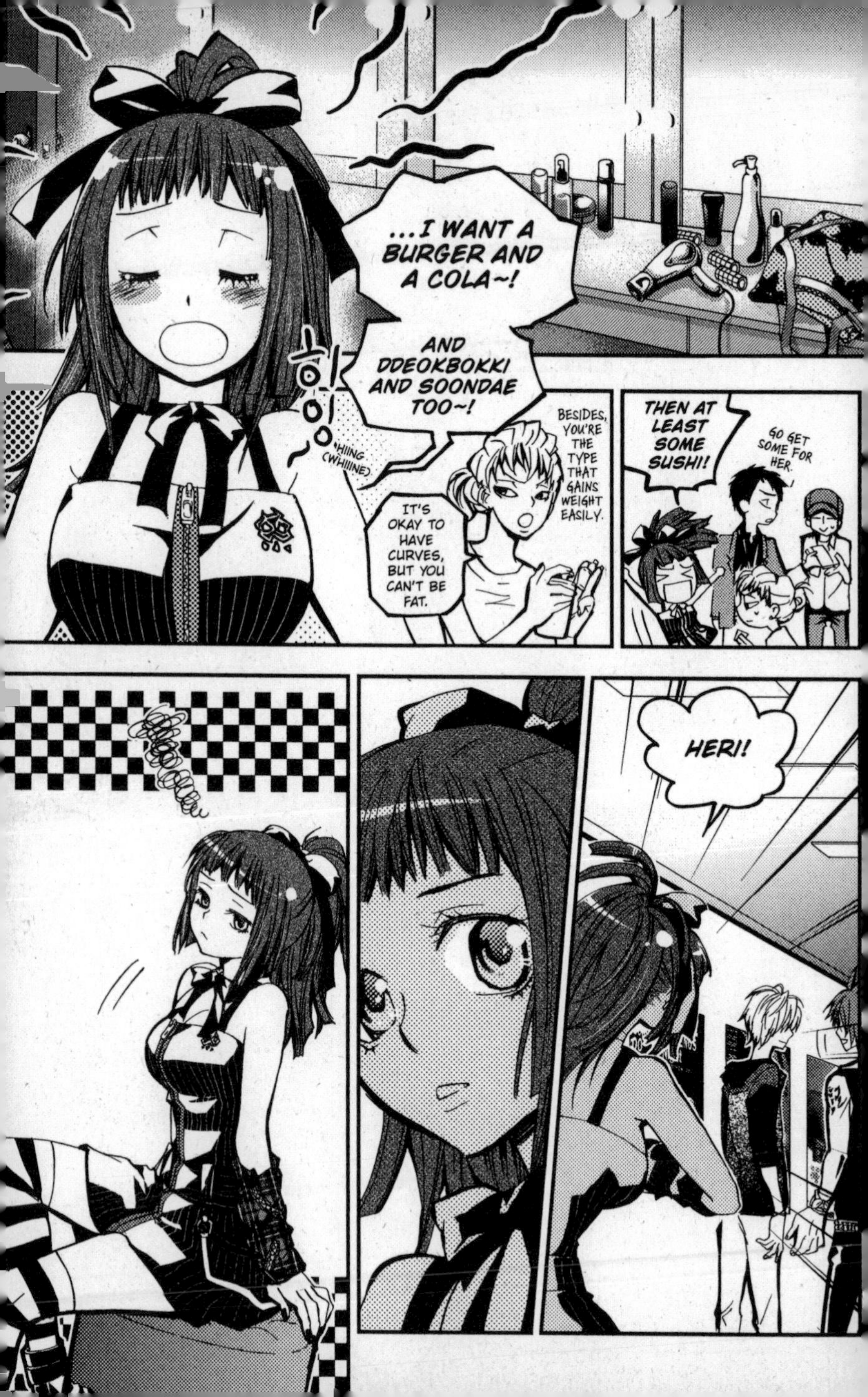
...I WANT A BURGER AND A COLA~!
AND DDEOKBOKKI AND SOONDAE TOO~!
HIING (WHIIINE)
IT'S OKAY TO HAVE CURVES, BUT YOU CAN'T BE FAT.
BESIDES, YOU'RE THE TYPE THAT GAINS WEIGHT EASILY.
THEN AT LEAST SOME SUSHI!
GO GET SOME FOR HER.
HERI!

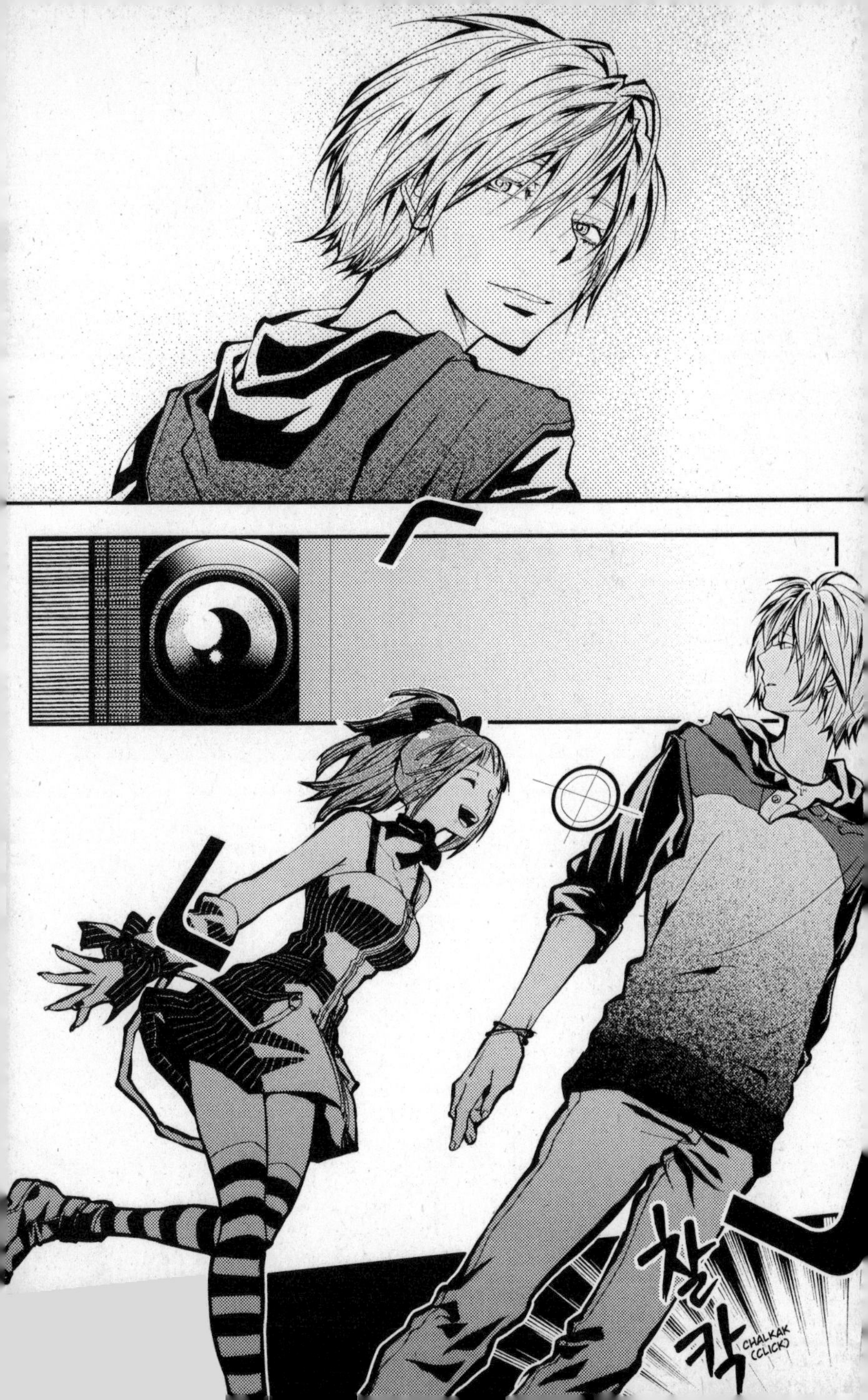
찰칵
CHALKAK (CLICK)

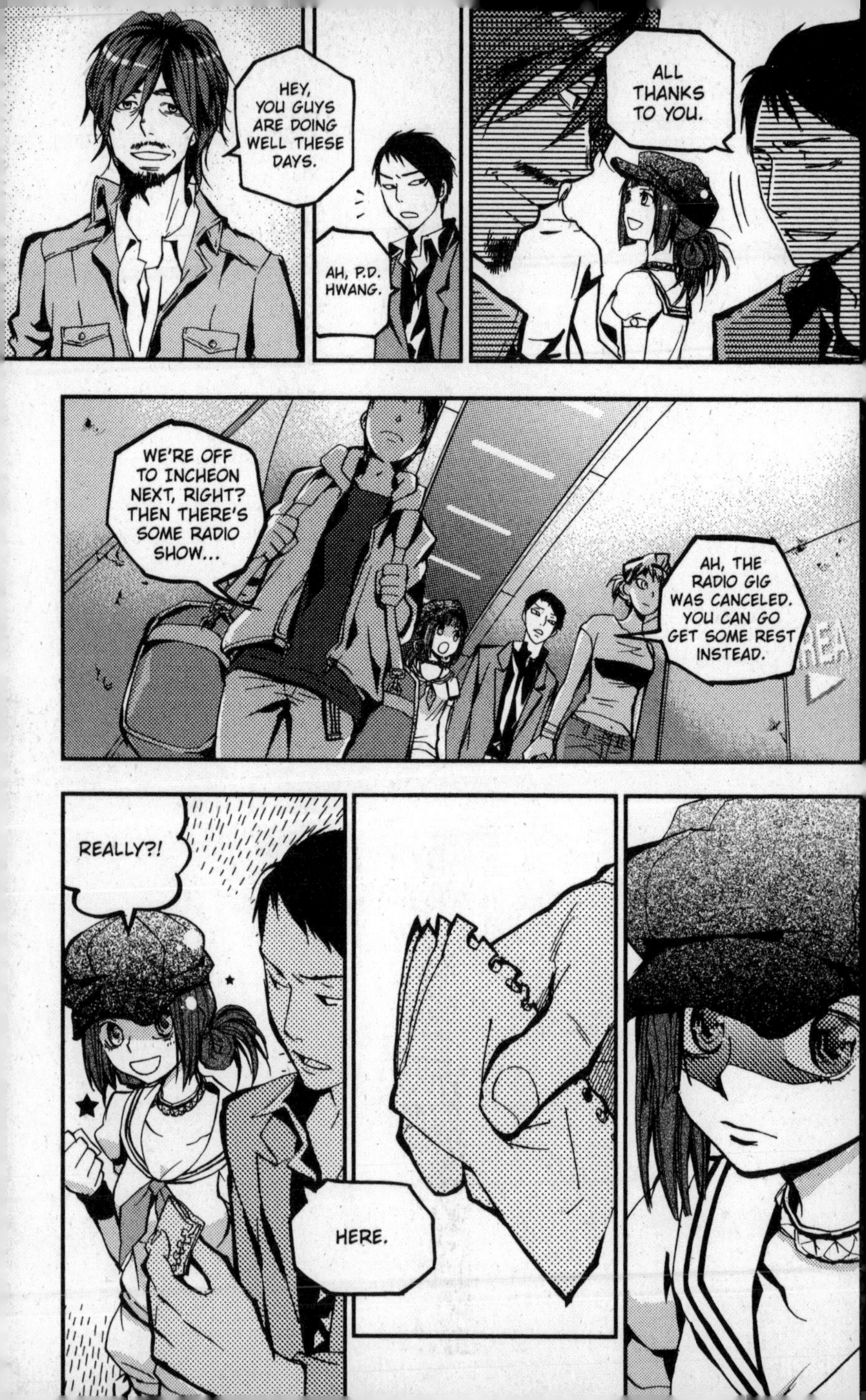
HEY, YOU GUYS ARE DOING WELL THESE DAYS.
AH, P.D. HWANG.
ALL THANKS TO YOU.
WE'RE OFF TO INCHEON NEXT, RIGHT? THEN THERE'S SOME RADIO SHOW...
AH, THE RADIO GIG WAS CANCELED. YOU CAN GO GET SOME REST INSTEAD.
REALLY?!
HERE.

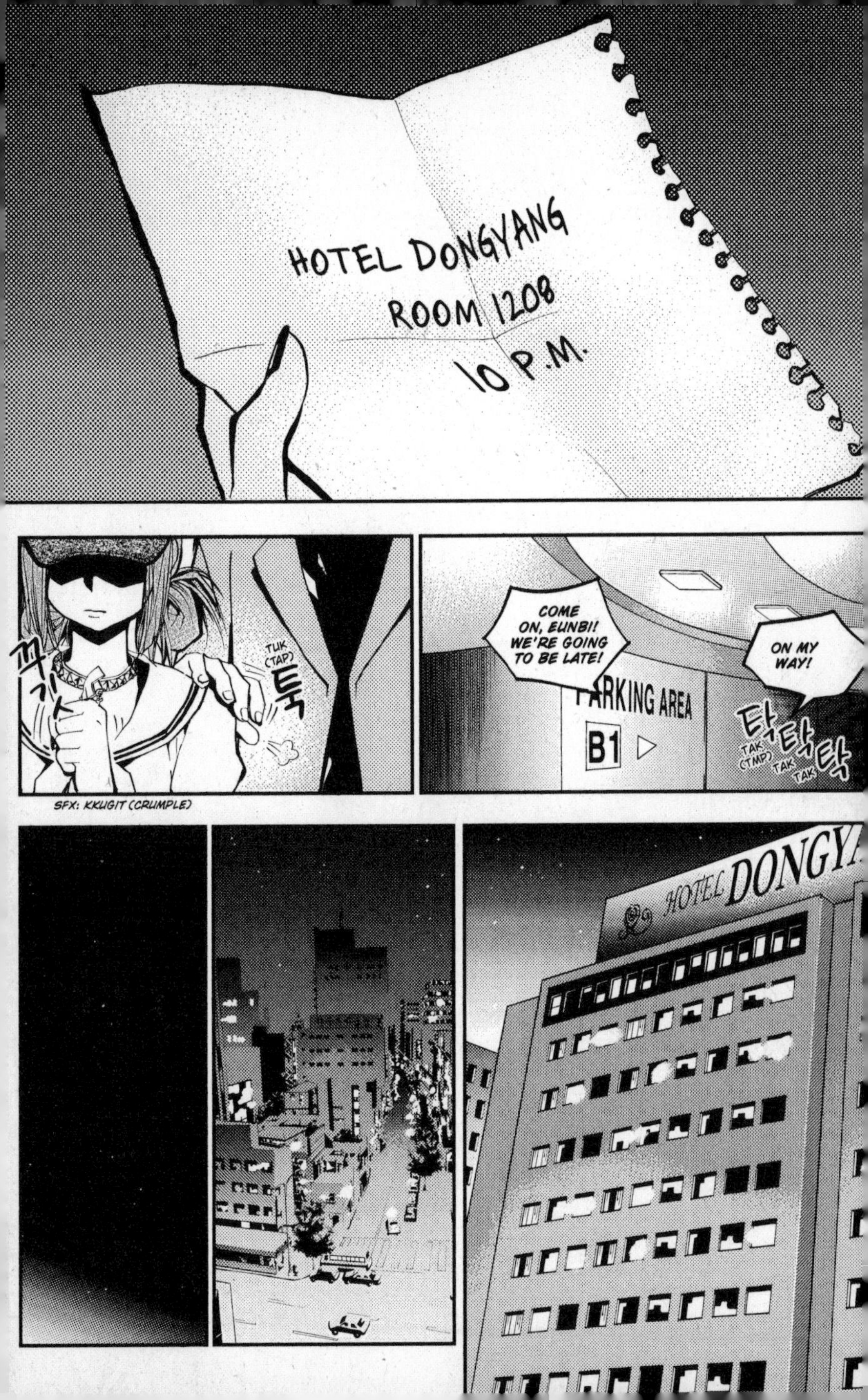
HOTEL DONGYANG
ROOM 1208
10 P.M.
꾸깃
TUK (TAP)
툭
SFX: KKUGIT (CRUMPLE)
COME ON, EUNBI! WE'RE GOING TO BE LATE!
PARKING AREA
B1
ON MY WAY!
탁 탁 탁
TAK (TMP) TAK TAK
HOTEL DONGYA

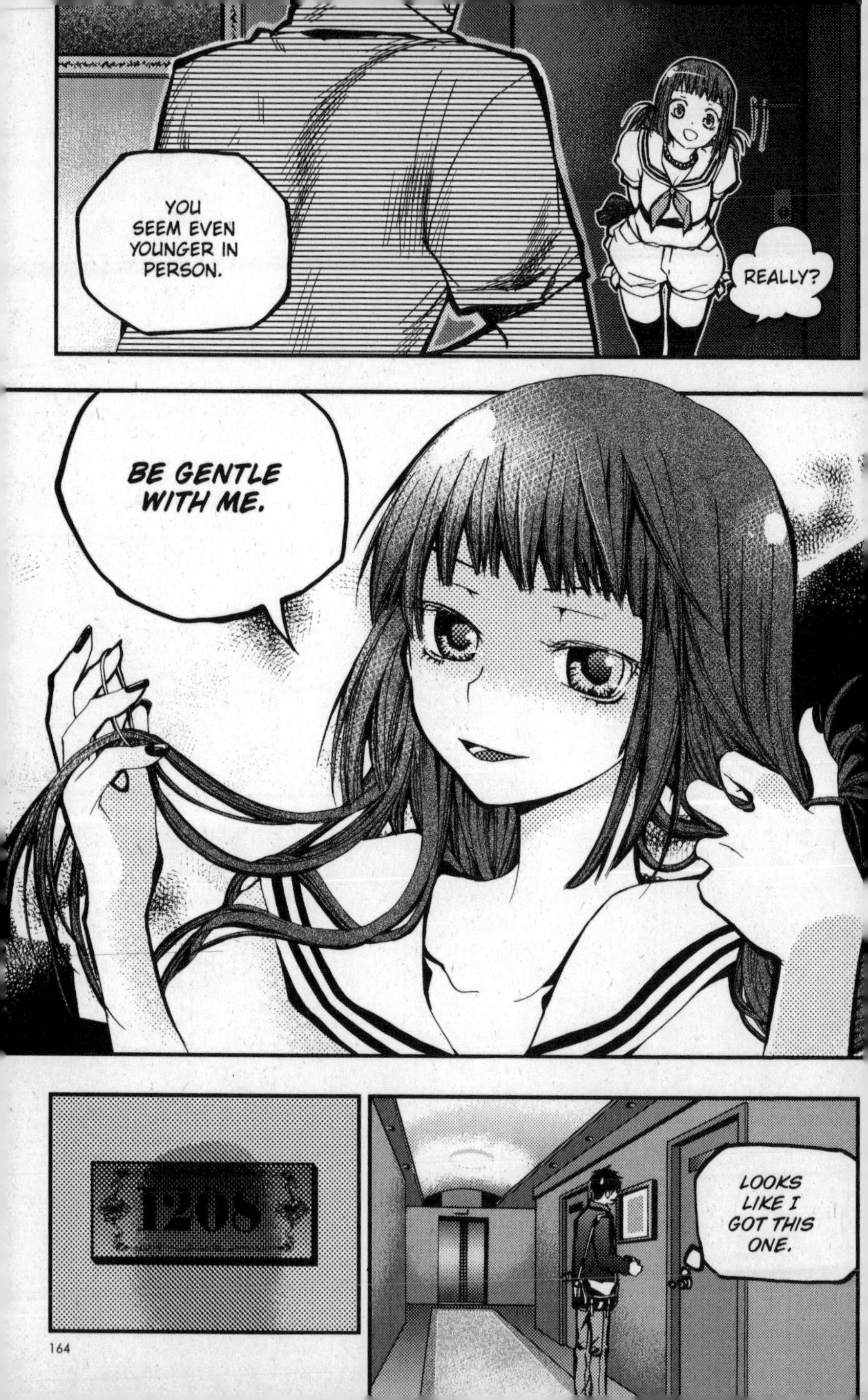
YOU SEEM EVEN YOUNGER IN PERSON.
REALLY?
BE GENTLE WITH ME.
1208
LOOKS LIKE I GOT THIS ONE.

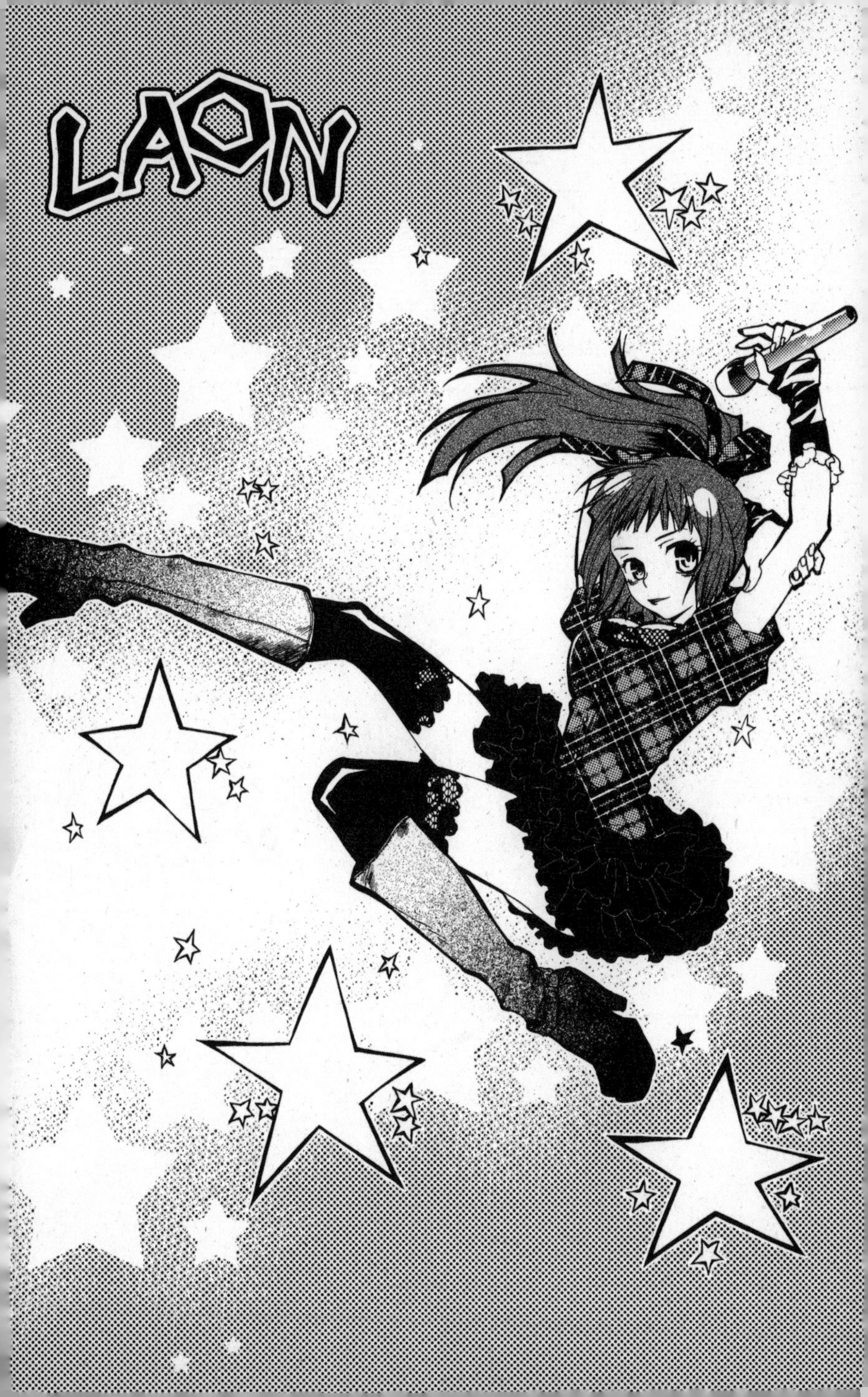
LAON

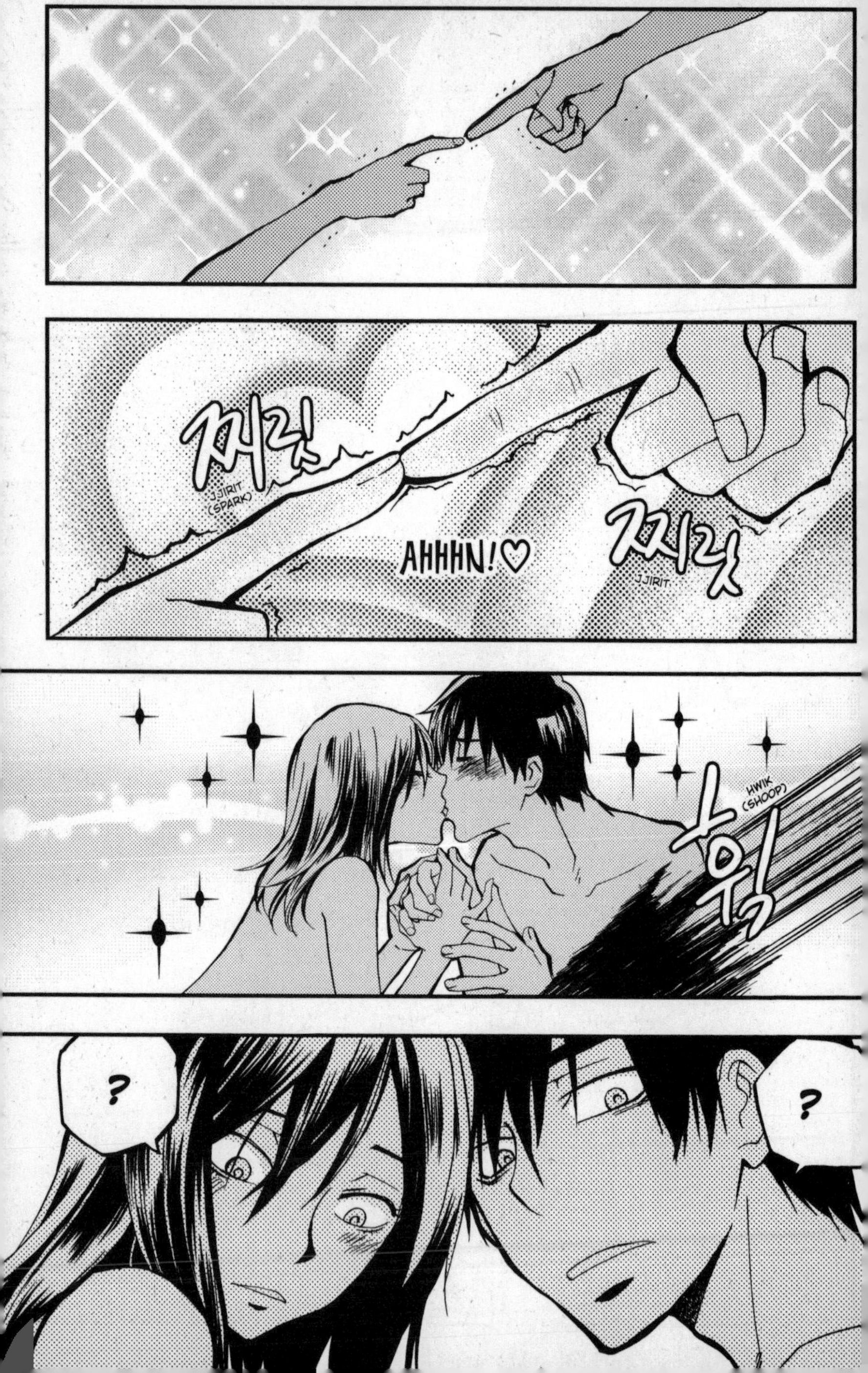
찌릿!
JJIRIT (SPARK)
AHHHN!♡
찌릿
JJIRIT
휘익
HWIK (SHOOP)
?
?

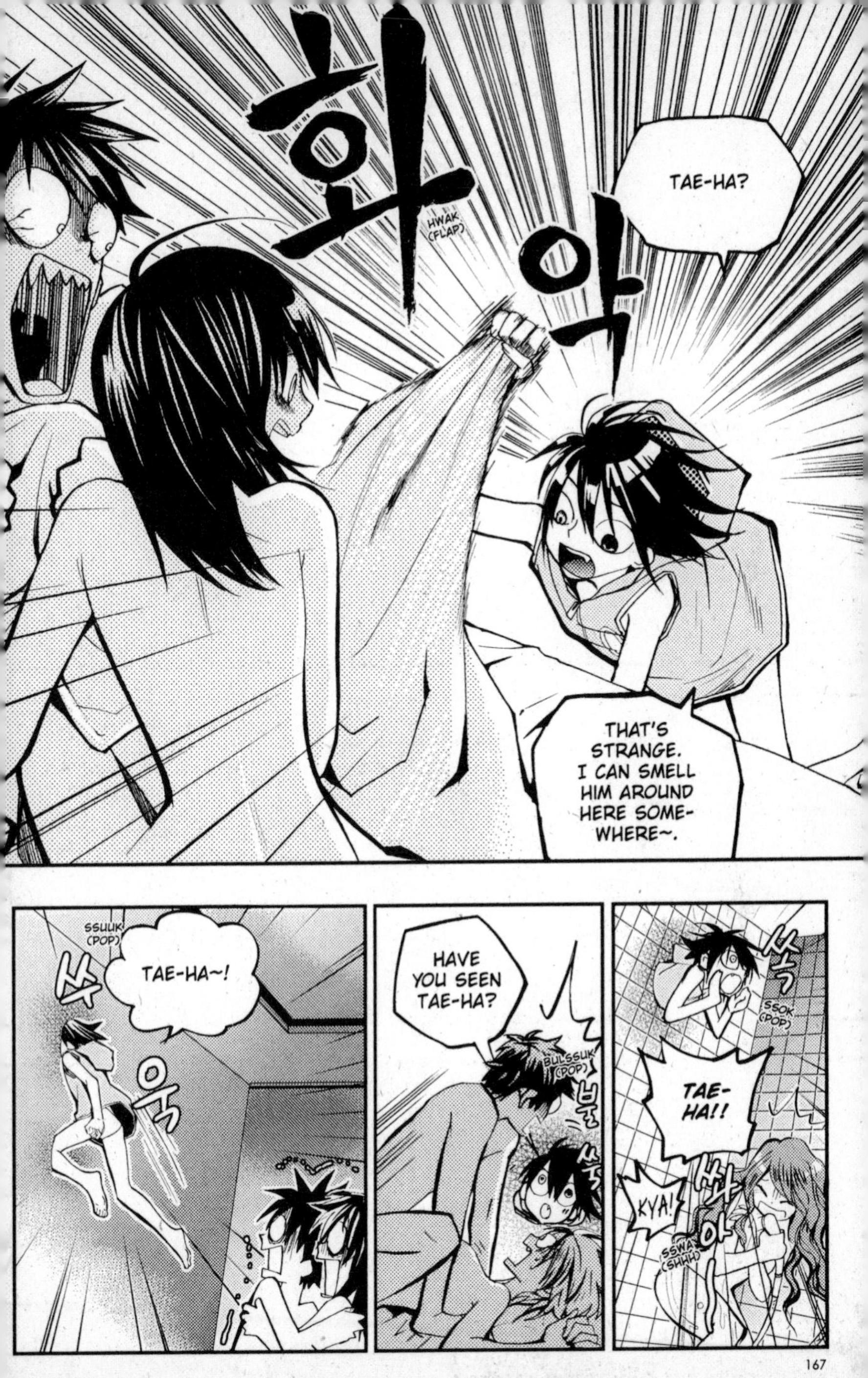

HWAK (FLAP)
TAE-HA?
THAT'S STRANGE. I CAN SMELL HIM AROUND HERE SOME-WHERE~.
SSUUK (POP)
TAE-HA~!
HAVE YOU SEEN TAE-HA?
BULSSUK (POP)
SSOK (POP)
TAE-HA!!
KYA!
SSWA (SHHH)

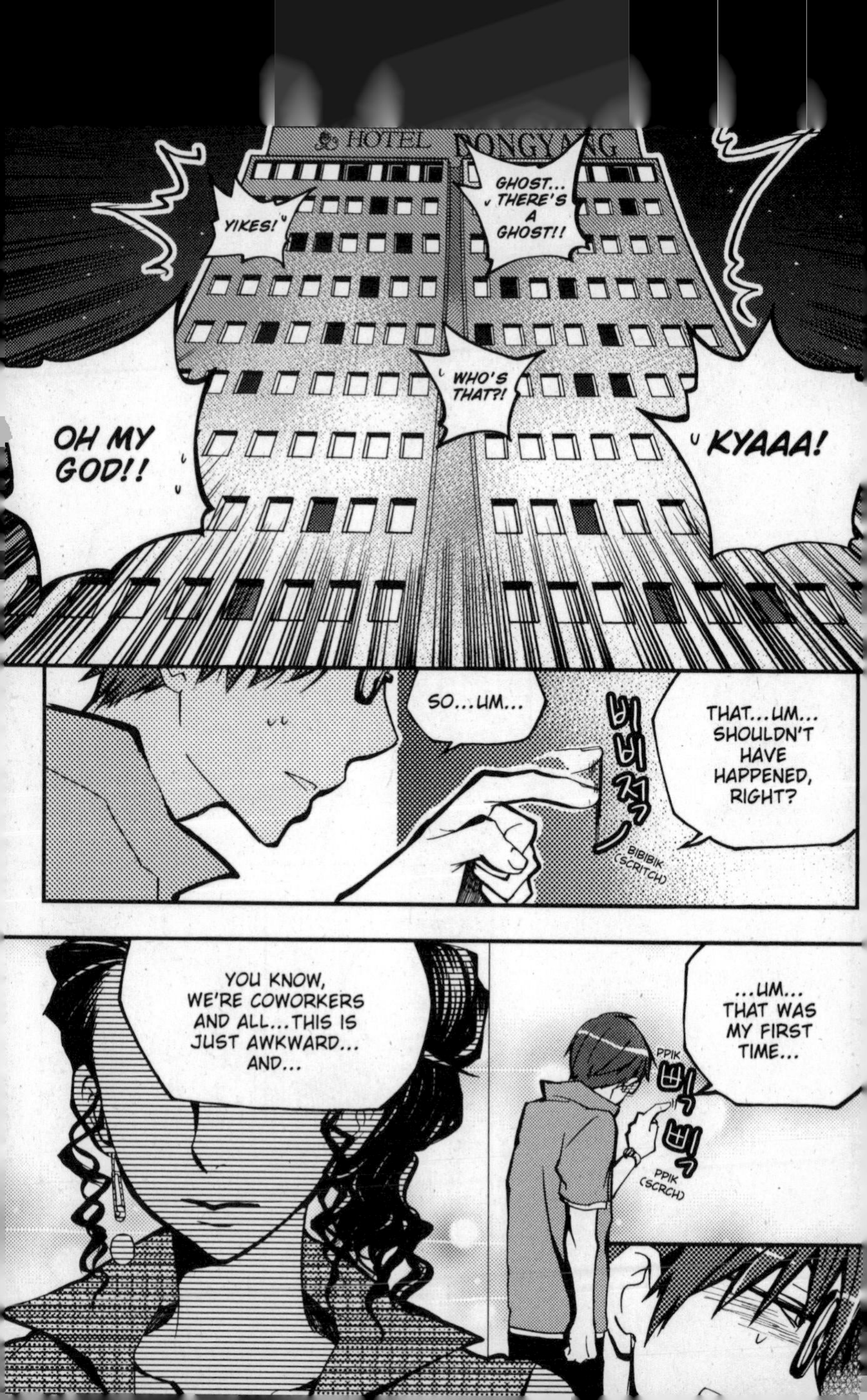
HOTEL
YIKES!
GHOST... THERE'S A GHOST!!
OH MY GOD!!
WHO'S THAT?!
KYAAA!
SO...UM...
비비적
BIBIBIK (SCRITCH)
THAT...UM... SHOULDN'T HAVE HAPPENED, RIGHT?
YOU KNOW, WE'RE COWORKERS AND ALL...THIS IS JUST AWKWARD... AND...
삑 삑
PPIK PPIK (SCRCH)
...UM... THAT WAS MY FIRST TIME...

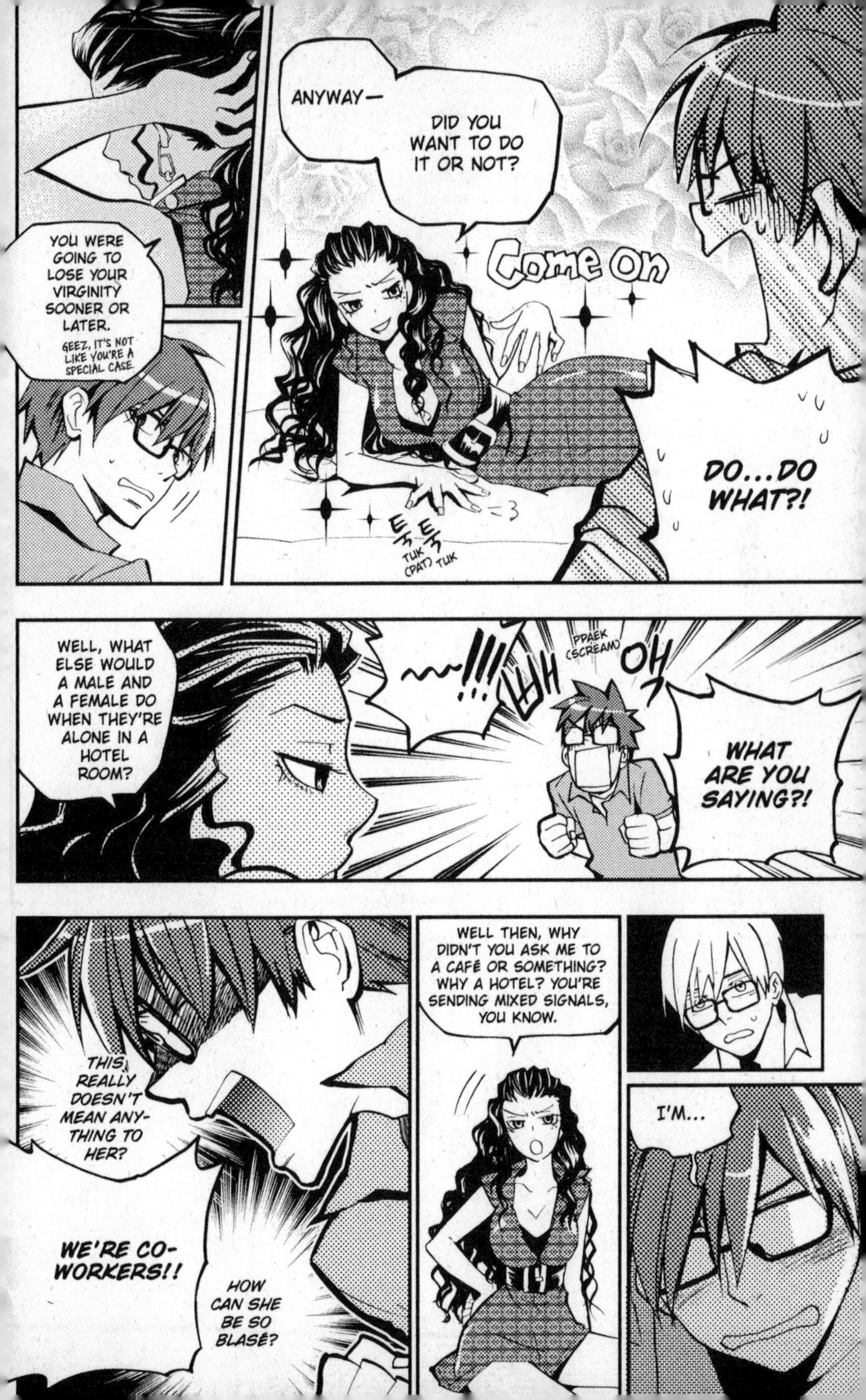
YOU WERE GOING TO LOSE YOUR VIRGINITY SOONER OR LATER.
GEEZ, IT'S NOT LIKE YOU'RE A SPECIAL CASE.
ANYWAY—
DID YOU WANT TO DO IT OR NOT?
Come on
TUK (PAT) TUK
DO...DO WHAT?!
WELL, WHAT ELSE WOULD A MALE AND A FEMALE DO WHEN THEY'RE ALONE IN A HOTEL ROOM?
~~!!!
PPAEK (SCREAM)
WHAT ARE YOU SAYING?!
THIS REALLY DOESN'T MEAN ANY-THING TO HER?
WE'RE CO-WORKERS!!
HOW CAN SHE BE SO BLASÉ?
WELL THEN, WHY DIDN'T YOU ASK ME TO A CAFÉ OR SOMETHING? WHY A HOTEL? YOU'RE SENDING MIXED SIGNALS, YOU KNOW.
I'M...

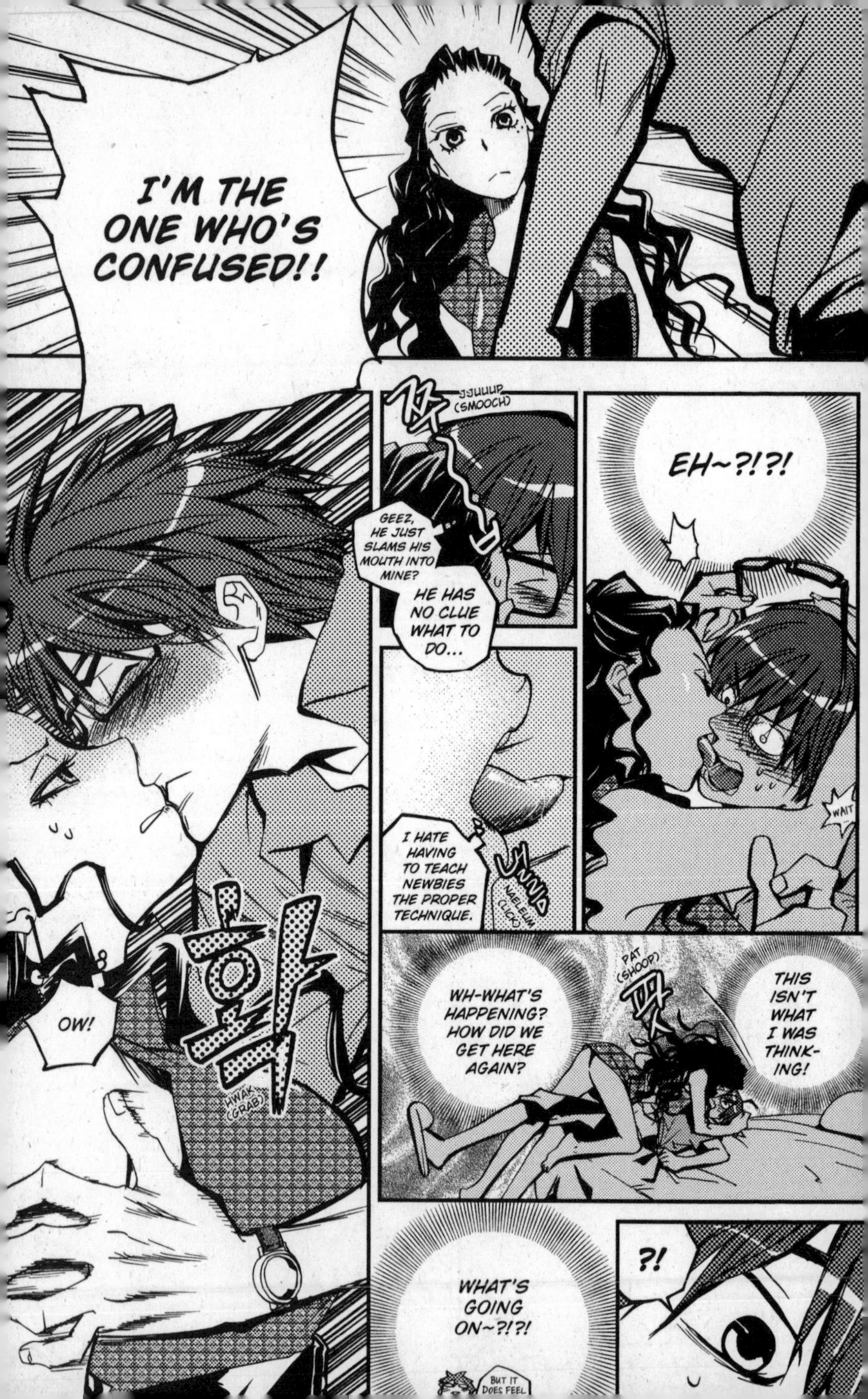
I'M THE ONE WHO'S CONFUSED!!
OW!
HWAK (GRAB)
JJUUUP (SMOOCH)
GEEZ, HE JUST SLAMS HIS MOUTH INTO MINE?
HE HAS NO CLUE WHAT TO DO...
I HATE HAVING TO TEACH NEWBIES THE PROPER TECHNIQUE.
NAELEUM (CLICK)
EH~?!?!
WAIT...
WH-WHAT'S HAPPENING? HOW DID WE GET HERE AGAIN?
PAT (SHOOP)
THIS ISN'T WHAT I WAS THINKING!
WHAT'S GOING ON~?!?!
?!
BUT IT DOES FEEL

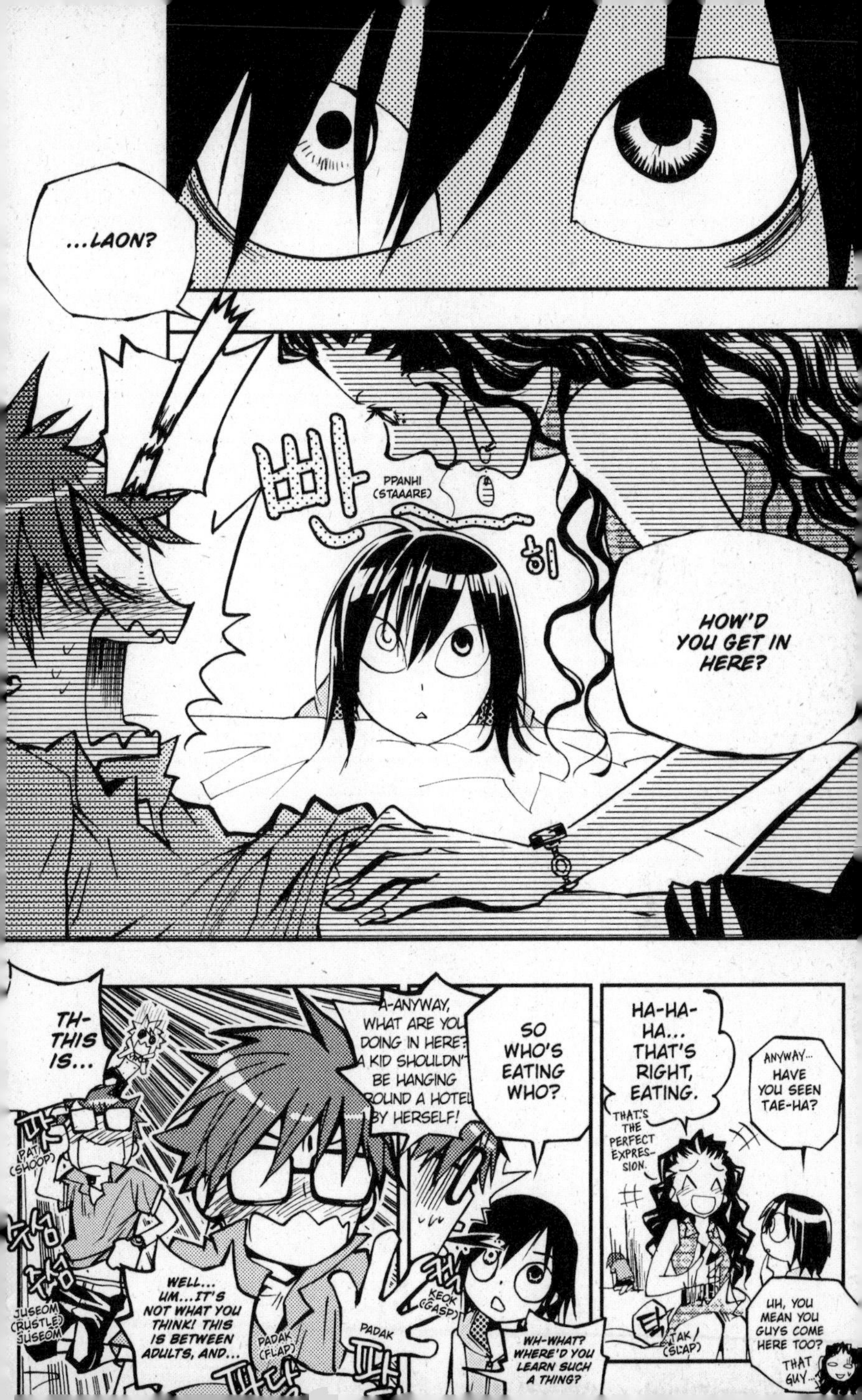
...LAON?
빤히
PPANHI (STAAARE)
HOW'D YOU GET IN HERE?
TH-THIS IS...
PAT (SHOOP)
JUSEOM (RUSTLE) JUSEOM
A-ANYWAY, WHAT ARE YOU DOING IN HERE? A KID SHOULDN'T BE HANGING ROUND A HOTEL BY HERSELF!
WELL... UM... IT'S NOT WHAT YOU THINK! THIS IS BETWEEN ADULTS, AND...
PADAK (FLAP)
PADAK
KEOK (GASP)
SO WHO'S EATING WHO?
WH-WHAT? WHERE'D YOU LEARN SUCH A THING?
HA-HA-HA... THAT'S RIGHT, EATING.
THAT'S THE PERFECT EXPRESSION.
ANYWAY... HAVE YOU SEEN TAE-HA?
탁
TAK! (SLAP)
UH, YOU MEAN YOU GUYS COME HERE TOO?
THAT GUY...

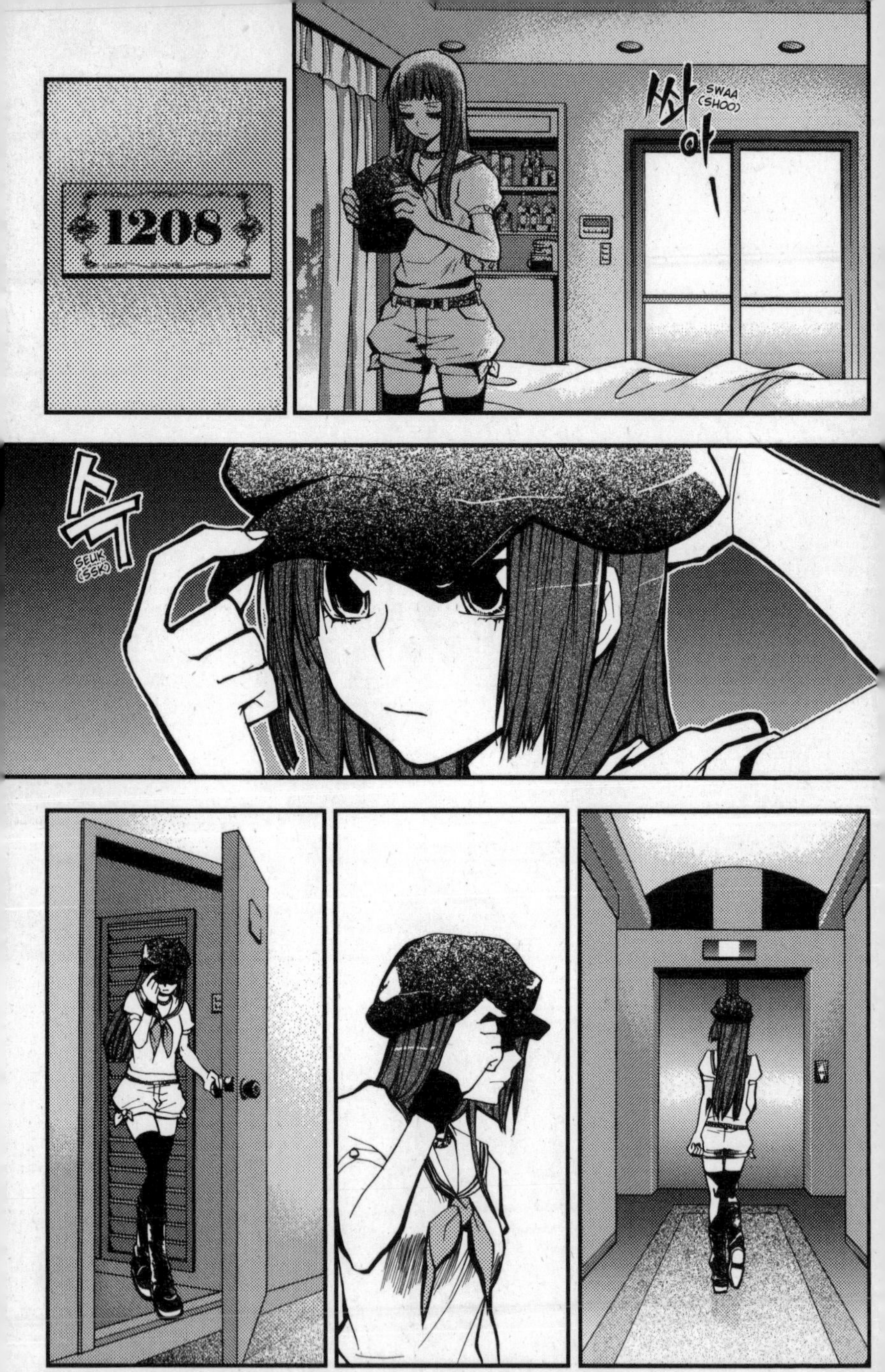
1208
쏴아
SWAA (SHOO)
슥
SEUK (SSK)

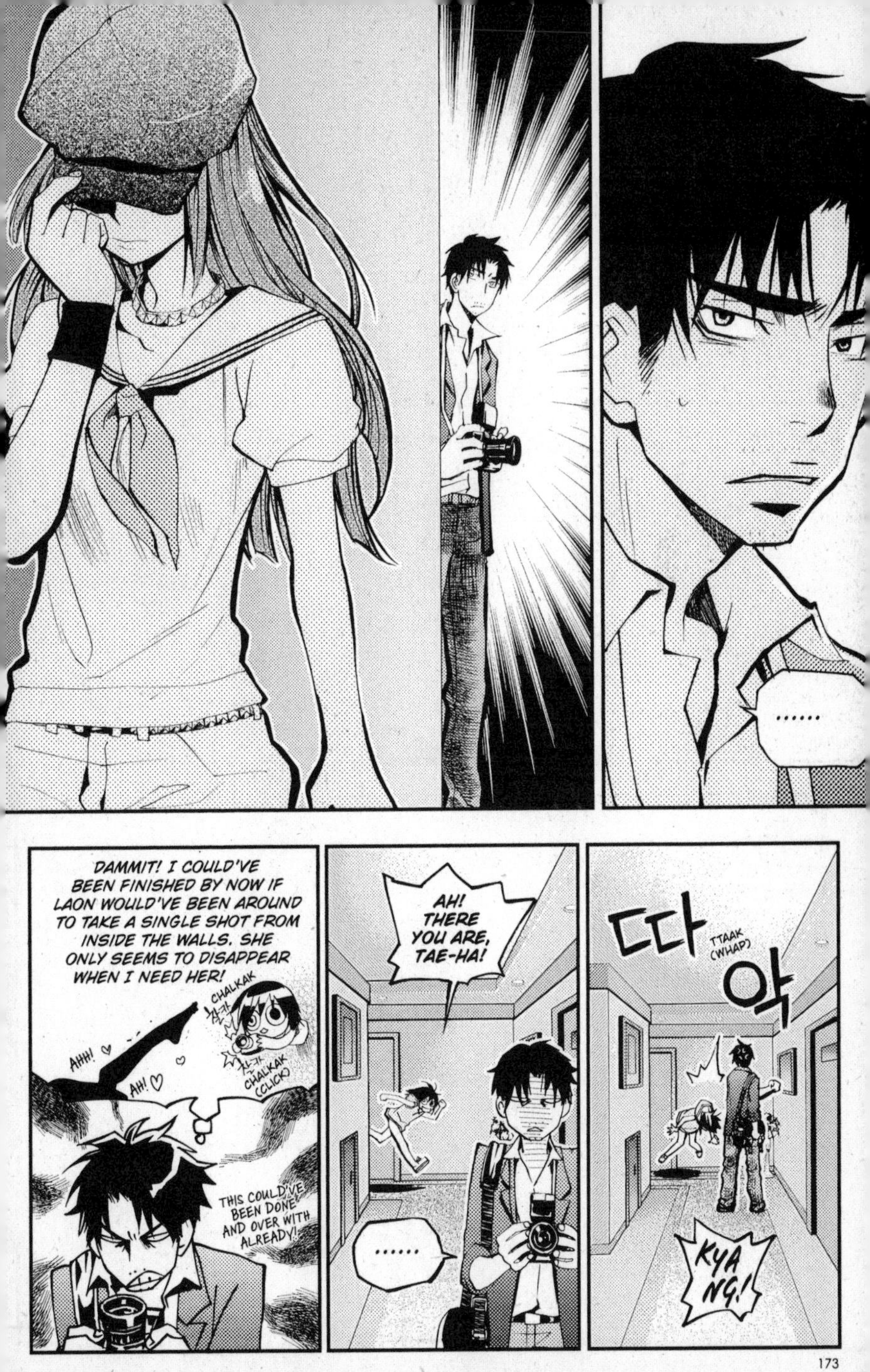

......
DAMMIT! I COULD'VE BEEN FINISHED BY NOW IF LAON WOULD'VE BEEN AROUND TO TAKE A SINGLE SHOT FROM INSIDE THE WALLS. SHE ONLY SEEMS TO DISAPPEAR WHEN I NEED HER!
CHALKAK
찰칵
AHH! ♡
AH! ♡
찰칵
CHALKAK (CLICK)
THIS COULD'VE BEEN DONE AND OVER WITH ALREADY!
AH! THERE YOU ARE, TAE-HA!
......
따악
TTAAK (WHAP)
KYANG!

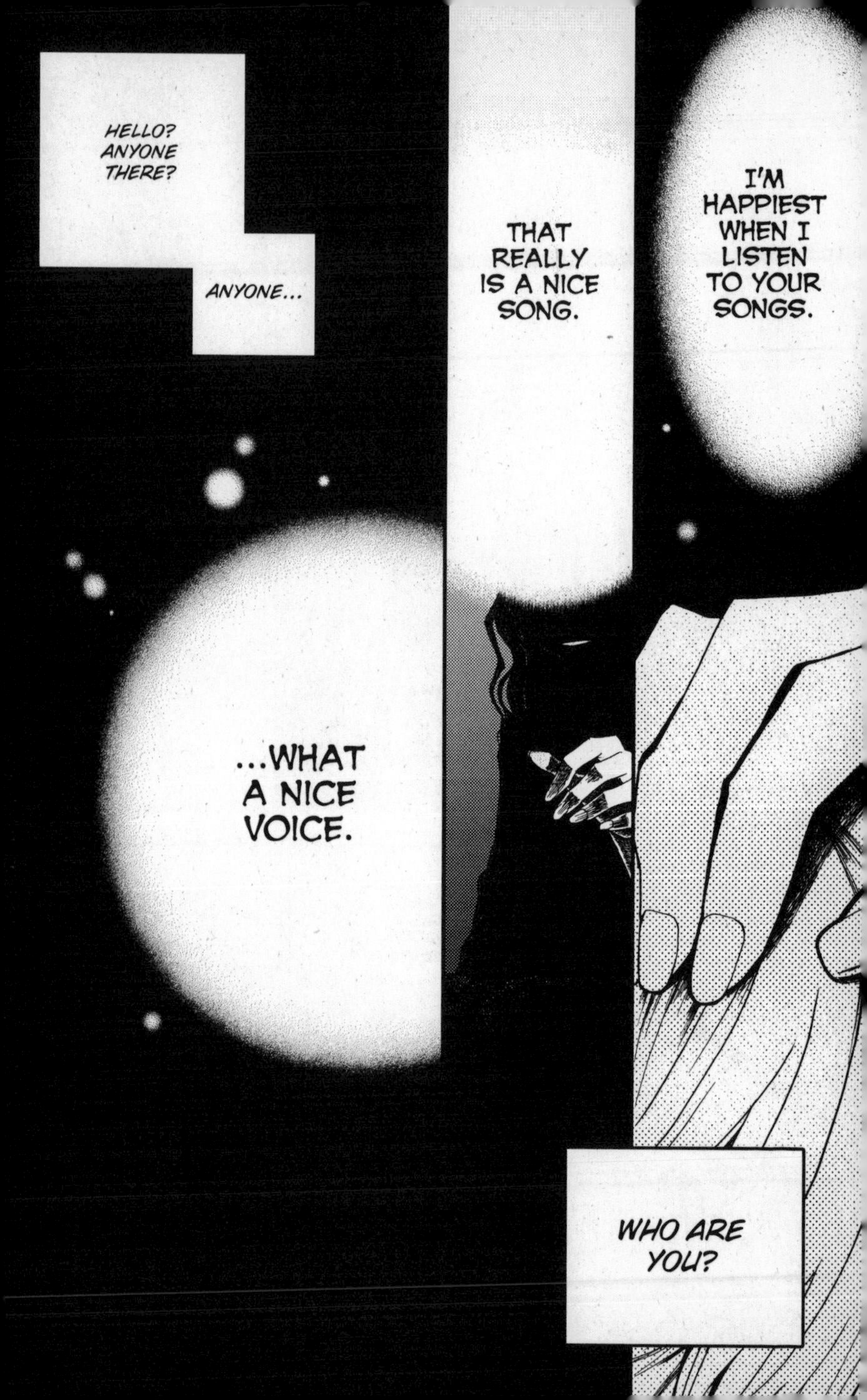
HELLO? ANYONE THERE?
ANYONE...
...WHAT A NICE VOICE.
THAT REALLY IS A NICE SONG.
I'M HAPPIEST WHEN I LISTEN TO YOUR SONGS.
WHO ARE YOU?

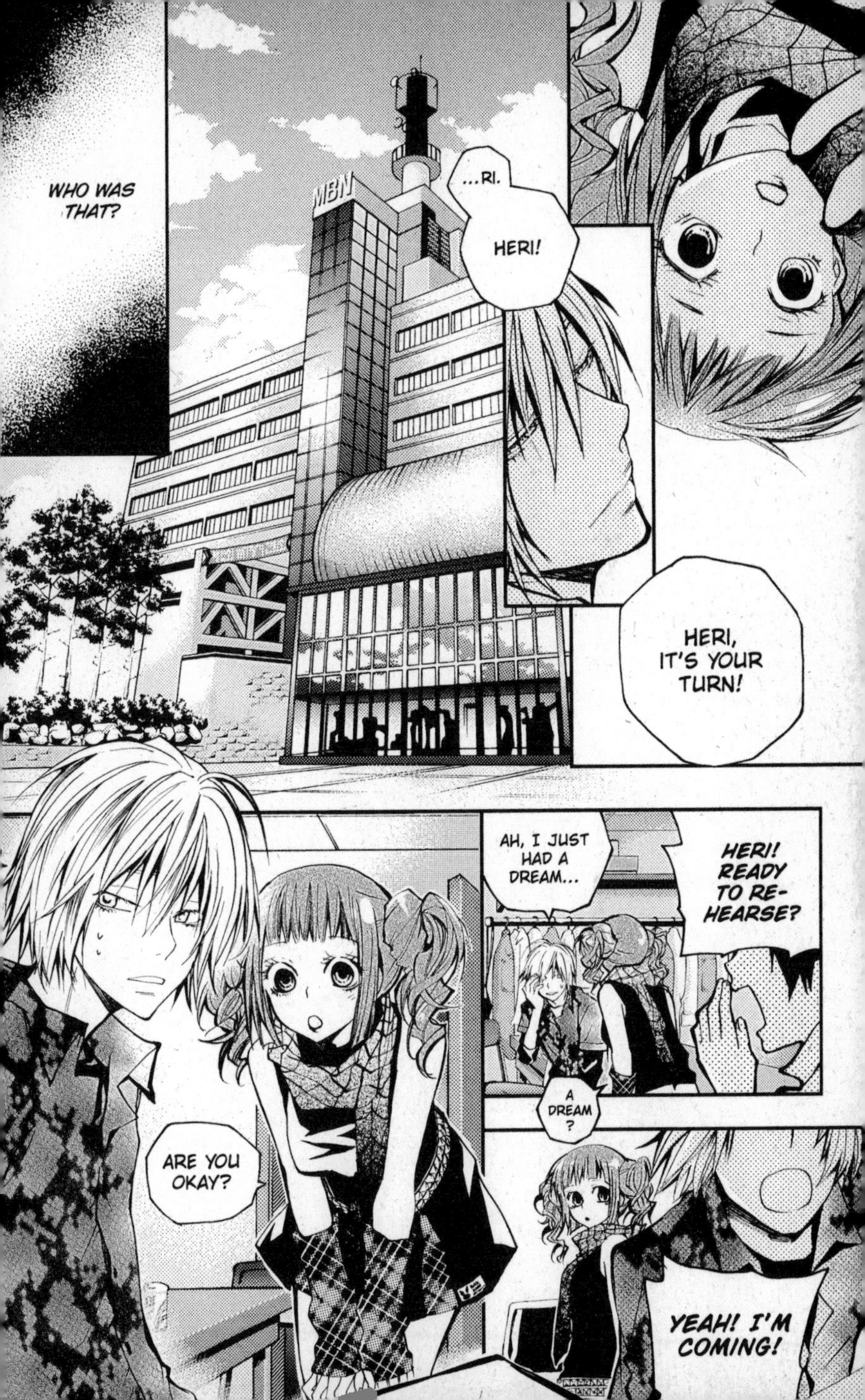
WHO WAS THAT?
...RI.
HERI!
HERI, IT'S YOUR TURN!
ARE YOU OKAY?
AH, I JUST HAD A DREAM...
HERI! READY TO RE-HEARSE?
A DREAM?
YEAH! I'M COMING!

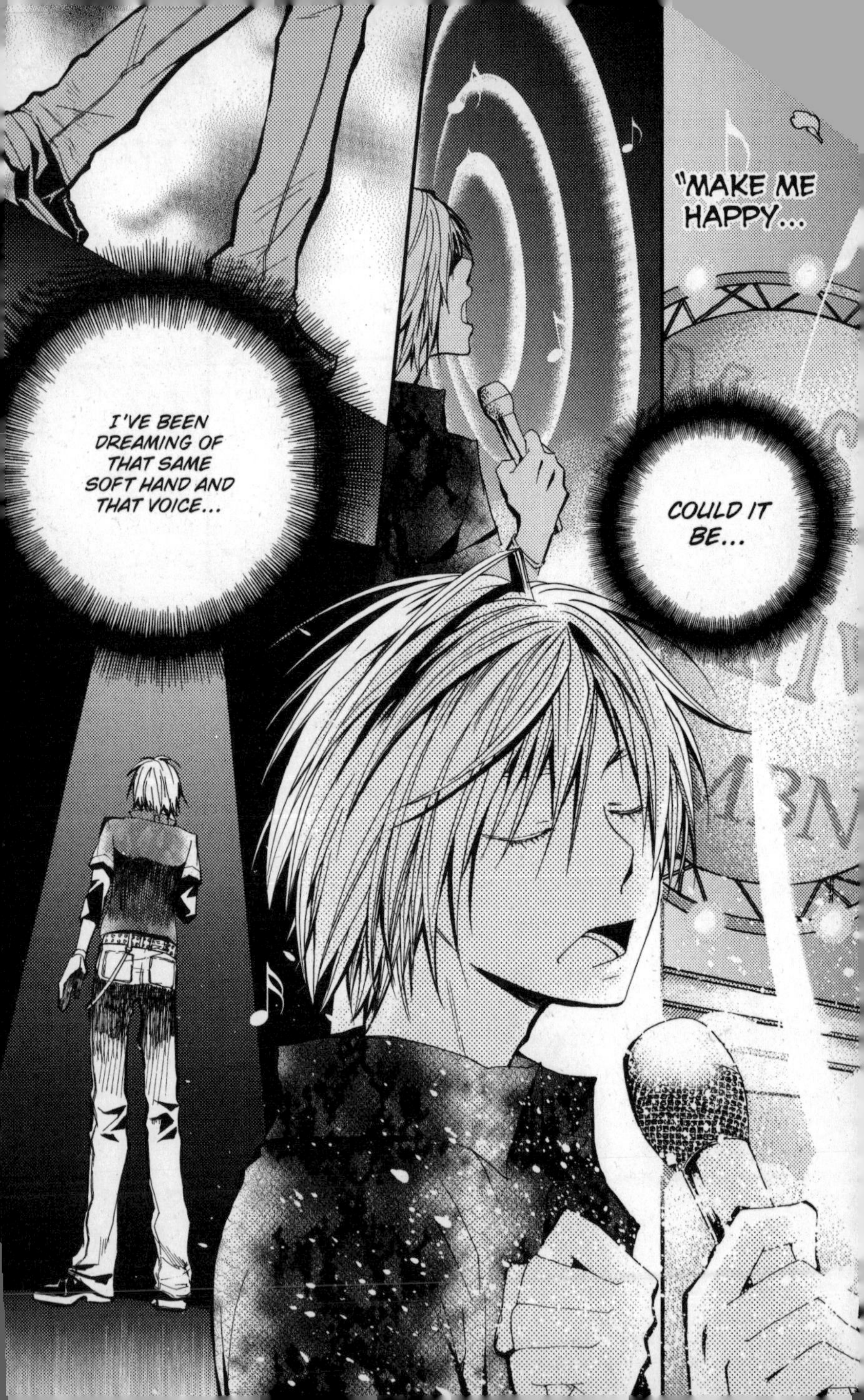
I'VE BEEN DREAMING OF THAT SAME SOFT HAND AND THAT VOICE...
"MAKE ME HAPPY...
COULD IT BE...

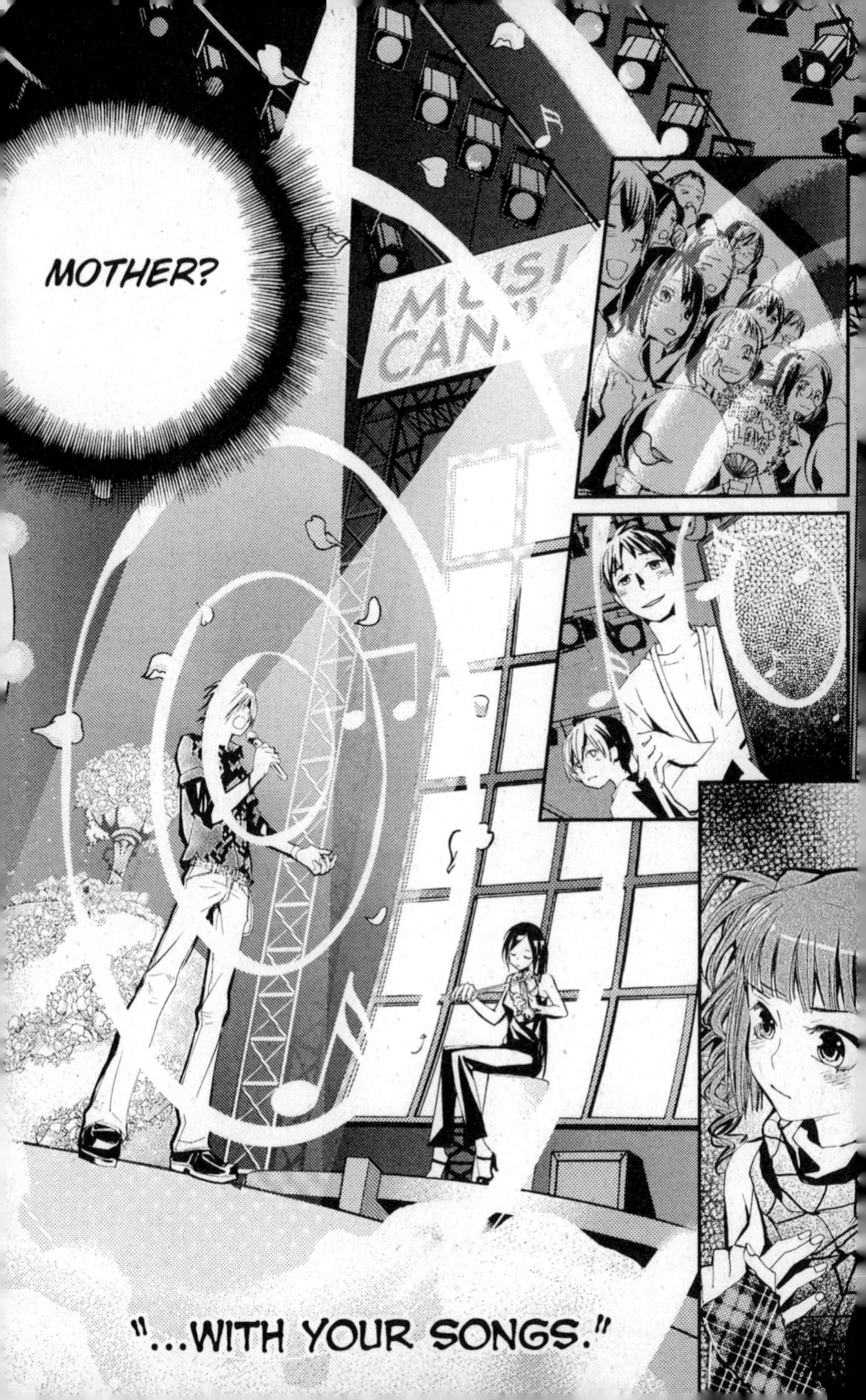
MOTHER?
"...WITH YOUR SONGS."

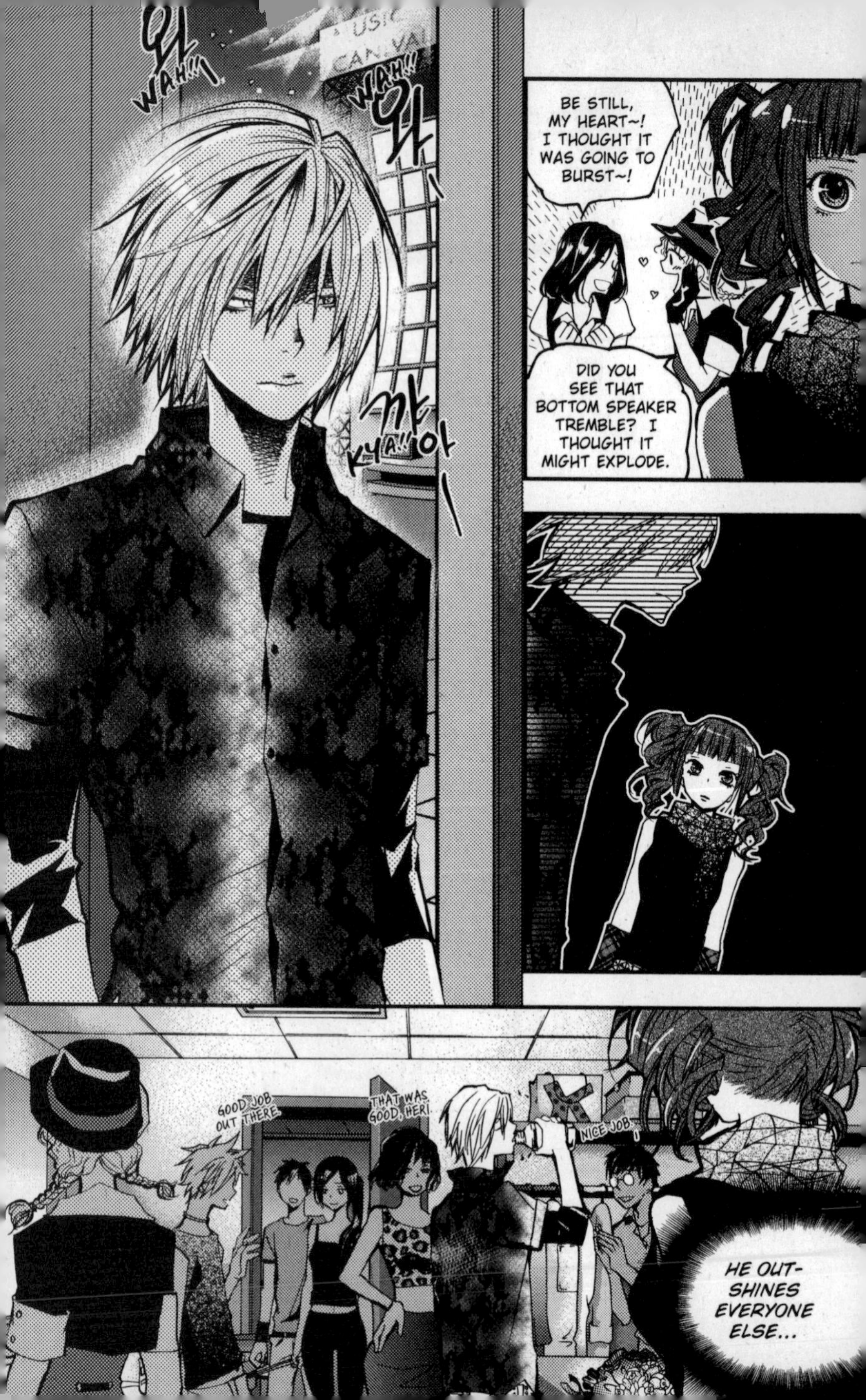

WAH!!
WAH!!
KYA!!
BE STILL, MY HEART~! I THOUGHT IT WAS GOING TO BURST~!
DID YOU SEE THAT BOTTOM SPEAKER TREMBLE? I THOUGHT IT MIGHT EXPLODE.
GOOD JOB OUT THERE.
THAT WAS GOOD, HERI.
NICE JOB.
HE OUT-SHINES EVERYONE ELSE...

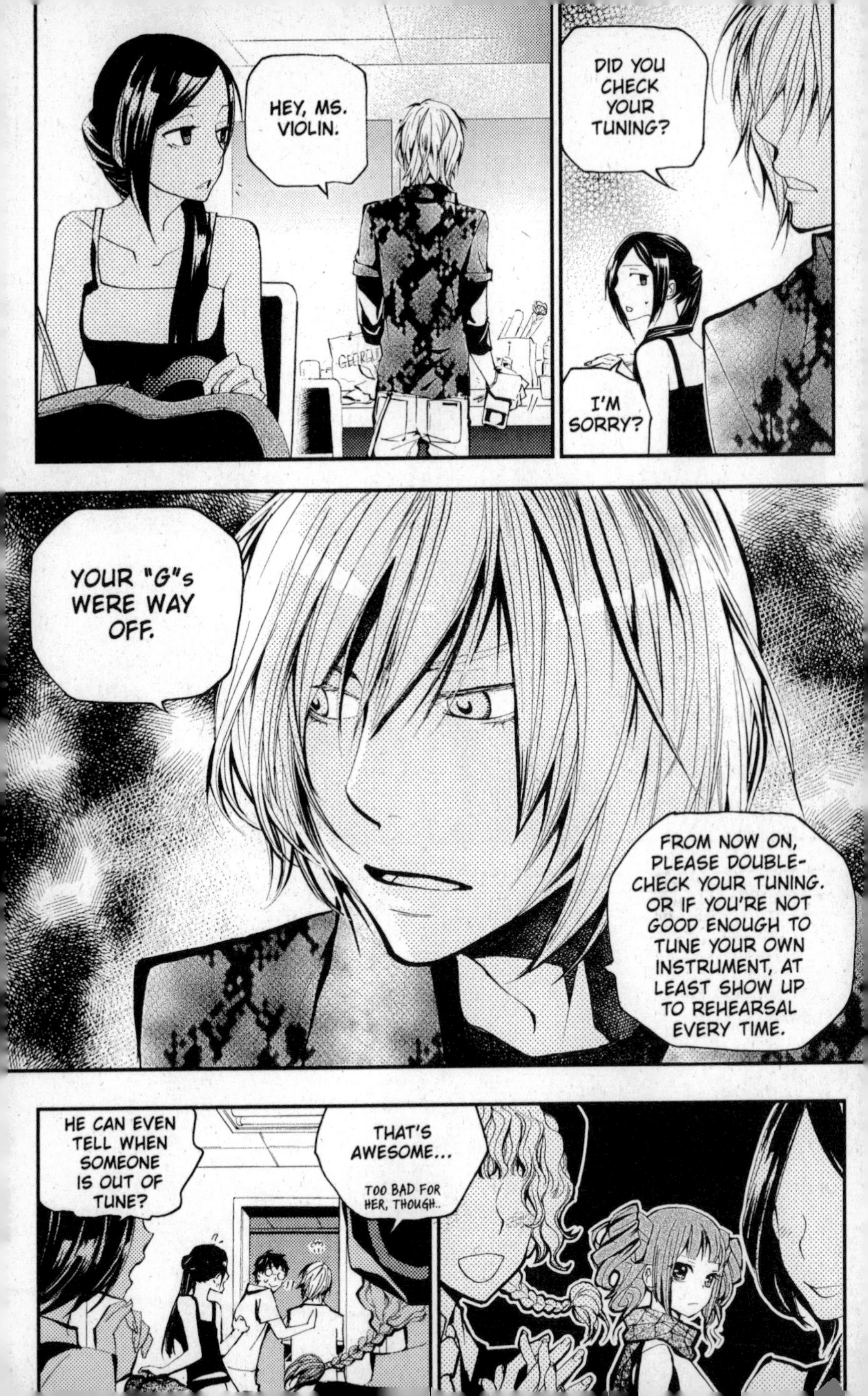

HEY, MS. VIOLIN.
DID YOU CHECK YOUR TUNING?
I'M SORRY?
YOUR "G"s WERE WAY OFF.
FROM NOW ON, PLEASE DOUBLE-CHECK YOUR TUNING. OR IF YOU'RE NOT GOOD ENOUGH TO TUNE YOUR OWN INSTRUMENT, AT LEAST SHOW UP TO REHEARSAL EVERY TIME.
HE CAN EVEN TELL WHEN SOMEONE IS OUT OF TUNE?
THAT'S AWESOME...
TOO BAD FOR HER, THOUGH..

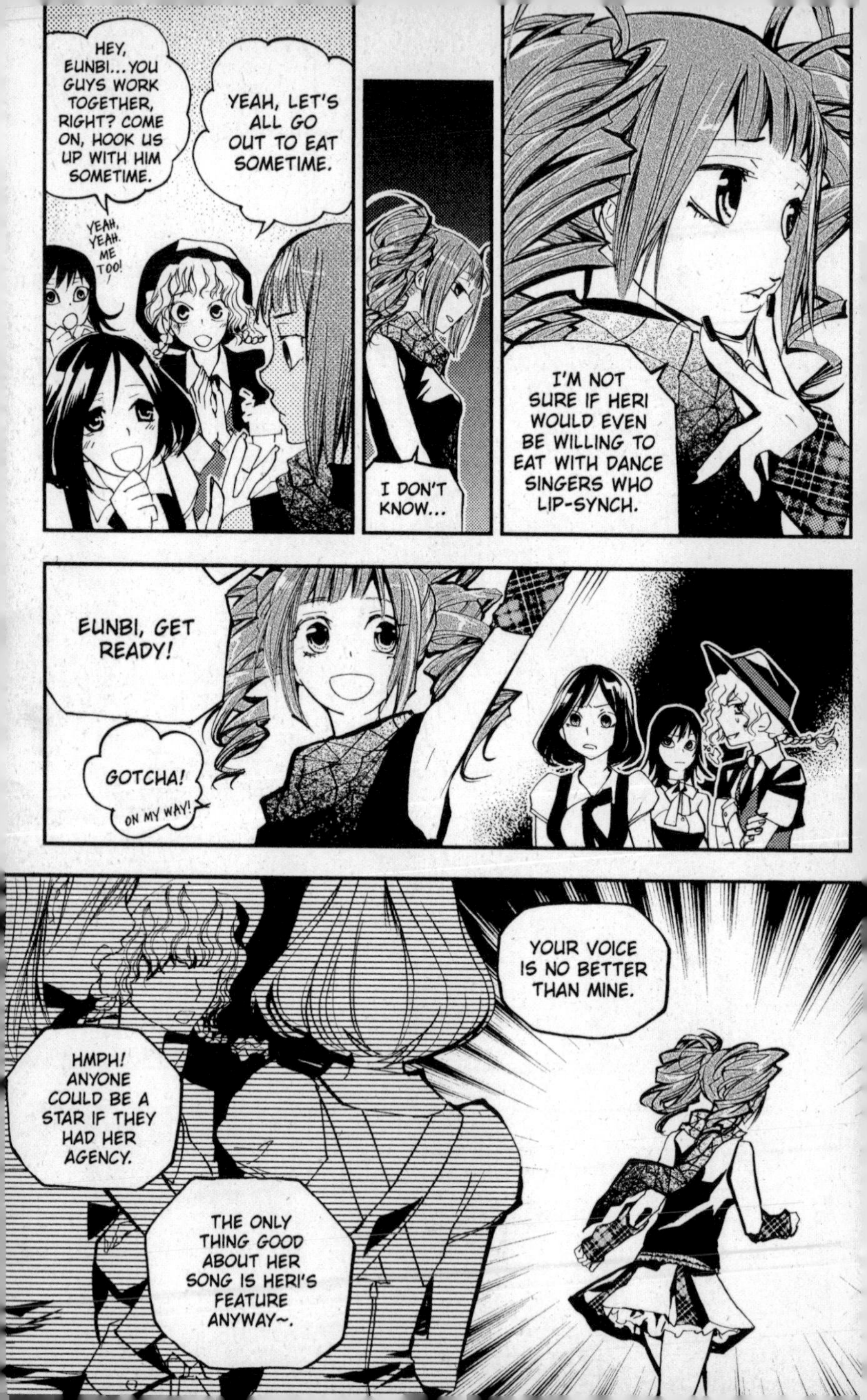
HEY, EUNBI...YOU GUYS WORK TOGETHER, RIGHT? COME ON, HOOK US UP WITH HIM SOMETIME.
YEAH, LET'S ALL GO OUT TO EAT SOMETIME.
YEAH, YEAH. ME TOO!
I DON'T KNOW...
I'M NOT SURE IF HERI WOULD EVEN BE WILLING TO EAT WITH DANCE SINGERS WHO LIP-SYNCH.
EUNBI, GET READY!
GOTCHA!
ON MY WAY!
HMPH! ANYONE COULD BE A STAR IF THEY HAD HER AGENCY.
THE ONLY THING GOOD ABOUT HER SONG IS HERI'S FEATURE ANYWAY~.
YOUR VOICE IS NO BETTER THAN MINE.

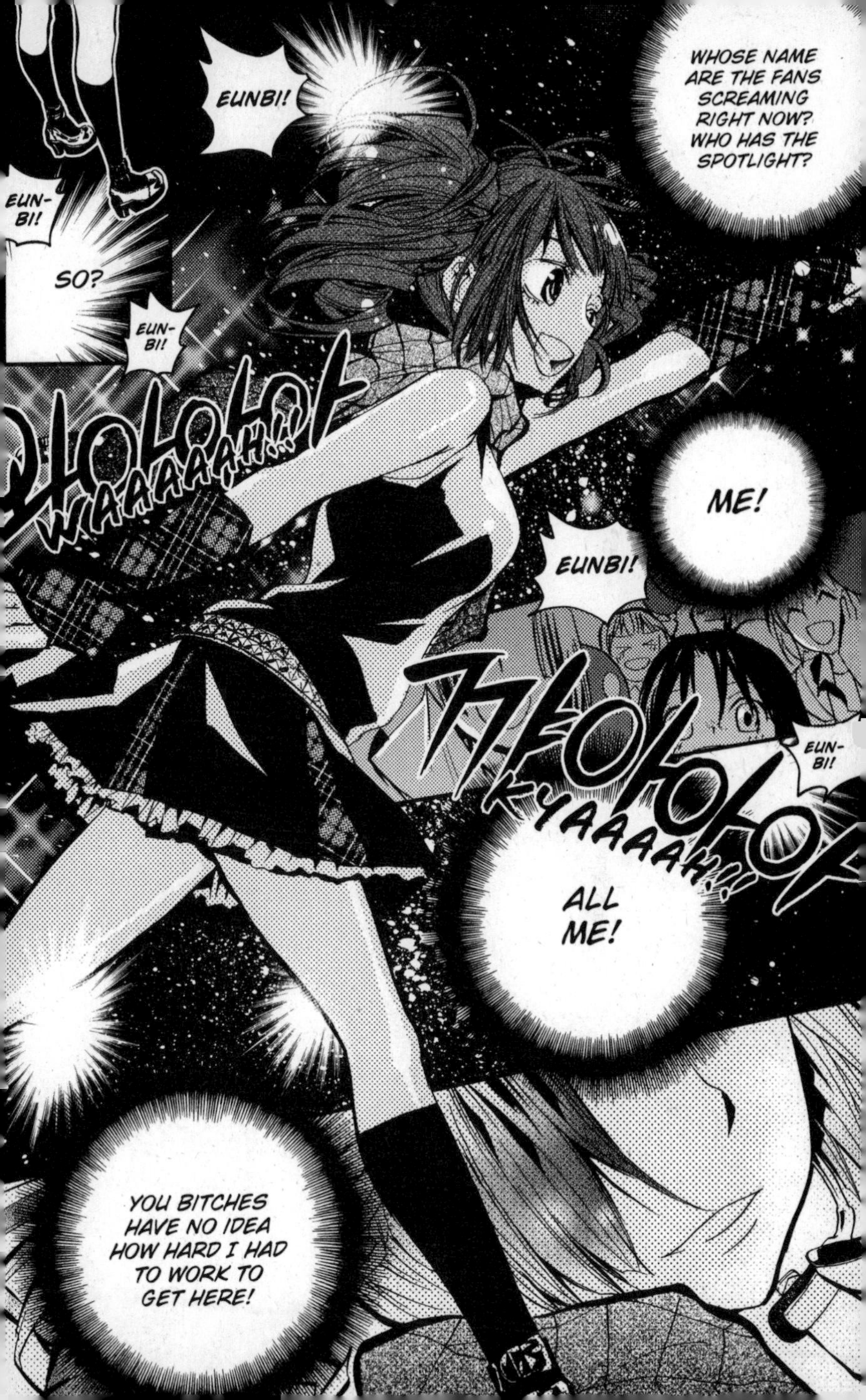
EUNBI!
EUN-BI!
SO?
EUN-BI!
WHOSE NAME ARE THE FANS SCREAMING RIGHT NOW? WHO HAS THE SPOTLIGHT?
WAAAAAAH!!
ME!
EUNBI!
KYAAAAAH!!
EUN-BI!
ALL ME!
YOU BITCHES HAVE NO IDEA HOW HARD I HAD TO WORK TO GET HERE!

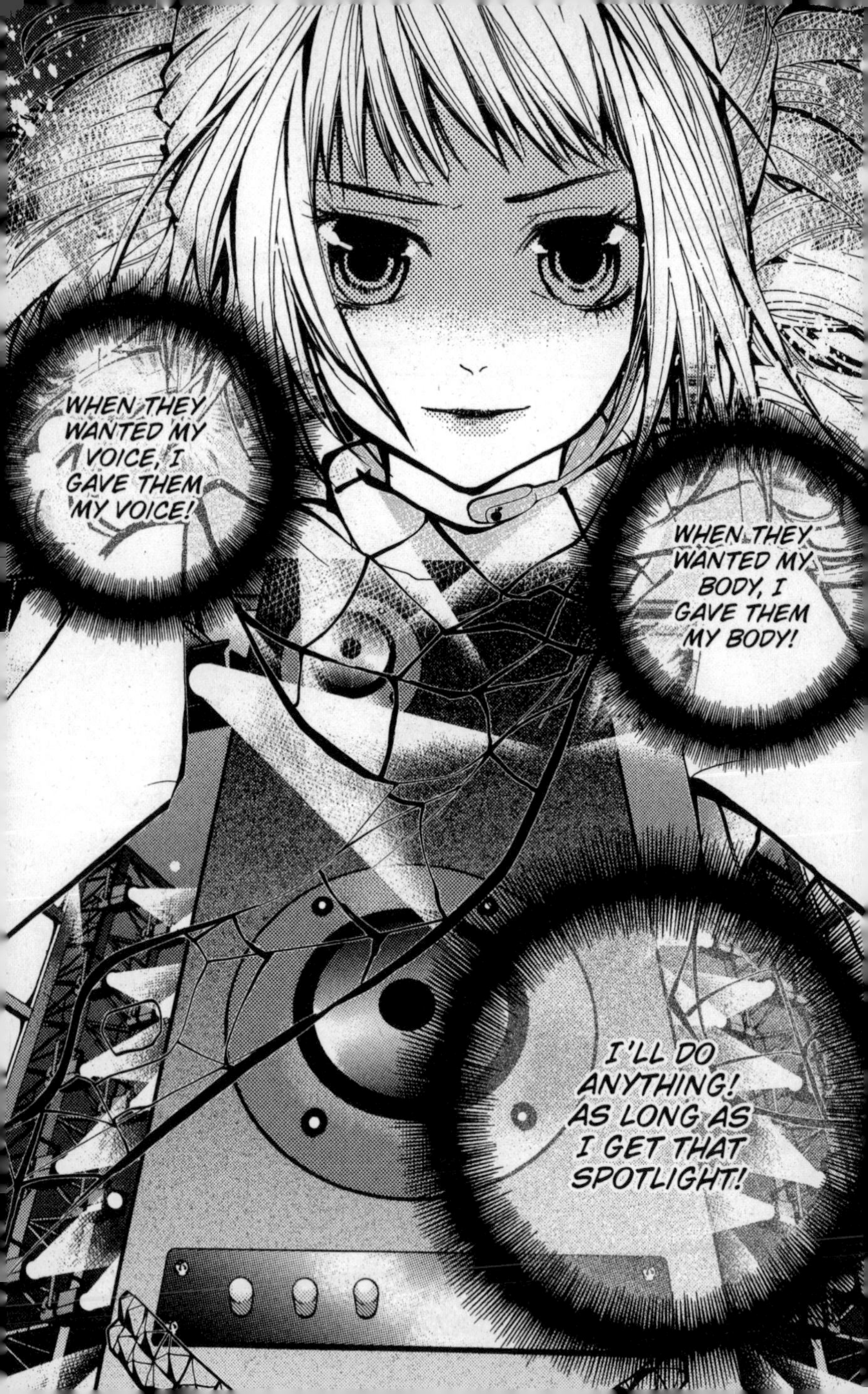
WHEN THEY WANTED MY VOICE, I GAVE THEM MY VOICE!
WHEN THEY WANTED MY BODY, I GAVE THEM MY BODY!
I'LL DO ANYTHING! AS LONG AS I GET THAT SPOTLIGHT!

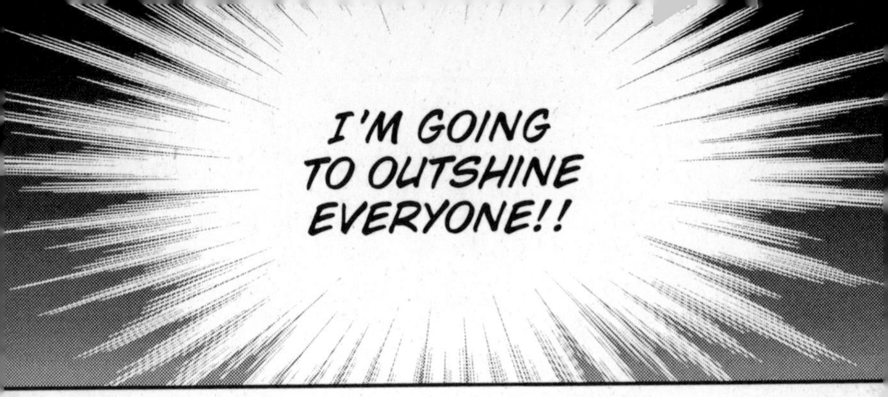
I'M GOING TO OUTSHINE EVERYONE!!

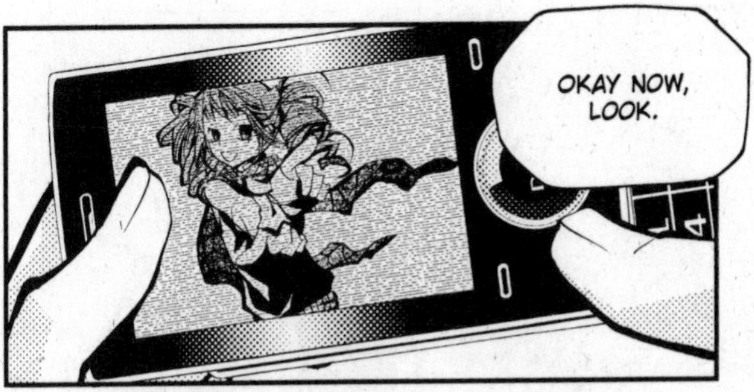
OKAY NOW, LOOK.

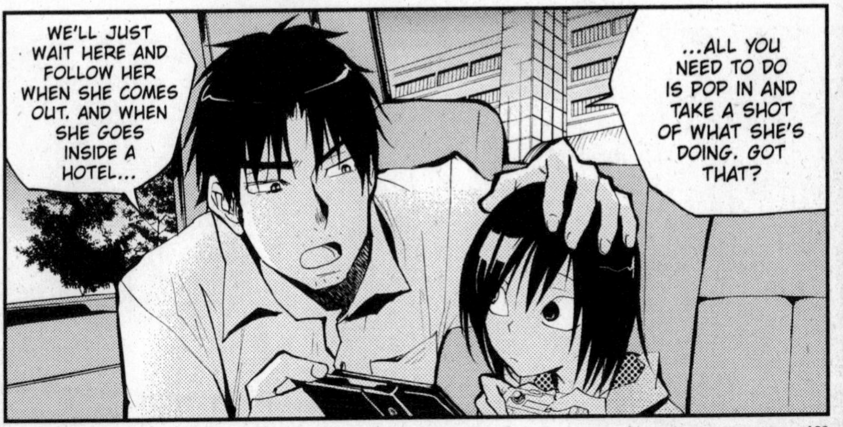
WE'LL JUST WAIT HERE AND FOLLOW HER WHEN SHE COMES OUT. AND WHEN SHE GOES INSIDE A HOTEL...
...ALL YOU NEED TO DO IS POP IN AND TAKE A SHOT OF WHAT SHE'S DOING. GOT THAT?

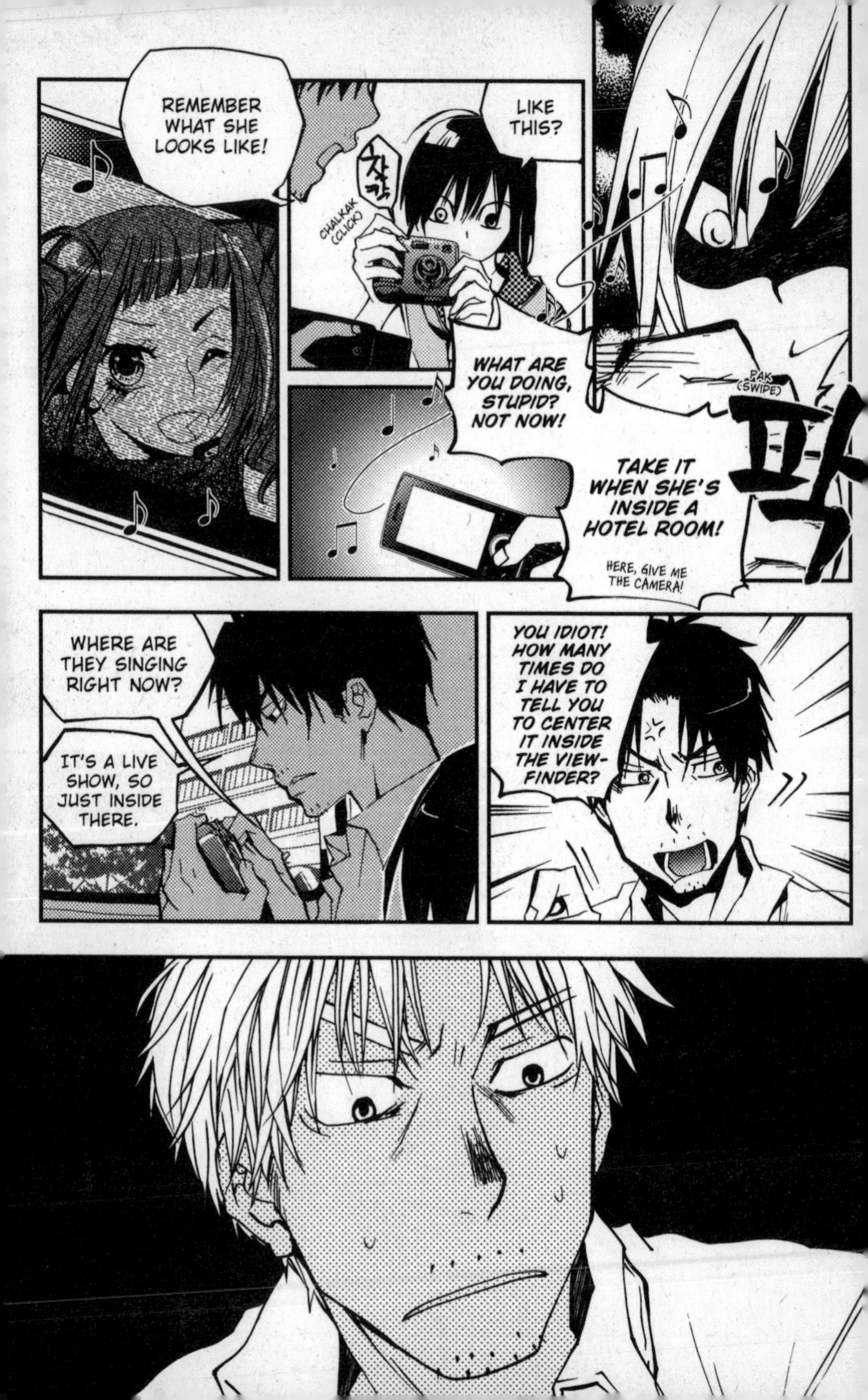
REMEMBER WHAT SHE LOOKS LIKE!
LIKE THIS?
찰칵
CHALKAK (CLICK)
WHAT ARE YOU DOING, STUPID? NOT NOW!
PAK (SWIPE)
팍
TAKE IT WHEN SHE'S INSIDE A HOTEL ROOM!
HERE, GIVE ME THE CAMERA!
WHERE ARE THEY SINGING RIGHT NOW?
IT'S A LIVE SHOW, SO JUST INSIDE THERE.
YOU IDIOT! HOW MANY TIMES DO I HAVE TO TELL YOU TO CENTER IT INSIDE THE VIEW-FINDER?

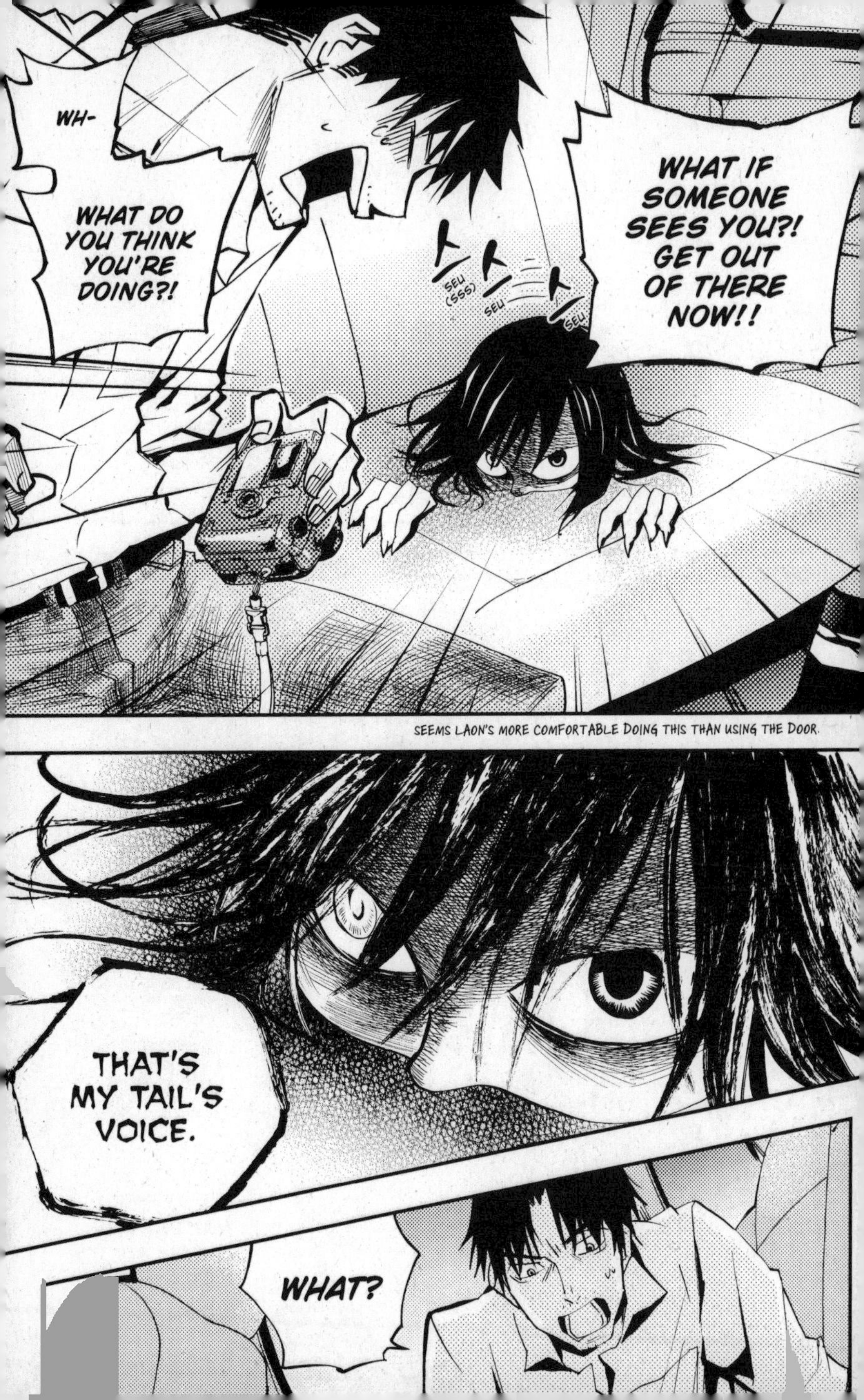
WH-
WHAT DO YOU THINK YOU'RE DOING?!
SEU (SSS)
SEU
SEU
WHAT IF SOMEONE SEES YOU?! GET OUT OF THERE NOW!!
SEEMS LAON'S MORE COMFORTABLE DOING THIS THAN USING THE DOOR.
THAT'S MY TAIL'S VOICE.
WHAT?

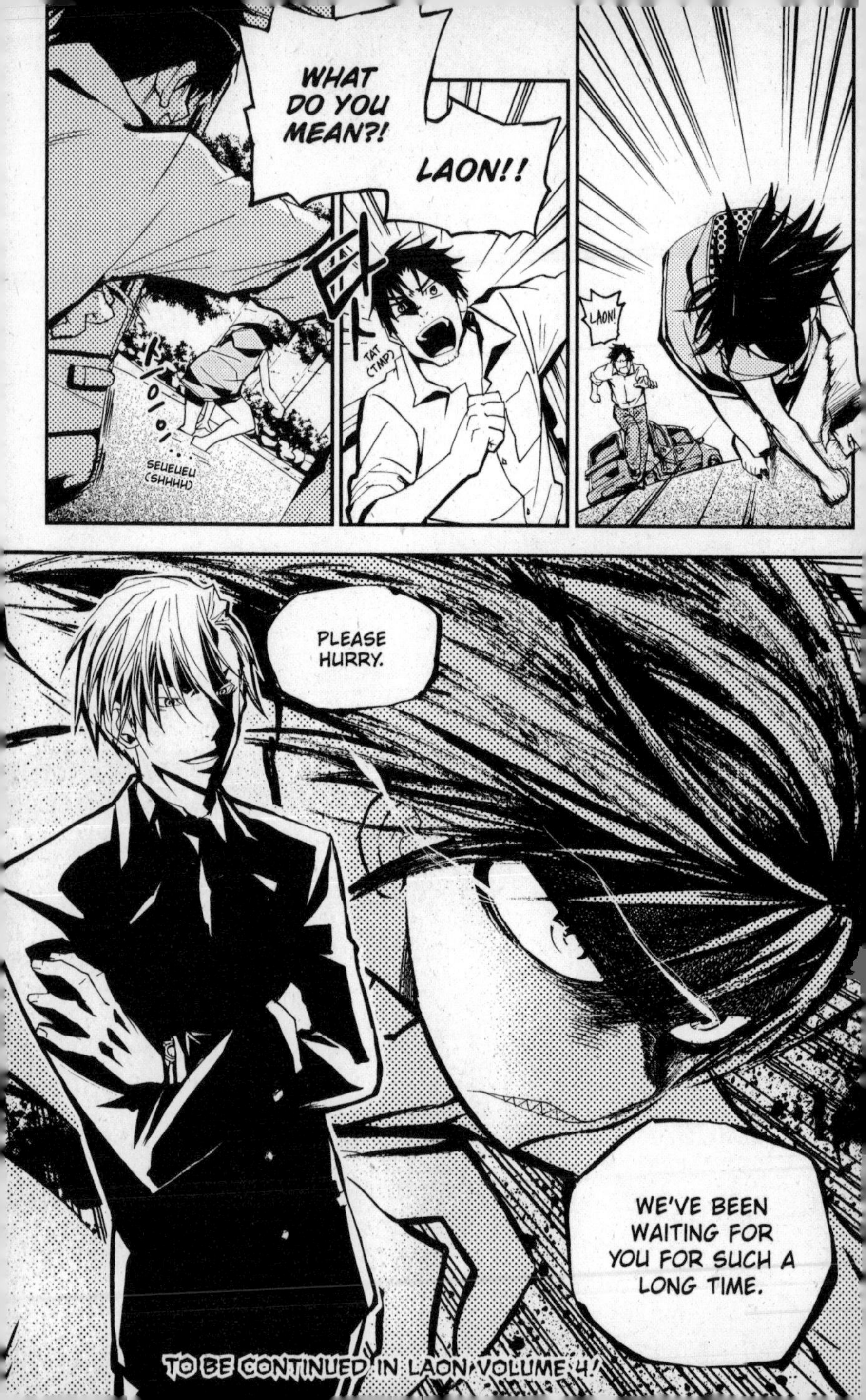

WHAT DO YOU MEAN?!
SEUEUEU (SHHHH)
LAON!!
TAT (TMP)
LAON!
PLEASE HURRY.
WE'VE BEEN WAITING FOR YOU FOR SUCH A LONG TIME.
TO BE CONTINUED IN LAON VOLUME 4!

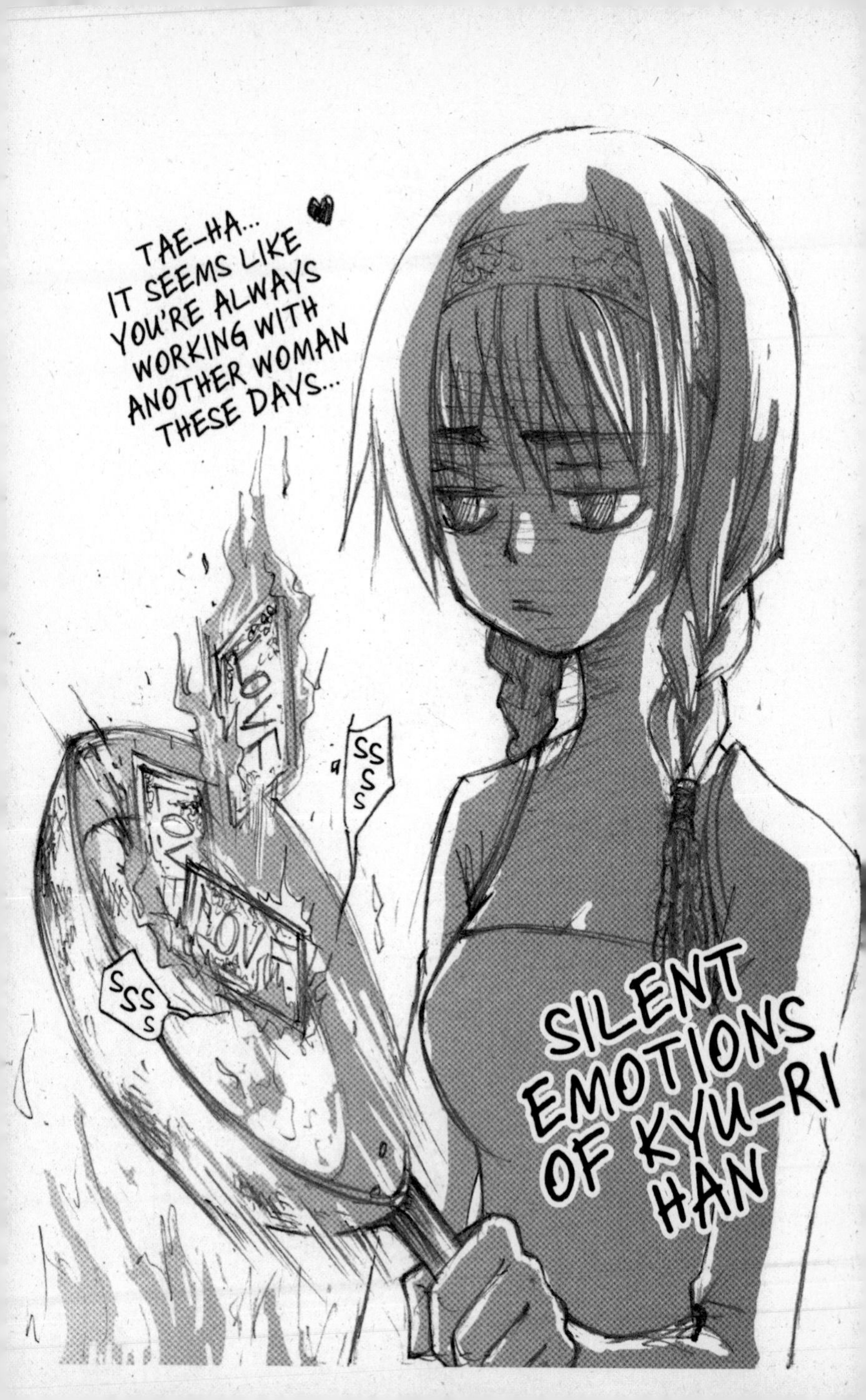

TAE-HA... IT SEEMS LIKE YOU'RE ALWAYS WORKING WITH ANOTHER WOMAN THESE DAYS...
LOVE
SSSS
LOVE
LOVE
SSSS
SILENT EMOTIONS OF KYU-RI HAN

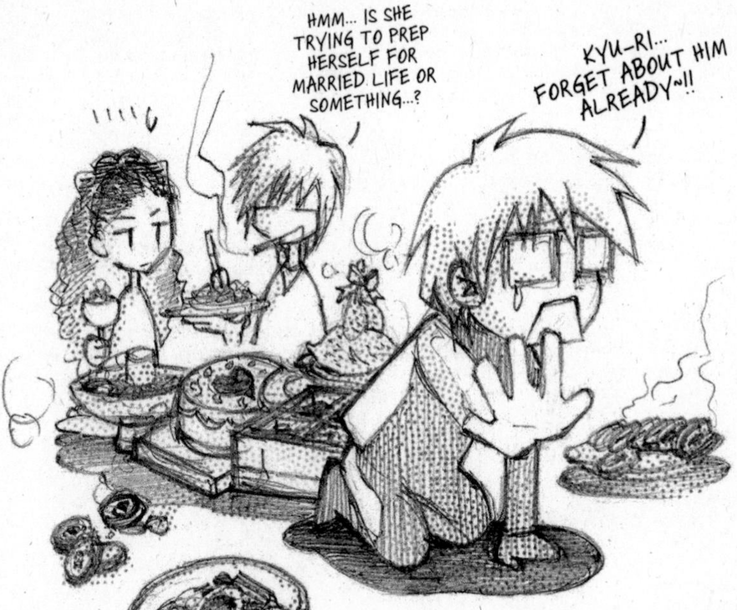
HMM... IS SHE TRYING TO PREP HERSELF FOR MARRIED LIFE OR SOMETHING...?
KYU-RI... FORGET ABOUT HIM ALREADY~!!

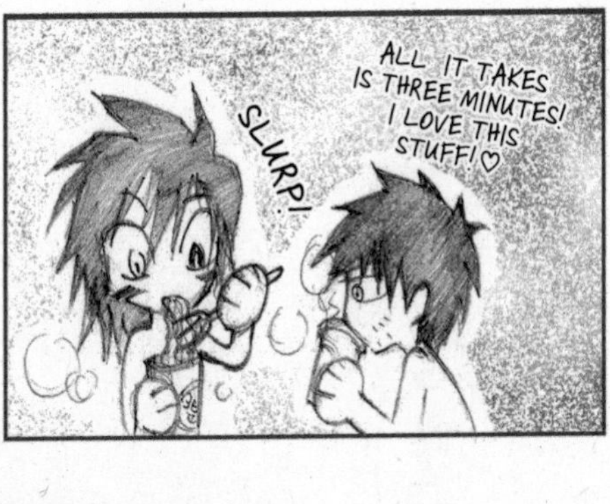
SLURP!
ALL IT TAKES IS THREE MINUTES! I LOVE THIS STUFF! ♡

Translation Notes

A **gumiho** (literally, a nine-tailed fox) is a mythical Korean fox creature with nine tails. Gumihos are able to transform into human form, generally beautiful women, in order to seduce men. Some versions have them eating human livers in order to regain their strength. This story follows the version that a fox creature becomes incrementally more powerful as it ages. From a common fox, it first becomes a white fox, then a red fox, then a gumiho, then finally rises to the level of a *cheonnyeonho* (literally, a 1,000-year-old fox). At this stage, it can ascend to the heavens, achieving the status of a god.

Hwan (幻) is a Chinese character used for words that indicate strangeness, change, illusion, and magic. In this series, it's used to describe parasitic supernatural creatures.

Page 36
The idea of yin and yang is an East Asian philosophical concept that describes how opposing forces counteract each other to keep everything in a state of balance.

Page 54
Koreans observe a ritual called *Jesa*, which is held once a year to honor one's ancestors. In modern times, some only hold rituals for their deceased parents, which seems to be the case in these pages. Often a lot of preparation time is required as many different kinds of foods and wine need to be offered for the ritual.

Page 55
Soju is a strong, clear distilled liquor made from rice or other starches.

Page 63
Dried pollack soup is one of many home remedies for hangovers used in Korea.

Ppo-Ppo-Ppo is a long-running morning children's TV show in Korea.

Page 66
In Korea, addresses are given from largest zone to the individual unit (the opposite of the U.S. system). Therefore, the callers were only able to tell the staff that these mysterious things were happening in a section of a suburb in northern Seoul before all were simultaneously cut off. The exact address of these occurrences remains unknown.

Page 67
"People's X" is a slogan used for goods that are affordable to any common citizen, much like how the VW Beetle was supposed to be the "People's Car" for Germans.

Page 71
The buzzing here represents the sound of cicadas chirping in the summer.

Page 73
Though exchange rates fluctuate daily, a good estimate to use is 1,000 Korean won to 1 U.S. dollar.

Page 80
Kimbap is a Korean dish similar to Japanese sushi rolls. The Korean version does not use raw fish, but rather uses various meats and vegetables.

Makgeolli is a Korean rice liquor that is sweet and has a milky color.

Page 83
Wild ginseng roots are highly prized in Korea and are often mentioned in folk tales as a cure-all herb.

Page 103
Ki, or sometimes *chi*, can be loosely translated as "living energy" or "life force."

The White Tiger of the West and Black Tortoise of the North are two of the four mythical deities that guard four cardinal directions (the other two being the Blue Dragon of the East and the Red Bird of the South).

Page 117
The extended pinkie finger refers to a girl.

Page 122
Honey diluted in water is a common Korean home remedy to minimize the effects of a hangover.

Page 126
In Korean, the word "negative" can also be read as "flesh" in this context, which is why Kyu-Jin is startled in this scene.

Page 127
Again, "color" can be understood as "lust" in this context.

Page 156
Maegu is another native Korean word for a *cheonnyeonho*, a fox that has lived 1,000 years. (See note at left for *gumiho*.)

Page 160
Ddeokbokki and *Soondae* are typical "junk foods" that Korean teenagers enjoy. *Soondae* is a type of blood sausage; the most common fillings are clear noodles, pork blood, and vegetables, though there are many local varieties throughout Korea. *Ddoekbokki* is a dish of rice cakes with a spicy red sauce. Both are common street foods.

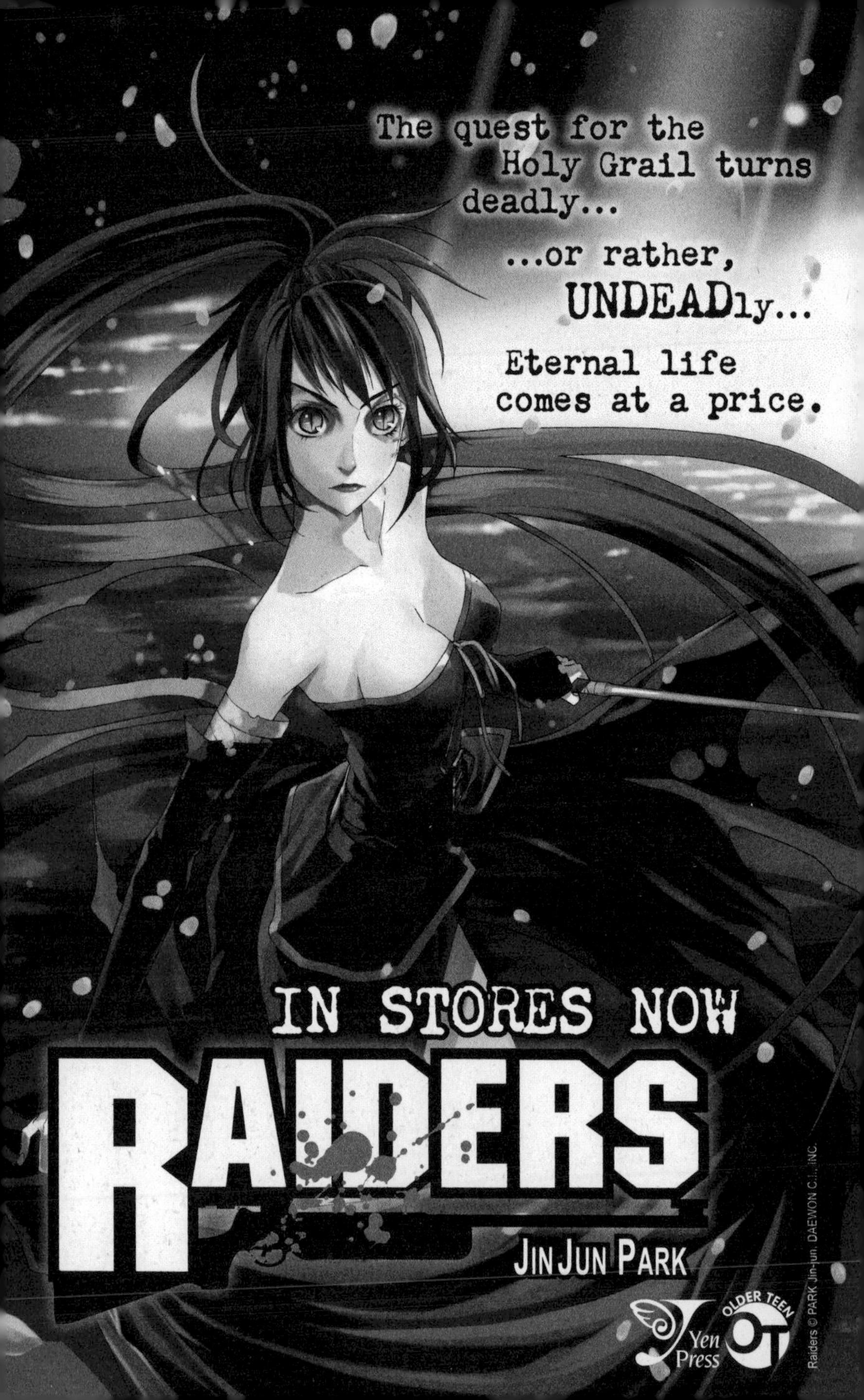
The quest for the Holy Grail turns deadly...
...or rather, UNDEADly...
Eternal life comes at a price.
IN STORES NOW
RAIDERS
JIN JUN PARK
Yen Press
OLDER TEEN
OT
Raiders © PARK Jin-jun, DAEWON C.I., INC.

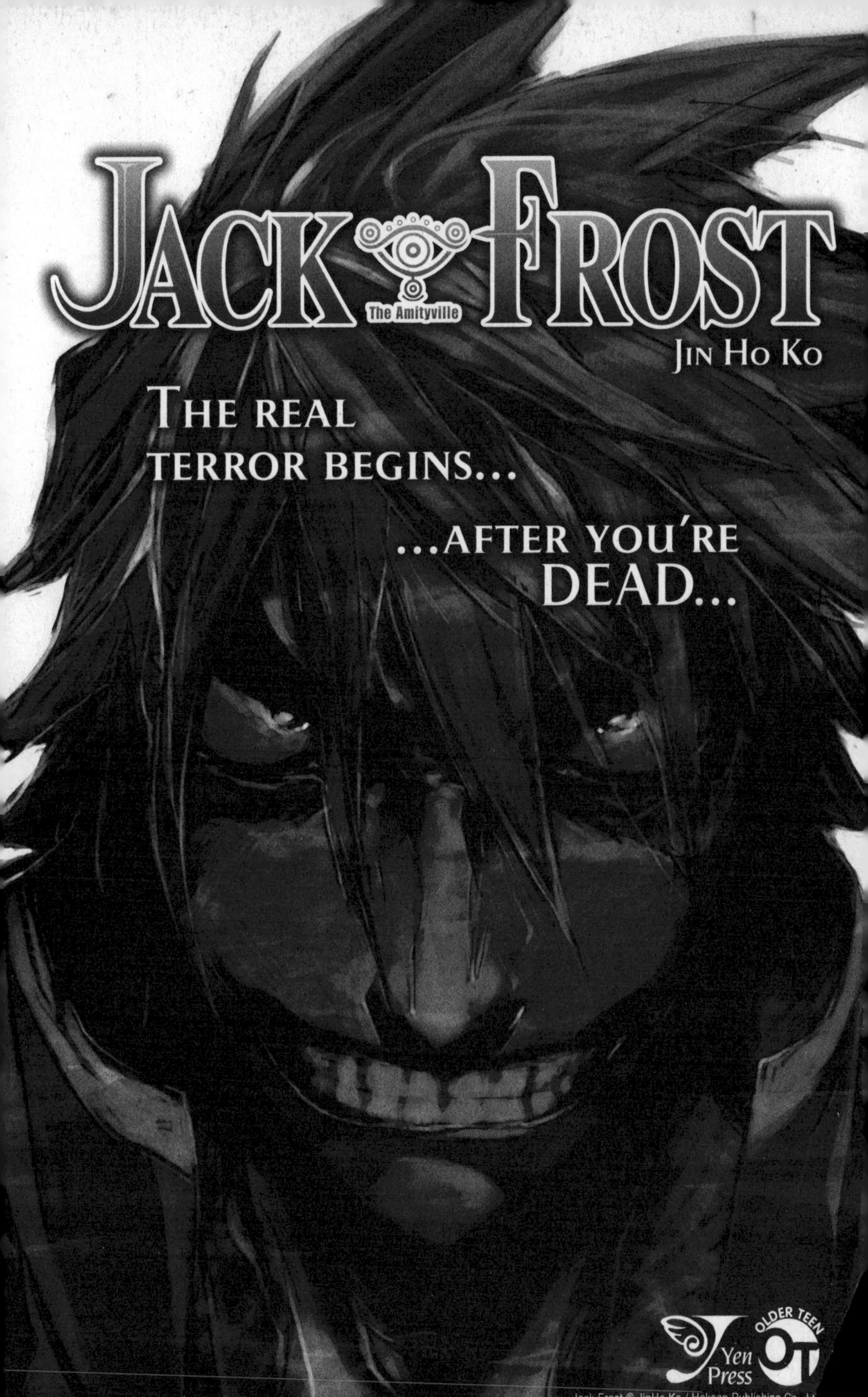
JACK FROST
The Amityville
JIN HO KO
THE REAL TERROR BEGINS...
...AFTER YOU'RE DEAD...
Yen Press
OLDER TEEN
OT

LAON

YOUNGBIN KIM
HYUN YOU

Translation: Woo-Sok Park

Lettering: Abigail Blackman

LAON, vol. 3 © 2007 by KIM Young-bin and YOU Hyun, DAEWON C.I. Inc. All rights reserved. First published in Korea in 2007 by DAEWON C.I. Inc. English translation rights in USA, Canada, UK and Commonwealth arranged by Daewon C.I. Inc. through TOPAZ Agency Inc.

Translation © 2010 by Hachette Book Group, Inc.

Yen Press
Hachette Book Group
237 Park Avenue, New York, NY 10017

www.HachetteBookGroup.com
www.YenPress.com

Yen Press is an imprint of Hachette Book Group, Inc. The Yen Press name and logo are trademarks of Hachette Book Group, Inc.

First Yen Press Edition: September 2010

ISBN: 978-0-7595-3054-6

10 9 8 7 6 5 4 3 2 1

BVG

Printed in the United States of America